Shakespeare's Typological Satire

The Cobham Family Portrait.

SHAKESPEARE'S TYPOLOGICAL SATIRE

A Study of the Falstaff-Oldcastle Problem

ALICE-LYLE SCOUFOS

OHIO UNIVERSITY PRESS
Athens, Ohio

Library of Congress Cataloging in Publication Data

Scoufos, Alice-Lyle,
    Shakespeare's typological satire.

    Includes bibliographical references and index.
    1. Shakespeare, William, 1564–1616—Characters—
Falstaff. 2. Shakespeare, William, 1564–1616—Histories.
3. Shakespeare, William, 1564–1616—Knowledge—History.
4. Shakespeare, William, 1564–1616—Humor, satire, etc.
5. Cobham family. 6. Typology (Theology) in literature.
I. Title.
PR2993.F2S3   822.3'3   77-92256
ISBN 0-8214-0390-7

For my sons, Harry and Doug

TABLE OF CONTENTS

LIST OF ILLUSTRATIONS

Preface

IN SHAKESPEAREAN CRITICISM FALSTAFF HAS BEEN quite literally "the cause that wit is in other men." Complex, contradictory, gigantic in dramatic stature as well as girth, Falstaff remains today as he was in the nineteenth century, a lodestone for controversy. Essays written on this famous Shakespearean character equal–indeed, in our present century surpass–those written on Hamlet; moreover, the history plays in general have been the subject of a number of critical studies in recent years. It is, therefore, with a marked degree of temerity that I add yet one more volume to the endless file; I do so because of certain materials I have found in the historical records of England, materials which seem to me of considerable value for an understanding of Falstaff, of the Elizabethan interpretation of his character, and of his essential function in the history plays and in *The Merry Wives of Windsor.*

My research concerning the Falstaff-Oldcastle-Cobham problem has led me through reams of manuscripts in the Public Record Office, the British Museum, the Bodleian Library, and Alnwick Castle, through many volumes of chronicles, *Acts of the Privy Council,* Elizabethan gossip collections, biographies, histories, and letters. I have found, to my surprise, an abundance of material on the Brooke family, lords of Cobham. Much of it is irrelevant, some of it is pertinent, and a bit of it is vital. This material, I believe, provides some explanation for the more exasperating problems concerning Shakespeare's history plays and suggests resolutions for many another. It has created for me an irrefragable conviction that two centuries of the Cobham family are satirized in the panorama of the *Henry IV* and *Henry VI* plays and in *The Merry Wives*–a panorama of satire that moves from the outlawing of Sir John Oldcastle, Lord Cobham, in 1413, continues through the Eleanor Cobham witchcraft trial of 1441, touches the Cobhams of Wyatt's Rebellion (1554) and the Cobhams of the Ridolfi Plot (1571), and looks forward to the Cobhams of the Main and Bye plots of 1603–wherein lies enough sedition to break a dozen white staffs. It is not a pretty story: as Thomas Nashe once said to his indifferent readers, *"Nil nisi flere libet,* Gentles, heere is no joyfull subject towardes: if you will weepe, so it is."

This study of the Falstaff-Oldcastle-Cobham problem had its provenance in a brief paper that I wrote on the structure of the comic scenes in the *Henry IV* plays. The rowdy characters seemed to me to be functioning in echo-chambers. It also seemed obvious to me that Shakespeare's exploitation of aesthetic parallelism was related in some way to his basic conception of history, but my various probes kept ending at the frustrating hulk of the Oldcastle figure, which blocked further inquiry into the poet's artistic processes and structures. Why did this huge impediment defy analysis, I asked. Why had not earlier scholars laid the beastly problem to rest?

I soon learned that the nucleus of the complex problem lay in the first quartos of the plays, where traces of original character names remain. Nicholas Rowe, in his early edition of Shakespeare's plays, printed the story of the noble family who objected to Shakespeare's use of their ancestral name, consequently bringing to pass the renaming of Falstaff and his crew. Writers of the late eighteenth century in general rejected this story; however, with the increase of historical scholarship in the nineteenth century, Shakespeare critics accepted the story but "denied the minor," turning curtly from the embarrassing question of why Shakespeare chose to portray an early Protestant martyr as a roisterous buffoon. Twentieth-century scholars have acknowledged the facts and concluded that Shakespeare was satirizing the Brooke family, barons of Cobham. But whether the intended victim was William, Lord Cobham, or his son Henry, is disputed; and to the question of why they were satirized there is little in the way of answer.

The neglect of the Falstaff-Oldcastle-Cobham problem in our time is related to the changing critical mores of the twentieth century. Modern critics of Shakespeare's art have in general rejected the historical approach to litera-

ture as an unproductive or (in some instances) an invalid
one. Despairing of the whimsies of a Fleay or a Collier or
later "topical detectives," they have condemned the
method as well as the irrational users of the method–a condemnation which is itself irrational. Twentieth-century
criticism has brought its own kind of wealth and values to
literary studies. These have been profitable, but there is
still work to be done in all areas of investigation. My own
position should be clear: it is no more essential that we
know the topical background for the enjoyment of Shakespeare's plays than it is to know the personalities of the
Athenian politicians whom Aristophanes lampooned when
we read those intellectual comedies of the ancient world.
But it is puerile to ignore any information that can be recovered from the social milieu of either poet simply because the twentieth-century climate of literary criticism is
hostile to topical investigation.

Another reason for the neglect of the Falstaff-Oldcastle
problem in recent decades is the stickiness of the religious
problems involved in the satire. Oldcastle was (indeed, is
still) considered by many to be a martyr of the pre-Reformation period. Since our image of the bard includes adula-
tion, we find Shakespeare too wholesome, too universal to
be preoccupied with neurotic religious pressures. It is difficult, therefore, to reconcile our image with the implications of the problem. I have found no answers to the
question of Shakespeare's fidelity to either the Anglican or
the Roman Catholic church. It has become apparent to me
that the Falstaff-Oldcastle satire grew out of hostilities
between the actors and inhabitants of the Blackfriars precinct and tensions among the political factions in Queen
Elizabeth's court in the 1590s. This is not to say that religious differences were absent from the scene. I simply have
not found proof that they entered fundamentally into the
conflict other than through the satire of the Lollard-Puritan stance that was condemned by moderates among both
Anglican and Roman Catholic groups.

This study of the function of the comic characters in the
history plays has led necessarily to a consideration of
Shakespeare's attitudes toward history in general. In recent scholarship concerned with our poet's conception of
historiography, advances have been made. Irving Rib-

ner's study, *The English History Play in the Age of Shakespeare,* is based upon the broad generalization that "the use of history for the exposition of political theory has its roots distinctly in Italian humanism".[1] This assertion is obviously true, but Ribner fails to point out the basic conflicts and disagreements among humanists that evolved from Machiavelli's seminal work.

M. M. Reese, in *The Cease of Majesty,* suggests that Shakespeare, like Raleigh, "used history to glorify England, to teach moral and political lessons, and to assert the intrusive sway of providence".[2] Again, this thesis is true, but Reese fails to explore the complex and unconservative aspects of the ambiguity and satire that run consistently through the history plays.

In *A Kingdom for a Stage,* Robert Ornstein emphasizes the uniqueness—the individualistic elements—in Shakespeare's use of chronicle material. This certainly is a valid and valuable approach to the history plays, but Ornstein's conclusion is in itself conventional when he states that Shakespeare was concerned with the personal, familial, and communal relationships that constitute our social lives.[3]

I have surveyed Renaissance ideas of historiography closely. I believe that Shakespeare was aware of the rapid changes that were occurring in sixteenth-century conceptions of history. Critical theory was evolving as a result of new emphasis placed upon the distinctions between history, philosophy, and poetry. Epistemological conceptions of "politic" history with its innate skepticism were creating pitfalls for the idealists; the antiquaries were literally digging up evidence by the tun to demonstrate that the differences between the past and the present were vast, and in doing so they were breaking up the conflated image of past and present that the medieval mind, without aid of perspective, had created. Shakespeare's sophisticated use of chronicle materials reveals, I believe, his own solution to the problem of the function of history. The Renaissance idea of historical change made it imperative that a new idea be found to explain the relevancy of history. Shakespeare appears to have seized upon the idea of the poet as extrapolater of the universal human element from the vast panoply of events and eras. The artist with his critical mind and eye could draw nearer to truth than the historian who was tied to facts and deeds, with their changing lessons and values. It was an idea that Sir Philip Sidney exploited in his *Defense;* it was a classical idea, but its revival was new in England.

Having gained this fundamental stance, Shakespeare could then remold the medieval typological approach to history for his satiric purposes. The early patristic writers had developed typological exegesis as a means of relating the older Jewish writings to Christian doctrine. They believed that characters and events in the Old Testament prefigured events in the life of Christ and that events in the New Testament prefigured the apocalyptic era to come. This method, technically, was neither symbolic nor allegorical because both type and antitype were real. Shakespeare adapts this older method to his satiric mode in the *Henry IV* plays. He uses the secular chronicle characters as types of their Elizabethan antitypes, and in doing so he develops a two-edged sword that cuts both ways in time. The Lollard-Puritan stance is mocked, and the disordered and dangerous political activities within the Elizabethan milieu are exposed. It was both witty and brilliant—until the adventure got out of hand. But this is enough of adumbration.

I should like to add a word on the place of speculation in historical criticism. A friend of mine once remarked about a nineteenth-century historian that "he wrote history in the subjunctive mode." It is a sharp statement. Speculation can easily get out of hand (and inadvertently so) in the writings of an exuberant scholar. I have tried to keep my speculations tied to the evidence that I have found. I have borne in mind constantly John Selden's sage example: "In conjectures I durst not be too bold, but when they seem to offer themselves, they deserve the choice of judgment." I pray I have used the choice of judgment.

It is with gratitude and humility that I acknowledge my debts. First of all, my obligations to three dear friends are limitless: the late John M. Raines, whose classic objectivity and good humor made a grotesque project lighter, and the late Kester Svendsen, whose insights into literary art first introduced me to the magnitudes of Renaissance literature. Professor Calvin G. Thayer's assistance with this book has gone far beyond the call of duty: from the inception of this project to its end he has been a learned critic and loyal friend. My gratitude here is boundless. I should like also to state my gratitude to the late T.J.B. Spencer, director of the Shakespeare Institute, for his invitation to read my paper on "The Montage Technique in *Macbeth*" at the Fifteenth International Shakespeare Conference in Stratford-upon-Avon. I am obligated as well to the editors of *Shakespeare Studies*, who published portions of chapters four and ten in article form: *Shakespeare Studies II* (1966), 174-91; *Shakespeare Studies V* (1970), 25-52; to the editors of *Modern Philology* for permission to reprint portions of my article, "Nashe, Jonson, and the Oldcastle Problem," that appeared in their journal, volume 65 (May 1968), 307-24; and to the editors of *A Journal of English Literary History* who hold the copyright on my article, "Harvey: A Name-Change in *Henry IV*," that appeared in volume 36 (June 1969), 297-318. For more general obligations I can only say that it is impossible to acknowledge all the debts I owe to my predecessors and to contemporary Shakespeare scholars. The fact that I have gone back, when possible, to the original sources for my information should not imply that I have neglected or willfully ignored later commentary. I have tried in my notes to list important criticism. Any serious scholar in this field knows the large, unencompassed body of intellectual materials shared by all of us. If there were a void between me and my primary sources, I should find it impossible to write; the bridge with the past has been constructed by many hands.

I am indebted to a number of premier institutions. For many years the staff of the Henry E. Huntington Library have made scholarly work among their resources an occupation of the prelapsarian kind. It is a perfect setting. The staffs of the Manuscript Room and the North Library of the British Museum have been more than competent, as have the assistants in the Public Record Office in London. The Duke Humphrey Library at the Bodleian has been another ideal place for research. I am especially indebted to His Grace, the Duke of Northumberland, for permission to use the manuscripts in his collections at Alnwick Castle and Syon House. Mr. David Graham, Estates Manager at Alnwick Castle, was courteous and responsive to my requests for manuscripts. The staff at Lambeth Palace Library have been exceptionally competent in finding materials for me in their collections of medieval manuscripts. The assistants at the municipal libraries in Bristol and Gloucester have been helpful, and I received exceptional aid and encouragement from Dr. William Urry, former Archivist at Canterbury Cathedral.

I owe additional thanks to my own university for several grants that expedited the acquisition of materials that I needed, and I am grateful for grants from the Huntington Library, the American Philosophical Society, and the National Endowment for the Humanities, that provided funds which alleviated the burden of expenses accumulated in my travel and research. My typist, Mrs. Sherrill Pieschel, deserves commendation for her impeccable work. To all, my sincere thanks.

Alice-Lyle Scoufos
California State University, Fullerton

Shakespeare's Typological Satire

CHAPTER ONE

History and a Sanguine Epistemology

MANY SCHOLARS IN OUR DAY HAVE BEEN CONCERNED with Shakespeare's uses of history, as any cursory glance at twentieth-century bibliographies of the *Henry IV* and *Henry VI* plays will reveal. I too am concerned with our greatest playwright's adaptations of historical materials for dramatic presentation. The present study, however, is based upon a broader, more eclectic view of the theories of history in the sixteenth century than hithertofore has been used for an analysis of Shakespeare's history plays. At the same time, this study depends upon a more detailed investigation of the playwright's deviations from his historical sources. In general, my work is concerned with the Falstaff-Oldcastle problem and the type of satire the poet created as he took liberties with his sources; but the very problems of the Falstaff-Oldcastle character lie embedded within the extremely complex attitudes toward history that had become a part of the later Elizabethan intellectual milieu. I believe that the sanguine Shakespeare of the 1590s developed sophisticated theories of history and the uses of history in art that go far beyond the commonplace moral statements which the English chroniclers of the period used in their prefaces and which dominated the thinking of history writers in Tudor England.[1]

My intensive study of one segment (I could say "faggot") of English history, which the playwright used with skill, has led me to conclude that the poet's developing sense of the philosophy of history prepared a theoretical foundation for his new conception of the nature and func-

3

tion of dramatic satire. For when Shakespeare began to write the fresh and dynamic comic prose of the *Henry IV* plays, he appears suddenly to have reached a mature stage of development in his thinking about the relationship between drama and history, and even more specifically about the relationship between satire, comedy, and history. The playwright's position at this period belongs, it seems to me, in the definable trend of resistance, the countermovement, against the sixteenth-century currents of historical skepticism and Pyrrhonism that had swept across both Continental Europe and England before the 1590s. One recent scholar has remarked that "an understanding of the havoc they [the philosophical skeptics] wrought in the ranks of orthodoxy is imperative to any real appraisal of those enigmatic and volatile individuals whom we term the Elizabethans."[2] And with this opinion I wholeheartedly agree. I believe that Shakespeare's youthful answer to the nihilists comes through clearly in his confident and creative use of history in the second tetralogy, and particularly in the bold, innovative satire which livens the chronicle materials in the *Henry IV* plays. These dramas are sanguine and exploratory; they serve in a sense as prologues to the later tragedies in which the older Shakespeare turned to examine those dark recesses of questioning and doubt that the probing minds of the sixteenth century had created for thinking men.[3]

The broader background for sixteenth-century historical Pyrrhonism includes an eclectic skepticism in all disciplines of knowledge.[4]

I should like to make clear at this point, however, that I am not suggesting that all perceptive minds of the fifteenth and sixteenth centuries were interlinked by doubts of the universality of virtue, the innate dignity of man, or the viability of history. Such was not the case. There was great variety in the views on the true essence of human nature and the problems of written history. Those problems were too complex to permit any simple or single answer. But in general it has been popular in recent times to think of the Renaissance as a period of ebullient optimism in which humanistic minds delighted in the affirmation of unlimited potential for greatness and grandeur.[5] More recently, scholars have begun to emphasize the pervasive and deeply rooted pessimism that existed concomitantly with the views of mankind's excellence, and we learn that the period was a splendid but unhappy one.[6] I have no desire to step between the big guns of these warring factions of our modern Renaissance philosophers. Let me say simply that both groups reveal from diverse views the undeniable fact that Renaissance thought was extremely complex, frequently contradictory, even within the works of one man, and certainly so in the composite writings of an academy, a movement, or an age. I can only offer a cursory overview to encompass my own conception of the evolution of thoughts on historiography in that vital period: first, the increase of skeptical thought early in the sixteenth century, and second, the emergence of the view of "ideal history" toward the end of that century.

As intellectuals in various fields of study sought the elusive flame of truth, they questioned the past in a new way. Legal minds were becoming intensely aware of the discrepancy between their law and the laws of ancient Rome; theologians, both orthodox and rebel, were suddenly concerned with the primitive church of the first three centuries of Christendom; philosophers, inextricably caught in the gulf that widened between Platonism and Aristotelianism as the Reformation currents intensified, were swept to polarities, and the ideas of Peter Ramus compounded the tensions; historians, aware now that the present was more than a conflation of past ages, began to probe the idea of historical change. This investigation had been sparked earlier by the success of the Italian humanists in their demands for corrected, purified texts of the authors of antiquity. Their new attitude toward the past was an inherently comparative view: the past could not have meaning nor be rightly understood, they said, unless the language, laws, and institutions of the distant eras were reconstructed and viewed within their own contexts. This view was of course the beginning of the modern conception of historiography, a conception that did not reach its formal investiture until the seventeenth century was well past its majority.[7] The intellectual excitement sparked by Lorenzo Valla's exposure of the fraudulent *Donation of Constantine* fueled numerous discussions not only of church doctrine and authority but of linguistics, law, and literature as well. This enthusiasm was banked, however, when pre-Reformation tensions compounded the resultant problems of inquiry into the past. Skepticism with its divers heads ambled onto the scene with the gracelessness of the Blatant Beast some-time before Erasmus found it expedient to remark in the *Praise of Folly* that "human affairs are so obscure and various that nothing can be clearly known." Erasmus was, of course, a humanist, but his remark is a far cry from the sanguine Italian humanists who plagiarized Terence for their witty motto, "I am master of all I survey."[8]

The past: what is it? Can it ever be recovered? What relationship does it have with the present? Can it be of importance now? Can man justify the basis of his knowledge of the past—or of any knowledge at all? Many of the early humanists had affirmative answers for these questions. Their positive replies were founded upon a confident epistemology. Man's boundless mind could explore virtually to infinity. But the mind, soon boggled by its own untrammeled exuberance, signaled retreat. In the sixteenth century the antiintellectual alarum sounded its metallic yet strongly appealing tones in all areas of thought: in the realm of theology intuitive perception of divine Truth was a doctrine that congealed upon more doors than those at Wittenberg. In the cool realm of philosophy both occultism and relativism disordered the house; in the field of ethics an early form of naturalism erupted most naturally as human nature came under the scrutiny of the naked eye; and in the ill-defined area of history the past slipped beyond all reach, irrecoverably lost. These are of course partial statements, generalizations. But they convey an idea of the complexity of the sixteenth century as it progressed through what we call the Reformation and toward what we call the birth of modern science. It was a violent period of gestation, and the mental appetites craved more than strawberries and wine.

In Italy Pico della Mirandola (Gian Francesco, the nephew) could turn his back upon the eclectic intellectual system that his famous uncle had developed for himself and his fellow humanists in an attempt to unify classical, Hebraic, and Christian ideals. The younger Pico turned instead to the writings of Sextus Empiricus, the obscure Greek Pyrrhonian skeptic whose thoughts later gained broad dissemination as they filtered through Montaigne's brain.[9] When Martin Luther proclaimed in "plain and unvarnished" terms his declaration of Christian liberty at the Diet of Worms, faith as a criterion of sacred truth stood bravely in its challenge to institutional tradition and the past. Ironically, Luther's energy was consistently exerted in efforts to eradicate doubt ("Anathema to the Christian who will not be certain of what he is supposed to believe, and who does not comprehend it"), and he excoriated Erasmus for his skepticism. But in the complex evolution of the religious problems of the sixteenth century the reformers were ultimately tagged with the skeptic's label. With their insistence upon "inner persuasion" Calvin and Beza strengthened the developing antiintellectual currents of fideism. The early Puritan movement in England, with its primitivism, its attack upon the formality, power, and pomp of the Anglican bishops, its insistence upon "the vanitie of the artes" and the "immoralitie of the stage shews," was a further development of the major currents of the skeptical age.

The Portuguese physician and professor of medicine at Toulouse, Francisco Sanchez, wrote his famous *Quod Nihil Scitur* in 1576. Sanchez taught philosophy as well as medicine, and his emphatic conclusion concerning the impossibility of man's gaining any true and complete knowledge was geared to a philosophical attack on Aristotelian epistemology. Man can only achieve a very limited and subjective knowledge of the world about him; and even this perception can be obtained only if the observer can exercise keen observation and sound judgment. Since few observers judge, concluded Sanchez, and even fewer judges observe, true knowledge lies beyond our human grasp.[10] The philosophic (and dogmatic) skepticism that we find in Sanchez's work is matched and surpassed in Montaigne's famous writings.

Montaigne was by all accounts the most influential skeptic of the later Renaissance. His probing, doubting translation of and commentary upon the *Theologia Naturalis* of the fifteenth-century naturalist Raimond Se-

bond (who had taught at Toulouse) anatomized all religious, classical, and scientific knowledge. Mankind is dependent upon sense impressions, declared Montaigne, and
those sense impressions are relative, indeed are inferior, to
the sense impressions of animals. But what does it matter,
asks the skeptic, for no knowledge has ever benefited mankind. Montaigne insisted that the natives of the New World
lived as nature's noblemen in simplicity and ignorance,
"without letters, without law, without king, without religion of any kind." Ethics and morals are relative, he insisted, to the society that invents them; "all that we see
without the lamp of His grace, is only vanity and folly."[11]
This attack upon all human knowledge became a foundation for the seventeenth-century crisis of doubt, as every
historian of the period recognizes. But it was a manifestation of the sweeping currents that had risen to a crescendo
by the 1580s in Europe.

The element of doubt crept into the writings of the
lawyers and jurists of the sixteenth century, for they were
disturbed by the widening gulf between the ancient di-
gests of Roman law and the unwritten, customary law, or
as it was called in England, the Common law. Most English students are aware of the idealization of Common
law by the jurists of the Jacobean period, but this was
a ramification of an ideological movement that had as-
serted itself on the Continent fifty years earlier. The effec-
tiveness, the relevance, of Roman law was questioned by
legal scholars at Bourges and Toulouse. In his study of
French customary law, *Anti-Tribonian* (1567), François
Hotman extols the unwritten customs of the French people
at the expense of Roman law, which he calls "the most
useless subject a Frenchman can study." Jacques Cujas,
speaking from his scholar's chair at Bourges, is said to
have remarked when asked to apply his great knowledge
to current problems, "Quid hoc ad edictum praetoris?"[12]
These upheavals in the traditional halls of jurisprudence
were a sign of the ferment that had spread to most disciplines of knowledge, and that ferment caused the jurists
to turn to a stratum of thought lying above the din of
worldly mutability, as we shall see.

Another major figure in the developing currents of skepticism in the sixteenth century was Henrie Cornelius

Agrippa, whose work, *Of the Vanitie and Uncertaintie of Artes and Sciences,* was first published at Antwerp in 1530. It was put through numerous editions and translations; James Sanford Englished the work in 1569 and re-issued it in 1576. The book contains a hard-swinging attack upon the honesty of historians in general: all historians are liars. From that blunt beginning Agrippa tells "why in no parte any credite may be throughly geven to Histories": because "Historiographers entermeddle lies with the truthe, for delections sake." Moreover, "well neare all Historians at this daie, are flatterers . . . a corrupte and liynge kinde of flatteringe Historiographers." Agrippa puts history at the bottom of the list of studies for the attainment of knowledge: "This Arte, albeit it doothe chiefely require an Order, Agreemente, and Truthe of all thinges: not withstanding, it perfourmeth it leaste of all."[13] Holding this view of history, Agrippa went on to excoriate the more ephemeral arts. He had a contempt for poets and players that led him to define poetry as "an Arte, that was devysed to no other ende, but to please the eares of foolishe men, with wanton Rythmes . . . and to deceive mens mindes with the delectation of fables, and with fardelles of lyes."[14] The staging of plays is called "a dishonest and wicked occupation," and even the beholding of plays "is a shamefull thyng." Agrippa looked at the past and concluded that "there was in times past no man more infamous than stage players, and moreover, al they that had plaide an Enterlude in the Theatre, wer by the lawes deprived from all honoure."[15] Agrippa died at Grenoble in 1535; it would seem logical to expect his pessimistic writings to fade with him, but this is not the case. Antiintellectualism was in the air, and it provided a fruitful ground for Agrippa's mental husbandry in ancient skepticism. Thus his popularity was far greater than might be expected from the highly negative and dogmatic aspects of his major work. One of his followers and imitators was Charles de la Ruelle, whose book *Succintz Adversaires* appeared at Poitiers in 1567. Ruelle's attitude was also extremely antiintellectual; he attacked the basis of all knowledge. For him history was impossible. One can never know the past, and even if one could, all knowledge is useless:

Reste à examiner l'autre partie, Rapport du Passé. La verité du quel est totalement incertaine; et bien qu'elle fust certaine, seroit neantmoins de nul usage et proffit: et ne rien sinon inutilement et frustoirement contenter une vaine et plus que puerile curiosité.[16]

These are primitive and nihilistic attitudes, but they caught on in the swirling intellectual patterns of thought at mid-sixteenth century. Even the more objective and balanced historians of the period reveal some of the negativism of the skeptics in their "politic" histories. For example, in the Storia d' Italia of Francesco Guicciardini, which is usually considered the finest history written in the Italian Renaissance, there is an essence of resignation. Guicciardini was writing the history at the end of his life when all of his hopes for a regeneration of society in Italy had collapsed. There is, in spite of the constant analysis of causation, a sense of helplessness as the author attempts to understand the processes of history. Human conduct is unpredictable; it is too complex for any sure analysis of the past or any certain understanding of the future, thought Guicciardini. Faith must ultimately rest in an unknowable power that guides erratically. Fortune, mysterious and vague, controls human life, and Guicciardini quotes Seneca's famous precept with approbation: the Fates lead those who are willing but drag those who are not. In Guicciardini's insistence upon the limits to man's ability to understand historical processes there is a kind of historical determinism that the English translator of the Storia d'Italia could not abide. When Sir Geoffrey Fenton turned the work into the English idiom, he saw to it that the vagueness of the deity and the pagan idea of Fortune (the Italianate elements) were altered so that the English reader received a pious and orthodox rendition.[17]

The English reader was not supposed to be reading the works of Niccolò Machiavelli in any form; secular censorship had forbidden that. But in spite of restrictions Machiavelli was being read, both in England and abroad. That "diabolic" Italian had been a close and influential friend of Guicciardini, though he was some fourteen years the elder. Machiavelli did not share the deterministic attitude with his friend; he was too concerned with searching for what he considered the *general rule* in history, a rule which he thought could be applied to current political conduct. We can see in his *History of Florence,* much of it plagiarized, that he is concerned not with the particular historical event but with the generalization to be drawn from it. Indeed, at times he altered the historical facts in order to make them illustrate a favorite maxim. When he insists, as he frequently does in all his writings, that human nature does not change but remains the same in every age, Machiavelli is not playing the Platonist—his conception of human nature was never ideal. Given the chance to be natural, he insisted, or given a little power, a man would immediately expose his cruel and dishonest nature. And he speculates that if one should admit any possibility for change in human nature, it would be not for the better but for the worse. For Machiavelli history tended to reveal a constant factor, but that factor was unideal.[18]

England, the ideal demi-Paradise, the moated isle, did not escape the deluge of doubt that swept the Continent. Every reader knows of Spenser's "Mutability Cantos" and of the megrim exploited in the early poetry of John Donne. This same vogue of skepticism is to be found in the prose of Sir Walter Raleigh, who evidently had read both Agrippa and Montaigne. In Raleigh's early work, the *Sceptick or Speculations,* the true skeptic is defined as he who "doth neither affirm, neither denie any Position: but doubteth of it, and opposeth his Reasons against that which is affirmed, or denied, to justifie his not Consenting." And his doubt about the very reliability of Nature and about sense impressions is evident when he writes, "If it be replied, that Nature hath ordained as many instruments of Sence, as there are sencible objects; I demand, What Nature. Some affirming it to be one thing, others another, few agreeing."[19] This same breath of skepticism had even crept into the quiet countryside where Sir John Davies was writing his long and tedious poem *Nosce Teipsum,* which he later dedicated to Queen Elizabeth. In boyish fashion he began:

> Why did my parents send me to the schooles,
> That I with knowledge might enrich my mind?
> Since the *desire to know* first made men fooles,
> And did corrupt the roote of all mankind?

Davies piously condemns the appetite, passion, and curiosity of Adam and Eve, then looks to the contemporary scene:

> But we their wretched Offspring, what do we?
> Do not wee still tast of the fruite forbid?
> Whiles with fond, fruitlesse curiositie,
> In bookes prophane we seeke for knowledge hid?
>
> What is this *knowledge*? but the Shie-stolne fire,
> For which the Thiefe still chaind in Ice doth sit?
> And which the poore rude Satyre did admire,
> And needs would kisse, but burnt his lips with it?[20]

Davies's poem was an attempt to prove the immortality of the human soul; he attacked reason and extolled faith to gain his end. His final conclusion was that man is "a proud and yet a wretched thing." Knowledge, for him, was a vain and fruitless pursuit. This was the same conclusion reached by John Norden in his skeptical poem, *Vicissitudo Rerum, An Elegiacall Poeme, of the Interchangeable Courses and Varietie of Things in this World.* Here we find again the idea of mutability: "Nature her workes doth tosse like Tennis balls, / Now rayz'd by force, then downe again by poyse."[21] And so on. The tedium wearies the modern reader, but the point is made. Skepticism had found its officious way into England, not by way of the historians, but by way of the poets and the Puritans. This is not to say that the Continental historians were being ignored in England. As early as the 1570s we find Gabriel Harvey noting (with distaste) that the students at both Cambridge and Oxford could be found reading Commines, Guicciardini, Bodin, and "many owtlandishe braveryes besides of the same stampe." And he remarks in addition that the students were "prettely well acquayntid with a certayne parlous booke callid . . . II Principe di Nicollo Machiavelli."[22]

It is to Sidney that we must turn for what was to become the answer of the more sanguine historians to their pessimistic brethren. Ironically, the idea that Sidney states in the *Apology for Poetry* is actually an attack upon the pedantic writer of history who is "tyed not to what should bee but to what is, to the particuler truth of things and not to the general reason of things." Sidney at this point in his argument is making the distinction between literal truth and ideal truth: the first he says is the goal of the unimaginative historian; the second, the goal of the poet.[23] This is an ancient conception, used by Aristotle in the *Poetics* when he insisted that poetry was more philosophical and more serious than history. The Italian literary critics of the Renaissance had of course capitalized upon this idea that poetry is concerned with the timeless and the universal, while history is concerned with the specific and the unique in time. Tasso had the contemporary critical statements of Cinthio and Castelvetro to reinforce his own position when he decried the historian who shackled himself to "the truth of particulars rather than attemping to the universal."[24] We can see something of this idealism as it began to make itself manifest in the theories of historiography that were put into print on the Continent as the sixteenth century progressed. Its appearance was the result of the tensions that the skeptics had created with their difficult questions about the value of history.

Throughout Europe the headlong assault by the skeptics in various fields upon historical credibility, upon the belief in the utility of the history of past events, upon the foundation of accumulated knowledge itself was first met by writers who at times did not wholly disagree with the skeptics. The very popular work by Louis Le Roy entitled, *De La Vicissitude Ou Varieté Des Choses En L'Univers,* contained an eloquent affirmation of the theory of mutability. Constant change and infinite variety were to be expected within the scope of man's experiences, wrote this Frenchman, and sense impressions which channel into the human mind all knowledge are untrustworthy. But Le Roy's work is not totally pessimistic. He could acknowledge "the difficultie of knowledge, and the weaknes of mans understanding," but "there was never age more happie for the advancement of learning, then this present: if weying the shortnes of mans life, we resolve to employ our whole endevour & industrie on the studie of true knowledge." That idiom belongs to Robert Ashley, who translated Le Roy's book in 1594, but the idea is the original author's. The Frenchman exhorted men to study diligently: "So must learning also be provided for, by seeking of new inventions, in steede of those that are lost, by changing that which is not well, and by supplying that which is wanting: to the end that it be not decayed." Le Roy's whole conception in this work is based upon the premise that only the finite world of man is mutable. The greater cosmos stands firm: "[Nature] is the same that she was in the former famous ages: The world is such as it was before: The heaven and the time keepe the same order which they did . . . and men are made of the same matter, & in the same sort disposed as they were in old time." Again and again Le Roy insists that there are two schemata.

> For the world being made of two things, whereof the one are perpetuall, and others mutable and corruptible: It is certain that those which are perpetuall, as the heaven, the sunne, the moone, and thother starres, remain constantly alwaies in one selfe the same state: But they that are moveable doe begin, and end; are borne, and die; do increase, & diminish uncessantly; endeavouring notwithstanding (as much as they may) to come neere and participate of eternity: not by remaining alwaies one and the same (as doe the superiour and divine thinges) but by continuing their kindes by the meanes of generation; *which is an immortall worke in this mortalitie.*[25]

Le Roy was able to balance the two world views by fitting one inside the other. He was having the best of two possible worlds. There were others who arrived at a similar balance.

And again we must turn to those Neoplatonic writers whose professional careers were centered in jurisprudence. The problem they faced in the middle of the sixteenth century was one concerned with the study of law in a modern world. They taught Roman law and they needed new answers. In their search for those answers they touched unexpectedly upon the problem of time. Did time obliterate the values and relevance of ancient law? The answer was a Neoplatonic one: Roman law contained a universal truth, an extractable universal value that could be applied in any society and in any age.[26] When we turn to the work of François Baudouin, *De Institutione Historiae Universae,* we find that scholar applying his philosophical learning to the solution of the relevancy problem. Baudouin, who taught Roman law at the University of Bourges, published his treatise in 1561, dedicating it to Antony of Navarre. In it he argues for a universalism in history:

history as well as nature itself contains a permanent and ineffaceable element. Baudouin insists that the study of history "is a way and means by which we may arrive at that understanding of divine and human things which can place our minds, uplifted, on a height from which we may observe, as in a mirror, whatever has been done within the world from its beginnings which is worthy of our notice and remembrance. Such priests, indeed, does history produce." Baudouin insists that this knowledge is possible because of the idea of continuity in time, what he calls the "indivisibility" of history. The universality in history is to be found in the "pattern" (Baudouin uses the term *pragmateia)*; this pattern of history is *integra* and *perfecta.* This insistence upon the unbroken sweep of history or wisdom is related to the Neoplatonic ideas of Ficino and his closely knit academy of scholars near Florence, who insisted upon the continuity of human wisdom through all movements of European history and the appearance of universal truth to all peoples in all periods of time.[27] Baudouin was not concerned with the idea of the prophetic schema of time and its relationship to the Old Testament as were the German historical writers of this period. Indeed, he was in the foreranks of the French writers who attacked the German historians on this point. The French Baudouin, resisting the Germanic theories of the four Monarchies on the one hand and the humanistic demands for history that was rhetorically correct and realistically vigorous on the other, created his own idealistic conception of what history is. This universal element in Baudouin's theory, with its similarity to nineteenth-century theories of history, has led scholars to call him the "precursor of Mommsen."[28] It is this Neoplatonic element in Baudouin's work that I find useful and important for my own study.

At about the same time another Platonist, Francis Patrizzi, was publishing his ideas on ideal history. In the *Dieci Dialoghi della Historia* (1560) Patrizzi insists that history is a narrative of earlier ages that enables man to contemplate himself. This view of history is correct, he states, because man's essential nature is unchanging and can be seen in the episodes of history. (This view resembles in some aspects Machiavelli's idea that human nature is unchang-

ing, remaining the same in all ages.) Patrizzi does acknowledge that the subjective element in written history to
some extent prohibits the complete knowledge of any one
action in the past, but he insists that generalized knowledge
(philosophy and history are very close at this point) reveals man's essential nature. Especially does the writer of
biographical history, one of Patrizzi's three categories of
history, create more than a shadow, an imitation, an effigy;
he creates or adumbrates a human *soul*.[29] Some of these
ideas of Patrizzi were adapted and abridged by Thomas
Blundevill in an English translation of 1574, but Blundevill
was interested in only the last five of the dialogues. Patrizzi's investigation into "the inward cause and the outwarde
cause . . . from which every deed that man doth, spring-
eth" fascinated Blundevill.[30]

In the political writings of Jean Bodin we find the enlargement of the Platonic ideas about universal history.
Bodin taught law at the University of Toulouse and was
witness to some of the tensions created between the tra-
ditionalist methods of teaching law (methods used by the
Bartholists) and the humanistic methods introduced into
France by Alciati and popularized by Cujas. In the *Methodus ad Facilem Historiarum Cognitionem* (1566) Bodin
divides history into three main categories, human, natural,
and divine; in the *Republic* (his "human" history) he
develops his ideas on the predictability of human actions.
He believed that there was a kind of certainty to be derived from human behavior as it was revealed in history,
especially as it pertained to the rise and fall of nations.
Bodin was certain, at least when he was writing the *Republic,* that a universal element was to be found in human
history which could be extracted as valid generalizations
about the affairs of men and states. Bodin was writing in
book four of the *Republic* about the rise and fall of com-
monwealths when he stated that there are "means to know
the changes and ruins" of great leaders and their kingdoms.
These means involve the close study of history–classical,
Hebraic, Turkish, Christian:."And in this sort it is lawfull
for a man looking into the yearly course of time, by writing
to commend unto posteritie the chaunges of cities and
commonweales, and so by things precedent and alreadie
forepassed to judge also of things to come."[31] Bodin's

interests were multifarious—numerology, astrology, the genealogical continuity of peoples, geographical influences upon the natural character of races, and so on. But through all this maze of polyglot ideas a strong Platonic idealism is discernible.[32] Bodin and Baudouin were resisting the theories of historical decadence which the skeptics of the sixteenth century had popularized, and their answers were derived from a newly developing relationship between the historian and the philosopher. But we can also see them borrowing some of their ideas from the literary critics. Bodin and Baudouin were searching for a system that would explain ideal and universalized history; they were groping toward some conception of the underlying (they would have said overlying) variables of historical causation. They turned to the most readily available philosophical doctrine, the conception of a Platonic ideal within history itself that could be discovered if history were read in the light of the new *ars historica*. The literary critics had condemned historians for centuries for failing to do just that.

This was the easy and ready answer to the historical skeptics in the last half of the sixteenth century. The idea of the universality of history can be seen, I think, in the epistle dedicatory which Richard Grenewey wrote to the earl of Essex and used as a preface to his translation of Tacitus (1598).

> For if Historie be the treasure of times past, as well as a guide, an image of mans present estate, a true and lively pattern of things to come, . . . Tacitus may by good right challenge the first place among the best . . . I present him therefore to your Honors favourable protection in regard of himself: but yet no otherwise then as a glasse, representing in lively colours of prowesse, magnanimitie and counsell; not onely woorthie personages of ages past and gone, but also your L. owne honorable vertues, whereof the world is both witnes and judge.[33]

The English chronicle writers throughout the sixteenth century had been a relatively stodgy group. The new idea of ideal history had not yet been applied to English chronicle material. Hall, Grafton, Holinshed, and Stow had plodded along, publishing in the more or less conglomerate and static form of the medieval writers. They willfully edited their materials of course, but structurally their works were still in direct line of descent from *The Brut*. Two men of Elizabeth's reign broke with the older form, each searching for a way to visualize and verbalize a *theme*. These two men, John Foxe and William Camden, were as unlike as two men could be, but each produced a new kind of history written around an idea. Foxe was intent upon creating a new conception of a church, and Camden a new conception of a nation. Both men were moralistic historians tied still to the idea of God's providence as the controlling force in human history. The first English historian to write amoral, thematic history was Sir John Hayward, who published his *Raigne of King Henry the IIII* in 1599. In this work Hayward was consistently concerned with probing beneath the surface of past events to prove that history reveals the universal elements of human nature. He analyzed historical characters, using newer conceptions of reason, will, and passion, and he freely invented and interpolated materials to emphasize this universal characteristic in his subjects. He was so successful in his attempts to prove that the universal elements found in history were active in contemporary England that he was locked in the Tower of London under suspicion of writing history with seditious intent.[34]

It was in this fermenting intellectual milieu that Shakespeare produced his *Henry IV* plays. These plays reveal certain attitudes toward history, I think, attitudes which fit into the more sanguine and idealistic conceptions of the function of the past. To make this statement more pointed, let us summarize.

In the latter part of the sixteenth century the secularization of history (with the exception of the German writers) had led to the abandonment of the older providential theory of history on the Continent. It was not so much denied as ignored. Interest had turned from the supernatural to the natural; the individual had taken the center of the stage, while the emphasis was upon variety and the unique in the sweeping movements of historical change. Realism and detail were valued. Fluctuation and change were accepted; the idea of progress was only a few decades in the future (the seeds of this important modern idea had been sown). But with this idea of historical change came the problem of the function and utility of history. How could history be of value if it were constantly changing? In the older, relatively static view, history had appeared to repeat itself; if one abandoned this conception, how could history still be maintained as a viable discipline? The old idea that history provided examples of virtues for emulation and vices for fearing was no longer enough. The old morality was still given lip service by chroniclers and pious men, but the new philosophy of historical change had "brought all in doubt." The Platonic idea of the unchanging nature of man in a flowing universe began to replace the older conception of history repeating itself: man remains the same in an ever-changing universe; hence history is neither useless nor dead. Nor is the past merely to be imitated. It is an active element playing a part in shaping the present, and it can help to predict the future, the theorists proclaimed.

In England in the 1590s Shakespeare was examining the chronicle histories carefully and turning some of the materials into history plays. The English writers of history had been slow to experiment with the new theories of historiography; it remained for the poet with sensitive and critical mind to apply the newer ideas of the function of history in a sophisticated way. The sanguine epistemology, based upon the timelessness of certain human characteristics that were extractable from history, can be seen working in the playwright's creation of the timeless Falstaff. The Platonic element, abstracting and universalizing human character, seems first to have been applied by the playwright in the comic mode as he blended it with the realistic demands for the unique and the individual. We find the dramatist making use of a conflation technique in which past elements of history are blended skillfully with recent and contemporary events; English historical characters are given three dimensions with the mannerisms of their Elizabethan descendants. This montage effect is achieved by a freely interpretive use of history and a frank manipulation of source materials. Shakespeare introduces at times the intentional anachronism with which he pulls together the past and the present in order to make implicit similarities in either character or action more forceful. There is even an attempt by the playwright to predict the future, an attempt which in one instance (the Falstaff-Cobham satire) succeeded admirably, and in another (the Percy story), failed with a shocking result. Shakespeare's views of history can be examined in the *Henry IV* plays, and those views reveal his youthful optimism and idealistic belief in a most sanguine epistemology.

CHAPTER TWO

An Accretion of Minuscule Clues

THE EVIDENCE FOR THE CASE OF SHAKESPEARE'S USE of an historical figure as a source for the famous character of Falstaff is varied and fragmentary. To many scholars the evidence has seemed insignificant; as a result, although it frequently has been quoted by editors, it has not been thoroughly investigated. The reasons for this neglect are multiple. First, Shakespeare's use of source material for his comic action in the *Henry IV* plays is sophisticated and complex. The playwright was drawing his imaginative and inventive comic characters out of an assortment of materials taken not only from the chronicle histories at hand but from contemporary Elizabethan events as well. This variety has increased the obscurity, since the underlying principle of conflation has not been understood or accepted as a Shakespearean dramatic technique. Another factor in the neglect of the problem, and perhaps the most rigid impediment of all, has been the idealistic image of Shakespeare which developed with the romantic movement and reached its height in the Victorian period. The image of the infallible poet rivals that of any image created by religious mystique. The idea that Shakespeare could be guilty of any breach of manners or good taste was anathema for many years. Even today some scholars are offended by the possibility. A friend of mine insists that Shakespeare did not write satire and was never interested in the politics of his day. This apotheosized image of Shakespeare is beginning to fade from the scene with the result that a more normal and objective view of Shakespeare the man is beginning to appear.

21

Another factor that has prevented the solving of the Falstaff-Oldcastle problem is the reluctance of competent critics to meddle with a touchy problem. There are religious overtones, or undertones if you prefer, to the Falstaff-Oldcastle business. In this area we find that some chauvinistic critics and determined sectarian scholars, using tunnel vision, tug at the poet as the women did the child before Solomon's chair. They would rather destroy than share. Many studies that touch on Shakespeare's religious beliefs tend to be frenetic and to lack objectivity. My own position on the question of Shakespeare's personal religious beliefs is epicene—i.e., neutral and silent. I simply do not know what Shakespeare's personal position on religious doctrine was. In the materials that I have found concerning the Oldcastle problem, there is an indication that literary and political tensions were involved in the affair, enough certainly to motivate the poet without insisting upon a religious motivation. And so I have chosen to place my stress upon those literary and political factors.

One more reason that the Falstaff-Oldcastle problem has been fusting so long is that the historical materials needed for a thorough study have been hard to get at. The series of *Calendars of State Papers* for Elizabeth I's reign is still not complete, and without calendars the mass of materials in the Public Record Office is a wilderness. Materials in private collections are now being put on microfilm, but this is a recent innovation. Moreover, financing international research travel is difficult, and for this particular study such travel has been a fundamental requirement.

There is one more obvious factor in the delay of the solution of the Falstaff-Oldcastle problem: the critical attitude that has reigned for over sixty years in the English-speaking world. The hostility toward historical criticism has been tantamount to warfare. There is still today a disdain for what is considered in some circles a dull and stuffy kind of scholarship which is concerned with "an author's laundry list." My own position on this point is firm: criticism without knowledge of the social context which produced the art is bodiless; and contextual scholarship without aesthetic sensitivity is dull.

The fragmentary evidence concerning Shakespeare's use of a chronicle figure for the comic character that dominates the *Henry IV* plays can be summarily reviewed.

Behind the character of Falstaff stands an obscure image as mammoth in size, as protean in shape, and as complex in character as Shakespeare's great comic figure. Ironically, the obscure image is that of a fifteenth-century Lollard martyr, a man who was burned at the stake in the reign of King Henry V. In the five hundred years since his martyrdom, the image of Sir John Oldcastle, Lord Cobham, has developed epic and mock-epic proportions in legend, drama, and literary criticism. Thus with this epic quality established, the survey of the minuscule clues upon which that most famous Shakespearean crux resides begins *in medias res*.

Approximately one hundred years after Shakespeare had completed his Falstaff cycle of plays, and time had begun to glamorize the Elizabethan age, John Dennis published a pertinent remark about *The Merry Wives of Windsor*, the Shakespearean comedy he admired enough to revise into his own stage play, *The Comical Gallant* (1702). As a good neoclassicist should, he prefaced his play with an epistle dedicatory to explain his actions. "I knew very well," he wrote to George Grenville, "that it had pleas'd one of the greatest Queens that ever was in the world. . . . This comedy was written at her Command, and by her direction, and she was so eager to see it Acted, that she commanded it to be finished in fourteen days; and was afterwards, as Tradition tells us, very well pleas'd at the Representation."[1] Dennis's remark seems to be the basis for Nicholas Rowe's similar comment in the first annotated edition of William Shakespeare's plays (1709–1710). Rowe repeats the colorful story about Queen Elizabeth, and then adds a casual detail of his own.

> She was so well pleas'd with that admirable Character of Falstaff, in the two Parts of *Henry the Fourth*, that she commanded him to continue it for one Play more, and to shew him in Love. This is said to be the Occasion of his Writing *The Merry Wives of Windsor*. How well she was obey'd the Play it self is an admirable Proof. Upon this Occasion it may not be improper to observe, that this Part of Falstaff is said to have been written originally under the Name of Oldcastle;

some of that Family being then remaining, the Queen was pleas'd to command him to alter it; upon which he made use of Falstaff. The present Offense was indeed avoided; but I don't know whether the Author may not have been some what to blame in his second Choice, since it is certain that Sir John Falstaff, who was a Knight of the Garter, and a Lieutenant-General, was a Name of distinguish'd Merit in the Wars in France in Henry the Fift's and Henry the Sixth's Times.[2]

Rowe's remark of course put the problem of Sir John Oldcastle before the subsequent Shakespearean editors of the eighteenth century. Even in Rowe's own edition, in an essay written by Charles Gildon on the contemporary stage, Gildon remarks that unlike Rowe he thinks Shakespeare "merits Applause" for his ingenuity in the substitution.[3]

For well over a decade the problem was ignored in literary circles, although theologians and historians kept the historical problem of Oldcastle, the fifteenth-century Lollard martyr, before the public eye. Thomas Fuller at mid-seventeenth century had faced the difficult Oldcastle issue in several passages of his *Church History of Britain* (1655). Fuller, prompted by both kindness and religious convictions of his own, tried to keep to the *via media* in his presentation, and so he attempted to temper the source material he was using—the fierce account of Oldcastle's martyrdom written by John Foxe, the martyrologist. Fuller acknowledges the merit of Foxe's account of Oldcastle and the pains Foxe undertook to give "Posterity a writ of Ease therin," but Fuller had read beyond Foxe and had found more objective accounts of Oldcastle's death, so in the *Church History* he describes his own hesitation to credit his source.

For mine own part, I must confess my self so lost in the Intricacies of these Relations, that I know not what to assent to. On the one side, I am loath to load the Lord Cobhams memory with causeless crimes, knowing the perfect hatred the Clergie in that Age bear'd unto him, and all that look'd towards the reformation in Religion. . . . On the other side, I am much startled with the Evidence that appeareth against him. Indeed I am little moved with what T. Walsingham writes, (whom all later Authors follow, as a flock the Belweather) knowing him a Benedictine Monk of St Albanes, bowed by partiality;

but the Records of the Tower, and Acts of Parliament therein, wherein he was solemnly condemned for a Traitor as well as Heretick, challenge belief. For with what confidence can any private person promise credit from Posterity to his own Writings, if such publick Monuments be not by him entertained for authentical: Let Mr Fox therefore, be this Lord Cobhams Compurgator, I dare not; and if my hand were put on the Bible, I should take it back again. Yet so that, as I will not acquit, I will not condemn him, but leave all to the last day of the Revelation of the righteous judgment of God.[4]

Poor Fuller's hesitation to condemn Oldcastle, and indeed, the tenderness of his whole account of Wyclif and the Lollards, aroused the ire of Peter Heylyn, theologian and historian, whose high church position left no room in his quire for such sentiment—the Lollards of the fourteenth and fifteenth centuries in their aggressiveness resembled far too closely the troublesome nonconformists of the seventeenth century. Heylyn published his *Examen Historicum: Animadversions on the Church History of Britain* in 1659; he exposed with sharpness Fuller's quasi-Puritan tendencies. He taxed him for his management of Wyclif's doctrine, Oldcastle's treason and heresy, Thomas Walsingham and the Latin chroniclers, and Foxe. And he concluded with a blast: "The wheat of Wickliffe was so foul, so full of chaffe, and intermingled with so many and such dangerous Tares, that to expose it to the view, were to mar the market." He ends by accusing Fuller of whitewashing the heretics to make them "better and more Orthodox than indeed they were." Those readers who know the ways of seventeenth-century polemics will understand how Fuller in a few short weeks got out his answer in *The Appeal of Injured Innocence.* In this hasty work (the highly irregular pagination indicates that even the printer was hasty) Fuller questions Heylyn's sympathy with the Reformation, and then he makes clear his position on the Oldcastle problem: "As for Sir *John Oldcastle* L. *Cobham,* his Case is so perplexed with contrary relations *much* may be said against him, and *little lesse* in his behalf; and I have cause to beleeve indeed, that his Innocence wanted not *clearnesse* but *clearing.*"[5]

In the same decade Sir Richard Baker's *Chronicle of the Kings of England* appeared. Baker's presentation of the Oldcastle story is abbreviated, repetitive, and bare of details; he seems to have been using the Elizabethan chronicles as sources. The original source materials were still rare or difficult to obtain, although Thomas Rymer in his official capacity as royal historiographer had begun to collect many of the historical government papers and to edit them for later publication.[6] In 1675 Sir William Dugdale, Garter king of arms, published his impressive *Baronage of England*. Dugdale's position is manifest clearly in his account of Sir John Oldcastle, Lord Cobham: "[Oldcastle,] being tainted in his Religion by those pretended Holy Zelots, then called Lollards, became one of the chief of that Sect, which at that time gave no little disturbance to the peace of the Church." Dugdale describes briefly Oldcastle's "obstinacie in those dangerous Tenents," his "design to Murther the King," his escape from the Tower and the "new commotions," his eventual execution.[7] The publication of Dugdale's prestigious volumes seems to have silenced for some years objections to the negative accounts of Oldcastle's history. Not until 1707 do we find Laurence Echard saying in his *History of England* that Oldcastle died a hero. "Thus dy'd the great Lord Cobham," he wrote, "and as this was the first Noble Blood that was shed in England on the Account of Religion by Popish Malignity, so perhaps never any suffer'd a more cruel Martyrdom."[8] Gilbert Burnet's *History of the Reformation*, published after his lifetime, begins with the reign of Henry VIII, and so the bishop avoided any detailed account of the pre-Reformation period. But Jeremy Collier brought out his *Ecclesiastical History* in 1708, and his coverage included the medieval period of church affairs. Collier condemns Oldcastle as a heretic and a traitor, and he takes John Foxe to task for falsifying the records.

> I had passed over these exceptions against Fox, had he not taken the freedom to blemish the public records and arraign the government. But when a man will venture thus far in defense of a favorite, it is necessary to acquaint the reader with this manner, and precaution him against believing too fast. To which I must add that though we are obliged to pity unfortunate persons, and be as favourable to the dead as truth will give us leave, yet we ought carefully to distinguish between martyrdom and treason, and not to be over fond of the memory of those who suffered for a practice against the state.[9]

Collier then follows Heylyn in an attack on Fuller's endeav-
our to blanch the character of Oldcastle, and Collier concludes that Fuller's notions were without foundation.

In 1724, the year before Alexander Pope published his
six-volume edition of Shakespeare's plays, John Anstis,
Garter king of arms, published *The Register of the Garter,*
the official records of the renowned Order of the Garter, to
which he added notes and commentary. In his account of
Sir John Fastolf, who had received his Saint George collar
from Henry VI, Anstis remarks that the playwrights had
traduced the valiant soldier's name as Aristophanes of old
had traduced Socrates:

> The Comick Writers have drawn Characters with unaccount-
> able Freedoms, and have run to that Length, as to burlesque
> the Best of their Poets from whom they derived their own little
> Knowledge, and therefore 'tis the less Wonder they should in
> their Plays distort Historical Facts, and like Harpies defile what
> they touch; which strange License can be only to the Taste of
> those who would rather leave behind them Stench than Per-
> fume, and choose rather to live in ridiculous Satyrs and Invec-
> tives, than in just Panegyricks and Commendations.

Anstis, having defended his knight, was put to it then to
defend the bard, for bardolatry had swept over England and
was infecting the Continent too by this time. Anstis ab-
solves Shakespeare of any gross motivation in the use of
Fastolf's name:

> Shakespear, however, cannot be charged with any premedi-
> tated Spleen against the Memory of our Knight, at the Time
> when he composed his Comedies; for Sir John Oldcastle was
> at first introduced by him upon the Stage and personated in
> the Drama, which being resented as an Affront, the Poet altered
> the Scene, and when there was nothing to fear from any Pre-
> sentment, or any Hope for Favour, he in its Room substituted
> the Name of Sir John Fastolf, which might be done at random,
> since his first Design was evidently no more, than to entertain
> the Theatre with the Character of Henry V. while Prince, as the
> Subject of Mirth and Ridicule: And it must be confessed, that
> he hath performed his Design with incomparable Wit and
> inimitable Humor, which have made such lasting Impression
> on the Generality of Spectators, that they have been induced or
> bewitched into a Belief, that this Drollery was a Piece of true
> History.[10]

This cursory review of the late seventeenth- and early eighteenth-century milieu suggests, I believe, that any well-read Englishman of the period would have been aware of the explosive nature of the Oldcastle problem, both in and out of drama. When Alexander Pope published his edition of Shakespeare's plays in 1725, he supplied a minimum of commentary; to the epilogue of 2 *Henry IV* he notes, "This alludes to a play, in which Sir John Oldcastle was put for Falstaff." And he repeats John Dennis's story about Queen Elizabeth's command for *The Merry Wives of Windsor*.[11] Pope's failure to add more about the Oldcastle problem is the result, I believe, not of haste or ignorance but rather of his own good taste and his alertness, as a Catholic, to the vulnerability of the subject—Pope's schooling in literary polemics was of course superb, as students of the Augustan age are aware. When William Warburton, the Anglican divine whom Pope had chosen for his literary executor, reissued Pope's edition of Shakespeare, he added to the original Oldcastle note, drawing obviously from his readings in ecclesiastical histories and, it would seem from his wording, Anstis's account in the *Register of the Garter*:

> The reason of the change was this, one Sir John Oldcastle having suffered in the time of Henry V for the opinions of Wickliffe, it gave offence; and therefore the Poet altered it to Falstaff, and endeavours to remove the scandal, in the Epilogue to the second part of Henry IV. Fuller takes notice of this matter in his Church-History. . . . But to be candid, I believe there was no malice in the matter. Shakespeare wanted a droll name to his character, and never considered whom it belonged to.[12]

This is a discreet management of the touchy problem, particularly so because Lewis Theobald, in his 1733 edition of Shakespeare's works, had gone into some detail to explain the vexing problem. Theobald refers to Rowe's remark, to Fuller, to a quarto, and also to the old plays, *The Famous Victories of Henry V* and *The History of Syr John Oldcastle*, and he concludes that the evidence proves that Shakespeare used the name of Sir John Oldcastle for his character of Falstaff in the first production of the *Henry IV* plays, but used it unwittingly of course.[13]

The British historians of the eighteenth century continued to produce valuable source material pertaining to the historical Oldcastle. Rymer's *Foedera* was issued twice in the first half-century; David Wilkins's *Concilia Magnae Britanniae* was published in 1737. Thomas Hearne, a dedicated antiquary and scholar, began to edit many of the medieval chronicles, editions of vast importance to students of history, some of them being still the only, editions in print. In 1716 he edited Tito Livio's fifteenth-century Latin life of Henry V, a biography which includes an adverse account of Oldcastle the heretic and traitor. And in 1732 Hearne published the Latin chronicle of Thomas Otterbourne, a fifteenth-century source containing an energetic account of Oldcastle's capture and execution.[14] But as few literary scholars think alike, so too the historians. The violently Protestant account of Oldcastle's life which John Bale had published in the 1540s was reissued in facsimile in a beautifully bound and gilt edition of Bale's works. This book defends Oldcastle's martyrdom and presents the Lollards as victims of the unscrupulous Catholic clergy of Henry V's reign. Also included in the volume as appendixes are the citations and proclamations of the archbishop and the king against Oldcastle.[15]

When the first edition of *Biographia Britannica* appeared in 1750, it contained a lengthy and well-documented article on Sir John Fastolf, written by William Oldys, Norroy king of arms. Oldys had written the article for Birch's *General Dictionary* in 1737, but he refurbished it for the new publication. He had worked through the wealth of resources available to him by now, and in some detail he listed the disparity between the historical events as they appeared in Shakespeare's plays and the dates and events of Fastolf's life. Oldys concludes that Shakespeare had not seriously meant to travesty the historical Fastolf:

. . . for the Poet first drew the character of his Sir John Falstaff, in Sir John Oldcastle's name; but being thereby thought to have displeased some descendants or at least, made too free with such an early and eminent instrument or advancer of, and sufferer for our Reformation, the Poet was obliged to change the name, from one that might have well enough implyed the old battered bravo we see represented, to one that might as well express other parts of the same character, by a staff that was false in its soundness, or strength for support, and as little to be relied, or depended on, as a broken reed.[16]

Oldys's article seems to have been the prick that brought forth the lamentation which appeared in a fall issue of the *Gentleman's Magazine* in 1752. The author of the article, who signs it only with the initials P. T., insists upon the absurdity, the impossibility of the idea that Shakespeare would have satirized or defamed the noble and valiant Oldcastle whom Foxe had extolled and who headed the list of Protestant martyrs in the English Reformation.[17]

But such objections seem not to have disturbed Samuel Johnson, for in his edition of Shakespeare (1765) he reprints the notes from Theobald's and Warburton's editions to the effect that Falstaff had originally been called Oldcastle.[18] In the same year that Johnson brought out his Shakespearean texts, William Gilpin published a popular collection of lives of John Wyclif, John Huss, Sir John Oldcastle, and Jerome of Prague; the work went into a second edition within a year.[19] Gilpin revised the account of Oldcastle and the other early church reformers that he found in John Foxe's *Acts and Monuments,* but he kept the high emotional tone and the same point of view. And this was the state of affairs that Edward Capell faced when he edited the plays in 1767. He and Johnson had been working at their respective tasks at the same time. Capell's project was ridiculed, and his competition with Johnson was called fantastical. Capell was an acute textual critic; he has been called the first of the new school of critics who set aside historical criticism and base their notes on an examination of variant readings and reasoned deductions. Whether it was a reasoned deduction, the competition with Johnson, or his own theological position that influenced his stand on the Oldcastle problem we do not know, but Capell ducked the historical evidence and took the easy way out; he insisted that the old play, *The Famous Victories,* was the cause of all the trouble, that Shakespeare was simply alluding to it in the epilogue of *2 Henry IV,* and that the fate of the old play should be "damnation!"[20]

It may be objected that the eighteenth-century editors of Shakespeare's works were not conscious of the historical and theological points of view on Oldcastle that were available in that day. But any student of the neoclassical age in England is aware of the homogeneous yet factious and overly sensitive character of the scholarly circles of

Augustan London; and the Shakespearean editors were educated and competent men. But to follow through: Edmond Malone edited the plays and poems of Shakespeare in 1790, and he seems to have found it easy to follow Capell in remarking on the Oldcastle problem. "Sir John Oldcastle was not a character ever introduced by Shakespeare, nor did he ever occupy the place of Falstaff. The play, in which Oldcastle's name occurs, was not the work of our poet."[21] Malone's statement seems to have carried the day until J. O. Halliwell-Phillipps collected as much historical and critical material as he could find on the Oldcastle problem, organized it in a sensible manner, and presented it persuasively as an endeavor "to place in a clearer light a question which has been frequently discussed, but still left in considerable obscurity."[22] In his own logical way he concluded that the Elizabethan stage was in possession of a rude outline of Falstaff under the name of Sir John Oldcastle before Shakespeare wrote either part of *Henry IV;* that the name of Oldcastle was retained for a time in Shakespeare's *Henry IV* but was changed to Falstaff before the play was printed; and that, in all probability, some of the theaters in presenting *Henry IV* retained the name of Oldcastle after the author had made the alteration. Since the publication of this work no well-read Shakespearean editor has disagreed with Halliwell-Phillipps's general thesis. Twentieth-century editors and scholars have continued to work with the problem of Sir John Oldcastle's appearance in Shakespeare's plays, and positive evidence has grown slowly by research and sedulous reading until today we have an accretion of facts and allusions which has transformed theory into acceptable conclusion. There is no longer doubt that Shakespeare used the name of Sir John Oldcastle for his character of Falstaff in an early version of his *Henry IV* plays. The evidence to support this conclusion is both intrinsic and extrinsic—evidence surviving within the quarto texts and that drawn from allusions and references by playwrights and seventeenth-century commentators. Most of this material has been reviewed many times, and it is the product of many minds—the authors of the allusion books compiled much of it in the nineteenth century; Sir Edmund Chambers prints some material in the appendixes to his *William Shakespeare;* and the Variorum and

New Arden editors have remarked upon the numerous references.

The primary evidence of the Oldcastle-Falstaff name revision in the *Henry IV* plays is that of the texts. There remains in the 1600 quarto of *2 Henry IV* the speech-prefix *Old.* before one of Falstaff's lines (I.ii.137). This irregularity has been accepted traditionally as an oversight of the transcriber who prepared a copy of the manuscript for the printer, and it was corrected in the first folio.[23] In the epilogue of the same play the actor-dancer is made to promise:

> If you be not too much cloyed with fat meat, our humble author will continue the story, with Sir John in it, and make you merry with fair Katherine of France. Where, for anything I know, Falstaff shall die of a sweat, unless already 'a be killed with your hard opinions, for Oldcastle died a martyr, and this is not the man.

The phrase "and this is not the man" can be taken several ways, of course: as a flat denial, as a sop for the censor—the tongue-in-cheek pose popular with Nashe and Jonson—or even as a contemptuous statement about Falstaff and Lord Cobham with a negative image of Oldcastle—"This is certainly not the kind of man to die a martyr." Preceding lines in the epilogue increase this air of ambiguity: "For what I have to say is of mine own making, and what indeed I should say will, I doubt, prove my own marring." This whole epilogue is spoken by way of apology, the actor explains, for "I was lately here in the end of a displeasing play, to pray your patience for it and to promise you a better." This last remark leads most modern editors to suggest that the displeasing play was *1 Henry IV* with the Oldcastle name in it, and the remark lends credence to Rowe's story of the displeasure of the "family then remaining." This family in Elizabeth's court was that of William Brooke, Lord Cobham, member of the queen's Privy Council, knight of the Garter, lord warden of the Cinque Ports, lord chamberlain of the Queen's Household, lord lieutenant of Kent, constable of the Tower, and holder of minor offices as well. He was also a close and intimate friend of Lord Burghley and father-in-law to Sir Robert Cecil. It is reasonable to assume that Lord Cobham's position in the Privy Council and his office in the queen's household gave him sufficient influence with Elizabeth to bring about the ameliorating name-change.

In *1 Henry IV* Prince Hal calls Falstaff "my old lad of the castle" (I.ii.40) which, among its multiple meanings, includes a pun on Oldcastle; and in the same play two various lines (II. ii. 103; II. iv. 456) are unmetrical with the name Falstaff but regularly decasyllabic with the name Oldcastle.[24] In the first quarto of *The Merry Wives of Windsor* the name *Brooke* appears (lines 540-43, 550-55), but this name is changed to *Broome* in the 1623 edition of the play, spoiling Falstaff's joke, "Such Brookes are alwaies welcome to me." And Master Ford's alias, Brooke, also suffers revision to *Broome* in the first folio version. In this same play there is a probable pun on the name of Oldcastle in the line spoken by the host to describe Falstaff, "Sir John, there's his Castle, his standing bed" (line 1305). These few tactile clues make up the body of intrinsic evidence of the name revision from Oldcastle to Falstaff at some time prior to the publication of the first quarto of *1 Henry IV* in 1598. The extrinsic evidence for this name-change is more varied, more salient.

In the older play, *The Famous Victories of King Henry the Fifth,* Sir John Oldcastle appears as a character in the entourage of young Prince Hal. On coronation day Oldcastle and two other knights are renounced by the new king as ungodly men whose characters are incommensurate with the new standards of royalty. This anonymous play has long been considered a part of Shakespeare's source material. Its relationship to the *Henry IV* plays is discussed in chapter six of this study; it is mentioned here only to reveal the existence of a dramatic characterization of Sir John Oldcastle at an earlier date than Shakespeare's plays.

In November of 1599, the Lord Admiral's Men produced a play, an historic compilation by Drayton, Munday, Hathaway, and Wilson, entitled *The First Part of the True and Honourable History of the Life of Sir John Oldcastle, the Good Lord Cobham,* in which the authors defended the Lollard martyr and in which, by way of prologue, they made an evident thrust at the by-now famous Falstaff:

It is no pamper'd Glutton we present,
Nor aged Councellour to youthfull sinne,

But one, whose vertue shone above the rest,
A valiant Martyr, and a vertuous Peere:
In whose true faith and loyalty exprest
Unto his soveraigne and his Countries weale:
We strive to pay that tribute of our love
Your favours merit. Let faire Truth be grac'd,
Since forg'd invention former times defac'd.[25]

This play portrays the historical Oldcastle as a devoted and loyal subject of the king, and we assume that Part Two (paid for by Henslowe, but no longer extant) carried the story on to Oldcastle's martyrdom. This assumption, however, may be false: Part Two may never have been completed even though Henslowe paid for it. The publicity had been gained and the rebuttal made with Part One; the defense of the martyr is overt. The political machinations of Oldcastle in Part One are contrived only to undo the factions plotting against the king; Oldcastle's role here goes beyond Foxe's account or any other extant version of the Lollard's heroic actions. But more importantly, the play contains numerous allusions to Shakespeare's works; the opening scene between Lord Herbert and Lord Powis is patterned on the opening street-brawl of *Romeo and Juliet* and on the conflict in act I, scene iii of *1 Henry VI;* the *Oldcastle* scene in which the summoner (who resembles Pistol) is forced to eat his summons is much like the leek-eating scene in *Henry V;* the first scene in act II of *Oldcastle* contains a speech by Richard, earl of Cambridge, in which he declaims on the rights of his family (York) to the English throne; it resembles the duke of York's speech in *2 Henry VI;* and of course the portrayal of Doll, a character who closely resembles Doll Tearsheet, the robbery scene, the tavern scenes, the corruption and wit of Sir John, the parson of Wrotham—all indicate an influence of Falstaff and his merry crew.[26] These allusions, broad and overt, reinforce the reading of the line in the prologue, "Since forg'd invention former times defac'd," as a reference to the defamation of Oldcastle in Shakespeare's plays.

The forged invention theme is repeated by John Weever in a long poem about the Lollard knight which he called *The Mirror of Martyrs* (1601), written, as he declared in his dedication, "some two yeares agoe." This poetic eulogy, a conglomeration of classical and Renaissance effusions,

proclaims Oldcastle as "that thrice valiant Capitaine and
most godly Martyre," and Weever's hero is made to question, somewhat bluntly, the classical gods of the Elysian
Fields: "Why am I thus in my remembrance rotten, And in
thy sweet saint-pleasing songs forgotten?" Oldcastle himself is made to suggest a remedy to this lamentable situation as he bids the god Mercury descend to the earth as a
dramatic herald and

> Deliver but in swasive eloquence,
> Both of my life and death the veritie,
> Set up a *Si quis,* give intelligence,
> That such a day shall be my Tragedie.
>   If thousands flocke to heare a Poet's pen,
>   To heare a god, how many millions then?[27]

This reference to the thousands who flock to hear a poet's
pen is a possible allusion to the popularity of Shakespeare's *Henry IV* plays; however, it could as possibly be a
reference to the lord admiral's play that was paid for in
November of 1599. If Weever's poem were written before
this date, the allusion is quite probably a Shakespearean
one.

Outside the theaters the wit of the dramatist is reflected
in allusive remarks in letters of the period. We know that
toward the last of February 1598, the earl of Essex wrote
to Sir Robert Cecil, who was at that time traveling to
France on a diplomatic mission for the queen. Essex included in a postscript to his letter what has been taken as a
mocking jest: "I pray you commend me allso to Alex. Ratcliffe and tell him for newes his sister is maryed to Sr. Jo.
Falstaff." Leslie Hotson, who discovered this allusion, has
suggested, quite convincingly, that by "Sr. Jo. Falstaff"
Essex meant Henry Brooke, the new Lord Cobham.[28] We
know from the detailed gossip which Rowland Whyte sent
to Sir Robert Sidney that Margaret Ratcliffe, daughter of
Sir Alexander Ratcliffe of Ordsall and one of the queen's
maids of honor, was a contender for the title of Lady Cobham.[29] Whether Essex's jest had point in fact or fancy we do
not know. There is no evidence of such a marriage. We do
know of Queen Elizabeth's peculiar and hostile attitude
toward many of the marriages of her courtiers and maids;
Essex, Southampton, and Raleigh all suffered periods of

disfavor because of their marriages. It is quite possible that Cobham, if there were a marriage or alliance, succeeded in keeping it a secret—at least from the queen. There was additional gossip in the following year. On 8 July 1599 the young countess of Southampton, in a letter to her husband who was with Essex in Ireland, passed on to him a piquant bit of gossip which had reached her at Chartley:

> All the newes I can sende you which I think will make you merry is that I reade in a letter from London that Sir John Falstaff is by his Mrs. Dame Pintpot made father to a godly milers thum, a boy that is all heade and veri litel body, but this is a secrit.[36]

Scholars have been quick to discover that the "small fish with the big head" is in Latin a *Cottus Gobio* and in English a *cob*, or, as early as 1440, a "myllars thowmbe."[31] The gossip that the countess of Southampton repeated apparently credited the new Lord Cobham with parenthood, if we agree that the Cobhams were victimized by the character of Falstaff. Whether the gossip was true or not we have no way of knowing. If there were a secret marriage or misalliance between Margaret Ratcliffe and Lord Cobham, it was shortly terminated by the mysterious death of that unfortunate young woman in November 1599.[32]

We are indebted to another letter of the period for a reference to *Henry IV* as an Oldcastle play. The reference is to be found in one of Rowland Whyte's weekly messages to his employer, Sir Robert Sidney, the governor of Flushing at that time. As steward, Whyte was obligated to keep his master informed on as much of the business and life at court as he could learn from his trips around London. In March 1600 Whyte sent several newsy letters to Sidney; the one written on the eighth contains a description of the entertainment which had been given Ambassador Vereken during his visit to London:

> All this weeke the Lords have bene in Londen, and past away the tyme in feasting and plaies . . . on Thursday afternoon the Lord Chamberlain's players acted before Vereken *Sir John Oldcastle,* to his great contentment.[33]

Since the lord chamberlain's players would not have been performing one of Henslowe's plays, Whyte's reference appears to indicate that the *Henry IV* play or plays were being performed as *Sir John Oldcastle.* Whether or not the character of Falstaff was actually called Oldcastle in the performance in 1600 is unascertainable.

Another vague reference of this sort is extant in an office book of the lord chamberlain, compiled in 1638-1639. It is to be found in a bill evidently submitted by the King's Men for payment from the lord chamberlain. The item indicates a court performance: "At the Cocpit the 29th May the princes berthnyght—ould Castel."[34] These are slight but important evidences of a lingering tradition in the theater.

There are in addition some indications that later playwrights of the Jacobean stage found allusions to Oldcastle/Falstaff as humorous as the courtiers of Elizabeth's reign. In 1604 an anonymous play, *The Meeting of Gallants at an Ordinarie,* was published with lines that contain an allusion to Oldcastle as a rogue:

> *Shuttlecock:* Now Signiors how like you mine Host? did I not tell you he was a madde round knave, and a merrie one too: and if you chaunce to talke of fatte *Sir John Old-Castle,* he wil tell you, he was his great Grandfather, and not much unlike him in Paunch if you marke him well by all descriptions.[35]

And as late as 1610 apparently Lord Cobham's complaint of the players' satire seems to have been remembered. Lines from Roger Sharpe's *More Fooles Yet* allude it would seem to the affront taken by that nobleman:

> How Falstaffe like doth sweld Virosus looke,
> As though his paunch did foster every sinne,
> And sweares he is injured by this booke
> His worth is taxt, he hath abused byn.[36]

Moreover, in 1618 Nathan Field included a reference to Oldcastle in his comedy, *Amends for Ladies,* a reference that associates Oldcastle with Falstaff's famous catechism on honor. The humor character, Seldon, speaks the following lines to Lord Proudly:

> Good morrow to your Honor, I doe heare
> Your Lordship this faire morning is to fight,
> And for your honor: Did you never see

The Play, where the fat Knight hight *Old-Castle*,
Did tell you truly what this honor was?[37]

This list of allusions can be continued, for Thomas Randolph, one of the Sons of Ben, seems to have composed his comedy, *Hey for Honesty*, while he was still a student at Trinity College, Cambridge. And though the play was not published until some years after Randolph's death, the allusion in it to a Bardolph-Falstaff-Oldcastle figure apparently was still understood. In a tavern scene the following description occurs.

> Every Cupboard is full of Custards, the Hogsheads replenished with sparkling Sacke. . . . The Sinke is paved with rich Rubies, and incomparable Carbuncles of Sir John Oldcastle's Nose.[38]

In addition to this growing list can be added a passage from the anonymous play, *The Wandering Jew* (ca. 1628), in which an allusion to Oldcastle seems also to allude to Falstaff. The Glutton of the play is described as a "Manningtree Oxe with a pudding in his belly." When Glutton enters, he exclaims:

> A Chaire, a Chaire, sweet Master Jew, a Chaire: All that I say, is this. I'me a fat man, it has been a West-Indian voyage for me to come reeking hither; a Kitchin-stuffe wench might pick up a living, by following me, for the fat which I loose in stradling: I doe not live by the sweat of my brows, but am almost dead with sweating. I eat much, but can talk little; Sir John Oldcastle was my greatgrandfathers fathers Uncle, I come of a huge kindred.[39]

It should be remarked that while the numerous progeny of Falstaff-Oldcastle strutted the stage, sensitive men were to be found who objected to such usage. And their complaints add to the evidence of Shakespeare's employment of the ill-famed martyr's name. The poet George Daniel of Beswick wrote a long historical poem in 1649 called *Trinarchodia*. In this difficult work Daniel is concerned with the thought that new ideas in religion are usually considered evil when introduced. This idea leads him to the subject of the Lollards and to Oldcastle:

The Worthy Sr whom Falstaffe's ill-us'd Name
Personates on the Stage, lest Scandall might
Creep backward & blott Martyr; were a Shame,
Though Shakespeare story, & Foxe legend write;
    That Manuel where dearth of Story brought
    Such Sts worthy this Age, to make it out.

Some one hundred stanzas later, Daniel once again takes up the subject of Shakespeare's Falstaff, but this time he is concerned with the misrepresentation of the character of Sir John Fastolf.

Here to Evince the Scandall has bene throwne
Upon a Name of Honour, (charactred
From a wrong Person, Coward and Buffoone;)
Call in your easie faiths, from what y'ave read
    To laugh at Falstaffe, as an humor fram'd
    To grace the Stage, to please the Age, misnam'd.

Daniel applies logic to the problem and concludes that it would have been impossible for the honorable knight to have been a clown:

But thinke, how farre unfit? how much below
Our Harrie's Choice, had such a Person bene?
To Such a Trust? the Town's a Taverne now
And plumpe Sr John, is but the Bush far-seene;
    As all the Toyle of Princes had been Spent
    To force a Lattice, or Subdue a Pinte.

Daniel then attempts to defend the name of the valiant knight.

Such Stage-Mirth, have they made Him; Harry Saw
Meritt; and Scandall but pursues the Steps
Of Honour with ranke Mouth; if Truth may draw
Opinion, wee are paid; how ere the heapes
    Who Crowd to See, in Expectation fall
    To the Sweet Nugilogues of Jacke, and Hall.

And the poet concludes by letting the chips fall where they may; he is assured he says that honor will right wrong.

This may Suffice to right him; let the Guilt
Fall where it may; unquestion'd, Harrie Stands

> From the foure Points of vertue, equall built;
> Judgment Secur'd the Glorie of his Hands;
>   And from his bountie, blot out what may rise
>   Of Comicke Mirth, to Falstaff's praejudice.[40]

There were other critics in addition to the poets and playwrights who contributed a share to the controversy. Even historians and scholars had something to say about the inappropriate use of the Lollard Martyr's name. Old John Speed, patriotic and devout, was an industrious chronicler whose bias against poets and players placed him close to Cornelius Agrippa's position in the right-wing, conservative faction of thinkers. Speed wrote an angry attack upon the Jesuit scholar Robert Parsons—that "arch-traitor," that "Machiavell"—an attack that included what is apparently a reference to Shakespeare. In his *Theatre of the Empire of Great Britaine* (1611) Speed strikes out at Parsons's reference to Oldcastle in the Jesuit's long work, *A Treatise of Three Conversions of England* (1603-1604). Speed writes:

> That N. D. [the pseudonym Parsons used], author of the three conversions, hath made Ouldcastle a Ruffian, a Robber, and a Rebell, and his authoritie taken from the Stage-plaiers, is more befitting the pen of his slanderous report, then the Credit of the judicious, being onely grounded from this Papist and his Poet, of like conscience for lies, the one ever faining, the other ever falsifying the truth.[41]

Speed's derogatory phrase concerning Parson's "Poet" has caused scholars to wince. It refers in all probability to Shakespeare, an idea which can be accepted, I think, with more equanimity today than in earlier ages. It should be added that no evidence has been found of a relationship between the Jesuit writer and Shakespeare other than Parsons's use of a dramatic mode of propaganda that Shakespeare developed in the Falstaffian satire of his history plays and *The Merry Wives of Windsor*. Parsons's *A Treatise of Three Conversions* was written to expose the "falsification" of English history that the Jesuit found in John Foxe's *Acts and Monuments;* but Parsons was writing in 1603-1604 when the contemporary Lord Cobham and his brother were involved in a treasonous affair; and thus Parsons's insistence upon the treason of an earlier Lord Cobham (Oldcastle) was relevant to the times.[42]

Speed's reference to the perverters of truth is similar in content to that made by Fuller in the *Church History;* Fuller kept returning to the Oldcastle problem—it worried him.

> Stage-poets have themselves been very bold with, and others very merry at, the memory of Sr. John Oldcastle, whom they have fancied a good Companion, a jovial Royster, and yet a Coward to boot, contrary to the credit of all Chronicles, owning him a Martial man of merit. The best is, Sir. John Falstaffe, hath relieved the Memory of Sr. John Oldcastle, and of late is substituted Buffoone in his place, but it matters as little what petulent Poets, as what malicious Papists have written against him.[43]

Fuller's attempts to refute the defamatory accusations brought him at length to the conclusion that the devil and the Catholics were to blame for corrupting Oldcastle's fame. In *The Worthies of England* he wrote of the martyr thus:

> As his body was hanged and burnt in an unusual posture at Tyburn, so his memory hath ever since been in a strange suspense betwixt malefactor and martyr; Papists charging him with treason against king Henry the Fifth. . . . But it hath ever been the practice of the devil and his instruments, angry with God's servants for their religion, to accuse them for sedition. . . . But I have so worn out the nib of my pen in my "Church History" about clearing the innocency of this worthy knight, that I have nothing to add new thereunto.[44]

Heylyn's attack on the *Church History* on this point seems to have stopped Fuller's further protestations about the treatment of Oldcastle's name. But "good ole John Trappe" mentions the stage players and their satire in his *Commentary Upon Nehemiah* (1657). He seems, from his wording, to have read Speed's account of the travesty. In the passage Trappe has just stated that God builds a marble wall around his saints to protect their memory:

> But if dirt will stick to a mudwal, yet to marble it will not. . . . N. D. Authour of the three conversions, hath made Sr. *John Oldcastle* the Martyr, a Ruffian, a Robber, and a Rebel. His authority is taken from the Stage-players, of like conscience for lyes; as all men know.[45]

To conclude this list of critical writers of the seventeenth century who objected to the Shakespearean satire of the history plays, we add the name of Richard James, the scholarly librarian for Sir Robert Cotton, who became concerned with the defense of Sir John Oldcastle sometime after 1625, when he was preparing for publication a manuscript copy of Hoccleve's poem on the heretical knight. James, oddly enough, considered the poem ample proof of Oldcastle's heroism. In his dedicatory epistle to his friend, Sir Henry Bourchier, James declared that Oldcastle "appeeres to have binne a man of valour and vertue" and that he became a martyr because he would not "bowe under the foule superstition of papistrie." James included in his epistle a reference to Shakespeare's version of the knight.

> That in Shakespeares first shewe of Harrie the fifth [*1 Henry IV*], ye person with which he undertook to playe a buffone was not Falstaffe, but Sr Jhon Oldcastle, and that offence beinge worthily taken by personages descended from his title, as peradventure by manie others allso whoe ought to have him in honourable memorie, the poet was putt to make an ignorant shifte of abusing Sr Jhon Falstaffe or Fastolphe, a man not inferior of vertue though not so famous in pietie as the other, whoe gave witnesse unto the truth of our reformation with a constant and resolute martyrdom.[46]

These are the references, allusions, and clues suggesting that Shakespeare was somehow involved in the Oldcastle problem. Each bit of evidence, standing alone, is a very slender thing upon which to base a study, but when the minuscule letters are accumulated and considered together, they form a substantial case for Shakespeare's involvement writ large. These late sixteenth- and seventeenth-century allusions add also to our knowledge of the tensions that existed in the period in which Shakespeare's history plays were written. The tensions were caused by the religio-political strife of that age. The image of Sir John Oldcastle had become a tangible focusing point upon which the controversialists could maneuver their partial views. Religious tolerance had not yet become a virtue; religion and politics had not ostensibly separated and gone each its own way. In Elizabeth's reign the chronicle stories of Oldcastle's life and death were still in an evolutionary stage, each editor tampering with the materials to present an image to his liking. We know that two contrasting images had developed in the legends about the Lollard knight, one an image of saintliness and virtue, the other an image of depravity and vice. Shakespeare appears to have known something of both legends—both were readily available to him in the chronicle accounts of Holinshed and Stow. But the playwright apparently found one version more useful than the other in his creative art.

CHAPTER THREE

Sir John Oldcastle: History and Legend

THE MATERIAL FOR A BIOGRAPHY OF SIR JOHN OLD-castle must be handled with caution and objectivity, for neither the contemporary writers, who were primarily of the orthodox clergy of that day, nor the Tudor apologists were impartial in their views. These fifteenth- and six-teenth-century writers were determined to condemn or commend the Lollard leader according to their own religious convictions. Therefore, the most reliable information concerning the knight is that drawn from the official government files or from those contemporary writers who have no moral or propagandistic point to make. I am reminded at this point of the sage remark made by Richard Bentley when he read a certain history of heresy distorted by religious passion.

> For History is indeed a serious matter, not to be written carelessly like a Letter to a Friend; nor with Passion, like a Billet to a Mistress; nor with Biass, like a Declamation for a Party at the Bar, or the Remonstrance of a Minister for his Prince; nor in fine, by a Man unacquainted with the World, like Soliloquies and Meditations. It requires a long Experience, a sound Judgment, a close Attention, an unquestionable Integrity, and a Stile without Affection.[1]

Few writers of his own century took Bentley's standards for their own when writing of religious controversy. And as for the subject of Sir John Oldcastle, only in the twentieth century have scholars been able to write objectively about him and his martyrdom. The conflict of conscience and the state is an ancient problem; the solution is rarely a happy one. In

44

our own time we have made attempts to protect the liberty of conscience that we have come to cherish, but the intellectual climate of the medieval and early Renaissance periods contained nothing of amelioration for such uniqueness of mind. The modern psychological analysis of martyrdom leads us only into another malaise, so it is with a sense of relief that I limit this account of Sir John Oldcastle to a brief survey of the historical events of his lifetime.[2]

Sir John was born in Herefordshire at a date given variously between 1360 and 1378. His grandfather, John, was prestigious enough to represent Herefordshire in Parliament for the years 1368 and 1372, as was an uncle, Thomas Oldcastle, in 1390 and 1393. The latter was also sheriff of Herefordshire for 1386 and 1391. Sir Richard Oldcastle, father of Sir John, was knighted in 1399; the family seems at this time to have had little in material possessions other than the manor of Almely near the river Wye.

We know that by 1400 Sir John was also a knight and that he accompanied Henry IV on an expedition to Scotland; he seems from this time forward to have been retained in the royal service. He was employed by the king in the Welsh affairs of the next few years, and it was in these Welsh expeditions that Oldcastle came into close contact with young Prince Henry. At the age of thirteen the prince had been given partial command over Wales, and by 1406 he had received complete charge of North and South Wales and the Marches with power to receive and pardon all rebels. Among the retinue at his command were Thomas and Sir Richard Oldcastle as well as Sir John, and Sir Roger Acton, Sir Thomas Clanvowe, Sir John Greindor, and others who had or were later to come under the influence of Herefordshire Lollardy.[3] In 1404 Oldcastle was returned to Parliament as knight of the shire for Herefordshire; in 1406 he served as justice of the peace, and in 1408 he became sheriff of that county. In the same year he was in the army that was sent against Glendower at Aberystwyth, and he was a witness to the agreement signed on 12 September between the two forces.

In June 1409 Oldcastle, now twice a widower, contracted a marriage with Joan Cobham, the granddaughter and heiress of John, third Baron Cobham. By this marriage Oldcastle gained not only the notable estates of the Cobham family, which included manors and land in five counties, but also the right to attend Parliament as one of the lords temporal. He was so summoned late in 1409 to attend the upper house, and he continued to receive such a summons until his accusation of heresy in 1413. This first Parliament, which Oldcastle attended as Lord Cobham, was the troublesome one of January-June 1410, in which the Commons proposed sweeping confiscation of church property and a modification of the *Statutum de haeretico comburendo.* Thomas Walsingham, the St. Albans chronicler, printed the petition of the "milites Parliamentales (vel, ut dicamus verius, satellites Pilatales)" who wished to seize possession of the church—"ut Ecclesiam Dei per Angliam spoliarent."[4] Oldcastle has been suggested as the leader of this antiecclesiastical movement in the lower house.[5] The petitions failed, however, and during the Easter recess John Badby, the tailor of Evesham who denied the doctrine of transubstantiation, was burned at the stake for heresy.

The first official record we have of Oldcastle's suspected Lollardy is a letter written in April 1410 by Archbishop Arundel to the dean of Rochester complaining that an unlicensed chaplain was preaching Lollardy in the churches of Cooling, Halstow, and Hoo.[6] The dean was instructed to place these churches under interdict and to arrest the chaplain, who was presumed to be living with Lord Cobham. Nothing more is known of this incident except that the interdict was temporarily lifted that same month to allow the wedding ceremony for Lady Cobham's daughter to be performed. This marriage between Joan Braybrook and Sir Thomas Broke (Brooke) of Somerset brought the title of Lord Cobham into the Brooke family, where it remained for two hundred years.

In 1411 we have direct evidence of Oldcastle's leadership in the Lollard movement. Two extant letters of congratulation, written in September of that year, were sent from England to the leaders of the reform party in Bohemia. One letter was written by Richard Wiche, a former priest of Hereford, and was addressed to John Huss; the other letter was written by Oldcastle and sent to Wok of Waldstein. Both letters mention the receipt of tidings from the brethren of Prague, tidings of the progress of the reform movement there.[7] Oldcastle's letter is in Latin and is filled with exhortations to perseverance and endurance; it reveals also that

Oldcastle accepted without reservation the doctrines of Lollardy.[8] Sometime later in this year Oldcastle wrote to King Wenceslaus congratulating him (prematurely) upon the support given to the reform party. It is possible too that Oldcastle corresponded with Huss; Thomas Netter of Walden, in his *Doctrinale,* declared that Oldcastle, at Huss's request, sent copies of Wyclif's writings to Bohemia.[9]

In September of that year the English Council, urged by Prince Henry, agreed to send an expeditionary force to France to assist the duke of Burgundy in his conflict with the Armagnac faction. This English force was placed under the command of the earl of Arundel, Sir John Oldcastle, Sir Robert and Sir Gilbert Umphraville, and Sir William Bardolph, the brother of the Lord Bardolph who had fallen with the earl of Northumberland at Bramham Moor.[10] This English contingent distinguished itself in the victory at St. Cloud and returned home in December, gift-laden. There is no particular mention in the chronicles of meritorious exploits by Oldcastle, but part of his reward seems to have been a jewelled buckle that he sold to Henry V in 1413.[11]

We hear nothing more of Sir John until the convocation called by Henry IV the week preceding his death (March 1413) met to consider the darkening problem of heresy. On the first day of convocation a chaplain named John Lay, "who had celebrated mass for Lord Cobham," was called before the registrar to produce his ordination papers and his license to preach. He excused himself, saying that his papers were in Nottingham, and the case was postponed. We hear nothing more of it, but it seems by now to have been common knowledge that Oldcastle was sheltering the unlicensed preachers. John Capgrave, one of the contemporary writers using the vernacular, describes the heretical pastors.

Thei trosted mech on the witte and on the power of a certeyn knyte thei cleped Ser Jon Oldcastelle. He was cleped Cobham for he weddid a woman ny of the lordis kyn. A strong man in Bataile he was, but a grete heretik, and a gret enmye to the Cherch. For his cause the archbishop gadered a Councel at London; for he sent oute prestis for to preche, which were not admitted be non Ordinarie; and he was present at her sermones; and alle thei that seide ageyn his prestis was he redy to smite with his swerd.[12]

On 10 March King Henry IV died, and the business of convocation was not resumed until June. In the continuing investigations of heresy Lord Cobham's name was brought sharply to the attention of the assembly. Some unbound quires of heretical material had been confiscated at a limner's shop in Paternoster Row. When questioned, the limner declared the work belonged to Sir John Oldcastle, Lord Cobham; upon this information the knight was summoned to appear before the king at Kennington.[13] When Henry read aloud the more appalling passages, Oldcastle declared that the ideas were indeed heretical, but he insisted that he had never read more than two pages of the material. The members of the convocation were less than satisfied with Lord Cobham's explanation, and charges were brought against Sir John, charges declaring "quod idem Johannes fuit, et est, principalis receptator et fautor, protector et defensor Lollardorum."[14] Although these charges were duly recorded, cautionary measures were recommended by Archbishop Arundel, for Oldcastle, as Walsingham the chronicler describes him, "erat iste Johannis fortis viribus, operi martio satis idoneus, sed hostis Ecclesiae pervicacissimus; Regi, propter probitatem, carus et acceptus. . . ."[15] Archbishop Arundel and others of the clergy returned to Kennington to consult Henry V about proceeding further against Lord Cobham.

Henry, optimistically it would seem, determined to apply personal pressure to the strayed lamb, but during the ensuing midsummer weeks the obdurate knight appears to have heedlessly refused the advice of the king.[16] One chronicler suggests that Oldcastle at this time attempted to convert the king.[17] Such obstinacy resulted at length in a complete breach of friendship between king and subject. Oldcastle, *plenus diabolo*, left the court at Windsor without permission and shut himself up in Cooling Castle in Kent. Arundel's summoner was dispatched to cite Sir John to appear and answer to the charges of heterodoxy. The summoner, accompanied by the king's usher, was refused admittance to the castle, and Sir John declared he would allow no man to summon him. On 11 September the archbishop's court met in Leeds Castle. When Oldcastle failed to appear, he was declared contumacious, and a warning was sent him to show cause immediately why he should not be declared a heretic. When the archbishop received only silence for answer, the king sent officers to Kent, and Oldcastle was arrested and imprisoned in the Tower of London.

On 23 September the ecclesiastical court, with Archbishop Arundel presiding, met in the chapter house at St. Paul's, and Oldcastle was brought before the judges. He had prepared a written statement of his belief which he was allowed to read:

> I Johan Oldcastell knyght, Lord of Cobham, wole that alle crysten men wyte and understonde, that y cleps Almyghty God in to wytnesse that it hath be, now is, and ever, with the help of God, schal be myn entent and my wylle, to byleve, feythfully and fully, alle the sacramentys that ever God ordeyned to be do in holy chirche.[18]

Oldcastle continued in vague and ambiguous language to state his views concerning the sacraments, penance, images, and pilgrimages. Arundel insisted upon a clearer statement concerning the sacraments of the altar and penance. Oldcastle refused to elaborate on his written confession of faith; however, to Arundel's explanation of the orthodox position according to the church fathers, Oldcastle did reply that he thought the popes, cardinals, and bishops were powerless to determine such things. The court was recessed for two days to allow a translation of the church's doctrine on these points to be made for Sir John so that he might better his understanding of them.

On Monday, the twenty-fifth, the court reconvened at Blackfriars, and Oldcastle was asked the "murderous question"—did the material bread remain after consecration? His answer was that "evene as Crist whil He went here was God and man, the Manhod mite men se; the bred may men se, but not Cristis bodi."[19] And if the church taught otherwise, Oldcastle continued, it was not from scripture but from "venenum infusum in Ecclesia."[20] His answer concerning the adoration of the holy cross was that Christ, not the cross, should be worshipped. He stated that contrition rather than confession was necessary for salvation, that no one possessed the power of the keys unless he followed Christ in purity of life and living, that the pope himself was a very antichrist, and so on. Then it is said that Oldcastle in complete abandonment cried out to the spectators with "alto voce, manibus expansis," warning that the judges "seducent vos omnes . . . et vos ducent ad infernem."[21] He was immediately declared a heretic and handed over to the secular arm.

Through an unexpected leniency Oldcastle was given forty days in which to recant his heresy. This time he spent in the Tower, where it seems both Arundel and the king hoped he could be brought to a more tractable state. Thomas Netter of Walden printed the formal retraction of Lollard beliefs which was prepared for the apostate, an abjuration stating that he had now come to his right mind and was willing to acknowledge the authority of the papal see; this document seems never to have been signed by Oldcastle.[22] The knight evidently spent his brief reprieve evolving a plan of escape, for on the night of 19 October 1413 he slipped from the Tower with the aid of Richard Wrothe and William Fisher, the latter a parchment-maker in whose house in Turnmill Street Oldcastle hid for some weeks.

With their leader snatched from death's door, the Lollards began an aggressive countermovement directed toward the complete overthrow of church and state.[23] First, bills were posted upon the church doors of London warning that 100,000 men were ready to rise. Letters and money were then sent throughout England to arouse the followers and to give the date of the planned insurrection. E. F. Jacob, who has examined the numerous reports of the commissions of inquiry appointed to investigate the revolt after it had failed, remarks that though the plan for the rebellion was in itself defective, the preparations for assembling forces in each county were made with thoroughness and were patterned upon the revolt of 1381.[24] The insurgents in the distant counties began moving soon after Christmas. They were primarily artisans, craftsmen, and husbandmen led by local chaplains; however, gentry names are not missing from the lists: the Cheynes of Drayton Beauchamp, John and Thomas Cook of Essex, Sir Roger Acton of Sutton in Worcestershire, Sir Thomas Talbot of Davington in Kent, Thomas Maureward, ex-sheriff of Warwickshire, and others were involved in the movement. The chronicler of St. Albans watched the insurgents passing by the abbey on their way to London and described them as crowds drawn by great promise from almost every county of the kingdom; when asked why they hurried so, they answered that they were hastening to London to join Lord Cobham who had sent for them and retained them with wages.[25] The designated date for the uprising was Twelfth Night; the Lollards from the outlying districts were told to gather in St. Giles Field and there to meet the "50,000 sympathizers" from London proper. The scheme of a mumming was planned to cover the approach of the leaders to Eltham, where the king and his brothers were celebrating the holidays. The plot may have been only to seize the king, "the priests' prince," and hold him while Oldcastle acted as regent; however, the official indictment, filed on 11 January against Oldcastle stated that the Lollard leader was guilty of treason for conspiring to kill the king, his brothers, the prelates, and other lords of the realm, both temporal and ecclesiastical, and to make himself regent, abolish religious orders, force monks to apply themselves to secular occupations, and plunder and level to the ground the cathedrals and other churches.[26]

Henry V was neither unaware of the plotting against his person and his regime nor impotent to act. He moved his retinue to Westminster and sent word to the mayor of London that any congregations of citizens were to be prohibited, suspicious persons arrested, and the city gates barred. Early in the evening of Twelfth Night the mayor arrested several suspected Lollards at the sign of the Axe near Bishopgate, and from these prisoners the exact details of the uprising were learned. The king took his forces to St. Giles Field; the insurgents were scattered, arrested, or slain, but Oldcastle managed to escape. Within the next fortnight sixty-nine rebels were executed in London for this insurrection; however, pardons were still being issued eighteen months later. Oldcastle seems to have remained in and about London for five weeks after the failure of the uprising; he was hiding in Westminster when the duke of Clarence came searching for him. Evidence has been found that the archdeacon of Westminster, the abbot of Shrewsbury, and the Cluniac prior of Wenlock were all involved in protecting Oldcastle and aiding his escape.[27] Before the first of March Sir John seems to have fled to the hills of Wales where he set up headquarters for directing his continuing resistance to church and state.

We do not know how much popular sentiment was aligned in favor of the Lollard leader or how much of it predicated his guilt. We do know from two extant poems that the rebel knight's actions were condemned by some as a breach of the code of chivalry. In the anonymous complaint "Against the Lollards" poetic use is made of Oldcastle's name to create an image of desuetude and decay.

> Hit is unkyndly for a knight
>> That shuld a kynges castel kepe
> To bable the Bibel day and night
>> In restyng tyme when he shuld slepe.
>
> An old castel, and not repaired,
>> With wast walles and wowes wides,
> The wages ben ful yvel wared
>> With suiche a capitayn to abide;
>> That rerethe riot for to ride
> Agayns the kynge and his clergie
>> With prive peyne and pore pride;
> Ther is a poynt of lollardie. . . .[28]

In Hoccleve's poem, written to censure the defected knight, we find a mélange of disparagement and pity.

> Allas that thow that were a manly knyght
> And shoonful clear in famous worthynesse
> Standing in the favour of everye wight
> Haast lost the style of Christenly prownesse
> Among alle hem that stand in the cleerenesse
> Of good byleeve, and no man with thee holdith
> Saif cursid caitifs heires of dirknesse.
> For verray routhe of thee myn herete coldith.
>
> O Oldcastel how hath the feend thee beent?
> Where is thy knyghtly herte? art thow his thrall?
>
> If yee so holy been as ye witnesse
> Of your self, thanne in Crystes feith abyde.
> The disciples of Chryst had hardynesse
> For to appere, they nat woude hem hyde
> For fere of deeth but in his cause dyde.
> They fledden nat to halkes ne to hernes
> As yee doon that holden the feendes syde
> Which arn of dirkness the lanternes.

This poem includes a passage which indicates Hoccleve's belief that Oldcastle was the instigator of the recent insurrection:

Ne nevere they in forcible maneere
With wepnes roos to slee folk and assaill
As ye diden late in this contree heere
Ageyn the king stryf to rere and battaill.

Look how our Cristen Prince our Lige Lord
With many a Lord and knyght beyond the see
Laboure in armes and thow hydest thee
And darst nat came and shewe thy visage
O fy for shame, how can a knyzt be
Out of thonur of this rial viage.[29]

Proclamations were sent out to the midlands and the western counties for Oldcastle's apprehension after his flight from London. The king offered a reward of one thousand marks, a tremendous sum in those days, or land worth twenty pounds a year for life to anyone who would capture the Lollard leader; any town, borough, or city was offered exemption from tax during the king's life if its citizens could produce the rebel knight. None of these offers availed. On 14 June Oldcastle was formally outlawed for treason at Brentford county court, and the remainder of his lands was seized by the king. Toward the end of the year, however, Henry, in an effort to harmonize the discordant elements at home in preparation for his French campaign, offered a pardon to the rebel if he would submit to his sovereign. As late as April 1415 the proclamation of grace was reissued, but Oldcastle, possibly fearing a trap or hoping for success in a newly plotted conspiracy, refused to answer.

By midsummer of 1415, as premature rumors spread of the king's departure for the Continent, Oldcastle sent a hostile note to Richard Beauchamp, Lord Abergavenny, threatening an attack upon him; there seems to have been an ancient grudge between the two men. Immediately Abergavenny gathered a strong force from his Worcestershire estates, led them against the Lollard, and, though failing to take the leader, discovered his cache of weapons, money, and standards. Among the latter was a banner bearing the image of the chalice and the host.

During this same summer it was rumored that Oldcastle
had met William Douglas at Pomfret, that he had offered
the Scot three thousand pounds to bring the pseudo-
Richard II, Thomas Trumpington, into England at the head
of a strong force. There was evidently some basis of fact in
these rumors, for the Cambridge-Scrope-Gray conspiracy,
which was crushed at Southampton on 1 August as the English forces prepared to embark for France, had ramifications which touched Oldcastle. Richard, earl of Cambridge,
Henry, Lord Scrope of Masham, and Sir Thomas Gray of
Heton agreed to combine their forces, declare Henry V an
usurper, and place young Edmund Mortimer, earl of March,
on the English throne. At the same time they planned to
restore young Henry Percy, Hotspur's son, to his heritage,
thus incurring the favor of the northern counties. They
planned also to let the Scots in at Roxburgh to increase
their forces, to arouse the Lollards under Oldcastle, and to
draw upon the rebel strength of Glendower, if possible. The
Lollards, some of whom were mustered in the army that
was ready to sail for France, were to mutiny and assist the
earl of March who was to unfurl his banner with the arms of
England upon it. The conspiracy failed when the earl of
March revealed the plot to the king on the eve of the day
planned for the assassinations.

Evidence exists that Oldcastle was sheltered at this time,
August of 1415, by John Prest, vicar of Chesterton in Warwickshire.[30] But for the next year we hear almost nothing of
the Lollard rebel. The victory at Agincourt seems to have
quieted the rebellious factions at home, at least for a time.
In the Christmas season of 1416 a squire of Oldcastle's was
caught in an attempt on the king's life as the royal family
celebrated the holidays at Kenilworth. Soon afterwards the
abbot of St. Albans learned that Oldcastle was hiding in
the house of a peasant near the abbey. A raid resulted in the
arrest of some of Oldcastle's followers and the confiscation
of some religious books and pamphlets in which the saints'
names and pictures had been defaced. It would seem that
Oldcastle moved freely from his hiding places in Wales to
various sectors throughout central England. He seems also
to have continued his negotiations with the Scots after the
failure of the Cambridge-Scrope-Gray conspiracy. The
chronicler Thomas Otterbourne relates that at about this

time a written agreement between Oldcastle and the duke of Albany was discovered and that Lollards were busy inciting the men of Northumberland and Yorkshire to proclaim King Richard when he should return from Scotland.[31] It is interesting to note that the Scottish exchequer rolls contain a memorandum to the effect that Albany had spent in excess of seven hundred pounds in maintaining the pseudo-Richard.[32] The Scottish forces, whose movements had been previously planned to coincide with the Cambridge-Scrope-Gray conspiracy of 1415, moved into England in August of 1417, one force under the earl of Douglas approaching Roxburgh, another under the duke of Albany threatening Berwick. The regent Bedford and the duke of Exeter with hastily gathered forces marched northward. The Scots soon abandoned their "foul raid" and retired beyond the border.

On 1 December 1417 word reached London that Oldcastle had been captured at Broniarth in Wales by retainers of Edward Charlton, Lord Powis. Sir Griffith Vaughan and his sons had indeed succeeded in capturing the outlaw after a violent struggle; one story adds that a woman broke the rebel's leg with a milk-stool in the scuffle. Oldcastle was carried to London in a horse litter and presented before Parliament, which was in session. On 14 December Chief Justice Hankford read the indictment of treason and Archbishop Chichele read the sentence of excommunication; Oldcastle was then asked if he could present reasons why the sentences should not be carried out. It is reported that Oldcastle talked at first of mercy, saying that vengeance belonged only to God. At length, being directed to answer more to the point, Oldcastle declared that the present regime had no right to pronounce judgment, that he was a loyal subject of the true King Richard who was living in Scotland. Parliament immediately declared that the sentence of death should be carried out. Oldcastle was drawn to St. Giles Field on a hurdle, hanged in chains, and burned as a traitor to God and the king. Before his death it is reported that Oldcastle asked Sir Thomas Erpingham to secure tolerance for the Lollards if he should return to life in three days. This promise of resurrection brought a considerable crowd of Oldcastle's followers to St. Giles Field on the appointed day where they awaited the miracle; when

Oldcastle failed to appear, they gathered his ashes to rub in their eyes.

Such was the life and death of Sir John Oldcastle, Lord Cobham. The contemporary chroniclers called him Behemoth, Leviathan, faithless knight, perfidious follower of Wyclif, satellite of Satan, and so on. Thomas Walsingham, Thomas Netter, John Capgrave, Thomas Otterbourne, Thomas Eltham, Hoccleve, and the anonymous poet all tell a similar story of the strong soldier who turned against church and king. Today, we are disturbed when we read that so stalwart a man (like many another) was burned to death for devotion to his convictions. Our modern sensibilities are conditioned by what the medieval mind would have called soft and specious reasoning. This medieval tough-mindedness is well documented as late as the sixteenth century. Sir Thomas More, indulging his polemic prose in 1528, attacked the inimical problem of heresy in his *Dialogue Concerning Tyndale*. In this work, written when the Roman Catholic Church was fast losing its grip upon the English nation, More resolved

> . . . to aunswere the poyntes whyche ye moved at youre fyrste metynge, when ye sayde that manye menne thoughte it an harde and an uncharitable waye taken by the clergy, to put men convict of heresy sometime to shame, sometyme to death, and that Christ so farre abhorred all such violence, that he would not any of his flocks shoulde fyght in any wyse, neither in the defence of Christ himself, for which he blamed Saint Peter, but that we should all live after hym in sufferance and pacience. . . .

These objections, explained More, were soon answered, for no fault offends God more than heresy. The heretics themselves, he said, had resorted to violence since the early days of the Donatists when Saint Augustine was brought at length to advise the use of force to prevent the tormenting and killing of the true Christian flock; Saint Jerome and other virtuous fathers allowed the use of force against heresy; sore punishment by fire had been necessitated by the great outrages committed against the peace and quiet of the people in divers places of Christendom. Continuing, More cites the burning of Oldcastle as an English example of the wise use of fire to control destructive forces:

The Burning of Sir John Oldcastle, Lord Cobham.

Courtesy of the Henry E. Huntington Library.

> In the time of that noble Prince of moste famous memorye
> Kynge Henrye the fifth, while the Lorde Cobham mainteined
> certayn heresies, and that by the meanes therof, the noumber
> so grewe and encreased, that within a while though hymselfe
> was fledde into Wales, yet thei assembled themselfe together in a
> fielde nere unto London, in suche wise and such noumber, that
> the Kyng with his nobles were faine to putte harnesse on their
> backes for the repression of them, whereupon they were dis-
> tressed and many putte to execucion, and after that the Lorde
> Cobham taken in Wales and burned in London, the King his
> nobles and his people therupon consideryng the greate peryll
> and jeopardie that the realme was lyke to have fallen in by
> those heresies, made at a parliamente very good and substan-
> ciall provisions beside all suche as were made before, as wel
> for the withstanding as the repressing and grievous punishe-
> ment of any suche as should be founded faultie thereof, and by
> the clergye lefte unto the seculer handes.[33]

A heretic, More continued to explain, endangered the
whole Christian community with infection. The clergy,
though charitable and compassionate, had no choice but to
turn over an obdurate heretic to the secular arm. The loss of
one human soul was infinitely less than the destruction of
God's church.

If we are repelled by the asperity of these medieval conceptions, it will add little in the way of palliation to recall
that many of the early religious reformers were seeking
not the tolerance and freedom that we prize today (these
are neoclassical ideals) but the substitution of their own
rigorous forms of doctrine and church government. Oldcastle was ready to "smite with hys swerd" those who
complained of his priests. Some reformers were equally convinced that God's church was endangered, but for them its
salvation lay in complete reformation, and if that reformation required militant action against temporal and ecclesiastical powers, then revolution was to be undertaken for
God's glory and the edification of man. The sixteenth-
century Protestants had no trouble accepting Oldcastle's
revolt against the church, for by 1536 the English Reformation had begun; but they found that Oldcastle's treason
to the king rescinded his martyr's glory. Thus we find the
Tudor controversialists concentrating on the insurrection
of St. Giles Field, either minimizing its importance, reeval-
uating its purpose, or crediting its misconception to Sir
Roger Acton and others.

Until Tyndale glorified Oldcastle (ca. 1530) the accounts of the rebel knight were derivative versions taken from the writings of Walsingham, Netter, and Otterbourne. Tito Livio, the Italian scholar who had been attracted to England by the fame of Humphrey, duke of Gloucester, as a patron of literature, wrote his *Vita Henrici Quinti* before mid-fifteenth century, using in addition to these sources the official records and some version of *The Brut*.[34] The fifteenth-century vernacular chronicles of London gave brief, summarized accounts of the uprising,[35] and Caxton, printing his continuation of Higdon's *Polychronicon* at the close of the century, added his own editorial note of satisfaction at the failure of the rising:

> . . . but blessyd be God, the kynge and lordes had knowleche of theyr entente, and toke the felde to fore them, and awayted on theyr comyng, and toke many preestes, clerkys, and other lewd men that were of theyr sect fro alle the partyes of England, wenyng to have founded theyr Captayne there, Syre Johan Oldcastell, but they were deceyved.[36]

When the translator of Tito Livio's *Vita Henrici Quinti,* writing in 1513 to provide Henry VIII an example of a noble and virtuous prince, came to the "marvelous insurrection of hereticks," he named Lord Cobham as being "amongst the aforesaide," and he too thanked God that "the first victorie of that noble Kinge after his Coronacion was against these cursed supersticious heretiques for Christ and the defence of the Church of God, in the defence and supportacion of our Catholique faith."[37]

This point of view changed only when the heresiarchs Tyndale and Bale began to produce their controversial writings. William Tyndale's polemical pamphlets, shipped into England from the Continent, where he lived in exile, included a small work entitled *The Examinacion of Master William Thorpe . . . and of the Honorable Knight Syr Jhon Oldcastell Lord Cobham.* This "Bok of Thorpe" contained an account of Oldcastle's trial before Archbishop Arundel, an elaboration of Oldcastle's belief on the four points of doctrine that had entered his testimony, and a dramatic description of the knight's declaration of faith which Tyndale introduced with certain addenda:

And with that he kneled downe on the pavement / and helde
up his handis & said. I shryve me to god and to you all sirs /
yt in my youthe I have synnyd greatly and grevously in lecherie
and in pride and hurte many men & done many other hor-
rible synnes / good lord I crie thee mercie.[38]

To conclude this work Tyndale produced a letter, reputedly
Oldcastle's, which contained a warning to the Lollards that
any abjuration which the clergy might announce he had
made would be a false document designed to mislead and
destroy them.

Sir Thomas More decried this work of Tyndale's, declaring that any man of natural wit or learning

. . . shall not onely be well able to perceyve hym for a foly-
sshe heretyke & his argumentes easy to answere / but shall
also se that he sheweth him selfe a false lyar in hys rehersall
of the mater / wherin he maketh the tother parte somtyme
speke for hys commodite, such maner thynges as no man
woulde have done that were not a very wylde gose.[39]

Tyndale's little book was among those ordered burned in
1531, but this and More's ridicule were no deterrents to
John Bale who, by 1544, had expanded Tyndale's account
of Oldcastle's trial into a brawling attack upon the "beastly blockheads, these blody bellygods" who with their "un-
savory interrogations" had put an innocent lamb to
death.[40] The language of the fifteenth-century chroniclers,
who had found Oldcastle's conduct abhorrent, was now
turned by the pensmen of the new faith with triple invective upon the prelates who had condemned the rebel.
Bale's *Brefe Chronycle* was printed three times within four
years, though he himself was residing in Basel and returned
to London only after the accession of Edward VI. Bale's
torrent of abuse continued to flow in the first English edition (1563) of John Foxe's *Acts and Monuments of the
Church*. The martyrologist's primary intention in his relation of the Oldcastle story was to clear the knight's name
of the charge of treason, but, following the accepted syllogistic procedure of polemic debate, he attacked the Catholic clergy first:

No small number of godly disciples left that good man [Wyclif]
behind him to defend the lowliness of the gospel against the

exceeding pride, ambition, simony, avarice, hypocrisy, whoredom, sacrilege, tyranny, idolatrous worshippings, and other filthy fruit of those stiff-necked pharisees; against whom Thomas Arundel, the archbishop of Canterbury (as fierce as ever was Pharaoh, Antiochus, Herod, or Caiaphas) collected, in Paul's church at London, a universal synod of all the papistical clergy of England, in the year of our Lord 1413 (as he had done divers others before), to withstand their most godly enterprise. And this was the first year of king Henry V., whom they had then made fit for their hand. The chief and principal cause then of the assembling thereof, as recordeth the Chronicle of St. Albans, was to repress the growing and worthy lord Cobham, who was then noted to be a principal favourer, receiver, and maintainer of those whom the bishop misnamed to be Lollards.[41]

To the official condemnation of heresy and command to hand Oldcastle over to the secular jurisdiction, power, and judgment, Foxe, following Bale, added the words, "to do him thereupon to death." Foxe then argued that this was proof that Oldcastle was not a traitor in the condemnation of the first trial.[42] The insurrection of St. Giles Field is turned by Foxe into an evangelical meeting of the gospellers who sought sanctuary in the groves and byways.

In the Christmas following were sir Roger Acton, knight, master John Brown, esquire, sir John Beverly, a learned preacher, and divers others, attached, for quarreling with certain priests, and so imprisoned; for all men at that time could not patiently suffer their blasphemous brags. The complaint was made unto the king of them, that they had a great assembly in St. Giles field at London, purposing the destruction of the land, and the subversion of the commonwealth. As the king was thus informed, he erected a banner, saith Walden, with a cross thereupon; as the pope doth commonly by his legates, when he pretendeth to war against the Turks, and, with a great number of men, entered the same field, where he found no such company. Yet was the complaint judged true, because the bishops had spoken it at the information of their priests. . . . yet never a blow was given, never a stroke was stricken, no blood spilled, no furniture nor instruments of war, no sign of battle, yea no express signification either of any rebellious word or malicious fact, described either in record, or yet in any chronicle.[43]

Foxe suggests then, by way of afterthought, that the "high and tragical words" in the official indictment against Old-

castle and his followers ". . . may peradventure seem
to the ignorant and simple reader, some heinous crime
of treason to rest in them, for conspiring against God, the
church, the king and their country. But what cannot the
fetching practice of the Romish prelates bring about
where they have once conceived a malice?"[44]

Foxe's adventitious account of Oldcastle's trial and insurrection soon encountered a vitiating attack from the
pen of Nicholas Harpsfield, the former archdeacon of Canterbury under Queen Mary, who was imprisoned in the
Fleet from 1562 until his death in 1575 for refusing to
subscribe to the new religion. Harpsfield's *Dialogi Sex*
was published in Antwerp in 1566 under the name of Alan
Cope, a young English refugee who saw the work through
Plantin's press. In the last dialogue of the work Harpsfield attacks the pseudomartyrs whom Foxe had installed
in his calendar of saints, declaring that Foxe had fraudu-
lently and corruptly commended traitors of the crown.
Harpsfield cites the various sources, Polydore Vergil,
Fabyan, the Latin chroniclers of Henry V's reign, as proof
of Oldcastle's leadership in the insurrection of 1413.[45]
When Foxe brought out his second edition of the *Acts and
Monuments* in 1570, he added a thirty-page "Defense of
the Lord Cobham" in which he attacked not only "Alanus
Copus Anglus" for trying to prove him a "liar, a forger, an
impudent, a misreporter of truth, a depraver of stories, a
seducer of the world" but also the inaccuracies in the
chronicles of Robert Fabyan, Edward Hall, Polydore Vergil, Thomas Cooper, and Richard Grafton to destroy the
validity of their accounts of Oldcastle—the "ready sources"
with which Harpsfield taunted him.[46] The martyrologist
seems to have had in his possession a manuscript copy of
Hall's chronicle containing a cancelled passage on Oldcastle, for Foxe describes it and attributes the emendation to the influence of Bale's *Brefe Chronycle*, which had
been slipped into Hall's desk by one of his servants. Foxe
describes Hall's interest in Bale's "true" account of the
story and Hall's revision of his own writing:

> The matter which he cancelled out, came to this effect. Where-
> in he, following the narration of Polydore, began with like
> words to declare how the sacramentaries here in England,
> after the death of John Huss and Jerome of Prague, being

pricked, as he saith, with a demonical sting, first conspired against the priests, and afterwards against the king, having for their captains sir John Oldcastle the Lord Cobham, and sir Roger Acton, knight; with many more words to the like purpose and effect, as Polydore, and other such like chroniclers do write against him. All which matter, notwithstanding, the said Hall with pen, at the sight of John Bale's book, did utterly extinguish and abolish; adding in the place thereof the words of Master Bale's book.[47]

Hall's account of Oldcastle as a "valiant capitain and a hardy gentleman" is certainly a mitigated version of the original story, but it scarcely "followeth Bale." Hall omits Oldcastle's name in the account of the insurrection and describes it thus:

After this tyme in a certain unlawfull assembly was taken sir Robert Acton knight, a man of greate wit & possession, Jhon Broune Esquire, Jhon Beverly clerke and a great numbre of other whiche were brought to the kynges presence, and to hym declared the cause of their commocion and risyng. . . . Some saie that the occasion of their death was the conveighance of the Lorde Cobham out of prisone. Other write that it was bothe for treason and heresy as the record declareth. Certain affirme that it was for feined causes surmised by the spiritualitic more of displeasour than truth: the judgement whereof I leave to men indifferent. For surely all conjectures be not true, nor all writinges are not Gospell, & therefore because I was nether a witnes of the facte, nor present at the deede I overpasse that matter and begin another.[48]

Pynson's edition of Fabyan's *Chronicle* (1516) contained the standard account of Oldcastle and his adherents assembling in St. Giles Field where they "entendyngd thi destruction of this land / and subvercion of thi same."[49] And Rastell's edition of this same work admitted no changes to the story;[50] although the 1542 and 1559 editions contained alterations and omissions to bring them into conformity with the Reformation, the history of Oldcastle remained untouched: Sir John, for heresy and treason, is "hanged upon a newe peyer of galowys with chaynes, and after consumed with fyre."[51]

Polydore Vergil's account of Oldcastle followed the *Vita Henrici Quinti* of Tito Livio, *The Brut*, and Fabyan, and he blames the leader, Lord Cobham, for the treasonable uprising.[52] The chronicle of John Hardyng, who was a contemporary of Oldcastle and had spent his youth with the Percy family in Northumberland, was published in 1543 in two dissimilar editions by Richard Grafton. In the Stow-Grafton quarrel which later ensued over editorial policies, Stow twitted Grafton about the inconsistencies that occurred on almost every page, but the account of Oldcastle is identical in both editions. Hardyng's history is in verse form and relates the insurrection in three stanzas:

> In his fyrste yere, the Lorde Cobham heretike
> Confedered with lollers insapient
> Agayne the churche arose, and was full lyke
> It to have destroyed by theyr entendment
> Had not the kyng then made suppowelment
> And put hym from the felde, by good direccyon,
> That sembled were, by greate insurreccyon.
>
> Then fled the lorde Cobham hexxorious
> To Wales, so with lollers many one
> Musyng in his opinyon venemous
> Howe that he myght destroye the churche anone
> But God that syt in heven above alone
> Knowyng his herte, naked of all good entent
> Let hym be take, to have his judgement
>
> And brent he was to ashes deed and pale
> Through cursed lyfe, thus came he in greate bale.[53]

Sometime between 1536 and 1544 Robert Redmayne composed a Latin life of Henry V which praised the "king of famous memory" but also revealed the author's sympathy with Oldcastle's cause. Redmayne spoke of Oldcastle's family as "militis, fortis viri et optimi equitis descenderint" and characterized the clergy who pursued him as "perditi homines." This manuscript was dedicated to the earl of Huntingdon, but there is no evidence that it was published in the sixteenth century.[54]

Thomas Lanquet edited Cooper's *Chronicle* in 1560; the story of Oldcastle's heresy and treason follows the older accounts of the uprising. There is nothing in this work about Oldcastle's death.[55] In 1568 Richard Grafton published his own historical work, *This Chronicle of Breteyn*, but in it we find the author sidestepping the touchy issue of Oldcastle's treason and referring the reader to Foxe's history:

And in this first yere, Syr John Oldcastell, which by his wife was called Lorde Cobham, a valiaunt Captaine and an hardie Gentelman, was accused unto the Archebishop of Cantorbury of certeine poyntes of heresie. But for that I have not purposed in this historie to write of any matter that specially concerneth religion, I will therefore referre you to the booke of Monumentes of the Church, where the whole historie of this Gentelman and many others is at large described and set foorth.[56]

Among these sixteenth-century accounts of the Oldcastle story by far the most interesting is that printed by John Stow. Stow was a tailor for many years, but he pursued his antiquarian interests all his life. In spite of his poverty, he managed somehow to buy the collection of rare books and manuscripts of Reginald Wolfe (the projector of Holinshed's *Chronicles*) upon that antiquary's death in 1573. When Stow published his first account of the Oldcastle affair in *A Summarie of Englyshe Chronicles* (1565), he listed only Hall as his source, and his brief description of the St. Giles insurrection proclaims that it was a meeting of "adherents of Syr John Oldcastell" who were so numerous that all the prisons in and about London were full.[57] Although Stow was called before the Privy Council in 1568 for his possession of "curious books" and his antique religion, he was befriended by Archbishop Parker. It was Stow who edited the beautiful editions of Walsingham's *Historia Brevis* (1574) and *Ypodigma Neustrae* (1574) for the archbishop.[58] And when Stow brought out the enlarged edition of his *Annales of England* in 1592, he dedicated it to Archbishop Whitgift. Stow had by this time examined the available sources, and he wrote a lengthy account of the Oldcastle affair. "This John was a strong man," Stow explained, "and a meetely good man of war, but he was a most perverse enimie to the state of the church at that time." Stow's account of the uprising is detailed. He describes the alacrity of the mayor who

. . . about X of the clocke at night went himselfe with a strong power, to the signe of the Axe withoute Bishops gate, where they apprehended the man of the house called John Burgate carpenter and vi other, one of them being an esquire belonging to Sir John Old-castell, and sent them to Eltham, where they confessed before the k. that they were confederate with Sir John Old-castell, to fight against him and his lords in S. Giles field above Holborne.

Stow describes the king's determination to take the field when he heard of the plot to destroy his realm, and his success in defeating the surprised rebels:

> . . . he went into the field when it was lettle past midnight, with a great armie, for hee was warned that Sir John Old-castell, and Sir Roger Acton, would bee in the same field on the next day following with 25000 people: and the same night were taken more than four escore men in armor of the same faction, for many that came fro far, not knowing the kings campe to be in the field, were taken by the same and sent to prison, & being demaunded whom they sought, made answere the lorde *Cobham*. The rumour of this, comming to the eares of the captaines that were the kings enimies, they were woonderfully discouraged, and that the more, bicouse none came to them out of London, from whence they looked for many thousands, whereupon they fled to save themselves, and the kings men following them tooke some, and slein other, but where their captain was become would not be known.[59]

Stow's account of Oldcastle's final appearance before Parliament and his execution is lengthy and includes much from Walsingham and Otterbourne. This detailed version from Stow's *Annales* must of course be compared with Holinshed's *Chronicles*, where we find a fascinating example of political and social pressures shaping editorial policy. First, it should be remembered that Stow helped edit the *Chronicles* after Holinshed's death in 1580, and he wrote the continuation that brought the history up to the date of the second edition (1585-1587). The checks and censorship Stow encountered as one of the co-editors of this work may account for the detailed description of Oldcastle in his own *Annales*; and his frustration may account also for the vehemence in his reporting of the Main and Bye plots in 1603 which he later indexed as "another Lord Cobham arraigned, and the manner of it is a fine story."[60] It should be remembered too that both the 1577 and the 1585-87 editions of Holinshed's *Chronicles* were dedicated to "the Right Honorable and his singular good Lord and maister, S. William Brooke Knight, Lord Warden of the Cinque Portes, and Baron of Cobham." The epistle dedicatory and the *Description of England*, which is used as an introduction to the *Chronicles*, were written by William Harrison, the former household chaplain of Lord Cobham.

Furthermore, the account of Elizabeth's reign in book 3 is followed by a seventeen-page "treatise of the Lord Cobham" written by Francis Thynne, a Kentish antiquary who later became Lancaster herald. This eulogy contained a history of the three branches of the Cobham family, a history that exaggerates the heroic deeds of the Lords Cobham and excises all the treason.[61] The Privy Council (of which Cobham was a new member) ordered the expurgation of Thynne's treatise and approximately one hundred additional pages from books 2 and 3 of the *Chronicles*. The only explanation which has been suggested for these censures is that Lord Cobham was out of favor at court at this time. We do know that Archbishop Whitgift took an active part in this expurgation of Holinshed's books.[62]

In Holinshed's account of Sir John Oldcastle the knight is called "a valiant capteine and a hardie gentleman." He is made to thank the king for having "lovinglie admonished him," and he offers "an hundred knights and esquires to come to his purgation, or else to fight in open lists in defense of his just cause." The leadership and responsibility for the uprising are attributed to Sir Roger Acton, and Oldcastle's presence at St. Giles Field is questioned:

> But whether he came thither at all, or made shift for himselfe to get awaie, it dooth not appeare; for he could not be heard of that time (as Walsingham confesseth). Although the king by proclamation promised a thousand marks to him that could bring him foorth, with great liberties to the cities or townes that would discover where he was. By this it maie appeare, how greatlie he was beloved, that there could not one be found, that for so great a reward would bring him to light.

At this point Holinshed was apparently drawing upon Foxe for his material, but in his description of Oldcastle's capture and death he preferred simple and heroic language:

> About the same season was sir John Oldcastell, lord Cobham taken . . . not without danger and hurts of some that were at the taking of him: for they could not take him, till he was wounded himselfe. . . . shortlie after he was brought before the duke of Bedford, regent of the realme, and the other estates, where in the end he was condemned, and finallie was drawne from the Tower unto saint Giles field, and there hanged in a chaine by the middle, and after consumed with fire, the gallowes and all.[63]

Ⅎ Brefe Chronycle concernynge the
Examinacyon and death of the blessed
martyr of Christ syr Johan Oldeca-
stell the lorde Cobham/collected to-
gyther by Johan Bale.

☛ Syr.Iohan.Oldecaſtel.the.worthy
lorde.Cobham.and.moſte.valyaunt.
warryoure.of.Ieſus.Chriſt.
ſuffred.death.at.London.Anno.1418.

☛ In the latter tyme ſhall manye be
choſen / proued / and puryfyed by fyre/
yet ſhall the vngodly lyue wyckedly ſtyll
and haue no vnderſtandynge. Dan.12.

The Militant Sir John Oldcastle, Lord Cobham.

Most of these disparate accounts of the history of Sir John Oldcastle, Lord Cobham, were available to the English dramatists who, in the last decade of the sixteenth century, were sifting through the chronicles for plot materials that would captivate their audiences and flatter their patrons. The materials for a raucous pasquil of Oldcastle were provided by the conflicting reports of that knight's heroism (tarnished or ideal), his morality (mundane or evangelic), and his martyrdom (saintly or simply the result of his culpability). Oldcastle's appearance upon the Elizabethan stage is not surprising; it would have been strange indeed had the knight *not* made his entrance in a dramatization of the life of Henry V. The idea that Shakespeare would satirize a religious martyr has been repugnant to many. This attitude, I think, has been conceived without knowledge of the complex background of the Oldcastle legend and without knowledge of the contemporary Cobhams who bore the brunt of Shakespeare's satire. It would be fond and extraneous to state here that Shakespeare's portrayal of comic character is untrammeled by twentieth-century inhibitions or to lecture on the humanity of the poet. The evidence is extant to suggest that Shakespeare made use of the Oldcastle story. A number of the events of Oldcastle's life are subtly suggested in the actions and characterization of Falstaff, and with these historical allusions are ployed jibes at the contemporary lords of Cobham—badinage based upon the questionable loyalty of that family to Elizabeth's crown.

CHAPTER FOUR

The Henry IV Plays

THE GREAT BODY OF PARAMYTHIC CRITICISM THAT adheres to any discussion of Shakespeare's famous comic character is based upon the complex presentation of Sir John Falstaff in the two parts of *Henry IV*; it is therefore with these history plays that this discussion of Shakespeare's allusions to the lords of Cobham begins, although chronologically these dramas do not contain the first of such satire. The earlier lampooning began with the Falstaff of *1 Henry VI* and with the figure of Eleanor Cobham in the second play of that early tetralogy. But that story will follow.

We gain our first introduction to Falstaff in the *Henry IV* plays in the second scene of act I. We are aware of the playwright's refined sense of structure when we perceive that the second scene mirrors, with a difference, the theme of the opening scene of the play: the first scene has introduced us to the disorder in the political realm of England with the speeches of the weary king. We learn that the unstable Percies are angered and that a northern rebellion is brewing. Rebellion with the Percies is a timeless action that Elizabethans could associate with the idea that history repeats itself, because the Percies of the north country had anger and rebellion in their blood. Not only did they mount insurrection twice against Henry IV, they also rebelled against Henry VIII in the famous "Pilgrimage of Grace" and against Queen Elizabeth in the even more famous "Rising of the North." When Shakespeare writes of rebellion in these history plays, he writes with an Elizabethan veracity. And he also writes with a sense of the new theories of history:

There is a Historie in all mens Lives,
Figuring the nature of the Times deceas'd:
The which obseru'd, a man may prophecie
With a neere ayme, of the maine chance of things,
As yet not come to Life, which in their Seeds
And weake beginnings lye entreasured:
Such things become the Hatch and Brood of Time.

[*2 Henry IV*, III.i.83–89]

"The Hatch and Brood of Time"—paradoxically, time is used to prove the timelessness of certain characteristics in men. Human nature does not change. To the sophisticated twentieth-century reader this idea seems facile. But it should be remembered that the sixteenth century was an age in which men's minds were for the first time willing to give up the idea of the deterioration of human nature; the medieval notion of man's slide from Eden *downward* to the last days, when evil and decadence should overtake nearly all of humanity, had been jogged out of its position of supremacy. In the seventeenth century the idea of moral progress was intoxicatingly new. It was an idea which so fascinated John Milton that he created his magnificent epic around it. But the sixteenth century was a fulcrum intellectually, and the idea of a tangible human stability in the midst of incessant change was an exciting and sanguine idea. In these history plays Shakespeare is being relatively sophisticated, not puerile.

Human nature does not change; it was an idea that appeared to be true both of loyal and of disloyal men.

And though wee here fall downe,
Wee haue Supplyes, to second our Attempt:
If they mis-carry, theirs shall second them.
And so, successe of Mischiefe shall be borne,
And Heire from Heire shall hold this Quarrel up,
Whiles England shall have generation.

[*2 Henry IV*, IV.ii.47–52]

This idea of the permanence of the spirit of rebellion in certain men is again reinforced in the lines

For treason is but trusted like the Foxe,
Who neuer so tame, so cherisht and lockt vp,
Will haue a wilde tricke of his ancesters.

[*I Henry IV*, V.ii.9–11]

Generations of families provide evidence, the playwright is saying in these plays, of the transmission of a dominant character trait that appears to be timeless. In the sonnets Shakespeare was concerned with not only the immortality that art brings but also with the defeat of time through marriage and the generation of children. Ceaselessly, beauty and virtue are passed on, the sonnets proclaim. Continuity through children is the means by which mankind touches the eternal realm beyond time. The idea resembles the panegyric which Louis Le Roy wrote in his discussion of the two kinds of immutability:

> But they that are moveable doe begin, and end; are borne, and die, do increase, & diminish uncessantly; endeavouring notwithstanding (as much as they may) to come neere and participate of eternity: not by remaining alwaies one and the same (as doe the superiour and divine thinges) but by continuing their kindes by the meanes of generation; which is an immortall worke in this mortalite.[1]

In his last plays Shakespeare was to experiment with the idea of family resemblance, of patterns of human nature handed down through children that would be essential for recognition and identity. This idea is an extension of the theme of the history plays. In the second tetralogy Shakespeare experiments with the idea of the timelessness of human characteristics, but he is concerned in these plays with the obverse side of the idea as well. In these dramas he probes the idea of the permanence of disorderly characteristics in noble families. The proclivity of rebellion, the trend toward treason, the ingrained infidelity of certain nobles lines, the continuity of patterns of human nature which again and again created havoc and disorder in the English realm—these thoughts fascinated the poet at this time. There is a strong element of repetitiveness in both the structure and the theme of the *Henry IV* plays, a repetitiveness that has annoyed modern critics. They have worried the problem of unity in these plays to death. I believe that the playwright is employing in these plays every aesthetic device he can create to stress the reappearance of human traits, generation after generation. Repetition is such a device, and it enforces the idea of timelessness. Shakespeare has adopted, I think, the new theory of historiography that the continental writers had been developing: history provides insight, they were saying, into the permanent center of human character.

The second scene of *I Henry IV*, mirroring the first scene, portrays disorder, but here the disorder is in the private sector of the realm. The prince carouses with the morally disoriented crew, and the point is made: both public and private, both political and moral realms are caught in the throes of rebellion. But the prince's sanction of the behavior of the frequenters of Mistress Quickly's tavern is dissimulated. This action of dissimulation is so important that the playwright will forgo the element of dramatic suspense to emphasize it. There is no qualification of meaning here; Hal's soliloquy at the end of this scene is forthright: "Ile so offend, to make offence a skill, / Redeeming time when men thinke least I wil." Dramatic critics have regretted the poet's naiveté in this disclosure of intention so early in the play, but the *Henry IV* plays are not modern in this sense. They are ironic and classical. Shakespeare is using history with an idealistic (it is also frankly propagandistic) conception of function. The prince knows the natures of his rowdy companions just as he knows the natures of the nobles and his father the king. Hal's final reformation at the end of *2 Henry IV* is the ultimate example of the permanence of nobility and grace, but the actions of the Percies and the satiric comedy of Falstaff reveal the continuity of infidelity and ultimately of defeat. The playwright is insisting that human nature does not change.

Scene two begins when Prince Hal enters to find Falstaff rousing from sleep. This action of awakening is repeated in the "resurrection" of Falstaff at the end of Part One. There is a sense of revival in the nonverbal image of the huge figure rising from his bed, just as there is a symbolic element in the pseudoresurrection of the fat knight on the field at Shrewsbury. The idea of the timelessness of Falstaff's character is presented verbally as well. The dialogue in this scene begins with the old knight's query, "Now *Hal*, what time of day is it lad?" And the prince answers, " . . . What a diuell hast thou to do with the time of daie?" This statement on time is surrounded with realistic dialogue filled with graphically colorful "capons," "clockes," and "cups of sacke," and obviously the prince is making a point concerning Falstaff's nocturnal activities. But these colloquial comments should not obliterate the emphasis the poet is making on the timelessness of character in this scene. The structure of the scene is circular, and the pattern is contrived by these opening and closing references to time, as critics have noted.[2] Why is this emphasis upon time so important in Falstaff's character? It is important because the playwright is beginning to develop his idea of the repetition of disorderly actions in the commonwealth as deeds of treason are performed in a family line, generation after generation. Behind Falstaff's dramatic figure lies the historical image of Sir John Oldcastle, Lord Cobham. Shakespeare's allusions to the Oldcastle legend take the form of foreshadowing remarks, usually made by the prince, which are saturated with dramatic irony, for the playwright has given Prince Hal an awareness of the true nature of the Falstaff-Oldcastle character and his ultimate treasonable end. Shakespeare can develop his Sophoclean mode of irony against the chronicle background. His technique at this point is quite similar to that used by the ancient Athenian tragedians who adjusted the details of their heroic myths to fit their dramatic purposes, depending upon perceptive response from an audience well informed in the legends of the past. Shakespeare is writing historical comedy in these plays in an extremely allusive vein.

In this first comic scene the prince taunts Falstaff with ambiguous references to the gallows and to Falstaff's having "the hanging of the theeues" and becoming "a rare hangman" (lines 55, 63-64). Almost every chronicler of the fifteenth and sixteenth centuries noted in his account of the death of Sir John Oldcastle the rare manner in which the martyr had been hung horizontally in chains and burned. (The method was probably devised to hasten death. There are records of burnings at the stake in which the victim's legs were burned off while he was still alive. Apparently the authorities in 1417 were attempting to avoid such an occurrence. Oldcastle also had a broken leg, an injury he received in the fight in Wales when he was captured, and this may have been a factor in the strange manner of his execution.) In this same scene Prince Hal dallies with the idea of the robbery at Gads Hill and threatens to tarry at home. "By the lord," replies Falstaff, "ile be a traitor then, when thou art king" (line 141). In the dramatic context these lines are comic and made in broad fun, but in the historical context they are ironic and true: the official indictment filed against Sir John Oldcastle after the 1413 insurrection charged the outlaw with treason for conspiring to kill King Henry V and all his brothers.[3] In this scene Falstaff's banter is loaded with historical relevance. If the character were actually called Oldcastle in some of the early performances of *1 Henry IV*, as we think he was, the irony would have been overt and easily perceived by most of the audience.

In the tavern scene that follows (act II, scene iv) Falstaff and the prince perform a "play within a play." He and Hal act out dramatically "in King Cambyses vein" an imaginary interview between the king and the prince. The dialogue is concerned with the merit or lack of merit of the prince's wild companions, and the descriptions of those wild companions provide two versions of the great hulk of a knight who leads the group. Falstaff, portraying the king, declares that "a goodly portly man i'fayth, and a corpulent, of a cheerful looke, a pleasing eie, and a most noble cariage" is near the prince and should be maintained there, "for Harry, I see vertue in his lookes" (lines 394-99). Hal in turn portrays the king while Falstaff pretends to be the prince. The view is reversed: "a diuell haunts thee in the likenesse of an olde fat man, a tun of man is thy companion. . . . a rosted Manningtre Oxe. . . . Falstaffe, that olde white bearded Sathan" (lines 419-21, 424, 434). It would be difficult to ignore what has occurred here. Critics have noted that this scene looks forward to Hal's redemption at the end of Part Two, but it also looks backward toward the Oldcastle legend. This scene depicts the two images of Oldcastle's character that had come down through the chronicles. The earlier version drawn by the monastic writers of a perfidious knight, a Behemoth, a satellite of Satan is contrasted with the later Protestant version of Oldcastle as a valiant knight and a virtuous Christian. Shakespeare is presenting the dual view of the chronicle legend, and the euphemistic description of the "portly man" is obviously the hypocritical one.

This same dialogue continues with Falstaff playing the

king. He declares with pomp: "This chaire shall be my
state, this dagger my scepter, and this cushion my
crowne." These lines contain an allusion, I believe, to
Oldcastle's ambitions to become the regent of England.
The same idea is expressed when Falstaff, now the brag-
gadocio, proclaims, "If I do not beat thee out of thy kingdom with a dagger of lath, and driue all thy subjects afore
thee like a flock of wild geese, ile neuer weare haire on my
face more, you prince of Wales" (lines 120-23). This is
play-acting, and it is funny; but the historical background
is there, overshadowing the humor. This scene also contains ironic adumbration in the reference to the hurdle
that Oldcastle rode to his execution (it was a medieval
custom); Falstaff himself retorts when the sheriff is at the
door, "If I become not a Cart as well as another man, a
plague on my bringing up" (lines 466-67). Thomas Walsingham gave a long description of the hurdle trip
through the streets of London to St. Giles Field. The trip
was interrupted at several points when the hurdle was
stopped and Oldcastle was allowed to kneel and pray.
There are several other references in the *Henry IV* plays
to Falstaff and the gallows (Oldcastle's chains were hung
from a gallows): in Part Two Prince John threatens the
old roisterer with his someday breaking the gallows' back
(IV. iii. 31), and Prince Hal taunts him in Part One with
the "ridge of the gallowes" (I. ii. 36). These references are
self-contained and humorous; but with the historical implications exposed, the wit is gruesome. The same is true
with the teasing of Doll Tearsheet. When she calls Falstaff a "whorson little tydie Barthomew Borepigge," she
is using her own unique terms of endearment; but the Bar-
tholmew Pig, as well as the Manningtree Ox, was roasted
over an open fire. If the reader is repelled by this kind of
humor, he should skip to the next page. Falstaff is sensitive
too. When Doll asks him when he will patch up his body
for heaven, the fat knight moans, "Peace (good Dol) doe
not speake like a Deathshead: doe not bid me remember
mine end" (Part Two, II. iv. 345-36). No one wishes to
think of his own death, so Falstaff's line is understandable. But with the character called Oldcastle, the reference to his final day is especially pointed. The Elizabethan audience would, I think, have found these remarks

filled with double meanings and overt references to the burning of the Lollard. I suspect that even the pitlings would have comprehended the allusions.

There are other suggestive lines in these plays. The prince calls Falstaff a "whorson Candly-myne" (melted tallow) in the same scene, and in Part One he refers to a dish of melted butter, then remarks of Falstaff: "Behold that compound" (II. iv. 108). Of course Falstaff is fat, and of course he "lards the earth," but against the background image of the burning martyr the wit is grisly. Examples of this kind of satire accrue: when Falstaff thinks of Bardolph's face, it acts as a *memento mori*. "I neuer see thy face, but I thinke vpon hell fire, and Diues that lived in Purple: for there he is in his robes burning, burning. . . . O thou art a perpetuall triumph, an euerlasting bonefire light." And Bardolph replies, "Zbloud, I would my face were in your belly" (III.ii. 29–31). In addition, Falstaff shudders at the mention of a roasted applejohn in *2 Henry IV* (II. iv. 1–10). This reference is understandable when one recalls that the variety of apple called the Kentish Codling was roasted and sold in sixteenth-century London as a "hot codling." Even such an indirect reference to burning causes Sir John to shudder.

There are more than just burning references to the Oldcastle legend. The thousand-marks reward offered by Henry V, for the capture of Oldcastle, a reward that Foxe made much of, is perhaps alluded to when Falstaff meets the lord chief justice in Part Two. In bragging of his own youthfulness the fat knight remarks, "He that will caper with mee for a thousand Markes, let him lend me the money, & have at him." The two men have just been discussing Falstaff's failure to answer a citation by the lord chief justice to come to court. Shakespeare probably had in the back of his mind the Oldcastle legend, for a parallel action is available at this point. The chroniclers related how Oldcastle refused to answer the summons of the archbishop to ecclesiastical court, and they told also how Oldcastle mistreated the king's servant who brought the citation to Cooling Castle and how he had locked himself within the castle and had refused to appear in court. These incidents seem to have supplied the playwright with ideas.

Allusions to the Oldcastle story are compounded in

the tavern scene (act II, scene iv) of *1 Henry IV*. Perception here is difficult and depends upon a knowledge of the great importance that the Lollards had placed upon their resistance to the doctrine of transubstantiation. During Oldcastle's trial in the Parliament chamber in Blackfriars (ironically, the chamber that was to become the Blackfriars Theater, the same chamber that Burbage bought in 1596), he was asked the "murderous question"—did the material bread remain after consecration? This was one of the major points of doctrine that trapped him. The Lollards insisted that the bread remained bread, becoming after consecration the *symbol* of Christ's body. This part of Oldcastle's testimony was a favorite with the Protestant writers. Tyndale, Bale, and Foxe had placed emphasis upon it. In addition, Oldcastle's standard had been a flag bearing the chalice and the host. In the tavern scene Falstaff has hidden himself behind the arras to avoid the hue and cry of the sheriff (Oldcastle had hidden, of course, to avoid the arms of the law), and when Poins discovers the "oily rascall" asleep, he searches his pockets for valuables, which turn out to be tavern bills for bread and sack: "O monstrous! but one halfepeniworth of bread to this intollerable deale of sack?" Obviously Falstaff is no bread-eater. Under the guise of wit is ridicule, I think, of the doctrinal position of the Lollards of the fifteenth century.[4] The Falstaff-Oldcastle figure carries only a symbolic amount of bread.

Contrasted with the vague bit of bread is the ragged army that Falstaff recruits for the wars: there is no symbolism here. Sir John's soldiers are "revolted tapsters, and ostlers trade-fallen, the cankers of a calm world" whom he leads to Shrewsbury as "food for powder." They march through St. Albans where one soldier steals a makeshift shirt from the host of the inn (IV. ii. 43). We are reminded immediately of the chronicler of St. Albans (Thomas Walsingham) who wrote the colorful description of the army of laborers and husbandmen who passed by the abbey on their way to London to join Sir John Oldcastle, Lord Cobham. The government records list the followers of Oldcastle as bakers, braziers, carpenters, cordeners, curriers, drapers, dyers, fullers, glovers, hosiers, ironmongers, laborers, mercers, parchmenters, plowmen, tailors, saddlers, spurriers, smiths, webs, and the like.[5] Shakespeare appears to have known of the St. Albans chronicler's satiric description of that ragged group. But there is more to this satiric depiction than a simple dramatization using an old chronicle story as a point of departure. The satire at this point is double-edged; it appears to have been written with a special contemporary relevance in mind. The playwright at this point is using a conflation process that relates the fifteenth-century actions and characteristics of an historical figure with the Elizabethan characteristics of a descendant of that same family line.

We know from the military records of the Elizabethan period that one of Lord Cobham's brothers, Sir John Brooke (he called himself Sir John Cobham, using the title name rather than his family name), led foot-soldiers to battle, and we know that, like Falstaff, his method of paying those soldiers as well as his technique of mustering them was questionable. The playwright is developing in this process of conflation a kind of satirical montage or three-dimensional artifact. With his view of history as an instrument for revelation, the playwright can select and combine older materials in such a way as to create an entity that is lifelike in the sense that it mirrors the living representatives of certain noble houses in Elizabethan England. It is a process the poet will use to create living Percies, and it is a process that is doubly important for an understanding of the Oldcastle satire. Moreover, in the Oldcastle satire, there is a lateral movement within the dramatized montage. The Elizabethan family of Sir William Brooke, Lord Cobham, was a large one. His brothers, John, Thomas, and Henry, as well as his eldest surviving son and heir, also named Henry, figure to some extent in the satire. They all apparently were vulnerable to the prick of the satirist's pen. Lord Cobham's brothers signed themselves "Cobham" not Brooke most of the time. The ambassador was Sir Henry Cobham, the seaman and black sheep of the family was Thomas Cobham, the soldier was Sir John Cobham, and so on. They were proud of their noble name, and apparently they were proud of their martyred ancestor, Sir John Oldcastle, also Lord Cobham. Shakespeare can make the one satiric figure of

Falstaff (his girth could encompass a dozen such men)
spread broad enough to touch all the members of the Cobham family. The montaged image of Falstaff works
therefore in a complex way; its meanings accrue from
chronicle history and contemporary events. Ultimately,
because of his new theory of the function of history, Shakespeare will also make that dramatic montage prophetic.
The future will be foreshadowed as well as the past.

We know nothing of Shakespeare's activities in that
period after he left Straford-upon-Avon about 1583 and
before he started writing plays in the early 1590s. Scholars have speculated about the sensitive young man in the
formative period of his early adulthood. Did he go to sea?
He seems later to know much of the world of ships and
seafaring men. Did he go to the Low Countries as a soldier when Queen Elizabeth sent reinforcements across the
Channel under the earl of Leicester? As a young recruit
did the playwright-to-be encounter such a captain as Sir
John Brooke? We, of course, do not know. Had Shakespeare been forced to experience literally every activity he
described in his plays, he would have had to have been a
Methuselah or more. (Erasmus put it well when he remarked much earlier that "A fool learns only by experience, a wise man, vicariously.") Shakespeare would not
have needed to know Captain John Brooke; apparently
that soldier's recruitment practices were common and
well known. His malfeasance had come to the attention
of Sir John Norris, commander of the English forces in
the Low Countries, early in the 1580s. The plight of the
English soldiers on the Continent was serious; they were
being riddled by disease and warfare, and many of the
soldiers in Sir John Brooke's company were dead. We
know from the reports of Norris that Captain Brooke attempted to collect the pay of his dead men. When Sir
John Norris received money from the Estates to pay the
English troops, he distributed it to eight of the eleven
companies, but he refused to give Brooke the money for
his three companies. Brooke wrote to Sir Francis Walsingham in complaint stating, "He [Norris] says that
rather than I should have the money which remains in
hands for my 'dead pays,' he will deliver it back to the
Estates on his account and reckoning."[6] We do not know

whether Sir John Brooke received the money for his troops who had been "food for powder" or not. We do know from a letter written in November of 1588 that another complaint was lodged against Sir John Brooke; this time the complaint was written by Sir Thomas Randolph, the English ambassador to Scotland, a Kentish gentleman and a friend of Lord Cobham. Randolph's letter is addressed to Secretary Walsingham and has an air of resignation about it. He states that Sir John Brooke was

appoynted to be a captain as others were of divers selected soldiers within Kent—what benefit he got in the choice of his men, taking up and leaving out as many as for money he liked, I speak not of—but for that which is complained unto me by my neighbors of Milton and most of them her majesty's tenants, is, that their captain having received pay of her majesty for a time for such soldiers as served under him that he retaineth their whole wages in his hands and payeth them nothing to whom it is due, your honour considereth whether this be born with or not, though I fear it be too common with other captains that use the like.[7]

This was the Armada year, in which every able-bodied Englishman had taken up arms. Sir John Brooke, a shrewd opportunist, apparently made a profit with the mustering and the nonpayment of his fellow Kentishmen. His dishonesty was common enough in the sixteenth century, as Randolph noted. Sir John Brooke's desire for money was and is common in any age. His brother, Lord Cobham, was one of the wealthiest men in England at that time; his annual income exceeded £7,000. A family of such great wealth would not ordinarily be associated with the more common forms of dishonesty. But younger brothers were, and sometimes are, hard-pressed financially. This comic theme of dishonesty is spread broadly through the Henry IV plays.

A more important dramatic incident of this kind is the Gads Hill robbery which provides a great action for the witticisms of the prince and Poins. It also provides a complex basis for some extremely serious satire created through the careful interweaving of legend, chronicle history, and current Elizabethan events. Indeed, the Gads Hill episode in 1 Henry IV is so exquisitely constructed over a recoverable framework of historical incidents that its structure, including the inversions and exaggerations involved, is graphically revealed. Moreover, by recovering the historical framework something of the pragmatic functions of the comic plot with the combined artistic and practical intentions of the poet can be revealed. It is important then to examine in detail the scene and its prototypal elements.

Much of the comedy that is so carefully woven into the actions, themes, and symbolic statements of the *Henry IV* plays is basically unhistorical material. But the Gads Hill episode is based upon the legend of Prince Hal's antics as highwayman, and that legend is derived from extant chronicle sources. When John Stow published his version of the legend of the wild prince in 1580, he noted his source with a marginal reference to Titus Livius. What Stow was using at this point, however, was not the Latin *Vita Henrici Quinti* of the Italian chronicler, Tito Livio Frulovisi, but rather the vernacular translation of that work which had been written about the year 1513 and which is known today as *The First English Life of King Henry The Fifth.*[8] The legend of the princely robberies makes its advent in extant historical sources through this anonymous translator in Henry VIII's reign who labeled the story a commonplace tale, "as the common fame is." This first account of Hal's penchant for good-natured thievery relates that

> He delighted in songe and musicall Instruments, he exercised meanelie the feates of Venus and of Mars, and other pastimes of youth, for so longe as the Kinge his father liued; by whose life (as I haue learned of the credence before rehearsed, and also as the common fame is) accompanied wth some of his younge Lords and gentlemen would awaite in disguised aray for his owne receauers, and distres them of theire money. And some time at such enterprises both he and his Companie weare surelie beaten; and when his receauers made to him theire complaints, howe they were distressed and robbed in theire comminge vnto him, he woulde giue them discharges of so much money as they have lost, and besides that they shoulde not depart from him wthout greate rewards for theire trouble and vexacions. And he that best and most manly had resisted him and his companie in their enterprise, and of whome he had receaued the greatest and most stroakes, should be sure to receaue of him the greatest and most bounteous rewards.[9]

This colorful passage is an interpolation which the translator added to his Latin source.[10] Modern historians have accepted the writer's statement that he had the story of the prince's highwaymanship from James Butler, the fourth earl of Ormonde (d. 1452) who lived during the reigns of Henry IV and Henry V, and who was familiar with the court and the events of those times.[11] John Stow's own copy of the translator's manuscript has not been found. The extant copy (Bodley MS. 966, the source for C. L. Kingford's edition) was transcribed about 1610 for Sir Peter Manwood, a Kentish antiquary, and it was known and mentioned by Thomas Hearne when that scholar edited the Latin *Vita* in the eighteenth century.[12]

This story of Prince Hal's irresponsible conduct had been used for stage material before Shakespeare adapted it to his own purposes. And it has been assumed by some drama critics that the robbery episode enacted in the first scenes of *The Famous Victories of Henry Fifth* is based upon John Stow's 1580 version of the princely robbery.[13] In addition, this older anonymous play, entered with the stationers in 1594 and published in 1598 by Thomas Creede, has frequently been referred to as a source for Shakespeare's own *Henry IV* and *Henry V* dramas. Some critics have even suggested the existence of a prototypal play that lies behind both *The Famous Victories* and Shakespeare's plays.[14] Whether the old anonymous play was a direct source for Shakespeare or whether it too was derived from an even older play which served as a source for both playwrights will perhaps never be determined. What is important for this study is that both Shakespeare and the author of *The Famous Victories* depict a robbery at or near Gads Hill in which Prince Hal and his riotous companions are involved. And even more important is the fact that one of the riotous companions is called Sir John Oldcastle, alias Jockey, in the anonymous play, and was called Oldcastle and then Falstaff in Shakespeare's version of the action.[15] It is against this warp of legend and chronicle materials concerning the wild prince and his highwaymanship that the weft of contemporary events is woven to form a dramatic satire that competes with Aristophanic lampooning in complexity. For there is historical evidence that links Lord Cobham and his brothers to incidents of importance that occurred near Gads Hill.

When Queen Elizabeth ascended the throne of England in 1558, she drew around her the nobles and friends who had endangered themselves for her sake during Queen Mary Tudor's reign. Among those noblemen was of course William Brooke, seventh Lord Cobham, who had been imprisoned in 1554 for his involvement in Wyatt's rebellion. This nobleman was an intimate friend of William Cecil, and he soon received from the new queen the important appointment to the wardenship of the Cinque Ports, the five harbors on the east coast of Kent which face the Continent.[16] The warden of the Cinque Ports controlled the egress and ingress of traffic to and from France, Spain, and the Low Countries, and during this period of history the special couriers of the foreign ambassadors residing in London could not leave England with their diplomatic packets without a special passport signed for each trip by the lord warden. Thus no packet could enter or leave the country without Lord Cobham's knowledge. In the early part of Elizabeth's reign there were important robberies near Gads Hill in which diplomatic packets were stolen from the foreign couriers, and Lord Cobham was involved in these intrigues.

Gads Hill was a lonely stretch of the main highway from London to Dover; it lay between Gravesend and Rochester and was approximately three miles northeast of Cobham village, the site of Cobham Hall, family manor of the barons of Cobham. We know that Gads Hill was notorious for robberies even before Elizabeth's reign; indeed, it had become a subject for ballads at mid-century. Thomas Phaer entered a poem in the *Stationers' Register* in 1559 which he entitled "The Robery at Gaddes Hill."[17] We know also that Alexander Nowell, when going to his new benefice in Kent in May of 1559, was robbed of his purse, his gown, and his cap at "Gaddys Hill," and that he wrote to his friend, a Mr. Abell, warning him to "take heed you come not there."[18] Gads Hill was not a safe place for the lonely traveler, but the incidents in which Lord Cobham was involved were not related to the snatching of a purse or a gammon of bacon but rather to far more serious affairs concerned with Lord Cobham's official position as lord warden. These episodes of diplomatic highwaymanship provided the later playwrights with materials for subtle satire: let us therefore survey the historical scene carefully.

Holbein's drawing of Sir George Brooke, Lord Cobham.

Courtesy of Her Majesty, Queen Elizabeth II.

William Brooke, seventh baron of Cobham, succeeded to the family title in September 1558, after the death of his father, George, sixth lord Cobham. In July of that year Sir Thomas Cheyne, lord warden of the Cinque Ports, had also died, and his important office was still unoccupied when Queen Mary died in the following November.[19] After her coronation Queen Elizabeth appointed Lord Cobham to the post; she trusted this young nobleman (he was thirty years old at this time), and she also selected him to be the special ambassador to carry the formal announcement of Queen Mary's death and of her own accession to Philip II in Brussels. Lord Cobham conducted himself well on this trip; Richard Clough, Sir Thomas Gresham's agent in Flanders, described him as "a very gentle and sage young lord of whom he wished there were more in England."[20] But the Count de Feria has left us evidence that the young Lord Cobham was also ingratiating himself with the Spanish in the Low Countries. "Cobham has been, and is, so zealous with his letters from Brussels," the count's secretary wrote, "that it has been necessary to manage him a little, and his lordship has therefore thought well to promise him a pension, although he has not told him how much it will be." The writer added further that the marchioness of Northampton, Cobham's sister Elizabeth, "has served His Majesty [Philip II] when opportunity has occurred."[21]

By 1562 tensions between Spain, France, and England had greatly intensified, and European diplomatic maneuvers were becoming much more complex. France was facing civil war after the atrocity at Vassy; Elizabeth was being urged by the Protestants to send tangible assistance to the prince of Condé in his conflict with the Guise family, while Philip was making every effort to keep Elizabeth neutral. Mary Stuart, now in Scotland after the death of her husband, Francis II, was urging Elizabeth to announce publicly her approval of Mary as the heir-apparent to the English throne. At the same time the Guise faction in France, in an effort to gain double indemnity in their maneuvers to control the English succession, were seeking ties with Lady Margaret, countess of Lennox, and her eldest son, Darnley, whose claims to the English throne were derived through Henry VII's daughter Margaret. But

Spain too was interested in the claims of the countess of Lennox, and the Spanish ambassador, Alvarez de Quadra, bishop of Aquila, had been instructed to investigate her claims and the potential backing which the English Catholics might be expected to provide for her. De Quadra was living in Durham House in London, and he received there not only the disaffected Catholics who attended mass in his chapel but also information from a widespread network of spies and informers. De Quadra had recently suffered a setback in his secret negotiations to encourage Lord Robert Dudley's marriage with Elizabeth; the untimely death of Amy Robsart and Elizabeth's apparent return to a more stable emotional state in regard to the handsome Dudley had by the spring of 1562 placed Cecil once again in control of diplomatic affairs in England. Early in 1562 de Quadra sent Doctor Turner, a Catholic priest, to the duchess of Parma with information concerning the claims of the countess of Lennox and with a detailed list of the disaffected Catholics in England who were willing to back those claims. When Doctor Turner died unexpectedly in Flanders, de Quadra's secretary, Borghese Venturini, returned to England with the diplomatic papers, but he delivered them to de Quadra only after making secret copies of them, and these he offered to Cecil.

On 30 April de Quadra sent another Spanish courier to the Continent; at the instigation of Cecil the courier was robbed near Gads Hill by Lord Cobham's brothers, who were disguised as highwaymen.[22] The diplomatic packet was taken, and the next day two of the lesser English Catholics were lodged in the Tower. The Catholic noblemen who were implicated by this exposure were Lord Montague (grandfather of Shakespeare's patron, the third earl of Southampton), the earl of Derby, the earl of Westmoreland, and the earl of Northumberland. On 5 May de Quadra wrote again to the duchess of Parma, explaining what had happened:

On the 30th ultimo I wrote to your Highness giving advice of the arrival of the Count de Roussy here from France and the departure of Henry Sidney thither on behalf of this Queen. I thought it was of some importance that your Highness should have timely news of what was going on and, as by waiting for the ordinary post the letters would not reach you for at least 12 days, I despatched a Flemish courier, who is one of the regular men and a trustworthy person, with the idea that, seeing the fine weather we were having, he would arrive in three days. He left London on Wednesday after midnight, and went to Gravesend by water. Leaving his inn next morning he was accompanied by four horsemen in the dress of gentlemen, and these, with two others who had preceded them on foot, stopped him two miles from Gravesend and kept him in a house all Thursday until Friday morning. They signified to him that they were after some money and jewels they said I was sending to Flanders, but really this was only to gain time for my letters to be sent to London and back again, which was done, and in fact the letters were brought to the palace here where they were opened and copies of them taken. The highwaymen were envoys of Secretary Cecil sent for the purpose of stopping the courier and were not common thieves. I could swear that this is the case although, as for proving it by evidence, that I cannot do, but I am certain of it. I do not know whether the courier will have dared to recount this insult in Flanders, or if your Highness had heard of it, but I have thought proper to inform your Highness of it and enclose a copy of the letter written by the courier to me. If the man is still in Flanders he can inform your Highness of full particulars and the names of those who attacked him, which he knows.[23]

De Quadra did not mention the fact that Cecil had taken the list naming the disaffected English lords, nor did he mention this when he wrote to Philip II. In his letter to the Spanish king he blamed Borghese for his troubles, and he again described the Gads Hill attack, but this time he named the attackers:

They presently took a courier whom I had sent to the Duchess of Parma, and who they thought was Gamboa, one of your Majesty's couriers here. They thought he carried letters of mine for your Majesty and verbal messages which they could get from him by torture. Those who took this courier were two brothers and other servants of Lord Cobham who were ordered to undertake it much against their will.[24]

Lord Cobham was playing both sides of the fence (if indeed the fence had only two sides). We know that six weeks before the robbery in April, de Quadra had written to the king that Lady Margaret's claims to the English throne were held in strong favor "both amongst catholics and others of the highest standing." And he continued with more detail, "I think one of these men called Cobham must have gone very far in this business, as he is very uneasy, and has sought an excuse for going to the baths of Liège."[25] The French interests of the Cobhams ran concurrently with their Spanish intrigues and were a carryover from Mary's reign when young George, another of Lord William's brothers, had ingratiated himself with François de Noailles, the French ambassador in London. George Brooke was an under-secretary to the Privy Council. In this position of trust he was able to inform the ambassador of the business of the Council in the tense days of 1557 that preceded Philip's return to England to persuade the Council that for both duty and expediency England should join Spain in an open declaration of war on France. In January George Brooke informed Noailles that orders had been sent out to seize one of the ambassador's packets on its way to France.[26] Noailles therefore supplied some bogus dispatches filled with conciliatory announcements and an abundance of praise for Queen Mary. These were placed in the diplomatic packet and were indeed seized by the English agents. After these papers reached the Council, Noailles was treated with renewed cordiality by the English leaders of government—until his deception was discovered when Henry II declared war on Spain. In another incident of this period Dr. Nicholas Wooton, the English ambassador in Paris, discovered a plot in February 1557 of "some of the best men in England" who planned to depose Mary and place Elizabeth on the throne without the "help of any strangers." Wooton's emergency dispatch to the Council was deciphered by George Brooke and passed on to Noailles. And again, in April of the same year Brooke was a witness to the dramatic meetings between the Privy Council and Mary and Philip in which the queen threatened, cajoled, and pleaded by turns to bring the Council to declare war on France. Ironically, George Brooke's reports to Noailles and that ambassador's reports to Paris give us the fullest accounts available of the Council meetings in Mary's reign.[27]

We will never know how many of these politically expedient robberies occurred on the highway from London to Dover, nor do we know how many were instigated by the Cobhams. Such robberies occurred, of course, throughout Europe. Similar episodes, including even the murder of couriers, are described in most of the foreign calendars of the period. The use of ciphers and secret codes became obligatory if a diplomat expected his messages to get through with any secrecy. In England the role the Cobhams played in the Gads Hill robberies apparently became known; the Spanish ambassadors in London were never ones to keep a quiet tongue. The Catholic noblemen, especially the lords of Montague, Westmoreland, Northumberland, Lumley, and Derby, were evidently warned. But Lord Cobham had ingratiated himself in all camps, and he was soon to cause another catastrophe among the unruly English Catholics.

Lord Cobham's questionable conduct involved him in trouble in a very short time. We know that in the fall of 1565 or the spring of 1566 he was placed under house arrest in William Cecil's home. The nature of his offence is unknown other than that he had something to do with the intrigue with the marquis of Baden and his wife, Lady Cecilia, the sister of the king of Sweden. We know that Lord and Lady Cobham met Lady Cecilia at Dover in September of 1565, that after the marchioness became disillusioned with Queen Elizabeth and the English court she corresponded with Guzman de Silva, the new Spanish ambassador in London who had replaced de Quadra, and that de Silva received letters from Lady Cecilia and her husband after they left England, letters in which they offered their services to Philip.[28] We know also that the Lady Cecilia was involved with the Flemish alchemist, Cornelius de Alento, who had promised to transmute base metal into gold for Queen Elizabeth. Lady Cecilia's extravagance in London had placed her at the mercy of her debtors and made her vulnerable to the sharp practices of the alchemist. De Alento was arrested and placed in the Tower in the spring of 1566; the margrave of Baden, Cecilia's husband, was thrown into a common prison at Rochester for debts.[29] Our knowledge of Lord Cobham's involvement with the marquis and his wife comes from Francis Thynne, the antiquary, who blamed ungrounded jealousy and envy for Cobham's trouble. Thynne wrote some time later:

So this noble lord Cobham by the complaint of others, was upon the same assigned over to the charge of the honorable

lord treasuror, untill further triall were made of his upright-
ness, but in the end, as gold the more it is purified by the
fire the brighter and better it becometh: so the Lord Cobham,
having well cleered himselfe of whatsoever was laid against
him, did like Joseph not onelie receive an honorable libertie,
but did also in following time rise to greater honor than he
had before.³⁰

This mishap does not appear to have warned or deterred
Lord Cobham in his machinations with the Spanish and
French governments; and if Cecil assisted Cobham in
"cleering himselfe" in this affair, it was only a prelude to
the effort which the Lord Treasurer was to expend in protecting his very foolish and untrustworthy friend when the
Ridolfi plot broke in the autumn of 1571. The Ridolfi affair was the final incident in a series of crises that erupted
in the turbulent years of 1569-1572—years which encom-
passed the failure of the Northern Rebellion and the intrigues of Mary Stuart and the discontented English Catholics. This series of intrigues ended in the execution of the
duke of Norfolk in June 1572.

Roberto Ridolfi was a Florentine financier who had
settled in London; his interests in diplomatic intrigue
involved him in the foreign machinations behind the uprising of 1569. In October of that year, when the duke of
Norfolk and the lords of Arundel, Southampton, Lumley,
and Pembroke were placed under arrest, Ridolfi too was
apprehended and detained at Walsingham's house; he was
accused of "intermeddling in causes of estate and matters
betwixt her majesty and other princes." As early as 13
March of that year La Mothe Fénélon had written to
Catherine de Medici describing the affairs of Ridolfi:

Le Sr. Roberto Ridolfy, Florentin, ayant receu charge et com-
mandement, de la propre personne du pape, de tretter de la
restitution et restablissement de la religion catholique en
Angleterre avec les seigneurs catholique de pays, il s'est
princepallement adressé au comte d'Arondel et à milord de
Lomeley. . . .

La Mothe continued by adding to the names of the earl of
Arundel and Lord Lumley the names of "les comtes Derby,
de Cherosbery, de Pembrot, de Northomberland, et aul-
tres plusiers" who had refused to accept the "nouvelle
religion." All these men, he said, were involved in the plot

to restore Catholicism in England.[31] The arrest of the principal Catholic intrigants in October followed closely
upon a Gads Hill incident that may possibly have had an
important bearing upon the failure of the 1569 rebellion.
Mary Stuart had written to La Mothe on 20 September
that she was being moved to Tutbury, where she was to
be placed in "les mains des plus grandz ennemys que j'ay
au monde," and that the planned revolt must be postponed.[32] William Cecil had begun to play his hand. On 3
October La Mothe wrote to Charles IX that his courier
had been sent to Lord Cobham's house for a passport and
had been delayed there for an hour and a half. On leaving
Lord Cobham's house he traveled some three miles
through a wood

> . . . à trois mille de lay mayson du dict lord Coban, au pas-
> saige d'ung boys, quelques ungs, montez à l'advantaige,
> ayantz les visages couvertz, mais non tant que l'ung d'eulz
> n'ayt esté recogneu, le sont venuz charger á coups de'espée
> par la teste, l'ont porté par terre, tout follé aulz piedz de leurs
> chevaulz, et luy ont demandé incontinent les lettres de
> France, puys les luy ayant ostées, l'ont garroté et attaché à
> ung arbre, et l'ont layssé là.[33]

This important robbery of the French courier was Cecil's
attempt to find out the degree of involvement of the French
in the machinations of the northern earls and in the plotting of the adherents of Mary Stuart for her release from
detention. The robbery was apparently carried out by
Lord Cobham's men who had been alerted while he kept
the courier at Cobham Hall for an hour and a half awaiting the lord warden's signature on the messenger's passport. The situation which developed after the robbery was
even more complex, as seen in a tantalizing note written
by an anonymous hand on the envelope of La Mothe's
letter to Catherine de Medici, dated 5 December 1569.
The note suggests some kind of triple-cross in the undercover intrigues. It is addressed to Monsier l'ambassa-
deur:

> Je vous laysse ces lettres, lesquelles ne me peuvent de rien
> servir, et vous asseure, sur ma foy, qu'elles n'ont jamais esté
> ouvertes, et le milord Cobham menacoit chacun que s'il pou-
> voit trouver celluy qui avoit pris les dictée lettres, qu'il le
> pendroit.[34]

Apparently the packet Lord Cobham's men had seized from the French courier had in turn been seized from him and returned to La Mothe. This is extremely vague evidence, and we cannot get beyond the merest suggestion of what happened in the late fall of 1569 when the diplomatic tensions were intense with the build-up of pressures as the Northern Rebellion erupted. We can only say that something devious, serious, and unexpected happened at Gads Hill at that time. Lord Cobham apparently was implicated in the action. Years later when the playwright of the *Henry IV* plays began to create the comedy of the Gads Hill scene, the famous figure of Falstaff (Oldcastle) was made the comic butt of the devious actions. One cannot say with certainty that the jest which the prince and Poins play on Falstaff is based upon the complex historical episode at Gads Hill in 1569 when a stolen diplomatic packet was taken from Lord Cobham, but the larger idea of the Gads Hill robbery as both Shakespeare and the author of *The Famous Victories* conceived it was apparently based upon the historical episodes at Gads Hill early in Elizabeth's reign. It is also clear that in spite of the fact that he was employed and trusted by William Cecil and the queen, Cobham used his position as lord warden of the Cinque Ports to advance his own personal aims.

We know that Lord Cobham's interests in 1569 were pro-Spanish; the Ridolfi plot itself was essentially an Hispano-papal plot, and Cobham was involved in the plot. So were other English noblemen. The Florentine merchant was an undercover agent and an emissary of Rome. In 1570, after the total collapse of the resistance in the north, Ridolfi wrote to Pope Pius V declaring that the English Catholics "have given the Duke of Alva to understand that, if he will aid them by placing at their disposal in one of these ports merely a certain quantity of arquebuses, and other arms and munitions, and some money to get a force of cavalry together on this side, they will undertake with the help of all the Catholics to deliver the Queen of Scotland safe out of the hand of this Queen, and to re-establish religion in this realm." Ridolfi continued in the letter to name the English noblemen and their followers: "They are the following: Baron Guglie [Willoughby], Sir Thomas Stanglei [Stanley], Sir Thomas Givarg [Gerrard] with the concurrence and support of all the country of the Earl of

Gauci [Derby]." He goes on to name Sir Thomas Fitzher-
bert, who had promised to raise 6,000 men, and the earl of
Southampton, Viscount Montague, the earl of Arundel,
Lord Lumley, and Lord Windsor "with their followers and
friends [who] promise to rise simultaneously with the rest,
and with 15,000 men make themselves masters of the
Court."[35] Ridolfi set into motion the new action that was
to end ultimately in the execution of the duke of Norfolk
and the increased discomfiture of the Catholic sympathizers in England. In 1570 Ridolfi brought from Rome a
number of copies of Pope Pius V's bull, *Regnans in Excelsis*, which proclaimed Elizabeth's excommunication; this
message, the papal faction believed, would free the Catholics in England from their doubts about rebelling against
their sovereign and would bring them into a solid rank
behind the duke of Norfolk and the queen of Scots.

Mary and Norfolk had agreed to the conspiracy by the
beginning of 1571, and in March of that year Ridolfi left
London with letters from them to the duke of Alva, to
Philip II, and to the pope. The duke of Norfolk's letter to
Pope Pius V is extant; he laments the deplorable state of
"this island of Britain" in which "misery and anxiety prevail on all hands by reason of the enfeeblement of religion
and by consequence of the civil power."[36] Norfolk also
sent with Ridolfi a long letter of explanation evidently intended for distribution among the European leaders; in it
he explains his willingness to be involved in the affair and
his willingness to marry the queen of Scots: "I am not
actuated so much by the desire to advance myself by marriage with the Queen of Scotland as by the hope of unit-
ing all this island under a lawful Prince, and re-establish-
ing the ancient laws and the true Christian and Catholic
religion." At the close of this long letter Norfolk added a
list of the adherents of Mary Stuart. The list includes the
names of forty English noblemen; among those named are
the earls of Arundel, Oxford, Northumberland, Westmoreland, Shrewsbury, Derby, Pembroke, and Southampton, Viscount Montague, and, of course, Lord Cobham.[37]

This list helps to explain some of the devious actions
that followed in the ensuing months. In April Ridolfi sent
a packet of letters from the Continent to London by a
Flemish carrier who was in the employment of John Les-

lie, the bishop of Ross (designate), Mary Stuart's ambassador in England. The packet contained letters from Ridolfi to Mary, to Norfolk, and to Lord Lumley; there were also letters in the packet from the exiled countess of Northumberland and from the earl of Westmoreland. Charles Bailley, the Flemish carrier, was searched in Dover, and the secret letters were found strapped to his back under his shirt. The guard at Dover sent the confiscated packet to the lord warden, who was at his London house in the Blackfriars precinct. But the news of the confiscation of a secret packet reached Cecil's ears. Alarmed, Lord Cobham sent the packet of letters to the bishop of Ross, who enlisted the aid of the Spanish ambassador. Hastily they compiled a bogus packet of old letters of the queen of Scots which were in cipher, and Lord Cobham sent this counterfeit packet to Cecil, keeping the original packet by him in the event the intrigue should fail. On 12 July Guerau de Spes, the Spanish ambassador, wrote to Philip II relating what had happened.

It was a most extraordinary piece of good fortune to save the packet taken by Carlos, the bishop of Ross's servant, which Ridolfi unsuspiciously entrusted to him at Brussels, knowing that he was the Bishop's secretary. It was written in a different cipher, and Carlos took an alphabet with him in order the more easily to decipher it in future. All of this was recovered through me by the good offices and help of Thomas Cobham before lord Burleigh heard of it, and another packet was made up with the same cipher characters: Burleigh has had a secretary at work upon it for days and has sent copies to France and Italy, but without effect for there is nothing in it. They are trying to cajole Carlos by means of the good Dr. Story. This Queen had some idea that Ridolfi was writing to certain personages here and that the Duke of Alva was going to send aid to the queen of Scots, but Carlos did not declare who these personages were for he did not know. I have no doubt I shall be able to throw them still further off the scent.[38]

On 14 July Philip wrote to Alva informing him that he was willing to back the enterprise and ordering him to prepare arms and supplies immediately.[39] Preparations for the invasion of England were seriously under way.

Where did the Spanish ships intend to land? We have some suggestion from a letter written by La Mothe Fénélon to Charles IX after the Ridolfi plot collapsed; La

Mothe's comment on Lord Cobham and the Cinque Ports indicates the serious degree to which that nobleman had involved himself in treason. The ambassador lists a number of noblemen who had been arrested, and then he remarks that Cobham too is in prison:

> . . . et desjà millord Cobham est miz on arrest, comme ayant esté de l'intelligence, et ayant offert, à ce qu'on dict, quelcun des cinq portz dont it est gardien, pour servyr à la descente des dicts Espaignolz.[40]

Had Lord Cobham sold out to Philip and Alva, and were the Cinque Ports being readied for Spanish ships? Apparently so. Some degree of Cobham's guilt is revealed by the depositions taken after Cecil discovered that he was trying to decipher worthless letters in the bogus packet Cobham had given him. Cecil also received intelligence from the Regent Lennox in Scotland concerning Mary's relationship and dealings with Alva; and the grand duke of Tuscany sent word of some of Ridolfi's plans and actions. Cecil had Charles Bailley, the Flemish carrier, racked. Gradually the story unfolded in the depositions of the prisoners. Bailley offered to betray the bishop of Ross if allowed to pursue his own course homeward.[41] Another stroke of luck enabled Cecil to apprehend Robert Higford, the duke of Norfolk's secretary, en route to Scotland bearing a large sum of money for the queen of Scots' followers north of the border. This money was part of the 12,000 crowns which Pope Pius V had sent from Rome to help relieve the suffering of the Catholics involved in the Northern Rebellion.[42] Higford's confession in September implicated Lord Cobham and his brother, Thomas, in Norfolk's plans, and in October the bishop of Ross broke under pressure and confessed nearly all he knew concerning the plot; he named most of the English adherents of the queen of Scots who were involved in the machinations. Norfolk was arrested on 3 October, and on the eleventh he was conveyed to the Tower. The earl of Southampton, the earl of Arundel, Lord Lumley, Sir Henry Percy, the earl of Derby's two sons, and a dozen lesser figures were arrested as well. Cecil wrote to the earl of Shrewsbury on 19 October that "this matter of the Duke of Norfolk grows daily larger upon examination. I am sorry to see so many touched therewith. My Lord Cobham is in my house as a prisoner, who otherwise should have been in the Tower. I loved him well, and therefore am sorry of his offence.[43]

With some historical certainty we can now say that some of the Gads Hill robberies that occurred in Queen Elizabeth's reign were planned by William Cecil (Lord Burghley since March 1571) and the queen in attempts to intercept the messages of foreign ambassadors. The queen and her secretary needed desperately to know more of the involvement of Philip II, Charles IX, the duke of Alva, and the pope in the affairs of Mary Stuart. Lord Cobham and his servants were personally involved in the diplomatic robberies, but Lord Cobham's interests were divided. He had aligned himself secretly with the Spanish ambassador and with Mary Stuart. He was so involved with the machinations set in motion to free the queen of Scots and in the plans for her marriage to the duke of Norfolk that the possibility of his treasonable consent to open the Cinque Ports to the invading Spanish ships is strong. Years later the Elizabethan playwrights would use these incidents as an historical foundation to give fiber to their dramatic satire. That satire contains an amalgamation of legend (Prince Hal's youthful misconduct), imagination (the involvement of the Oldcastle character in those princely robberies), and contemporary history (the activities of Lord Cobham, Oldcastle's titular descendant, at Gads Hill).

Shakespeare introduces his Gads Hill incident with some highly suggestive language. After Prince Hal has taunted Falstaff with sleeping days and carousing nights, Sir John defends himself: ". . . let vs be *Dianaes* forresters, gentlemen of the shade, minions of the moone, and let men say wee be men of good gouernement, being gouerned as the sea is, by our noble and chast mistresse the moone, vnder whose counteaunce we steale" (I. ii. 24–28). We transcend time. The center of this allusion is its reference to Diana, and Diana was a classical figure with well-known metaphoric significance in the court of Queen Elizabeth. Readers of late sixteenth-century poetry are aware of the use of the image of Diana or Cynthia, the moon goddess, as a device to flatter the queen herself. It had become a commonplace practice by the 1590s. The chastity of the ancient moon goddess and the myth of her power, her beauty, and her honor made her an ideal symbol

for England's maiden queen. And Elizabeth, as she began
to age, appears to have sanctioned this poetic use of hyper-
bole when it placed her, as it were, beyond time and
mortality. Thus in the poetry of the age Diana and the
English monarch become the same and share in the
grandeur of a new Renaissance conception of an ancient
Platonic Ideal.[44] But Falstaff's goddess takes on the attributes of St. Nicholas, for Sir John's Diana is the pa-
troness of highwaymen. If historical materials are
pertinent at all, it would seem that the queen's sanction
of the diplomatic robberies of the ambassadorial couriers
lies behind Falstaff's reference. Elizabeth's attitude concerning such "underhanded" diplomacy was bold and objective. Her remarks to the Spanish ambassador after
the first incident at Gads Hill are extant in a letter which
De Quadra sent to Philip II describing his interview with
the English queen. He told her that his master was upset
that his courier had been apprehended in England. Her
reply to that statement, wrote the ambassador, was that
"if she suspected anything was being written from here
against her interests she would, in such a case, not hesitate
to stop the posts and examine what concerned her." De
Quadra describes how he objected to her threat; he boldly
answered that it could not be done "without open offense
and enmity." Elizabeth (never one to be boggled by an
ambassador) had quickly pointed out that "it was offense
and enmity to act to her injury in her own kingdom."[45]
England's queenly Diana had something of the Patron St.
Nicholas in her spirit. This broad element of common sense
in her character apparently governed her response to the
dramatic satire in the *Henry IV* plays when those dramas
were produced at court. If the legend upon which we rely
for our knowledge of what happened is accurate, the queen
loved the plays, but she responded to the Cobham objections by asking for a change in the name of the leading
comic character. The satire and the comedy in the very
popular plays were not deleted, however. The queen, of
course, could have banned both plays entirely had she seen
fit. She did not. Indeed (again if legend leads critics aright),
she asked for more comedy with Falstaff falling in love.

    Falstaff's pretended defense of his nocturnal "purse-
taking" on Old Kent Road, his pseudoserious remark of

qualification, "Why *Hall,* tis my vocation *Hall,* tis no sinne
for a man to labor in his vocation" (I. ii. 100-101), has a
topical relevance in Lord Cobham's conduct as lord warden
of the Cinque Ports, the defender of the southeastern coast
of England. Lord Cobham's official position gave him the
authority to search and apprehend any suspected traveler
in Kent; the satire of the drama, however, bites deeper
than this and peers at the questionable use of that authority
in the diplomatic robberies of that period. Even more important than the lord warden's position for the topical
stratum of meaning in the Gads Hill satire is the office of
the lord chamberlain of Her Majesty's household, a post
which fell into Cobham's possession after the death of
Henry Carey, Lord Hunsdon, in the summer of 1596.

We know that the acting of plays had been prohibited in
London that summer. The Privy Council (of which Cobham
was an important member) sent letters to the justices of
Middlesex and Surrey on 22 July ordering them "to re-
strayne the players from shewing or using anie plaies or
interludes in the places usuall about the city of London."[46]
The letters mentioned fear of the plague in the city, but
there apparently was more to the order than simply a pre-
cautionary move to safeguard health. Thomas Nashe, the
poet and playwright, wrote a letter to Sir William Cotton
in the late summer of 1596. In this letter Nashe speaks
of his own strait circumstances and then remarks; "When
now the players as if they had writt another Christs tears,
ar piteously p[er]secuted by the L. Maior & the aldermen, &
howeuer in there old Lords tyme they thought there state
setled, it is now so vncertayne they cannot build vpon it."[47]
The actors were feeling the effect of Hunsdon's death.
Henry Carey, the queen's cousin (some historians say her
half-brother), was a blunt and somewhat rugged individual
with an unusually colorful speech habit (too profane to be
"truly Christian" one early writer says). As lord chamberlain, a post he held for eleven years, Hunsdon had complete control of those suboffices in the queen's household,
including the mastership of the revels (Sir Edmund Tilney
filled this position during the 1590s). The power of the
lord chamberlain's office gave Hunsdon control of all the
acting companies in London, both adult and children's
groups.[48] With his death at Somerset House on 23 July,

the Shakespeare-Burbage acting company lost its own personal patron, but the players also lost their title as the Lord
Chamberlain's Men. They became simply Lord Hunsdon's
Men under the patronage of George Carey, who succeeded
to the family title as his father's heir.

Within a fortnight of the elder Hunsdon's death the queen
had made her appointment of a new lord chamberlain, and
the Privy Council noted the fact: "This day, being Sonday
the 8th of August, the Lord Cobham, Lord Warden of the
Cinq Portes, was made Lord Chamberlain by her Majestie
in delivering to his Lordship the White Staffe before her
Majesty went to the Chapple in the foornoon."[49] Sir William
Brooke, Lord Cobham was now an elderly man of some
sixty-nine years, astute, proper, a respected member of the
establishment. He had received the honored Garter in 1584
and had been appointed to the Privy Council in 1586—both
honors, of course, were due to Lord Burghley's personal
favor. Lord Cobham had escaped disaster in the Ridolfi
affair through the protection of his powerful friend, and he
had become entrenched in the policies of the lord treasurer.
With his appointment to the lord chamberlain's post in
August 1596, a subtle mode of satire opened for the playwright. Shakespeare took advantage of this new appointment to create an even more pointed satire tangential to
the Oldcastle lampooning and aimed directly, I think, at
the new lord chamberlain and his office. The more pointed
satire begins with a pun on Oldcastle, as the character
Gadshill boasts of his colleagues in crime: "I am ioyned
with no footlande rakers, no long-staffe sixpennie strikers,
none of these mad mustachio purplehewd maltworms, but
with nobilitie, and tranquilitie, Burgomasters and great
Oneyers. . . . we steale as in a Castell cocksure" (II. i.
69–72, 82). Both Kittredge and Dover Wilson have noted
the probability of Gadshill's allusion in his pun on "Castell"
to the name of his leader, Sir John Oldcastle.[50] And this
allusion is related, it would seem, to the similar usage in
Hal's earlier jibe at Falstaff as "my old lad of the castle"
(I. ii. 40). Gadshill's "nobilitie" and "Burgomasters" ele-
vate the rank of the highwaymen even higher than that of
the knights who robbed in *The Famous Victories*. In Shakespeare's Rochester inn scene, Gadshill speaks to the
chamberlain of the inn where the travelers have spent the

night, and it becomes apparent immediately that the chamberlain is in league with the highwaymen. When the inn official greets Gadshill with the language of the underworld, "At hand quoth pickepurse," Gadshill responds in kind: "Thats euen as faire as at hand quoth the Chamberlaine: for thou variest no more from picking of purses, then giuing direction doth from labouring: thou laiest the plot how" (II. i. 46–49). And the chamberlain then describes for Gadshill the vulnerable travelers who are carrying money upon their persons. We learn also that the dishonest chamberlain will share in the "purchase" for his assistance in pointing out the franklin and the auditor.

What Shakespeare has done in this realistic scene of the inn life in Rochester is to depict on an inverted scale a corrupt chamberlain of the common variety who makes arrangements for the hijacking of his customers' purses. The action shadows forth what had occurred years before at Gads Hill; now that Lord Cobham had become lord chamberlain, he could be needled with some realistic satire that made skillful use of both history and literary symbolism. Years ago Halliwell-Phillipps suggested that Shakespeare had in mind the Crown Inn, the most famous hostel in sixteenth-century Rochester, when he wrote this realistic scene with its colloquial carriers and its picture of inn life. The Crown Inn was popular; Queen Elizabeth is said to have stayed there upon occasion.[51] Moreover, the name of this inn is suggestive. In Shakespeare's play the inn (possibly the Crown) with its crooked chamberlain becomes, I think, a very useful symbol. Shakespeare does not use a specific inn-name in the play, but in general the inn in poetry has been a traditional symbol for the society of the commonwealth. When Chaucer depicted the Tabard and its varied guests in the fourteenth century, he appears to have used the idea, and certainly Ben Jonson was aware of the allusive meanings of the symbol later when he wrote The New Inn with its broad social satire. In the Henry IV plays the Falstaff-Oldcastle character was established as a rollicking companion of the young prince, and Shakespeare could allude with some ease to certain elements in the lives of both the earlier Lollard and the Elizabethan Lord Cobham. The appointment of Lord Cobham to the position of the lord chamberlain, however, gave the playwright additional material for his already pointed satire. He created this tangential scene depicting a corrupt chamberlain in cahoots with the robbers. The scene is, I think, a covert reference to the man who now held the lord chamberlain's white staff.

Nashe's description of the "piteous persecution" that the players were enduring in the late summer of 1596 adds some evidence to support the conjecture that the Burbage acting company was suffering from the appointment of the new lord chamberlain. There was personal sorrow as well in Shakespeare's life at this time; young Hamnet, the playwright's eleven-year-old son, was buried on 11 August. The players had gone into the provinces after the close of the theaters at the end of July. We do not know that Shakespeare accompanied the troupe in its country rounds. We do know that he was named in a petition for surety of the peace in November 1596; it was the same month in which the residents of the Blackfriars precinct presented their petition to the Privy Council to forestall the remodeling of the Blackfriars Theater by Burbage and his sons.[52] The players were playing a losing game with Lady Fortune for some months in 1596, but the records reveal that they returned to court at Whitehall to present entertainment for the Christmas and New Year's holidays.[53] It was during this hectic autumn, I believe, that Shakespeare started composing Part One of the *Henry IV* plays. By November, I think the playwright was at work upon the comic scenes depicting the famous roisterer whom we call Falstaff. But in the first version of the play Falstaff was called Oldcastle; the players were too unhappy in their misfortune to be overly subtle. This first play, and again I conjecture, was apparently finished and produced before the death of Lord Cobham on 6 March 1597. The Gads Hill satire would have lost its point after that date, for Henry Brooke, eldest son and heir of Lord Cobham, was a pretty courtier, a man made of much softer material than his father: Henry Brooke was a fop.

There is, of course, more to the comic satire of the *Henry IV* plays than the Gads Hill episode. In Part Two Shakespeare creates an imaginative biography for Falstaff when he allows the senile Justice Shallow to remark that Jack Falstaff in his youth was a page to Thomas Mowbray, duke of Norfolk (III.ii.27-29). There is no historical evidence to indicate that Sir John Oldcastle was ever such a page. It has been suggested that in his youth the historical knight, Sir John Fastolfe (a figure that lies behind the satire of *1 Henry VI*), was attached to the household of the duke of Norfolk, but again there is no historical evidence upon which to ground such speculations. These conjectures arose with the statements of John Weever and Francis Blomefield in the seventeenth and eighteenth centuries; both writers were basing their remarks upon Shakespeare's play.[54] And in the play Shakespeare appears to fabricate this bit of history to make a pointed reference to Elizabethan political events—it was Sir William Brooke, Lord Cobham who had served as a "page" or follower of the duke of Norfolk. The evidence of Cobham's association with Thomas Howard, fourth duke of Norfolk, has been slighted or completely ignored by most historians, but it is colorful material, and it helps to explain some of the subtlety of Shakespeare's satire.

The reader will recall that Lord Burghley wrote to the earl of Shrewsbury in October 1571, saying that Lord Cobham was a prisoner in his house when he should have been in the Tower for his involvement in the Ridolfi plot. "I loved him well," wrote the famous secretary, "and therefore am sorry for his offence." Lord Burghley was protecting his untrustworthy friend. He wrote an account of the Ridolfi plot which he apparently intended to publish as an official statement on the affair. In it he described the arrest of the carrier, Charles Bailley, and the discovery of the letters of Ridolfi, but he carefully suppressed the role Lord Cobham played in the questionable dealings. Burghley concluded his account of the events with the arrest of the duke of Norfolk (3 October), and he conceded that the discovery of the whole plot was the result of two accidents, the capture of Bailley's packet and the apprehension of Norfolk's gold shipment to Scotland. This work did not reach the press. As late as 1595 Lord Burghley was still reworking his papers on the Ridolfi affair; he wrote a second account of the plot, an account which adds nothing to the story. It too went unpublished.[55]

The lord treasurer's secretiveness did not of course hide all the historical evidence. Lord Cobham's deposition is extant in the British Museum. He was quick to put the blame for his precarious position upon Thomas, his "ingrate brother," but he admitted that he had sent Thomas's wife (the daughter of Sir William Cavendish) to the duke of Norfolk with a warning.[56] Brother Thomas denied many things too; in a letter to the Privy Council on 2 October he declared that both Higford and Bailley were lying, for, he insisted, "I never named either Therle of Westmorland's or Ridolphi's Letters, nor knewe of anye sutch Letters, nor come neere the Mallet [packet], to do any sutch Thing." Bailley and Higford had repeated in their confessions the boast made by Thomas Brooke that he had slipped certain letters from the packet while Lord Cobham was talking to Bailley.[57] Thomas denied knowing the bishop of Ross or having any connection with the duke of Norfolk, but the confessions of others had placed too much evidence in Burghley's hands concerning the guilt of Cobham and his brother for the secretary to be further beguiled.[58]

As early as October 1570, Burghley had received a confession from one John Moon, a servant of Lady Lennox, who had been caught dealing in Mary Stuart's intrigues. Moon confessed that Thomas Brooke had offered him one thousand crowns to deliver a certain packet that had come out of Scotland to Alexander Leslie or Andrew Abercrombie.[59] But it was the bishop of Ross's confession that uncovered Thomas Brooke's role in the intrigues of the duke of Norfolk. Ross confessed that Thomas Brooke's wife had begged him in 1564, when Thomas was in the Tower for piracy (a racy historical episode that lies beyond the scope of this study), to intervene with the Spanish ambassador in an effort to have the Spanish charges of piracy withdrawn or mitigated. The bishop of Ross confessed that he had agreed to help and had given his own bond for surety in 1565, and

so Thomas Cobham comying fourth, fell with Thanks in Acquaintaunce with this Examinate [Ross], and so from Tyme to Tyme, he and Francis [Barty] wold tell this examinate, who were Freends and who were Enemyes to the Scots Quene. . . . ones he [Ross] sent a letter by Thomas Cobham to the Duke, but the Duke liked not to have hym a Messenger and so he used him no more.[60]

This last statement was not exactly true; Thomas Brooke (he is called Cobham throughout most of the historical papers) had been working for the duke of Norfolk for some time, and his actions had been described in detail by Higford, Norfolk's secretary, in a deposition dated 1 October. Higford related at length how messages or "tickets" were slipped into the Tower to his master in wine bottles, but he said that Norfolk was dissatisfied with that procedure and that another method was devised.

> Yet not contented with this, for my Lord coulde not be satisfied, I know not upon what Occasion (for it was also before my Returne to my Lord backe from Colde harbor) a Mayde of Mrs. Heyborne's, a Wydowe which keapt the Howse adjoyninge to the Prison wheare my Lord then laye, and now lyeth, upon a Pole's End, as I harde, put up a Writing to my Lord's Wyndowe, wheare the Chaplaine was looking out. This writinge, as we said, was delivered to the Mayde by Mr. Thomas Cobham, to be conveyed to my Lord. Upon the Perusall of this Letter, which, by like, commanded the Trustines of the Wench, Meanes was founde that Mr. Sewell [Norfolk's chaplain] spake with her downe from a Hoole in a Privie-howse, in an uther Chamber, over a Privie-howse also in her Mistris Howse. And so after this, he used to convey my Lord's Writings to the said Mr. Cobham, who sent them out by a Man of his to Howard Howse, or els delivered them to some of my Lord's Men, I know not wheither. And this was then thowght to be the surest Waye from all Daunger, and ther fore was bothe longer and more used. The Maide's Name is Nell, and now is Servant to my Lord at Howard Howse.

Higford continued in this lengthy deposition to name those to whom Norfolk communicated in this secret manner: "My said Lord hath written owt of the Tower to my Lord Lumley, my Lord Cobham, Mr. Dyer, Sir Nicholas Throgmorton, and others before named; and from them he hathe receaved also Letters againe."[61]

In the bishop of Ross's confession only a partial truth had been revealed concerning Lord Cobham's role in the disastrous proceedings; Ross attempted to shield his cohort as much as possible. The bishop confessed that through Thomas Brooke and Francis Barty (a Flemish salt-maker who acted as a messenger between Ross and Lord Cobham) he had had news of the apprehension of Charles Bailley and the letters from the Continent. Ross confessed

that the packet contained letters to the duke of Norfolk
and Lord Lumley and that there were letters in the packet
from the exiled Lady Northumberland and the earl of
Westmoreland. The bishop of Ross related how the counterfeit packet of letters was made up of old letters to the
queen of scots. He went so far as to implicate the French
ambassador in the actions: "yt was devised emonge them,
that the French Ambassador should say they were his Pacquet, and so demand it if Nede be." A few more details
concerning Lord Cobham's actions appear in this deposition. Ross related that Cobham had demanded to know
the contents of the cipher letters and had insisted that
"if there be any Letters in the pacquet concerning the
Queene my Mistris, or hir Estat, he wold not deliver them
to hym, nor no other, but to hir Majesty only; but if it
were but for small Maters of [hiatus] or Relief of those
which were beyond the Seas, and now in Misery, he would
be glad to help them."[62] But Burghley by this time had got
to the bottom of the whole ugly business. The Catholic
noblemen were placed in the Tower, and the duke of Norfolk was brought to trial. This part of the story with Queen
Elizabeth's vacillation at the idea of executing her premier nobleman is well-known history. On 24 May 1572,
Antonio de Guaras wrote to the duke of Alva that

> It is generally asserted that when Parliament closes the duke
> of Norfolk will be executed. The bishop of Ross, the Queen
> of Scotland's ambassador, the earl of Southampton, son-in-
> law of Lord Montague, two sons of Lord Derby, the earl of
> Arundel, are still in prison, the earl of Arundel himself being
> under arrest in his own house, and Lord Cobham under guard
> at Burleigh House. Thomas Cobham, brother of Lord Cob-
> ham, is in the Tower with over thirty other gentlemen of high
> position, all of them for being concerned with the queen of
> Scots and the duke of Norfolk.[63]

De Guaras was correct; a fortnight later Norfolk was beheaded. It was an ugly and tense time for the young earl of
Southampton (father of Shakespeare's patron) and for
the sons of the earl of Derby (one, the father of the Lord
Strange who was later to have an acting company with
which Shakespeare would be associated). Lord Cobham
came out of this mess unscathed. Sir William Dugdale
wrote many years later that Lord Cobham, "being one of

the Lords commited to the Tower of London for complying
with the Duke of Norfolk, in his design of marrying the
Queen of Scotland, upon hope of pardon discovered all he
knew therein."[64] Cobham "squealed," turned informer on
his colleagues in the plot. Lord Burghley in his written
account of Cobham's confession put the action of that lord
in more gracious terms: "The lord Cobham tolde me that
he would declare to me the whole truthe of the matter
whereof he was charged trustinge that I would save his
honor & name. . . ."[65] In the twentieth century we can
only guess at the intensity of the hatred that this bungling
action and confession made by Cobham to save his own
honor aroused in the Catholic noblemen and other rebels.
Many years later Shakespeare could refer to Jack Falstaff as a "page" to the duke of Norfolk, and at least some
of his audience, aware of the complexity of the satire,
could appreciate the jibe. For the playwright was not making a literal reference to a small household page; he was
using his dramatic pseudo history as a stalking-horse from
which to shoot his barbed shafts of satire at a man who in
his earlier years had served as a secret follower to the
fourth duke of Norfolk and his treasonable plots.

Something of the complexity of Shakespeare's satire is
beginning to be revealed. The poet was concerned with
ridiculing the new lord chamberlain through an established dramatic character who had stridden the stage
when the Queen's Company produced *The Famous Victories of Henry V* in the 1580s. But this character was
only the point of departure for Shakespeare's wit. He developed within the chronicle material context a broad
comic plot in which the Falstaff-Oldcastle character could
be manipulated to reflect not only the image of the ancestral Lollard martyr but also certain aspects of the life
of the contemporary Lord Cobham, Sir William Brooke.
Such a satiric mode was not difficult to create, for both
Oldcastle and his Elizabethan titular descendant were
vulnerable to the charge of treason.

Certain members of Shakespeare's audiences would
have been especially perceptive of this kind of wit, I
think. We know very little of the relationships between
poets and their patrons during the Elizabethan period.
The prefaces and dedicatory epistles from the volumes of

that age exist in abundance, but the language of those dedications is usually effusive, and there is little historical evidence to indicate that the writers were closely associated with their patrons. We know even less about Shakespeare's association with the earl of Pembroke, with Lord Strange (the earl of Derby's son), or with the earl of Southampton, though legends have left us some room for conjecture concerning the latter's special patronage. The fathers of Pembroke, Strange, and Southampton had been caught in the collapse of the Ridolfi affair, an affair which from an historical long-view was doomed to failure but which to the participants seemed to have collapsed (Burghley acknowledged it) because Lord Cobham bungled in the confiscation of the secret letters. The older earls of Pembroke and Southampton and the sons of the earl of Derby had personal grounds for despising Sir William Brooke, Lord Cobham.

The comic plot and the serious historical plot of the *Henry IV* plays meet frequently in the actions of the dramas. Scholars have noted the niceties in the structure of the plays as the comic crew again and again is used to augment, reinforce, or complement the serious political and moral themes of the plays. One important juncture at which the serious and the comic plots fuse is the battle scene at Shrewsbury. It is here that Falstaff produces his famous catechism on honor; and when he takes the dead Hotspur upon his back as a trophy of victory, we have a strong iconographic, nonverbal image drawn straight from the morality plays. The ancient Vice has won another victim and is carting him off to hell. But there is more than dramatic tradition in this famous scene. Falstaff brags of his own "resurrection," and this introduces an Oldcastle element into the satire. He then brags of his own prowess to the prince and claims to have killed Hotspur: "there is Percy, if your father will doe me anie honour, so: if not, let him kill the next Percie himselfe: I looke to bee either Earle or Duke, I can assure you" (V. iv. 138–41). This passage introduces an important and difficult episode in Elizabethan history and a role played in that episode by an Elizabethan "Gunpowder" Percy. First, the Oldcastle reference.

Falstaff's "resurrection" comes on the battlefield at

Shrewsbury after he has counterfeited death in his encounter with Archibald, earl of Douglas. The reader will
recall the dramatic action: Hotspur and the prince have
met with drawn swords, exchanged taunts, and set to fighting. Douglas enters, spies the grandstanding Falstaff who
is cheering on the prince, leaving his own great back un-
protected. Douglas starts the fight with the fat knight,
and in short order Falstaff "fals down as if he were dead"
(V. iv. 76–77). When the stage is clear of all except Falstaff and the dead Percy, Sir John explains, "Zbloud twas
time to counterfet, or that hot termagant Scot had paide
me scot and lot too." Then Falstaff looks at the dead Hotspur: "Zounds I am afraid of this gunpowder Percy,
though he be dead, how if he should counterfet too and
rise?" It is fine comedy, but with the character of Falstaff
called Oldcastle the idea of comic resurrection is also grotesque. The chronicle story of Sir John Oldcastle's final
statement of his planned resurrection hangs over the action of the great hulk of comic mirth rising slowly to life
again upon the stage. Thomas Walsingham, the St. Albans chronicler, described the incident in his account of
Oldcastle's death.

Ubi presens affuit rector regni cum
multa milicia et personis honorabili-
bus. Inter quos domino Thome de
Erpingham novissima verba locutus
est ut dicitur, adiurans eum ut, si
cerneret eum resurgere die tercia,
pacem procuraret secte sue. Tanta
fuit ardalionis demencia ut putaret
se post triduum a mortuis resurrec-
turum.[66]

[At this point in
the margin John
Bale wrote in his
copy, "Nota de
insania Cobam."]

John Stow printed this part of the legend in his account
of Oldcastle's history in the 1592 edition of *The Annales
of England.*[67] Shakespeare makes use of the chronicle
material with thematic irony; the spirit of rebellion will
rise again in England in the figure of a Lord Cobham just
as it will rise again in the figure of a Percy. Shakespeare
is creating universal figures here. The chronicle materials
had provided him with evidence that history reveals the
unchanging patterns of behavior in human nature; familial patterns of conduct reappeared in succeeding genera-

tions in much the same way that noble titles are handed down to heirs. The high spirit of a fifteenth-century Hotspur seemed to burn in the veins of an impetuous Elizabethan Percy; the choleric character of a fifteenth-century Lollard appeared to have survived in an irritable and unstable Lord Cobham. Reason or passion, fidelity or treason, the stamp of the past can be seen, says the playwright, in the unfolding events of the Elizabethan reign. Shakespeare found that the chronicle stories could be lifted from their parchment pages, gently reshaped with newly created details, and made into mirror art. But that art is sophisticated; it is not a static art depicting an unchanging history repeating itself for the moral edification of mankind. It is art which extracts a universal element from the flow of history by utilizing artistic traditions (the Vice, the Braggart Soldier, etc.), chronicle legends (the Oldcastle story), and a new Platonic psychology ("universal" human nature). These basic materials are amalgamated into indelible and individualistic dramatic character. The universal decked out in unique raiment—that is Shakespeare's art.

An ancient and revered mode of interpretation of the past is also being used by the playwright, but used in a satiric way. Centuries before Shakespeare's age the medieval churchmen had established the typological method of scriptural interpretation when they read the episodes of the Old Testament as symbolic or figurative history that functioned proleptically as a type or pattern for an event which would happen later in history. Thus the sacrificial episode of the young Isaac upon the altar with Abraham standing above him, knife poised, was recognized as a crucifixion scene depicting Christ's sacrificial death. Scriptural typology became an integral part of medieval culture, as most scholars know. The stained glass windows and elaborate wall paintings at Canterbury, Peterborough, and Worcester cathedrals depicted famous typological cycles.[68] The mode was used in medieval drama when the stories of the scriptures became subjects for the art of the pageant wagons; Judeo-Christian history was transformed into figurative dramatic designs.[69] When Shakespeare turned to the chronicle histories, he could perceive, I think, that some of the secular events of the early fifteenth century were "types" or figurative designs that could be considered proleptic events in the way that sacred history had been patterned in the older exegeses. Especially were the Percy episodes and the Oldcastle story illuminative. But these chronicle materials not only were secular, they dealt with insurrection and treason, revolt and anarchy in the political realm. Hotspur and Oldcastle bore no resemblance to an Abraham or Isaac, or Christ as a Second Adam, or Elijah as a Resurrection figure (although John Foxe, the martyrologist, had indeed seen in Oldcastle's fiery death a likeness to the death of Elijah in the chariot of flames). Shakespeare could turn to his new theories of history and psychology for ideas of dramatic characterization, but his vehicle for this new characterization was a secular and satiric use of ancient typology. The old chronicles contained types or figurative designs that could be utilized in a new satiric way. There is an inversion in the mode from sacred to secular; prefiguration descends to the diabolic.

Lily Bess Campbell pointed out some years ago that Shakespeare was apparently aware of the similarities in pattern between the rebellion of Hotspur against Henry IV and the Northern Rebellion of 1569. She concluded in her scholarly study of the history plays that "the rebellion which Shakespeare drew was motivated and carried out with greater resemblance to the rebellion of 1569 than to the three rebellions under Henry IV, which it telescopes."[70] Her perception of the montage device was keen; however, she was concerned primarily with the general sweep of history in Shakespeare's plays, and she did not pursue her ideas into the details of Shakespeare's telescoped history. A pursuit of details is necessary to understand the full satiric meaning of Shakespeare's artistic exploitation of historical patterns.

The final episode with the dead Hotspur and its relevance to Elizabethan matters can be introduced best with the character of Shakespeare's Lady Percy, Hotspur's wife. Shakespeare calls her Kate. A reference to the older chronicle stories reveals that Hotspur's wife was Elizabeth Mortimer.[71] Scholars have therefore amused themselves with speculating on the playwright's special fondness for the feminine name Catherine or Kate. Shake-

spear's choice of the name in the *Henry IV* plays is meaningful, I think, because the contemporary Elizabethan
Lady Percy was *Catherine*, eldest daughter and heir of
John Neville, the cantankerous and wealthy Lord Latimer.
She had married her cousin, Henry Percy, in January 1562,
when he was thirty years of age and before he inherited
the earldom following the execution of his brother, Francis,
seventh earl of Northumberland in August 1572. This Lady
Percy became the mother of eight sons and two daughters,
and at least two of those sons saw and admired Shakespeare's art. Both Sir Charles and Sir Josceline Percy were
among those followers of the earl of Essex who arranged
for the Lord Chamberlain's Men to perform *Richard II* on
the eve of the Essex rebellion.[72] Augustine Phillipps, one of
Shakespeare's fellow actors, mentioned the two Percy
brothers in his deposition taken on 18 February 1601. "On
Thursday or Friday sevennight, Sir Chas. Percy, Sir Josceline Percy, Lord Monteagle, and several others spoke to
some of the players to play the deposing and killing of King
Richard II, and promised to give them 40s. more than their
ordinary, to do so."[73] It is safe to say, I think, that history
plays were considered provocative art by at least some of
the contemporary viewers. We know from Sir William
Lambarde's letter that the queen herself saw a covert
meaning in one of the plays. "I am Richard II, know ye
not that" she quizzed Lambarde who had been made her
keeper of the Rolls. And after his courteous response she
added, "this tragedy was played 40^{tie} times in open streets
and houses."[74] I also think it is safe to assume that the
younger Percy brothers took an interest in more than
Richard II. When Shakespeare altered Lady Percy's name
to Kate and added Elizabethan lineaments to his Henry
Percy, the younger Percy sons in all probability sharpened
their wits to have a careful look at the *Henry IV* plays.
We too should sharpen our wits and examine the character
of Hotspur.

Shakespeare's Hotspur is a composite character made of
dramatic elements drawn from the historical figures of a
number of Henry Percies. And the composite image is
meaningful. From the chronicle stories of Hotspur's
impetuosity and valor Shakespeare drew the major outlines
of his dramatic rebel, but the playwright alters drastically

one pronounced aspect of the historical Hotspur's character. The chronicle accounts of the battle of Shrewsbury told of the strong superstition of the famous Percy. The medieval writers related that when Hotspur entered the battle, he found he had left his favorite sword, the one he had used so victoriously at Homildon, at the campsite of the previous night in the tiny village of Berwick near Shrewsbury. A soothsayer had told Hotspur that he should die at Berwick, but the famous soldier had assumed Berwick to be the northern border city. "Now I see that my ploughshare is drawing its last furrow," he despaired. There were other bad omens to cast gloom over the forces of the rebels. A comet was seen in the sky over the head of the brave Percy ("super caput Henrici Percy apparuit stella comata, malum significans eventum"). It was all too much; Hotspur is reported to have said a sad farewell to his troops before the conflict: "It is better to fall on the battle-field in the cause of the republic than to die after the battle by the sentences of our enemies."[75]

Shakespeare ignores this colorful element in the historical Hotspur and creates instead a Percy who draws his sword at the battle of Shrewsbury and announces, "Here draw I a sword, / Whose temper I intend to staine / With the best bloud that I can meet withall, / In the aduenture of this perillous day, / Now esperance Percy and set on . . ." (V. ii. 93-97). Moreover, Shakespeare's Hotspur is contemptuous of superstition, especially the superstition of the Welsh Glendower. Act III begins with the humorous scene in which the friction among the rebels is heightened by the irritability and lack of finesse in Hotspur. The reader will recall Percy's laconic reply to Glendower's description of how "the front of heauen was full of fiery shapes / Of burning cressets, and at my birth / The frame and huge foundation of the earth / Shaked like a coward." With a prick of wit Hotspur assaults the inflated Welsh ego: "Why so it woulde haue done at the same season if your mothers cat had but kittend." And Percy then expands with a scientific explanation of why the earth at times trembles.

Diseased nature oftentimes breakes forth,
In strange eruptions, oft the teeming earth

Is with a kind of collicke pincht and vext,
By the imprisoning of vnruly wind
Within her wombe, which for enlargement striuing
Shakes the old Beldame earth, and topples down
Steeples and mossegrown towers. At your birth
Our Grandam earth, hauing this distemprature
In passion shooke.
[III.i.26-34a]

Shakespeare's Hotspur has a rationalistic mind and an interest in scientific theory. This alteration of historical character is relevant to what we know of the late sixteenth-century Percies. One of the foremost advocates of the new scientific learning was Henry Percy, ninth earl of Northumberland. In the 1590s his interests in experimental science involved him in the "School of Night" clique to which Sir Walter Raleigh and Thomas Hariot, the mathematician, belonged. Northumberland later built a scientific laboratory on the grounds of Syon House for Hariot, who had constructed a telescope and was using it to examine sun spots years before Galileo built his "tube."[76] This earl of Northumberland was the Henry Percy who in 1594 married Dorothy Devereux, Essex's high-tempered sister. But he was becoming disenchanted with the politics and people of the Essex faction by late 1596. He tells us in his *Advice To His Son*, written many years later, that after his marriage he "grew out of Hope within one or two Years; for Essex and I were at Warres within that Tyme, and Hindrance grew rather than love."[77] When Shakespeare was writing the *Henry IV* plays, Henry Percy, ninth earl of Northumberland, was making a political transition from the Essex party to the opposing faction led by Sir Robert Cecil, Sir Walter Raleigh, Lord Cobham, and his eldest son, Henry Brooke.

In the final act of *1 Henry IV* the dead Hotspur is addressed by Falstaff as "this gunpowder Percy." Then with the body over his shoulder Falstaff confronts the prince with, "there is Percy, if your father will doe me anie honour, so: if not, let him kill the next Percie himselfe."[78] The reference to gunpowder is an anarchronism, of course, but it is, I believe, an intentional anachronism. When Shakespeare was writing this play, the death of the *eighth* earl of Northumberland, also named Henry Percy, the

father of the ninth earl and of Sir Charles and Sir Josceline
Percy, and husband of Kate Percy, was a very recent and
disturbing historical event. Henry Percy, the eighth earl,
was found dead in the Tower of London, his body covered
with gunpowder burns. There was mystery surrounding
his death, mystery and controversy. This Henry Percy had
escaped the calamity of the Northern Rebellion and had
received the earldom in 1572 when his brother Thomas,
the seventh earl of Northumberland, was executed for his
role in the northern insurrection. Henry, the eighth earl,
was involved in the Ridolfi affair; he was arrested for intrigue in November 1571 and was enlarged from the
Tower in May 1573. A decade later he once more became
involved in questionable activities and was returned to
the Tower after the Throckmorton plot was broken by the
authorities at the end of 1583. For eighteen months Percy
remained in the Tower while Lord Burghley and Attorney
General Popham compiled the case against him. About
midnight, 20/21 June 1585, Henry Percy, the eighth earl
of Northumberland, either committed suicide or was murdered in his apartment in the Tower. At least four versions of his death circulated throughout Europe. The official English report, written by Lord Burghley, stated that
the earl "knowing thereby howe haynous his offences were,
fearing the justice and severity of the Lawes, and so the
ruyne and overthrowe of his house, fel into desperation,
and so to the destruction of himselfe."[79] Lord Burghley's
enemies at home said the earl was innocent of any treasonable acts, but, seeing himself helplessly condemned by
political foes, he killed himself to save his estate for his
sons. Gossip also circulated freely at home; Sir Christopher Hatton was named as the man who murdered Percy
in his bed. The Catholic faction both at home and on the
Continent accused Queen Elizabeth of having plotted and
carried out Northumberland's "foul murder."[80] Richard
Verstegan's volume, *Theatrum Crudelitatum Haereticorum
Nostri Temporia*, published on the Continent in 1587,
contained a dramatic woodcut depicting three assailants
firing pistols at the helpless earl.[81] Moreover, the French
and Spanish ambassadors in London wrote to their governments that Northumberland had been assassinated at
the order of the queen; and at Cologne a pamphlet entitled

The Murder of the eighth Earl of Northumberland.

Crudelitatis Calvinianae Exempla duo Recentissima ex Anglia accused the leaders of the English government of Percy's murder. This pamphlet was translated into French, German, Spanish, Italian, and English; it was this propaganda that Lord Burghley sought to squelch when he wrote *A True and Summarie Reporte of the Declaration of Some of the Earle of Northumberlands Treasons*.[82] We do not know today what happened in the Tower apartment at midnight on 20 June 1585, nor do I insist that Shakespeare knew what happened. Lord Hunsdon examined the earl's body with its three gaping wounds (wounds which made the suicide theory impossible, it was rumored). But there is no factual basis to suggest that the playwright knew more than most other Englishmen about the death of Henry Percy, eighth earl of Northumberland.

In the final act of *1 Henry IV* Shakespeare apparently was exploiting the mystery surrounding the late earl's death. And this exploitation was indulged in, I believe, to influence the actions of the young Henry Percy, eldest son of the eighth earl who had succeeded his father in the peerages of Percy and Northumberland. In other words the playwright, using archetypal literary images and altered chronicle materials, created a suggestive scene which members of the Percy family (and hopefully the young ninth earl of Northumberland) would find not only exciting but applicable to the contemporary situation. Henry Percy, the ninth earl of Northumberland, was moving out of the political sphere of the earl of Essex and into the influential group surrounding Sir Robert Cecil and the Cobhams. Cecil had married Elizabeth Brooke, daughter of the elder Lord Cobham, in 1589. The friendship between Lord Burghley and Lord Cobham had matured and ripened, and the families of the two men were now closely linked. When Falstaff remarks, "Zounds I am afraid of this gunpowder Percy, though he be dead, how if he should counterfet too and rise? by my faith I am afraid hee woulde proue the better counterfet, therefore ile make him sure, yea, and ile sweare I kild him," Shakespear is writing effective comedy, and modern audiences enjoy the buffoonery. But the playwright, in allowing his comic clown to demand false credit for the death of Henry Percy, is also creating mockery and satire. It is comic mockery that easily could have aroused suspicion in a turbulent Percy mind, and it easily could have opened old wounds. With Falstaff called Oldcastle (a name closely associated with Lord Cobham) the scene becomes grotesque with innuendo. The state papers reveal that the ninth earl of Northumberland had sound grounds for grievance against the Cobham family. Tensions had developed between the young Lord Percy and Sir Henry Brooke, Lord Cobham's brother who was Queen Elizabeth's ambassador in Paris for a number of years. The trouble erupted in the tense spring of 1582.

It was a year and a half before the Throckmorton plot would collapse and destroy the eighth earl of Northumberland. The earl was still restricted to the area around Petworth and the city of London, cut off by royal order from his strongholds in the north of England. His restless nature invited trouble, and it came in the secret visits of Lord Paget and his firebrand brother Charles. Later, Attorney General Popham would insist in writing that these secret visits of the Pagets to Petworth were proof of Northumberland's treason.[83] Charles Paget was of course involved up to his chin in the machinations of Mary. His abode in exile was Paris, and in that capitol city he took some pains to seek out the young Lord Percy, who was studying there in the spring of 1582. The information that young Henry Percy was meeting with dangerous renegades was sent from Paris to Secretary Walsingham by Sir Henry Brooke, the English ambassador in residence there.[84] The whole Percy family was living under the shadow of suspicion, and the high-tempered young lord was incensed when he learned of the ambassador's spying upon him. Lord Percy wrote to Walsingham in anger:

Righte Honnorable: I doe understande that Sir Henry Cobham, Ambassador here for her maieste, hathe not long agoe informed your Honnor, both against me and Mr. Pagett, for conversing some tymes one with the other, and that Mr. Pagett should not onelie seek to dissuade me from the Religion I have been nourished and bredd upp in, but also deale with me in undewtifull Practises. When I hard of this Manner of my Lo: Ambassador's proceedinge, it greved me very muche, in respect of his place, what force his Advertisement might carie against me, to bringe me in Disgrace with her Maieste, and Displeasure with my Lo: my Father. . . .[85]

By the same carrier young Lord Percy sent another letter to England, this one to his father. In it he explained the injustice of the "bare Reporte of my Lo: Ambassador, grounded without Reason or Trewth." He described how he had gone to the ambassador's house to confront him:

> So soone as I harde what Course my Lo: Ambassador had taken against me (whiche is thre weekes agoe) I presentlie went vnto him, being desirous to satisfie him in Trewth, and offred to conforme my selfe to anie Course that he should wishe me vnto. But my goode Meaninge was refused by him withe verie appassionate Speeches, whiche were neither agreable to the Place (in my humble opinion) he beareth, nor the Freindshippe he semed to professe vnto me. I did finde by the Conference I had with his Lo: his Inclination more redie to take holde of false Accusations against me then of the trew Allegations I broughte in my defence.

Lord Percy continued by explaining to his father that Sir Henry Cobham was now afraid that he might be discredited by the staunch disavowal of any wrongdoing which Percy was making: "he will thinke it muche to his Discreditt yf it should be knowen he hath aduertised Vntrewthes against me."[86]

This unpleasant episode was only a preamble to the troubles awaiting the Percies. The Throckmorton plot was revealed late the following year, and the elder Henry Percy was once again confined in the Tower.[87] His mysterious death in 1585 seems to have left a notable mark upon his eldest son's mind.[88] In 1587 the young Henry Percy wrote to Sir George Carew (later earl of Totness) of his "present discontent."[89] We do not know which version of his father's death the young earl came to accept as the true one, but many years later in the remarks he set down as *Advice To His Son* he wrote, "If ever father loved a son, he did me (and whether his death was such as vulgarly it was bruited, is not for this place), only this I must say and conclude, that his care was to leave me well to maintain the honour of his house behind him."[90] The version of the eighth earl's death which was "vulgarly bruited" was that which insisted he was murdered at the instigation of Lord Burghley. But in 1596 and 1597 the young earl of Northumberland was swinging into the circle of power around Lord Burghley, his son, Sir Robert Cecil, and the Cobhams. Lord Burghley at this time was coaxing the ninth earl of Northumberland with special favors. In July 1596 the earl was asked to take the Garter to Henry IV of France. He refused. In June 1597 the earl was offered the post of warden of the Middle Marches and the lieutenancy of three shires. Again he refused.[91] But by the end of the decade he had succumbed to the pressures and had settled in as a member of the Cecil-Cobham faction. In Shakespeare's *1 Henry IV* the actions of the Falstaff-Oldcastle character, the stabbing of the dead Hotspur, and the insistence upon credit for the defeat of "Gunpowder Percy," are relevant, I believe, to recent Elizabethan history. The playwright appears to have been motivated while writing the *Henry IV* plays by the cross-currents of contemporary political rivalry. He was using in these plays a dramatic device to catch the conscience of a Percy. We do not know that the living Henry Percy, earl of Northumberland, saw the poetic creation of his ancestor which Shakespeare presented upon the stage. Northumberland had a sensitive, eclectic mind. If he viewed the popular historical drama that the Lord Chamberlain's Men (Lord Hunsdon's Men for a few months) produced in the late 1590s, he saw the playwright's conflation of history and a boldly drawn composite figure of a Percy who had both fifteenth- and sixteenth-century lineaments. But Shakespeare's use of the dramatic montage to create a Percy figure is not limited to the fifth act of *1 Henry IV*. There were other historical materials for the playwright to draw upon, and he did.

In these two plays several elements are drawn from the array of historical Percy figures and their chronicle actions; these elements contribute to the complexity of the dramatic characters and events in the dramas. The creative conflation in these plays occurs in an artistically controlled sequence, a sequence which offers the critic an insight, I think, into the poet's sense of structure and also into his experimentations with the idea of time. The first manifestation of the playwright's manipulation of historical Percy characters in the *Henry IV* plays is that described above: the substitution of a caustically rational Hotspur for the superstitious chronicle figure (Part One, act III). This new dramatic element was drawn from the character of the then living Sir Henry Percy, *ninth* earl of Northumberland. The second artistic manipulation of the Percy chronicle material is the addition of the death of the "Gunpowder Percy" (Part One, act V), a dramatic episode which contains, I think, allusions to the death of Henry Percy, the *eighth* earl of Northumberland, in 1585. The third intentional use of Percy "history in the subjunctive mode" is to be found in the playwright's introduction of materials related to the *seventh* earl of Northumberland. This material is used overtly in the character of Morton, an invented figure, at the beginning of Part Two.[92] Shakespeare opens this second play with Henry Percy, first earl of Northumberland, at Warkworth Castle, the "worm-eaten hold of ragged stone" where he has lain "crafty-sick." In the first scene Northumberland receives false news of victory at Shrewsbury from both Lord Bardolph and Travers, a servant. At line 72 the character named Morton enters bringing the ugly news of defeat and death: "I ran from Shrewsbury (my Noble Lord)," he says, "Where hatefull death put on his vgliest Maske / To fright our party" (I. i. 79–81). With some difficulty, caused by Northumberland's passionate interjections, Morton describes the death of the "neuer-daunted" Hotspur. Morton's next lines contain a stoic restatement of the possibilities of defeat that the rebels had discussed earlier and had seriously weighed (I. i. 179–95). To this point the invented role of Morton has been used for dramatic expediency; the character has presented the news from Shrewsbury and has drawn from Northumberland the impassioned responses needed to define for the audience his volatile Percy character. But with the next speech the role of Morton takes on a much more pointed function. He brings news not only from Shrewsbury but from the rebel archbishop as well.

I heare for certaine, and do speake the truth;
The gentle Arch-bishop of Yorke is vp
With well appointed Powres: he is a man
Who with a double Surety bindes his Followers.
My Lord (your Sonne) had onely but the Corpes,
But shadowes, and the shewes of men to fight.
For that same word (Rebellion) did diuide
The action of their bodies, from their soules,
And they did fight with queasinesse, constrain'd
As men drinke Potions; that their Weapons only
Seem'd on our side: but for their Spirits and Soules,

This word (Rebellion) it had froze them vp,
As Fish are in a Pond. But now the Bishop
Turnes Insurrection to Religion,
Suppos'd sincere, and holy in his Thoughts:
He's follow'd both with Body, and with Minde:

[I.i.204-19]

This is one of the passages cut from the text in the quarto
edition (1600) of the play.[93] These lines provide an introduction to the character of the "gentle" but militant
churchman who is the true leader of the Percy rebellion
of *2 Henry IV.* The abridged version of the quarto depicts
the archbishop as a subordinate figure, but in the longer
text of the folio edition (1623) the role is a dominant one.
In this later text of the play the medieval archbishop
espouses the "ultra-modern doctrine that the citizen has
the right to rebel against the authority of the State."[94]
Westmoreland accuses him: "[You do] seale this lawlesse
bloody Booke / Of forg'd Rebellion, with a Seale divine /
And consecrate commotions bitter edge" (IV. i. 100-102).[95]
If we look to the sources we find that Holinshed had described the archbishop of York's appearance among the
rebels: "comming foorth amongst them clad in armor, [he]
incouraged, exhorted, and (by all meanes he could) pricked
them foorth to take the enterprise in hand."[96] Shakespeare
uses the chronicle suggestion, but he telescopes this
rebellious action with the events of 1403, and at the same
time makes his dramatic history relevant to the unruly Percies of the Elizabethan reign. This he accomplished with
the invented character of Morton.

In the 1569 Rising of the North an important role was
played by Nicholas Morton, described by contemporaries
as "the most earnest mover of the rebellion." Camden said
the northern earls were "boldly and powerfully incited
hereunto by Nicholas Morton, a Priest, sent from the Pope,
to denounce Queene Elizabeth for an Heretike and therefore deprived of all power and governement."[97] And Lord
Burghley wrote in his *Execution of Justice in England* that
the Northern Rebellion was precipitated by Morton: "one
D[r]. *Mooreton,* an olde English fugitive and conspirator,
was sent from *Rome* into the North partes of England, to
stirre up the first rebellion there."[98] This "Dr. Mooreton"
was a native of Yorkshire, a graduate of Cambridge, and,

during the reign of Mary Tudor, one of the six clergymen appointed by Cardinal Pole to serve in the cathedral church of Canterbury. After Queen Elizabeth's coronation he went into exile in Rome where he received his doctoral degree, and it was he whom Pope Pius V dispatched to England in the spring of 1569 with the title of apostolical penitentiary. He was to give instructions to the isolated English priests of the old faith, but part of his mission was to carry financial aid to the northern earls and to inform them that the papal bull *Regnans in Excelsis* was being prepared in Rome. In it, he was instructed to tell the earls, the pope planned to excommunicate Elizabeth and deprive her of her "pretended right" to the English throne.[99] Nicholas Sanders, the leader of the exiled English Catholics at Louvain, described the mission of Morton in his *De Visibili Monarchia Ecclesiae* soon after the rebellion failed:

Pius Quintus Pontifex Maximus ad vnicam, quaetam graui morbo adhiberi poterat, medicinam se conferens, anno Domini 1569. reuerendum Presbyterum *Nicolaum Mortonum Anglum, S. Theologia Doctorem,* vnum ex Presbyteris, qui poenitentiis indicendis Romae praeerant, in Angliam misit, vt certis Illustribus, & Catholicis viris authoritate Apostolica denunciaret, Elizabetham, quae tunc rerúpotiebatur, haereticam esse: ob eamq̃; causam omni dominio & potestate, quam in Catholicos vsurpabat, iure ipso excrdisse, impuneq̃; ab illis velut Ethnicam & publicanam haberi posse: nec eos illius legibus aut mandatis deinceps obedire cogi.[100]

During the Northern Rebellion of 1569 the earls of course stressed the issues of religion. Their first proclamation of 15 November stated that they intended no harm should come to the queen, but they wanted to reform the new modes of worship: "For as muche as the order of things in the churche and matters of religyon, are presentlye sett furthe and used contrarye to the auncyent and Catholicke faythe: therefore there purposes and meanynges are, to redewce all the said cawses in relygyon to the ancyent customes and usages before used, wherein they desyre all good people to take their partes."[101] The unhappy northern earls were very willing to "consecrate commotions bitter edge," and to "turn insurrection to religion." They were encouraged in this by Nicholas Morton and his message that the bishop of Rome backed their enterprise. Indeed, Morton carried twelve thousand crowns with him from Rome to help finance the uprising.[102] Northumberland, in his answers to the interrogation that Lord Hunsdon conducted after the earl was turned over to the English authorities at Berwick, attempted to hide his relationship with the papal messenger: "As for Dr. Morton, he was once at my house, and I spake with him about an howre; and he opeind unto me no suche matter of any bull, or promise of aide from the Pope; but lamented he sawe so greate wante of sound and catholick priests, that he might give authoritie to them for reconciling suche of the people as would seeke. More than this delt I not with him."[103] We know, however, that such was not the case. In a letter written afterwards by one of the participants in the rebellion, the influence of Morton is described: "Dr. Morton was the most earnest mover of the rebellion, who used strong persuasions to the Earl and this writer's father showing many reasons for this purpose . . . his first persuasion was to give them to understand of the excommunication, which threatened danger as well to their souls as to the loss of their country."[104] The authorities in England were aware of the role Nicholas Morton was playing in the insurrection. When he fled to Scotland with the retreating earls, he resided some weeks in Fast Castle where he conducted mass as "the Pope's patriarch." He succeeded in escaping the trap that Thomas Randolph set for him and other fugitives off the Fern Islands. Later with Egremont Ratcliffe he made his way safely to the Low Countries.[105]

It is against this historical material that Shakespeare's intrusive character of Morton should be placed. The poet, working carefully at the task of conflation, has created a messenger in the play who describes the slack followers of Northumberland as being "but shadows and the shows of men." The idea of rebellion has divided "the action of their bodies from their souls," and they cannot fight against the monarch because the word *rebellion* has "froze them up." Shakespeare has provided in this passage a literal description not only of Northumberland's followers in the early fifteenth century but of the northern earls and their retinue in 1569 when indecisiveness characterized their actions

for weeks before they received reassurance from Morton
that the pope had declared rebellion in religious causes to
be lawful and not a sin. They were told that their duty lay in
obedience to Rome, not to "that abandoned woman," the
queen.[106]

Shakespeare creates the messenger Morton as a mouth-
piece through which the militant archbishop is presented
as the setter-on of rebellion. The archbishop is of course an
English figure, not a pope, but the playwright, writing for
an audience still sensitive to the tragedy of the Northern
Rebellion of their own day, succeeds in bringing the
historical events together in his art. He superimposes the
image of the 1569 insurrection upon the very similar events
of the early fifteenth century, and in doing so he isolates
a universal element in history.

The same technique can be observed in the playwright's
manipulation of historical characters in the Gaultree Forest
episode of 2 Henry IV. The "dastardly treachery" of Prince
John of Lancaster in the ugly and unheroic action has
distressed Shakespeare's critics from Dr. Johnson's day
to the present. Most modern readers are uncomfortable if
not bewildered at the playwright's apparent condonation
of the slick violation of faith which Prince John is guilty of
when he reaches for victory without honor. The Elizabethans of the 1590s were becoming accustomed to the
use of stratgems in diplomatic affairs, and many perhaps
would have acknowledged the necessity of a breach of
military faith under dire political circumstances, as
modern critics have suggested.[107] But Shakespeare's
peculiar presentation of distorted chronicle materials
should warn us that at this point we ought to look more
closely at the Percy rebellions of the past to detect the
complex implications being made in the Gaultree Forest
scene.

The perfidious action of Prince John is strikingly similar
to the questionable conduct of the royal leaders in two
episodes in Tudor history, the so-called Pilgrimage of Grace
in 1536–37 and the unheroic ransoming of the seventh
earl of Northumberland in 1572. A sense of compromised
integrity on the royal side hovers over both incidents of
sixteenth-century history. The Pilgrimage of Grace was a
complex series of rebellions originating in the religious and

economic discontentment of the northern gentry and nobility. Its leaders were the Percies, Nevilles, and Dacres.
Many of the subtle problems of the uprisings (there were
four major branches of the insurrection) are still debated
by modern historians, but the climax and terminal debacle
are relatively clear.[108] Henry VIII sent the duke of Norfolk
northward with the royal troops in the fall of 1536 to put
down and punish the northern insurgents. Norfolk's army
was sadly outnumbered and outmatched by the militant
followers of the northern noblemen. When the leaders of
the two forces met at Doncaster, Norfolk was compelled
to stall for time. In one of his letters to the king his intended
duplicity is made clear: "I beg you take in good part whatever (at the advice of others) I may promise the rebels;
for surely I shall observe no part thereof, for any respect
of that others might call mine honor dystayned . . . for
I think no promise made to serve you can 'dystayne',
me."[109] Henry's answer came two days later: he was aware
of the need for expediency; Norfolk could promise the
rebels anything, but the obloquy must fall upon Norfolk's
head, not upon the royal crown. "We doubt not you will
have such a temperance as our honor shall remain untouched by any certain grant of what you cannot certainly
promise."[110] On 6 December Norfolk met with the "Pilgrims" at Doncaster again and granted them the king's
pardon; by 8 December the insurgents had been persuaded
by their leaders to disband and retire to their homes. Early
in the new year there were commotions among the common
people in the northern parts. These disturbances were
minor in character, our historians assert, but the disruptions were an excuse for the king to send the sword of
revenge sweeping through the northern parts of the kingdom. All pardons were rescinded, and summary executions were conducted in most parts of the north country
and in the Tower of London.[111] Sir Thomas Percy and his
brother Sir Ingram Percy played important roles in the
uprising. George Lumley, son of Lord Lumley, wrote in his
deposition that Sir Thomas Percy was the "lock, key, and
ward of this matter."[112] By early summer the executions had
been carried out according to order. In addition to Sir
Thomas Percy, Lord John Hussey, Lord Thomas Darcey,
George Lumley, Sir Robert Constable, and some two

hundred other northerners had been executed as traitors to the crown.

From the point of view of the northern Englishmen, this major smudge upon the Tudor honor was deepened in the Elizabethan reign when the seventh earl of Northumberland was bought from his Scottish hosts in 1572 for a handful of silver. The principal agent on the English side of this "pacta pecunia" was Lord Hunsdon, who became the patron of the Burbage-Shakespeare company in the 1590s. The diplomatic episode is well documented by Hunsdon's letters to Lord Burghley and the queen in London and to his contacts in Scotland. Hunsdon was warden of the East Marches toward Scotland and governor of Berwick. After the rebels of the 1569 insurrection fled into Scotland Lord Hunsdon was instructed to speed all attempts to intercept their flight, harass their supporters when possible, and hinder their escape to the Continent. Hunsdon had contacts planted in many of the noble households in Scotland. By the spring of 1572 he knew that the countess of Northumberland had made her way safely to the Low Countries and that she was offering a reward of ten thousand crowns for the escape of her husband, who by that time was a "guest" of William Douglas at Lochleven. Queen Elizabeth instructed Hunsdon immediately to offer the earl of Mar two thousand pounds for the safe delivery of the earl of Northumberland to Berwick.

In the complex political relationship that existed between Scotland and England at that time, with Mary Queen of Scots a prisoner of the English, the regent of Scotland at length acquiesced to Queen Elizabeth's demands, but Mar made two stipulations in his agreement: he wanted the English to base the legality of their demand for the return of the earl upon previous treaty agreements (which actually were nonexistent) in order to provide "some colour to deliver him by." And second, Mar asked that Northumberland's life be spared. The transaction was carried out at the end of May; Hunsdon handed over two thousand pounds sterling for possession of the rebel earl.

The Scots in general were angered and humiliated by this base breach of the ancient tradition of sanctuary on the border. One of Burghley's men wrote from Scotland that " many are discontented with the delivery of the Earl of Northumberland—yea, the best." And in the north of England the earl began to be considered in the light of Christian martyrdom; he became a Christ figure, sold for a handful of coins. One ballad of the time suggests the general contempt of the northern people for the deed. Part of the ballad refers to the Scots:

> I lothe to tell howe nowe of late
>   That cruell Scotland hath procurde
> The slander of their realme and state
>   By promise broken most assurde:
> Which shamefull act from mynde of man
> Shall not departe, do what they can.

> The noblest Lord of Percie kinde,
>   Of honour and possessions faire,
> As God to him the place assigned
>   To Scottishe grounde made his repaire:
> Who, after promise manifolde,
> Was last betrayed for English golde.[113]

Almost everyone was upset. Count Stefano Angarani wrote to the Venetians, lamenting that "contrary to every human law" the earl of Northumberland had been ransomed and beheaded.[114]

Hunsdon appears to have been ill at ease in his task as keeper of the popular nobleman, a task that was difficult there in the bastion of Northumberland's own broad territories. In letter after letter Hunsdon requested permission to send the earl south to London. "I would fain be rid of my guest," he wrote Burghley in June; and in July he wrote again that he looked hourly to be discharged of his guest, of whom he was "right weary." In London the queen and the Privy Council were still debating Northumberland's fate, and early in July Hunsdon received with relief the news that the earl's life was to be spared. He wrote immediately to Burghley: "I am not sorry for the alteration of Her Majesty's resolution touching the Earl, considering what loss she will have by his death, *and the circumstances how he was procured to the same.*" But ten days later Hunsdon received the news that the queen had reversed her decision and now commanded him to take Northumberland to York and supervise his execution for high treason. Hunsdon was appalled at the duplicity in which he found himself enmeshed. Although he was a man trained in warfare and disciplined in the ways of the court, he nevertheless rebelled at the ugly assignment: "I can neither think that Her Majesty deals with me therein, nor have I any such friends about Her Majesty as I account of; and surely I will rather suffer some imprisonment than do it," he wrote indignantly to Burghley. The heavy task was carried out by Sir John Forster, and Northumberland was beheaded in York on 22 August.[115]

It is against this historical backdrop of duplicity that Shakespeare creates the Gaultree Forest episode in *2 Henry IV*. Three different generations of Percies had rebelled against their monarchs; those rebellions were terminated by the offer of royal pardon or some gesture of royal faith that was immediately violated or broken. The pattern is a curious one, and Shakespeare capitalizes upon it. He changes the leading role on the royal side. In the chronicle sources it was the earl of Westmoreland who offered the rebels the king's pardon. In *2 Henry IV* it is Prince John of Lancaster who faces the rebels and swears "by the honour of my blood" to speed the redress of their griefs. Why the substitution? I believe that the playwright wanted to place the responsibility for the "shrewd policie" directly upon the royal party rather than upon Westmoreland, who was only a spokesman for the king. Moreover, the name of Westmoreland was too recently associated with northern rebellion: the Elizabethan earl of Westmoreland was co-leader of the 1569 insurrection, and the playwright could not allow the Westmoreland of his drama the role of chief instigator of the policy on the royal side because it would have blurred the pattern he was attempting to create, the universal pattern drawn from the repetitions of historical actions.

The content of the dialogue over the articles of complaint, the paranoiac sense of abuse which the rebels reveal, the "time misordered" which doth "Crowd us and crush us to this monstrous form / To hold our safety up," all appear so broadly composed that they represent the complaints of the Pilgrims of Grace and of the rebels of 1569 as well as those of the insurgents of 1405-07. This generalization again appears to be the result of the playwright's application of the technique of conflation.

In both the Pilgrimage of Grace and the final events of the 1569-72 uprising the royal policy of duplicity determined the final outcome of the episodes. In his treatment of the similar action in 2 *Henry IV* Shakespeare appears to approve with a calm acceptance this Machiavellian political policy. It is a disturbing thought for idealistic critics. So I will add a possible explanation for the bald presentation of the Gaultree Forest scene. I believe that the playwright's determined loyalty to his patron surfaces in the presentation of the scene. Such an implication lies in the startling analogy between the actions of Prince John and those of Lord Hunsdon. When we remember that the sixteenth-century gossip pronounced Henry Carey, Lord Hunsdon, to be the half-brother of Queen Elizabeth (the *Complete Peerage* repeats the story today), then the actions of the earlier royal prince in capturing the northern rebels becomes a prelude to the recent defeat of the earl of Northumberland and the questionable role that Hunsdon played in buying that earl home.

There is only one more episode in the *Henry IV* plays that offers some evidence of the playwright's exploitation of recurring patterns of historical actions. That episode follows the Gaultree Forest incident and presents the comic Falstaff with his prisoner, Sir John Colevile of the Dale. Shakespeare, as usual, takes his initial clue from Holinshed. The chronicle account of the executions which followed the defeat of the rebels at Gaultree Forest lists among the victims one, "sir Iohn Colleuill of the Dale." Shakespeare turns this reference into comedy, but in doing so he once more welds a bit of relevant Elizabethan history to his source. We learn this by tracing the actions of the Scottish informer, Sir John Colville, in his intrigues in England and on the Continent during the 1580s and 1590s.[116]

Sir John Colville was a graduate of the University of Saint Andrews, and he was for a time chantor of Glasgow. In 1578 he was appointed master of requests at the Scottish court, and it was in this position that he found means of cultivating an intimacy with the English ambassador; through this friendship he was able to establish ties with the English government. We know that Colville was furnishing Walsingham with information from Scotland as early as 1583. In February of that year Walsingham wrote to Ambassador Cobham (Lord Cobham's brother) in Paris that Colville was expected in London soon to "treat of some more inward amity between her Majesty and the king his master."[117] Colville had been in Paris during Sir Henry Cobham's tenure there as ambassador, and Colville had been placed on Cobham's list of informers and promised some remuneration. When Sir Edward Stafford replaced Cobham in the Paris post, he wrote to Walsingham to ask which financial account he should use to pay the hundred crowns for intelligence from the Colvilles (Sir John Colville and his cousin, Sir James Colville of Easter-Weemes).[118] Sir John Colville was sent to London in 1589 as an agent for King James, and Burghley noted on 9 December that he had paid "to John Coleville, to the use of the said King of Scottes, MMM li" (three thousand pounds).[119] But Colville soon associated himself with Francis Stewart, earl of Bothwell, an association that was encouraged by Elizabeth, and in 1592 Colville was accused of treason by the Scottish authorities, and his lands were forfeited. Sir Robert Bowes wrote to Burghley that Colville, now an outlaw, needed to be "comforted and relieved with her Majesty's bounty."[120] Colville seems to have been responsible for the apprehension of Bothwell's brother, Hercules Stewart, who was executed in February of 1595. This act of disloyalty to his fellow outlaws secured him the favor of King James again, and Colville was granted payment of a debt of over a thousand pounds out of James's annuity from Queen Elizabeth.[121]

In 1597 Colville was acting as an agent for King James on the Continent, but something happened of which we have no record, and in 1598 Colville was in London and out of favor with his king once more. James apparently gained information of Colville's double dealing. Ambassador Nicholson wrote from Scotland to Sir Robert Cecil stating that King James demanded to know why Colville was so courteously entertained in London, his "good entertaunment, longe staye there, his courtiouse despatch, with licence to bring away 3 horse, and lettres to my Lord Willoughby to treat him; and the favour Mr. John findes there to have been better then is, without a great sute, granted to the King's best subjectes, mervayling what it should meane."[122] Whether the new Lord Cobham was helping to entertain Colville or not we do not know; certainly the Scotsman had known and had been of service to Sir Henry Cobham, the former ambassador. Colville's name and services had become ludicrous by this time, and so he makes a vulnerable target for satire. Using a suggestion from Holinshed, Shakespeare amplifies it with a bit of pointed wit and a relevancy that brought the historical actions depicted upon the stage up into the Elizabethan times.

The remainder of Sir John Colville's story is shabby. Sir Robert Cecil ordered him out of England in 1599, accusing him of lack of secrecy and belittling his former intelligence:

> When your dealing with me was more secret, it gave you better meanes to discover dangerous practises, then now it doth; for when you came to the Erle of Essex, it was in more private formes, then since your continuall aboade hath made it. But if you remember, the wonders offered from Bruce, and what treasures of the Popes should be intercepted, with other such lyke ouvertures, me thinke you might well aunsuer yourself, that your good will is better than your meanes.[123]

Then Cecil sent word to King James that "the Queene scorneth to geve creditt or suffer any dealinges with any soe turbulent humours."[124] Colville's servile character can be deduced from his letters to Cecil, his "Mecenas," in which he calls himself a worm and contends that "beat as you will, as a dog I must fawn."[125] Colville went to the Continent after his dismissal in England. He apparently became a Roman Catholic to further his aims, and he died in poverty in Paris a few years later. John Chamberlain wrote to Dudley Carleton in 1605 that "Old John Colville, that busy-brain'd Scot, who trubled our King so much in consorte with the Earl of Bothwell, having an ambition to be made Chancellor of Scotland, and ever since lived in exile, is dead in this town, within few dayes, in great want and misery."[126] Apparently the "busy-brain'd Scott" was well known in the upper echelons of London political life. Indeed, if the second part of the *Henry IV* plays was being presented in 1598, as I think it was, Colville had returned to London and was on the scene. In Shakespeare's play Falstaff captures the easily intimidated Colville. If there is more meaning to this comic action because of the current association of the contemporary Lord Cobham and the Elizabethan Scotsman, that meaning lies beyond recovery. The humorous captive with his ironic respect for Sir John Falstaff is obviously the butt of the inwit of the play. Beyond that point we cannot proceed.

CHAPTER FIVE

Henry VI, Parts 1 and 2

IT IS IN THE *Henry VI* PLAYS THAT WE FIND SHAKE-speare first experimenting with the Falstaff-Cobham satire. The Fastolf or Falstaff character in what is called Part One of this series of plays and the negative character of Eleanor Cobham in *The Contention* (which became Part Two in the folio editions of the dramas) have an antecedent relationship with the fat roisterer of *Henry IV*. In what apparently were his initial attempts at the craft of playwriting, Shakespeare tried his hand at the sophisticated Aristophanic type of lampooning, using old chronicle materials to shadow forth Elizabethan personages and recent events in Tudor history. The evidence for this assertion can be produced from a close examination of both the historical and the literary backgrounds of the 1580s and 1590s in Elizabethan England.

In the spring of 1592 Gilbert Talbot, who had recently become the seventh earl of Shrewsbury upon the death of his father, the sixth earl, was installed as a knight of the Order of the Garter.[1] It was customary for the poets of the day to write commendatory poems in honor of the new initiates. The installations offered a chance to an ambitious poet of gaining the recognition of a famous patron—if he were lucky. Such was the case in 1593 when George Peele composed his "Honour of the Garter" and dedicated it as "a Poeme gratulatorie: Entitled to the worthie and renowned Earle of Northumberland." We know that Northumberland ordered his steward to send Peele three pounds, a sizeable reward in those days for a poem of some five hundred lines.[2] Whether or not Shakespeare knew Gilbert

Talbot, earl of Shrewsbury, in 1592 cannot now be ascertained. But *1 Henry VI* is a "Talbot play," as scholars have pointed out for generations, and some of its important actions, particularly those concerned with the Talbots, are centered on the Garter. The heroic actions of Shakespear's famous character, his fight for England's claim to foreign territory, his steadfastness in his contest with the magic of the French "trull" and her followers, his sacrifice of life for honor's sake—all provide an important element in the thematic structure of the play. Talbot's death, like the confusion of England, is the result of a breakdown of order. There is political disorder in the intestine conflict between the English nobles, and there is moral disorder in the cowardice and betraying actions of Sir John Falstaff.[3] In many ways this paralleling relationship of the two plots resembles the parallel structure of the comic and serious scenes in the *Henry IV* plays, but in his earlier attempts with this mirror device, Shakespeare had not yet mastered the comic art. Indeed, comedy would not have been fitting in the serious Talbot-Falstaff scenes, for eulogy is the mode of the play. The eulogy is for the honor of the historical Talbots, but at the same time, using his conflation technique, Shakespeare can slant the play to compliment the contemporary Talbots of the Elizabethan reign. With slight contrivances, alterations, and addenda the playwright can make the older chronicle materials mirror the slur that fell upon the honor of George Talbot, sixth earl of Shrewsbury (Queen Elizabeth's "good old man") and the activities of Lord Cobham, who was involved in that defamation of good name. I am of the opinion that the young Shakespeare seized the opportunity of the upcoming Garter election of 1592 to create a work of art that would compliment the new earl of Shrewsbury and defend the honor of his name. I believe that the playwright, utilizing the newly developed form of the history play, turned to the English chronicle accounts of the heroic actions of the first earl of Shrewsbury to eradicate the suggestions of treason that now tarnished the house of Talbots, earls of Shrewsbury.

The Talbot scenes, particularly those concerned with the siege of Rouen, having long been considered topical allusions to the siege of Rouen which the English forces under the earl of Essex made in the autumn of 1591; and the eulogistic lines spoken over the corpses of the Talbots, "From their ashes shall be rear'd / A phoenix that shall make all France afeard" (IV. vii. 93-94), have been suggested as a reference to Essex's heroics in France.[4] The recital of Lord Talbot's titles (IV. vii. 60-71), taken from the epitaph on his monument in Rouen, has long been suggested as a device used to compliment the earl of Shrewsbury of Elizabeth's reign.[5] But there is more than just a complimentary nod in the Talbot scenes; I would like to suggest that these scenes were written to exonerate the actions of George Talbot, sixth earl of Shrewsbury, who died in November 1590 with his honor blemished by the intrigues of Mary Stuart, queen of Scots. George Talbot's warfare was not fought on the battlefields of France, but his difficult task as keeper of the queen of Scots had placed him in the line of fire in the international intrigues for over fifteen years, and when he was relieved of his post, it was with a suggestion of dishonor and disloyalty that was neither proved nor disproved in Elizabethan England.

We know that Shakespeare's portrayal of the heroic actions of John Talbot, first earl of Shrewsbury, is a dramatic exaggeration of that hero's deeds as they were related by the contemporary Elizabethan chroniclers. That the dramatist's intention was, in part, to reflect the actions of the sixth earl of Shrewsbury can be deduced best, I think, by looking carefully at the unhistorical scene in act II which is interpolated into the chronicle materials of the play. The scene is the chivalric meeting of Lord Talbot and the countess of Auvergne in which the countess attempts to capture the English commander by guile, underestimating both his strength and his integrity. This scene is pure fiction; no action of this kind is related in Shakespeare's source materials. Moreover, the scene stands alone in many respects, for nothing before it or after it relates it to the actions of the play, and the countess of Auvergne does not reappear in the drama.[6] It is possible that the scene was suggested to the playwright by the historical fact that Lord Talbot was captured by Joan of Arc's forces at Patay in 1429. In that battle the maid's stratagem of immediate attack, which gave Talbot and his archers no time to stockade themselves behind their stakes, won the day for her forces and gave her the credit for the capture of Talbot,

Scales, and Hungerford.[7] Shakespeare arranges his chronology to avoid just such an imputation; the defeat at Patay
is described by a messenger in act I, scene i, and the blame
for Talbot's capture is placed upon Sir John Falstaff (as
both Hall and Holinshed related). But in the following
scene (act I, scene ii) the Bastard of Orleans produces the
"Holy Maid," and she is brought before the dauphin for
the first time. This chronological arrangement makes her
historical humiliation of Talbot at Patay impossible in the
play. To avoid such a suggestion, Shakespeare brings the
maid and Talbot together in hand-to-hand combat in scene
v and ends the scene with Joan's withdrawal. Moreover,
when Talbot confronts Falstaff at Paris before Henry VI,
he accuses him of cowardice at the battle of Poitiers, not
Patay (IV. i. 19). This again seems motivated by the playwright's desire to avoid mention of the fateful battle by
name. If the Talbot-Joan of Arc scenes are arranged to
protect Lord Talbot's reputation on the battlefield, the
Auvergne-Talbot scene seems invented to emphasize the
chivalry and integrity of its hero. His conduct is discreet
and honorable in spite of the faint sexual overtones in
Burgundy's preceding speech and in Talbot's final lines in
this scene. This unhistorical episode of the drama can, I
believe, be related to events of the 1580s in both the
literary and the political milieu. In the Elizabethan setting
we can find a parallel situation in the life of George Talbot,
sixth earl of Shrewsbury, that provides an enlightened
explication of this scene.

First the literary milieu. John Lyly's *Endymion* was
entered in the *Stationers' Register* on 4 October 1591 and
was published before the year ended by John Charlewood
and the Widow Broome. This play contains court allegory
centering on Cynthia, a figure that almost all critics agree
is devised to flatter Queen Elizabeth. The female antago-
nist in the play is Tellus, whom Cynthia imprisons for her
misdeeds. As most readers will remember, Tellus is given a
jailer or keeper, a military man of some sensitivity, whom
she attempts to beguile. Her keeper, Corsites, becomes
enamoured of his captive to the extent that he betrays the
trust of Cynthia. He is extremely vulnerable to the beauty
and feminine wiles of his captive. Lyly's modern editor,
working with the very difficult problem of identification in

court allegory, suggests that Lyly was indeed writing about Mary, queen of Scots, and her relationship with her keeper, the earl of Shrewsbury.[8]

Most critics today are hostile to the conception of political allegory; such is the trend of our times. I will insist, however, that any Elizabethan audience who saw a performance of Lyly's *Endymion* would immediately have made a comparison between the beautiful prisoner, isolated with her needlework and helplessly at the command of Cynthia, and the imprisoned queen of Scots. It would be naive to think otherwise. To say today that Lyly meant only moral allegory in his dramatic art is to underestimate the love of complexity and verve of the Elizabethan artist. Working then from the assumption that the Elizabethan audience would have seen a relationship between the keeper of the beautiful Tellus and the keeper of the queen of Scots, we find a negative implication. Lyly's Corsites is beguiled in the play, made a fool of by the lovely prisoner. The gossip of the day contained essentially the same story about Mary Stuart and the sixth earl of Shrewsbury. His name was defamed in covert talk and backstairs tattling. I believe that Shakespeare's Talbot scenes were written to counteract the hostility that he and many another Elizabethan saw in the allegory of Lyly's *Endymion*.[9] This assumption is not, however, basic to the analysis of the Talbot scenes in *1 Henry VI* that were created to counter also the much broader publicity concerning the Talbots in the political arena.

As early as 1584, when George Talbot, sixth earl of Shrewsbury, was relieved of his office as keeper of the queen of Scots, the defamation of the earl had begun. In the famous propaganda piece *Leycesters Commonwealth*, which was circulated throughout the Continent, the anonymous author posed several pointed questions: "What meaneth also these pernitious late dealings against the Earle of Shrewsbury, a man of the most ancient and worthiest Nobility of our Realme?" And he continued with some knowledge of the private imbroglio going on between the earl and his wife: "What means the practises with his nearest both in bed and blood against him?" Then the author centers on his main point: "What means these most false and slanderous rumors cast abroad of late of his

GEORGIVS TALBOTVS
COMES SALOPIÆ
AN· ÆTATiS 58
S· H
1580

Sir George Talbot, sixth Earl of Shrewsbury.

disloyall demeanures towards her Majesty and his countrey, with the great prisoner committed to his charge?"
With those ideas posited, the writer makes his own conjecture: "Is all this to any other end, but only to drive
him to some impatience, and thereby to commit or say
something which may open the gate unto his ruine?"[10]
Even earlier than this publication there were unsettling
thoughts about the situation in which the elder Talbot
found himself. In May of 1579 Gilbert Talbot had written
from London to his father, repeating a remark made by the
earl of Leicester: "By the Eternal God, if they [Shrews-
bury's enemies at court] could ever bring the Queen to
believe it that there were jars betwixt them [Shrewsbury
and his wife], she would be in such a fear as it would sooner
be the cause of the removing of my Lordship's charge [Mary
Stuart] than any other thing."[11] The earl of Shrewsbury's
second wife was the famous Bess of Hardwick, a woman of
determination who had her own role to play in the political
game of chance focused on the succession to the crown.
Bess and the earl had been married only a year when he was
appointed the keeper of Mary Stuart in January 1569. In
the first years of Mary's imprisonment the countess and the
captive queen were friends, but the mutual devotion ended
with the marriage of Bess's youngest daughter, Elizabeth, to
Charles Stuart, the countess of Lennox's youngest son, in
October 1574, and with the birth of their daughter, Arbella,
in 1575. Because of this marriage and its lack of royal
approval, Bess of Hardwick spent a year in the Tower. In the
new grandchild, Bess had a contender for the title of heir-
apparent to the English throne, and the jealousy between
Mary Stuart and the countess of Shrewsbury grew as the
child did. The relationship between the earl of Shrewsbury
and Queen Elizabeth also grew tense during the years of
his custody of the Scottish queen. Frequent reports that
Shrewsbury's guardianship of Mary Stuart was lax reached
London; servants of the earl as well as his younger sons
were thought to be carrying messages to and from the imprisoned queen; and Henry Cavendish, one of the countess's sons by her previous marriage to Sir William Cavendish, was reported to be involved in an attempt to convey
the Queen of Scots to Scotland. Furthermore, Elizabeth
had been stinting in her payments to her "good old man" so

that the excessive expense of Mary's maintenance had become a heavy burden to the earl. Queen Elizabeth continued to compound the tensions by siding with the earl's tenants in a quarrel over rents on his estates. Thus the earl of Shrewsbury was not without motives for his actions in 1583-1584.

In the summer of 1582 Mary Stuart was visited by M. de Ruisseau, one of her councillors in France. When Queen Elizabeth heard the rumor that Mary had discussed with the Frenchman a proposed plan for the invasion of Scotland by the duke of Guise and the plan for her own escape from Sheffield, Elizabeth was furious. She was not yet sure of Shrewsbury's infidelity, but she cancelled his permit to come to London (a permit for which he had pleaded a number of years), and she ordered Mary's guard increased and placed severe limitations on her movements. In vain the earl wrote to London, "I have heard of late her Majesty hath expressed some very hard conceits of me." He continued by adding, "I am very well able to prove that she [Mary] hath showed herself an enemy unto me and to my fortune and that I trust will sufficiently clear me."[12] Meanwhile, information was coming in to Walsingham and Burghley from Scotland concerning the activities of Esmé Stuart, count d'Aubigny, whom James had created duke of Lennox. Esmé Stuart was a cousin of James; his French manners and ingratiating ways had endeared him to the young king, and after the fall of Morton the new duke of Lennox was virtually in control of Scotland. The English Council was soon aware of the grandiose scheme which Lennox and Guise, with the aid of Philip, the pope, and the Jesuits, hoped to put into effect—the invasion of England through Scotland and the restoration of Catholicism in the island.

In the complex and devious events of this period it is at times difficult to say exactly whose lines fouled whose or how much the English government was influencing Scottish actions, but suddenly the Protestants in Scotland captured their young king in August of 1582, and Lennox was forced to flee to France, via England. In London he gained an audience with Queen Elizabeth and proclaimed vehemently his loyalty to Protestantism and the English cause. In France he established contact with Sir Henry Cobham, the English ambassador, and he told an exciting tale. Whether his motive was to double-cross the duke of Guise or to beguile the English with half-truths, we do not know, but he began to expose the Hispano-Guise plot to Ambassador Cobham in March and April of 1583.[13] Cobham in turn relayed the information to Walsingham in London. Lennox gave the ambassador details of Mary Stuart's plans of escape from Sheffield, the Catholic plan to kidnap young James and carry him to France, and the plan of Guise and the pope to invade England. Cobham wrote also that Lennox wished to come to London to show Queen Elizabeth a letter he had received from Mary Stuart offering him the allegiance of her followers in Scotland and the favor of her confederates in England if he would stay in Scotland to direct the forthcoming plan of invasion. Lennox proposed, or so Cobham wrote, to discover the names of Mary's English adherents if Elizabeth were interested.[14]

Cobham's letter in which this offer was described was written on 1 May; a few days later Lennox was dead.[15] *D'une maladie de langueur* was said to have been the cause of his death; Mary Stuart said he had been poisoned; Froude suggests he was poisoned at the instigation of the duke of Guise.[16] Queen Elizabeth and her councillors had considered exterminating Lennox two years earlier before the Raid of Ruthven.[17] We do not know the actual cause of Esmé Stuart's death, but it was considered a stroke of luck by some in England. Young Roger Manner's remark, made in a letter to his brother in June (they were related to the earl of Shrewsbury), is indicative of the surge of relief that the nervous adherents of the queen of Scots felt: "The Duck of Lenoix is ded in France, wherat we here rejoyce."[18] Nor do we know what Ambassador Cobham would have done had he received the list of Mary's adherents in England; certainly one of the names on that list would have been Lord Cobham's.

Lennox's revelations had implicated Shrewsbury again in a plot for the release of the queen of Scots. Was the earl playing a double game with Queen Elizabeth? Recent scholarship suggests that he was. In September of 1583 Shrewsbury moved the royal prisoner to Worksop, his manor in Sherwood Forest. While there, the earl was visited by his nephew the earl of Rutland, a zealous Catholic who was reported to be an adherent of the Scots queen.[19] When Elizabeth heard of Mary's liberties in Sherwood Forest, she was incensed; she had already heard during the summer months the unpleasant gossip that Bess of Hardwick had sent to the court concerning an undue intimacy between the earl, her husband, and the captive queen. Mendoza, the Spanish ambassador, had picked up the gossip also, and he relayed it to King Philip in June. Mendoza said he had heard that the countess of Shrewsbury had sent one of her sons directly to Queen Elizabeth with her complaint and that Elizabeth referred him to the Council. The Spanish ambassador described how Bess's son had balked at this point: "He replied that as the matter was one between husband and wife, he did not think this course would be agreeable to his mother." Mendoza proceeded with his account of the gossip:

> The substance of the complaint is that, so long as the Queen of Scots was in the hands of the Earl of Shrewsbury, she would never be secure, as he was in love with her, and this the Countess sets forth with a thousand absurdities and impertinences, which the Treasurer and Walsingham have repeated, the Queen having shown them the statements.[20]

The twentieth-century biographer of Bess of Hardwick declares that the countess of Shrewsbury started the rumors to protect both her life and the earl's, knowing that Elizabeth would relieve him of his post when she heard the gossip, thus placing the earl out of the way of the conspiracy.[21] London was a hotbed of gossip, and soon the French ambassador there heard the unseemly talk, and he passed it on to Mary Stuart. The queen of Scots was both irate and frightened. She commanded Mauvissiere

> to publish everywhere as loudly as you can my offers hereupon and their answer, to the end to countermine the false rumors that you tell me they have already spread. You will have somewhat understood by my said letters my intention of touching indirectly the Countess of Shrewsbury, against whom, if I am not afraid of opening my mouth, I am sure that she and all her courtiers will have whereof to repent for having so cruelly and treacherously attacked me.[22]

The earl of Shrewsbury was of course inflamed when he heard the report of what his wife had done. He proceeded with the *Statute of Scandalis Magnatum* against William and Charles Cavendish, Bess's sons, and her steward, Henry Beresford, who had helped spread the gossip in the court. As late as March 1587, Shrewsbury was demanding of Walsingham some measure to force the countess to make a "public submission and retraction of her slanderous speeches."[23] And in June 1587, the earl petitioned the queen that the countess his wife might be banished from court "now that she hath so openly manifested her devilish disposition and defended her wicked servant Beresford in the defamation of my house and name."[24] The effect of the gossip plus the revelations gained from Francis Throckmorton's confession made it imperative that Shrewsbury be relieved of his position as keeper of Mary Stuart. Sir Ralph Sadleir was commissioned in March 1584 to replace Shrewsbury as Mary's host and guard. Sadleir spent the summer months with Mary and the earl at Sheffield. In September he moved the queen of Scots to Wingfield.[25] The earl of Shrewsbury, disillusioned and unhappy, was never reconciled with his countess. He died in November 1590, and the ugly atmosphere of dishonor still permeated the scene in 1592 when young Gilbert Talbot was elected to the Order of the Garter. It is against this background of historical events and conditions that Shakespeare's Talbot scenes should be viewed for full understanding.

In the puzzling scene between Lord Talbot and the countess of Auvergne in *1 Henry VI* the countess attempts to capture the hero by guile. Why did the playwright choose the name "countess of Auvergne" for his intriguing lady? One has only to turn to the *Dictionnaire de Biographie Française* to discover a logical reason. The dauphins of France in the sixteenth century bore the title "le Prince Dauphin d'Auvergne." The title had passed to the house of Bourbon after 1436, and in 1527 the last duke of Bourbon, the celebrated Constable Charles of Bourbon, had forfeited the title to the crown as a consequence of his treason.[26] Mary Stuart had married in 1558 the young "Prince Dauphin d'Auvergne" who became Francis II, king of France. With this knowledge, Shakespeare's allusiveness

suddenly has method behind it. The scene between the
stalwart Talbot and the beguiling lady does appear to
have been written to uphold the honor of the sixth earl of
Shrewsbury. In the play the staunch Talbot outwits and out-
plots the lady; at the same time he maintains himself as a
gallant courtier and competent military man. The lines
given to Talbot in the preceding scene appear paradoxi-
cal:

> . . . when a world of men
> Could not prevail with all their oratory
> Yet hath a woman's kindness over-rul'd.

[III.ii.48–50]

History suggests that the sixth earl of Shrewsbury did indeed succumb for a brief time to the pathos and perhaps
the intrigues of the imprisoned queen of Scots. If I have
interpreted this scene in *1 Henry VI* correctly, the young
playwright appears to have been unwilling to believe it so.

The cowardice of Sir John Falstaff is depicted three
times in *1 Henry VI*: first, by the messenger in act I,
scene i (lines 130–34); second, by Falstaff's flight at the
battle of Rouen (III.ii.105–8); and for the third time in
Talbot's recital of Falstaff's base actions when the former
appears before the king (IV. i. 13–26). In addition, by bearing Burgundy's letter of defection, Falstaff is implicated
in that betrayal. Thus we have four actions in the play
developed from one historical event related by the Tudor
chroniclers who were drawing from the biased account of
the battle of Patay given by Monstrelet.[27] This heavy
emphasis upon the dishonorable conduct of Sir John
Fastolf or Falstaff would seem to allude obliquely to the
strained relationship between the earl of Shrewsbury and
William Brooke, Lord Cobham. Much of the evidence of
Lord Cobham's connections with the queen of Scots and
the duke of Norfolk has been presented earlier in this
study. We know that Lord Cobham's name was on the list
of Mary's adherents thought to have been compiled by
Francis Throckmorton. We know that Sir Henry Cobham
sent the details of Mary's escape plan to Walsingham, im-
plicating the Shrewsburies. There is further evidence
that Lady Frances Cobham, mistress of the Queen's Wardrobe and a particular favorite of Queen Elizabeth, was involved in secret communications with Mary Stuart.

Early in Elizabeth's reign the Spanish ambassador had written to Philip that he was receiving intelligence about the English court from Lady Cobham.[28] And in 1565 De Silva wrote to the king that Lady Cobham had paid him a secret visit to beg leniency for Thomas Cobham. De Silva spoke of the "affection they all bore toward your Majesty."[29] In February 1575 Henry Cockyn, a prisoner in the Tower, wrote to Walsingham that his reticence was caused by his fear of "touching great personages, indeed, at first I was afraid to discover that which I knew of Lord Henry [Howard] and the Lady Cobham. . . . What favourers the Scottish Queen has in Court, I know not, other than Lady Cobham."[30] Frances Cobham's contact with the queen of Scots seems to have come about through her close friendship with the countess of Shrewsbury. Lady Cobham had had a hand in arranging the marriage of Bess and the earl in 1568. It had at one time been thought that Sir Henry Cobham was the suitor most likely to succeed in winning the hand of the widowed Bess, but Lady Cobham seems to have used her talents for matchmaking to help Bess catch the wealthy earl instead. Shrewsbury, in an endearing letter to his new wife written from Hampton Court on their first parting, gave Lady Cobham some credit for his happiness.

My Lady Cobham, your dear friend, wishes your presence here: she loves you well. I tell her I have the cause to love her best, for that she wished me so well to speed as I did [his marriage]: and as the pen writes so the heart thinks, that of all earthly joys that hath happened unto me, I thank God chiefest for you.[31]

An extant letter written by Gilbert Talbot from court to his stepmother, of whom he was very fond, contains more evidence of the closeness of Lady Cobham and the countess of Shrewsbury. "My Lady Cobham," he wrote, "asketh daily how your La: doth, and yesterday prayed me, the next time I wrote, to do her very hearty commendation unto your La:, saying openly she remaineth unto your La: as she was wont, as unto her dearest friend."[32] Bess at this time was in serious trouble over the marriage of her daugh-

ter to the countess of Lennox's son, so it was brave of
Lady Cobham to speak so openly.

Lady Cobham was dabbling in intrigue on her own, and
she received an unexpected humiliation as a result of these
activities. Her signature appears with those of Walsingham, Burghley, Hunsdon, and Shrewsbury as endorse-
ment on the back of a letter that Walsingham intercepted
in 1586. The letter was written by Thomas Morgan in
Paris and was smuggled to Mary Stuart via Walsingham's
spies. Morgan suggests that Mary resume her contact with
Lady Cobham.

> My Lady Cobham beareth a great stroke over her Husband,
> who towardes your Majesty is not evil inclined: Your Majesty
> may consyder how to revive your Intelligence with my Lady
> Cobham, and you may take Occasion to congratulate of the
> Estimation of her Husband [Cobham's appointment to the
> Privy Council], and that he had wronge that he was not called
> to that Place earlier, and that you doubt not but he will use
> his Creditt in that Place to the Honor and Good of the Realme,
> and to his own Commendation, and that he will ever favour
> Equitye and Honor in all your Causes.

Morgan then suggests several ways of contacting Lady
Cobham—through Francis Barty, the countess of Arundel,
or Lord Stourton.

> My Lord Stourton is a Catholike, and maried the Daughter
> of the Lord Cobham: and the Lord Stourton, being in that De-
> gree of Alliance with that Familye, were a fitt Instrument to
> be imployed towardes the Lord and Lady Cobham. Sir John
> Arundell were a fitt Man to pushe on the Lord Stourton for
> your Service.

Morgan at length decided that the countess of Arundel
would be the best means of reaching Lady Cobham, so he
enclosed in his letter a note to Lady Arundel that Mary was
to copy and send.

> We have written herewith a few Lines to the Lady Cobham,
> which we likewise desire to be delivered to her, and pray you
> further to buy for us of the best Silkes or Velvets that you
> can finde, as moch as will serve to make her a cople of Gownes
> to weare for our Sake.

The note continued with a reservation that if Lady Arundel thought the action unsafe, she was not to proceed with Lady Cobham. Morgan concluded his own letter with a warning that if the league between Lady Cobham and the countess of Shrewsbury "be still great, then is the Lady Cobham to be delt withall with more Discretion, or perhaps not to be delt with at all."[33] The Privy Council appears to have invited Lady Cobham to attend their meeting where the letters of Thomas Morgan were read. She was asked to initial the letter on the back, along with the other members of the Council.

These bits of evidence, collected from a range of years during which the intrigues of the imprisoned queen of Scots hazarded the careers of far too many of the courtiers surrounding Queen Elizabeth, do not of course give a complete picture of what happened in the fall of 1583. The reader will recall that when the Ridolfi plot collapsed in 1572, Lord Cobham escaped censure and punishment through the protective actions of Lord Burghley, and the Catholic nobles were incensed at what appeared to be his betrayal of their cause. In 1583 a similar situation appears to have developed. Lord Cobham's name once more appeared on the list of adherents of the queen of Scots, and once more the ports of England which faced the Continent were being surveyed by the intriguers. Bernardino de Mendoza, the current Spanish ambassador in England, working with the duke of Guise, who had agreed to land French forces on the coast of Sussex, the Jesuits and the pope, and his own master, Philip II, was in continuous contact with "incredible numbers" of English Catholics at home and with the ringleaders among the exiles on the Continent, Charles Paget, Thomas Morgan, and Charles Arundel. Francis Throckmorton, nephew of Sir Nicholas Throckmorton, was one of Mendoza's chief contacts in London. When Walsingham became suspicious of Francis Throckmorton's activities in the early fall of 1583, he had the young man's lodgings raided. It was a stroke of luck for the secretary. He found among Throckmorton's papers a list of the major ports of England, "Havens in every coast fitte for a landing of forces." It contained a description of their capacities, the prevailing winds, and other details. Also among the papers was a list of the Englishmen who would be willing to join the plot.[34] Lord Cobham's name

appeared on that list.[35] What was going on? The details
are difficult to find, but the general scope of events is relatively clear.[36] Cobham appears to have been open to suggestions and to contacts from the Catholic factions as
usual. But this time he was working carefully with Walsingham and Burghley. In Walsingham's personal journal,
which he kept as a reference to appointments, assignments,
and remembrances of things that must be done during
these months, there are numerous references to Lord Cobham: "a letter to the L. Cobham touchinge the portes," a
"Comyssion for Cobham," a note to be sent "to L. Cobham," a "reminder to remember the L. Cobham" concerning
one to be committed to prison, and so forth.[37] It would appear that Lord Cobham had by this time become a very
valuable instrument for gathering intelligence concerning
the unruly dissidents of the reign. He was related to some
of the unhappy Catholics, and he had been pliable in the
hands of the plotters at an earlier date. He was a known
sympathizer with the causes of Mary, and he had willingly
risked his career for her in the opening days of her campaign for the English throne. But in 1583 Lord Cobham
was fifty-five years of age, and he had learned through experience that his easiest and readiest way to prosperity
was through Lord Burghley and Queen Elizabeth. And he
was right. His most handsome rewards came immediately.
In the spring of 1584 he was elected as a knight of the
Order of the Garter, and in the first months of 1586 he
was appointed to the Privy Council.[38] Meanwhile, the earl
of Shrewsbury's name was slandered and maligned. The
story of his faithlessness as keeper of the queen of Scots
was broadcast everywhere through the account of Mary
Stuart which Francis Thynne included in his continuation
of the history of Scotland for the second edition of Holinshed's *Chronicles*.[39] The irate Shrewsbury forced Thynne
to write a retraction. Thynne complied with a palinode of
some grace, "least my error might be eyther offensyve to
his honor or honorable posterity, or injurious to his right
noble auncestors," and he gave an innocuous account of
Shrewsbury's dismissal from his post as keeper of the Scottish queen:

> The Earle of Shrewsburye, having many yeares had the Quene
> of Scottes in his custodie, finding by long experience how bur-
> denous and troblesom a charge she had bene unto him and howe

perilous yt might be yf she long contynued with him, she still
thirsting for libertie and dailye seking extraordinary courses
for her enlargment, made humble sute unto her Majestie to be
discharged thereof. . . . he was after long sutes disburdened of
his said charge.[40]

When Shakespeare's Talbot scenes are placed against
this miasmic backdrop of subterfuge and treason, the dramatic actions of a former Lord Talbot and his betrayal by
Sir John Falstaff's cowardice and disloyalty become symbolic drama. It would appear that the young Shakespeare
turned to the English chronicles for materials on the early
Lord Talbots which he could use to create a work of art
that would compliment the Elizabethan earls of Shrewsbury. The story of Sir John Falstolf or Falstaff (the latter
spelling is more fitting to depict the broken staff of command or office) and his cowardice, and especially the
account of the retraction of the Garter, afforded the playwright a brilliant chance to depict something of the contemporary tensions that had recently made the court of Queen
Elizabeth a hotbed of emotional unrest and danger. The
oblique references to the Cobhams in the emphasis upon Sir
John Fastolf's duplicity are based, I believe, upon the defamation of the earl of Shrewsbury appearing in Ambassador
Cobham's reports from Paris and upon the possible betrayal
of the Catholic intriguers in 1583 by Lord Cobham in his
important position as lord warden of the Cinque Ports. The
disclosure of the Catholic plot which Walsingham gained
from Francis Throckmorton, who was racked until he had
confessed all he knew of the proceedings, made it imperative that Queen Elizabeth remove Shrewsbury from his
post. Lord Cobham was working with Walsingham at this
time to gain that exposé.

The Fastolf-Falstaff story in the English chronicles
appears to have intrigued the playwright because it was an
apt vehicle for his satire, not because of any historical relationship between the fifteenth-century Fastolf and the sixteenth-century Cobhams. The chronicles had already deni-
grated Fastolf's name; Shakespeare increases that denigration. The question at this point arises: was there possibly
another reason for the young Shakespeare's desire to satirize the Cobhams under the guise of the Fastolf-Falstaff

characterlization? An affirmative answer lies in the close relationship of the Throckmorton plot and the troublesome case of the Arden-Somerville affair. The unfortunate episode of John Somerville's wild ride toward London to kill the "viper" queen occurred almost simultaneously with the Throckmorton exposé. There are a few elements in the case not generally known to readers of the twentieth century. Almost all historians follow the statements of numerous Elizabethan writers who declared that John Somerville was a disturbed young man ("crazy" the tactless said) who had ridden off to London to assassinate Queen Elizabeth. Most historians agree that there was no connection between John Somerville and Francis Throckmorton, as far as political plotting was concerned. But there is some historical evidence to the contrary.

John Somerville of Edstone, a young man in his early twenties, had married Margaret Arden. She was the daughter of Sir Edward Arden of Park Hall, who was obliquely related to Shakespeare's mother. On Friday, 25 October, Somerville, accompanied by a servant boy, set out from his home, six miles above Stratford, for London. The next day he was arrested between Banbury and Bicester, taken to Oxford, then to London, examined in the Gatehouse on 30 and 31 October, then committed to the Tower.[41] Somerville's examination as well as those of his wife, sisters, mother, and the Arden family are extant.[42] Thomas Wylkes, whom Walsingham had sent to Stratford to search the houses of the Catholics there, wrote to his master on 7 November to report what he had learned. He described Somerville's state of mind before he left home: "I perceave that there wilbe alleadged in his excuse to save him from the danger of the lawe, that he hathe ben sithence midsomer affected with a Frantike humor, growne (as it is said) of jealousie conceaved of his wife." Wylkes also explained that Somerville had not slept well because of the books he had been reading, seditious books procured for him by his sister Elizabeth.[43] And this is the story that was given to the public at large. But on 30 November Walsingham wrote to the earl of Derby relating how Somerville, thinking to do his country a great deed, had planned "to make awaie with her majestie." Walsingham explained his own interpretation of the case: "To excuse this intended action, yt hath bene geven out, that he was a man distracted, not know[ing] what he did, or intended. Howbeit, by sundry exam[inations] of himself, yt appear[eth] that there [is] no such destrac[tion] in the man."[44]

Lord Hunsdon and Judge Haywarde were commissioned to conduct the trial at the Guildhall, and on 16 December both Somerville and his father-in-law were found guilty of treason.[45] The night before the executions were scheduled to be carried out, Somerville was found hanged in his cell at Newgate. There is some interesting commentary on this incident. Two extant letters, both unsigned, repeat rumors that Somerville was hanged in prison "to avoyd a greter evell."[46] And the same story was repeated by Robert Batt, a Yorkshireman, in his letter to Stephen Waterhouse in December.[47] This was indeed rumor; certainly there is no evidence to suggest that Somerville was murdered in his cell to prevent him from making accusations at his execution. Sir Edward Arden was executed on schedule the next day. But the rumors help us to understand the air of mystification surrounding the events of October, November, and December 1583.

There is another puzzling letter. It was written to Walsingham by Sir Edward Stafford, who had just replaced Sir Henry Cobham as ambassador in Paris. On 2 December he informed Walsingham that Charles Paget, his brother, and Charles Arundel had "suddenly entered my dining chamber before anyone was aware of it" and that they had demanded an interview with the ambassador. They explained that they had fled from England "for fear, having enemies." They insisted that Somerville had warned that "there was to be a hard hand over all papists," so the young Catholics had slipped across the Channel to France.[48] The question arises: what contact had these ringleaders in the Throckmorton conspiracy with Somerville? The trial of Somerville had not occurred when this letter was written. Charles Paget and his followers could have been lying; they were up to their ears in intrigue. But Stafford's letter adds to the mystery of the case.

There are other curious elements in the Somerville case. Thomas Wylkes found a letter in his search of the Somerville home written by Elizabeth, Somerville's sister, while she was on the Continent: "I learne that this woman is a [*hiatus*] and a malitious papiste and hathe of late ben beyonde the seas as appereth by a letter written by her to her mother from St Omers in August, which I send herewith, and retourned into the Realme about three months past."[49] St. Omers was a Jesuit stronghold. Again, this is no evidence of a relationship between the Somerville case and the Throckmorton plot, but Somerville's range of contacts is broader than has been suspected. The matter of Hugh Hall, the priest in the Somerville case, adds to the mystery. Hall admitted in his examinations that he had worked as a gardener for both John Talbot and Sir John Throckmorton before he came to stay with Sir Edward Arden. He insisted that he "hath had no familiaritie with Fra: Thrikemorten these vi or vij yeres / and doth not remember that he hath seen him these iii or 4 yeres."[50] Thomas Wylkes described Hugh Hall, "the preiste," as being "a most dangerous practiser, a convayor of intelligence to all the capitall papistes in these partes, a reporter unto them under the cloke of a Gardiner, [who] countrfethe, reconcilethe, confessethe, saithe masses, and he [is] the most liklie to have persuaded this wreched traitor, to attempte her Maties destruction."[51] Wylkes, who was the clerk of the Privy Council, needed a victim, but there is other evidence which points toward broad contacts that Hugh Hall maintained. In a letter written by William Davison to the Council concerning intelligences that he had picked up in Scotland, he remarks that he had learned that "Hugh Hawll the priest" had been in Rome where he shipped "seditious" books home to England "very cunningly" hidden under the roots of plants and trees that were sent to his patrons. Davison adds that Hall was a "minister of messages and practices" and that he hoped that "this remembrance touching Hawll" would serve to bring other plots to light.[52] Davison is a responsible source of information. It would seem that Hugh Hall, who was pardoned when he complied with Walsingham's instructions, was a better informed man than the usual country priest of the sixteenth century.

What I am trying to establish is not that there was an explicit connection between the Somerville and Throckmorton plots (that is impossible at present) but rather that there was evidence enough to make even the authorities probe for such a relationship. It certainly was not to the advantage of Walsingham and Burghley to admit that there was a broad conspiracy reaching into the well-established families of the midlands. Such news would have frightened the general public even more. The Ardens were a respected family of the gentry; the Throckmortons had distinguished themselves in sixteenth-century diplomacy (Shakespeare was distantly related to them); and John Talbot, with whom Hall the priest had lived, was the son of Sir John Talbot, brother of the sixth earl of Shrewsbury.[53] We wonder naturally how the nineteen-year-old Shakespeare responded to these difficult events, and of course we have no direct answer. The cry for order which is unmistakable in the history plays gives us a clue to the rightness of his mind, but we should note as well the touch of family loyalty that appears in *The Contention* (generally considered Shakespeare's first play) where the character Sir John Somerville is made a loyal adherent to the crown (*3 Henry VI*, act V, scene i). My suggestion at this point is that Shakespeare too felt Lord Cobham and his brother to be in part responsible for the unfortunate "trap" in which so many of the Catholic families found themselves in 1583. The earl of Northumberland was once more in prison; the earl of Shrewsbury was being defamed; the Arundels, Pagets, Throckmortons, and Ardens were sinking under the weight of accusations and solid evidence of their adventures in intrigue. These people were not insurrectionists or rebels in the liberal sense of the word. They were conservative, old-fashioned families who were appalled at the "conspiracy" of the establishment to destroy the old way of life. From their point of view, they were gradually being exterminated by the politicians in power in London, and the younger members of those families determined upon extreme measures of resistance. It was a tense period in Tudor history, and it is out of this complex matrix of warring emotions, I believe, that the Falstaff-Cobham satire in Shakespeare's plays developed.

The same vortex of political affairs appears to have been the source for the satire involving the character of Eleanor Cobham, duchess of Gloucester. The story of this historical figure resembles in many ways the history of the Oldcastle legend. It came down through the chronicles as a story of treason, but the later Tudor historians reworked the material until Eleanor became a victim of political forces and at length, like her kinsman, she was enrolled in Foxe's calendar of martyrs. A typical mid-fifteenth-century version of Eleanor's story is described by William Gregory, mayor of London.

[A.D. 1440–41] And in the same yere there were taken certayne traytours, the whyche purposyd to slee oure lege lorde the kyng by crafte of egremauncy, and there instrumentys were opynly shewyd to alle men at the Crosse in Powlys chyrche yerde a-pon a schaffolde i-made there-for. Att the whyche tyme was present one of the same traytours, whiche was callyd Roger Bulbroke, a clerke of Oxforde, and for that same tresoun my Lady of Gloucester toke sayntwerye at Westemyster; and the xj day of Auguste thenne next folowynge she toke the way to the castelle of Lesnes. And on Syn Symon and Judeys eve was the wycche by syde Westemyster brent in Smethefylde, and on the day of Symon and Jude the person [parson] of Syn Stevynnys in Walbroke, whyche that was one of the same fore sayde traytors, deyde in the Toure for sorowe.[54]

When Edward Hall related the story of Eleanor Cobham he appears to have been well aware of George, Lord Cobham, and his prominent position in the royal court and on the Privy Council. In Hall's version of the story emphasis is placed upon the enemies of the duke of Gloucester, and he minimizes the treason of Gloucester's wife.

But venyme will once breake oute, and inwarde grudge will sone appeare, whiche was this yere to all men apparaunt: for divers secret attemptes were advaunced forward this season, against the noble duke Humfrey of Glocester, a farre of, whiche in conclusion came so nere, that they bereft hym both of lyfe and lande, as you shall hereafter more manifestly perceyve. For first this yere, dame Elyanour Cobham, wyfe to the sayd duke, was accused of treason, for that she by sorcery and enchauntment, entended to destroy the kyng, to thentent to advaunce and to promote her husbande to the croune.

Hall describes how she was tried and judged guilty through the influence of the crafty clergy and how others were drawn into the case: "At the same season, wer arrested as ayders and counsailers to the sayde Duchesse, Thomas Southwel, prieste and chanon of saincte Stephens in Westmynster, Jhon Hum priest, Roger Bolyngboke, a conyng nycromancier, and Margerie Jourdayne, surnamed the witche of Eye." Hall also described the charge concerning the image of the king formed in wax, which "litle and litle consumed, entendyng therby in conclusion to waist, and destroy the kynges person, and so to bryng hym death." But Hall emphasizes the statement of Roger Bolingbroke that "there was never no such thyng by theim ymagined."[55]

Fabyan's account of Eleanor's deeds followed the older Catholic version of the story, as we would expect. He did not hesitate to include a bit of gossip about Lady Eleanor that had circulated in the rumors of the court and which Monstrelet had described.

> And first this yere dame Elanoure Cobham, whom he [Glou-cester] was to famylyer with, er she were to hym maryed, was arrestid of certayne poyntes of treason, and therupon by xamynacion convict, and lastly demyd to dwell as an outlawe in the Isle of Man.[56]

Fabyan continued his account with a description of the execution of Bolingbroke and the Witch of Eye, and he described the wax image of the king with the attendant acts of treason by sorcery. Thus the two versions of the story existed side by side for sixteenth-century readers to compare. The "modern" version reclaimed the lady's honor; the "obsolete" one defamed her name. Twentieth-century writers suggest that Eleanor Cobham was the duke's "evil genius," that she mixed in affairs of state and performed illegal acts, and that she was probably guilty of the charge of witchcraft.[57]

By 1563 John Foxe had picked up the story of Eleanor Cobham, reknit it into a chivalric defense of the lady, and made her as well as her husband a victim of the malice of the unscrupulous bishop of Winchester. This incident for Foxe was one more example of the unlicensed depravity of Catholicism in general. But Foxe's account of the story contained flaws that Nicholas Harpsfield was quick to catch. The imprisoned archdeacon taunted Foxe for confusing the priest Bolingbroke with Sir Roger Only, knight, and for placing the Witch of Eye in his calendar of saints.[58] Foxe wrote "A Brief Answer to the Cavillations of Alan Cope's Concerning Lady Eleanor Cobham," that he printed in the 1576 edition of the *Acts and Monuments*.[59] He had not made the witch a saint, he insisted, but he had made an error in the name of Bolingbroke because his first edition was "so hastily rashed up in such shortness of time." And of this little matter "Master Cope, the pope's scout, lying in privy wait to spy faults in all men's works . . . taketh pepper in the nose, and falleth again unto his old barking against me." Foxe then defended Eleanor Cobham by syllogistic reasoning: Eleanor favored Lollardy, therefore she was hated by the papists; if she had intended treason she would not have made so many persons privy to her intentions; the Witch of Eye lived in the bishop of Winchester's see, and therefore she was probably his instrument; Polydore Vergil omitted the account of Eleanor Cobham from his *Angelica Historia*; his "mewing up of the matter" indicated to Foxe that he must have found something to make him mistrust the whole story. And so on. After ten such conclusions Foxe ended thus:

> Although these, with many more conjectures, may be alleged as some part of the defence of this duchess, and of her chaplains and priests, yet, because it may still not be impossible for the matter laid against them to be true, I leave it therefore at large, as I find it; saying, as I said before, that if that be true which the stories say in this matter, think, I beseech thee, gentle reader! that I have said nothing hereof.[60]

And thus Foxe left it hanging fire, as it were. The Elizabethan chroniclers, in this account, followed true to their previous commitments to the Oldcastle story. Grafton's account of the Eleanor Cobham episode (1569) is based upon Hall; his opinion of the charges of treason brought against the duchess was that they were part and parcel of the bishop of Winchester's plan to destroy the duke of Gloucester.[61] Holinshed relates the tragedy of Eleanor in which she is the victim of Gloucester's enemies.[62] Stow's version of the story goes back to the pre-Reformation account of the affair; he contends that the lady's "pride, false covetise, and lechery" were the cause of her "Confusion." Stow denigrates her character further by insisting that she was Gloucester's "paramour, to his great reproch." He describes her apprehension and indictment for treason with the other unholy conspirators, and adds:

> There was taken also Margery Gurdemaine, a witch of Eye ny
> Westminster, whose sorcerie and witchcraft the said Elianor
> hadde long time used, and by her medicines and drinkes en-
> forced the Duke of Gloucester to lofe her, and after to wedde
> her, wherefore, and for cause of relapse, the same witch was
> brent in Smithfield, on the twentie-seven day of October.[63]

Scholars are agreed that Shakespeare read and used the
Elizabethan chronicle accounts of Dame Eleanor's tragedy;
of equal importance with the chronicle accounts for analogues is the literary production of the story of the duchess
of Gloucester that appeared in the 1578 edition of the *Mirror for Magistrates*. George Ferrer's versified tragedies of
Eleanor Cobham and of the duke of Gloucester were indexed in the 1559 and 1571 editions of the *Mirror*; they
were not, however, included in the printed text. The 1578
edition of the *Mirror* indexed only the tragedy of the duke of
Gloucester, but the companion tragedy of Eleanor, his
duchess, was introduced in a cancel for folio 39 of this
edition. This unindexed and unfoliated gathering contained
a new prose link, the tragedy of the duchess, and a revised
prose link introducing the tragedy of the duke of Gloucester.[64] In this tragedy Eleanor's actions are motivated by
pride and ambition.

> An of pure pitty ponder wel my case,
> How I a Duches, destitute of grace
> Have found by proofe, as many have & shal
> The prouerbe true, that pryde wil hauve a fall.
>
> [lines 4-7]

Her birth is said to be base:

> A noble Prince extract of royal blood
> Humfrey sometyme Protector of this land
> Of Glocester Duke, for vertu cald (the good)
> When I but base beneath his state did stande
> Vouchsafte with me to joine in wedlockes bande
> Hauing in Court no name of high degree
> But Elinor Cobham as parents left to mee.
>
> And though by byrth of noble race I was,
> Of Barons bloud, yet was I thought vnfitte,
> So high to matche, yet so it came to passe.
>
> [lines 8-17]

Eleanor's ambition to wear the crown is described as one of the major reasons for her fall.

> For not content to be a Duchesse greate,
> I longed sore to beare the name of Queene
> Aspyring stil vnto an higher seate,
> And with that hope my selfe did ouerweene
> Sins there was none, which that tyme was betweene
> Henry the king, and my good Duke his Eame
> Heyre to the crowne and kingdome of the Realme.
>
> [lines 78-84]

In this version of her history Eleanor admits that she called in the Witch of Eye, Bolingbroke, and Southwell to cast certain divinations to discover who should succeed to the crown, but she insists that neither by "inchauntment, sorcery, or charme" did they ever plan "to work my princes harme" (lines 111-12). And she furiously denounces Beaufort, bishop of Winchester, as the perpetrator of the plot to destroy both her and Gloucester (lines 176-238). In the companion tragedy of the duke of Gloucester, however, the treasonable sorcery of Eleanor and the necromancers is described by the duke, and he does not deny the charges made against his wife, although he too says that Beaufort, the bishop of Winchester, used "this haynous crime an open wordly shame" as "a fyne fetch further thinges to frame."

> Yet besides this there was a greater thing,
> How she in waxe by counsel of the witch,
> An Image made, crowned like a king,
> With sword in hand, in shape and likenesse syche
> As was the kinge, which dayly they did pytch
> Against a fyre, that as the waxe did melt,
> So should his lyfe consume away vnfelt.
>
> [lines 274-280]

Ferrers was drawing upon an older tradition of verse that seems to have been popular in the fifteenth century. Several poems of that earlier period were sung as laments of the proud duchess, a lady "soo proude & highge of harte, that she hur-selffe thought pereles of estate," and there were verses on her "mutabilitie."[65]

Against this heterogeneous background of source materials Shakespeare's management of dramatic character becomes more significant. Shakespeare's version of the duchess's character is quite similar to that portrayed by George Ferrers. The playwright introduces the ambition of the duchess in her opening lines, addressed to her husband.

Why are thine eyes fix'd to the sullen earth,
Gazing on that which seems to dim thy sight?
What seest thou there? King Henry's diadem,
Enchas'd with all the honours of the world?
If so, gaze on, and grovel on thy face,
Until thy head be circled with the same.
Put forth thy hand, reach at the glorious gold.
What, is't too short? I'll lengthen it with mine:
And having both together heav'd it up,
We'll both together lift our heads to heaven,
And never more abase our sight so low
As to vouchsafe one glance unto the ground.

This characteristic of ambition is reinforced in the same scene by Eleanor's description of her dream in which she is crowned queen in Westminster cathedral (lines 36–40). Her dealings with the Witch of Eye, Roger Bolingbroke, Southwell, and Hume are dramatized in act I, scene iii. This scene was revised for the folio edition, possibly, as the New Arden editor suggests, to remove the direct part taken by the duchess in the treasonable proceedings.[66] It is significant, I believe, that the burning of the wax effigy is not mentioned in the play. When Buckingham announces Eleanor's apprehension to the king and Gloucester, he simply says,

A sort of naughty persons, lewdly bent
Under the countenance and confederacy
Of Lady Eleanor, the Protector's wife,
The ringleader and head of all this rout,
Have practis'd dangerously against your state,
Dealing with witches and with conjurers:
Whom we have apprehended in the fact;
Raising up wicked spirits from under ground,
Demanding of King Henry's life and death,
And other of your Highness' Privy Council
As more at large your Grace shall understand.
[II.i.159–69]

And when Eleanor is sentenced by the king, he only says "in sight of God and us, your guilt is great" (II. iii. 2).

Eleanor's stoic reply is, "welcome is banishment; welcome were my death" (II. iii. 14). Her last lines in the play are those of acknowledged guilt. When Sir John Stanley tells her to throw off her sheet in which she had done penance and prepare for her journey into exile, she laments,

> My shame will not be shifted with my sheet:
> No; it will hang upon my richest robes,
> And show itself, attire me how I can.
> Go, lead the way; I long to see my prison.
>
> [II.iv.107-10]

Shakespeare's Eleanor Cobham is not an innocent victim of either the bishop of Winchester or Fortune's wheel, although Beaufort makes advantageous use of her ambition and pride to undermine Gloucester. Shakespeare's suppression of the wax image which the conjurors made of the king is interesting. Lily B. Campbell suggested some years ago that the tragedy of Eleanor Cobham was written by George Ferrers to mirror the historical episode of 1555-1556 in which Princess Elizabeth and Dr. John Dee were accused of attempting to destroy Queen Mary Tudor by conjuration with a wax effigy of that queen. George Ferrers was one of the informers to the Privy Council in the affair.[67] This earlier allegoric use of the tragedy of Eleanor Cobham provides a possible suggestion for Shakespeare's cautious use of the conjuration scene and his failure to mention the effigy. We can assume safely, I believe, that Queen Elizabeth had been sensitized to the subject in any form.

To understand something of how the contemporary Cobhams were involved in the story of Eleanor Cobham, we must turn to the few extant biographical facts concerning George Ferrers.[68] He was a native of Hertfordshire; he attended Cambridge and then became a member of Lincoln's Inn. His services as a page of the chamber to Henry VIII earned him a legacy of one hundred marks, which the king left Ferrers in his will. In 1541 he married Elizabeth, widow and executrix of Humphrey Bourchier, illegitimate son of Lord Berners. This marriage brought him into contact with Henry Bourchier, second earl of Essex of that line.[69] In the same year Anne Bourchier, daughter of the earl of Essex, married William Parr, brother of Catherine Parr, who was Henry VIII's last queen. When Henry Bourchier died without male heirs, William Parr became the earl of Essex through his wife's claim to the inheritance of her father. But in 1547 by an act of Parliament William Parr (now marquis of Northampton) divorced Anne Bourchier on grounds of adultery. Before the legal proceedings were properly completed Parr married Elizabeth Cobham, eldest daughter of George, sixth Lord Cobham. The Privy Council was annoyed with Parr's haste, and Elizabeth Cobham was sent to stay with Catherine Parr until a decision was reached.[70] In 1548 Parr obtained another act of Parliament that made his children by Anne Bourchier illegitimate and denied them their rights of inheritance.[71] In 1552 a third act of Parliament legalized his second marriage to Elizabeth Cobham. This young woman, like her father, was a friend of the duke of Northumberland, and she helped in promoting the marriage of Guilford Dudley and Lady Jane Grey. When Queen Mary Tudor terminated the nine-day reign of Lady Jane, one of her first moves was to insist that Parliament repeal the act of 1552. The position of the marchioness of Northampton was, therefore, a dubious one during the reign of Queen Mary.

George Ferrers was the official master of the King's Pastimes in 1551 and 1552; he directed the pageants and masques presented at court during the Christmas season of those years. He remained in this position for the duration of Edward VI's reign, and Queen Mary retained him as her lord of Misrule. It has been suggested that Ferrers wrote the tragedy of the duke of Gloucester during Edward's reign or shortly thereafter to mirror the fall of Protector Somerset. Somerset's divorce, his second marriage, the treachery practiced against him, and his fall make such an allegory applicable in every sense.[72] It has also been suggested that the unfavorable presentation of Beaufort, bishop of Winchester, was offensive to Stephen Gardiner, bishop of Winchester, and that for this reason the *Mirror for Magistrates* was suppressed in 1555.[73] If these satirical patterns are correctly analyzed, Ferrers was using his tragedies to mirror contemporary political situations, but his presentation of the character of Eleanor Cobham seems to have had a dual purpose. In addition to a political level of meaning, the poem appears to have been created to denigrate Elizabeth Cobham or at least to embarrass the woman who had been the cause of the divorce and humili-

ation of Anne Bourchier, Ferrers's kinswoman. Like Eleanor, Elizabeth Cobham had married a peer whose former
marriage was still a matter of litigation. Contemporary
readers would have had little difficulty in marking the striking resemblances between the two women.

It perhaps should be noted at this point that Elizabeth
Cobham, when she became the marchioness of Northampton, had an acting company at her disposal. Records of
"ye M'ques off northamts players" are scant.[74] We can only
wish we knew what plays they performed and wonder
whether one of those plays was concerned with an heroic
version of the story of the fifteenth-century Eleanor Cobham. Elizabeth Cobham's father George, sixth Lord Cobham, had an acting company of his own in the late 1530s.[75]
But again, we can only guess at the content of the plays
those early actors performed and speculate about a possible prototypal play on Oldcastle, the "good Lord
Cobham."

George Ferrers seems to have retired from the court upon
Queen Elizabeth's accession, but he remained active in
political affairs. In 1567 he served in the office of escheator
for the counties of Essex and Hertford, and in 1571 he was
elected to represent St. Albans in Parliament. Unfortunately, Ferrers seems to have been involved with many
another Englishman in the Ridolfi affair of that year. In his
position as a member of Parliament he was able to relay
information of a political nature to Mary Stuart's ambassador in London, John Leslie, bishop of Ross. It will be
recalled that in October of that fateful year Burghley and
Walsingham broke the Ridolfi plot. In his confession the
bishop of Ross related how George Ferrers had sent him
information concerning the affairs before Parliament, and
the bishop also declared that Ferrers was the author of a
book written in Latin which advocated the queen of Scots's
claims to the English throne.[76] Lord Cobham's mismanage-
ment of Charles Bailley's packet of letters was one element
in the collapse of the Ridolfi plot. I think it is not too fanciful
a conjecture to suggest that this bungling of political matters served to increase the bad feelings between Ferrers
and Lord Cobham. The index of the 1571 edition of the
Mirror for Magistrates contained the two tragedies of
Eleanor Cobham and the duke of Gloucester, but the stories

failed to appear in the text. In 1578 Ferrers was successful in bringing his "royal ballads" out in print, the tragedy of Eleanor appearing in the cancelled gathering. His success may have been due in part to the disfavor Lord Cobham was in at court because of the failure of his mission to the Low Countries with Walsingham.[77] There is no evidence that the members of the Cobham family complained about the publication of these poems. The marchioness of Northampton had died in 1565. Upon her death she was eulogized in verse as a pure and virtuous lady:

> Mee thinkes I see her modeste mood
> Her comlie clothing plainlie clad,
> Her face so sweete her cheere so good,
> The courtlie countenance that she had
> But chefe of all mee thinkes I see,
> Her vertues dentie daie by daie,
>   Homblie kneeling one her knee
>   As her desire was still to praie.[78]

Shakespeare, Drayton, Christopher Middleton and Chettle and Day wrote versions of the story of Eleanor Cobham in the 1590s. Shakespeare's version is an unflattering portrait of that lady. It would be naive to assume that the playwright was motiveless in his dramatization of the story. That it was designed to annoy the Cobham family can be assumed from the playwright's continued satirical attacks upon William Brooke, Lord Cobham, and his son Henry. In the years of 1598–1600 when the dramas of *Henry IV, The Famous Victories of Henry V,* and *Sir John Oldcastle* appeared, the story of Eleanor Cobham reappeared in new attire. Michael Drayton published his version of Lady Eleanor's story in *Englands Heroicall Epistles.* Drayton calls the duchess "a proud, ambitious woman" who designed "by sorcerie to make away the King."[79] This unflattering portrait resembles Ferrers's and Shakespeare's versions of the story. In 1600 Christopher Middleton produced a chivalric defense of the duchess in his *Legend of Humphrey, Duke of Glocester.* His Eleanor is "a vertuous Lady, one of good account." She is the victim of the hatred and bigotry of the court, and she is sentenced to an unwarranted penance.

And after that perform'd, be banished hence,
Into the Isle of Man, and there should live,
A guiltlesse exile, for a small offence
Or none at all: and who so ere did give
That unjust sentence, hath ere this his doome,
Amongst th' condemn'd, where comfort nere shall come.[80]

Busy too with the reformation of Eleanor Cobham's character were Henry Chettle and John Day who wrote *The Blind
Beggar of Bethnal Green* for the Lord Admiral's Men in
1600. In this play we have only the early history of Eleanor
and how she was courted by both the cardinal of Winchester and the duke of Gloucester; her portrait here is one of
sweet virginity. The play was apparently a three-part thing,
but we have extant only this early portion. We can presume
with some degree of certainty that the duchess became an
innocent victim in the later parts of this drama.[81] This series
of plays seem to have been written as a response to Shakespeare's *Henry VI* plays, just as the Drayton-Munday-
Hathaway-Wilson play on Oldcastle's martyrdom appears
to have been written in response to Shakespeare's *Henry IV*
dramas. The subject of the Cobham's history had been
caught up in the literary warfare between the acting companies by the end of the sixteenth century. That such effusive performances as these works—Middleton's *Legend*,
Weever's *Mirror of Martyrs*, Chettle and Day's *Blind
Beggar*, and the *History of Sir John Oldcastle*—salved the
chagrin of the Cobhams is to be doubted. Henry, eighth
Lord Cobham, complained in 1603 that "exceapt ye hous of
Norfolk no one hous of England receved mor disgrace and
Jelozie for many years together in ye tyme past then my
powre house."[82]

The Cobhams were satirized in Elizabethan literature,
and by more than Ferrers's and Shakespeare's pens. Both
Thomas Nashe and Ben Jonson had some galled ink to use
in the same manner.[83] In the 1590s the rivalry between
literary patrons and dramatic companies provided fuel and
flame for the continuation of this battle of innuendo, allusion, and insult. But the pattern for this type of dramatic
satire was set by the older play *The Famous Victories of
Henry V*, in which Oldcastle strode the stage as "Jockey."
There is historical evidence to explain in part the reason
why.

CHAPTER SIX

The Famous Victories of Henry V

WE ARE NOT CERTAIN WHAT PROMPTED THOMAS
Creede, the pirating printer, to bring out an old play, *The
Famous Victories of Henry V,* in 1598. Greed probably
would be a fair guess, for Creede was a promoter. He did
more than his share of poaching upon Shakespeare's plays
throughout this period. We know, however, that this older
play belonged to Creede; he had entered it with the stationers in May 1594. It is possible, since he appears to have
been a shrewd businessman as well as an unscrupulous
one, that he did not foresee a profitable sale for the play
until public curiosity was aroused in 1597-1598 by the Lord
Chamberlain's Men, who were producing, we think, Shakespeare's *1 Henry IV* at the time. Whatever his motive, he
printed *The Famous Victories* in 1598, and on the title page
he added, "As it was plaide by the Queenes Maiesties Players." This information, plus the fact that the anonymous
author of the drama used the 1580 edition of John Stow's
Chronicles as one of his sources, helps to set the *termini a
quo* and *ad quem* for the composition of *The Famous Victories.* It would appear to be a play of the 1580s. Both style
and structure indicate as well that the provenance of the
play lies in that penultimate decade.

The similarities of content between this older drama and
Shakespeare's second tetralogy have provoked a broad
variety of responses from responsible critics. T. W. Baldwin, using the casting pattern of the Queen's Company, has
suggested that the play was written between 1583, when
that acting company was organized, and 1586.[1] B. M.
Ward, utilizing topical references and ignoring the source

166

problem, has suggested that the play had its origin in some court entertainment given by the Earl of Oxford's Players about 1574.[2] A. E. Morgan has suggested that the play was originally written in verse, then was passed to the Lord Admiral's Men, who revised the play as their production of *Henry V* in 1595-1596.[3] Sir Edmund K. Chambers suggested that the play was in all probability a two-part drama and that it was issued about 1594 when it became the source used by Shakespeare for his *Henry IV* and *Henry V* plays. Chambers also suggested that perhaps the play was used independently by a writer for the Admiral's Men.[4] C. A. Greer suggested that since there is no great similarity in phraseology between Shakespeare's plays and *The Famous Victories,* there must have been an older play that served as a common source for Shakespeare and the author of *The Famous Victories.*[5] And recently S. M. Pitcher, reading the older play from another point of view, has pointed to a number of similarities in phraseology which lead him to conclude that the play was a product of the Queen's Company in 1587.[6] Much of this criticism is saltatory, but necessarily so. The evidence for such speculation is fragile; however, we must utilize it or do without facts at all.

We know that the Queen's Company of players originated in 1583. John Stow, who seems to have admired the competent actors, mentions the formation of that group at the request of Queen Elizabeth and continues by commenting upon two especially talented actors who had become popular public figures through their art.

> Comedians and stage-players of former time were very poore and ignorant in respect of these of this time, but being nowe growne very skilfull and exquisite actors for all matters, they were entertained into the service of divers great Lords, out of which companies there were xii of the best chosen, and at the request of Sir Francis Walsingham, they were allowed wages and liveries as groomes of the chamber: and untill this yeere, 1583, the Queene hadde no players. . . . Amongst these xii players were two rare men, viz., Thomas Wilson for a quicke delicate refined extemporall witte, and Richard Tarleton for a wondrous plentifull pleasant extemporall wit, hee was the wonder of his time.[7]

Most critics accept the suggestion that Richard Tarlton played the role of the clown Derick in *The Famous Vic-*

tories. Tarlton's witty extemporizing in the scene following the slapping incident (in which Prince Hal strikes the chief justice) has survived in a jest book of the period. The writer describes how William Knell, another of the actors, struck Tarlton a ringing blow on the ear.

> At the Bull at Bishops-gate was a play of Henry the fift, wherein the judge was to take a box on the eare; and because he was absent that should take the blow, Tarlton himselfe, ever forward to please, tooke upon him to play the same judge, besides his owne part of the clowne: . . . And Knel then playing Henry the fift, hit Tarlton a sound boxe indeed, which made the people laugh the more because it was he, but anon the judge goes in, and immediately Tarlton in his clownes cloathes comes out, and askes the actors what newes: O saith one, hadst thou been here, thou shouldest have seene Prince Henry hit the judge a terrible box on the eare: What, man, said Tarlton, strike a judge? It is true, yfaith, said the other. No other like, said Tarlton, and it could not be but terrible to the judge, when the report so terrifies me, that me thinkes the blow remaines still on my cheeke, that it burnes againe. The people laught at this mightily: and to this day I have heard it commended for rare; but no marvell, for he had many of these.[8]

A complaint has been made that Tarlton could not appear as clown and judge at the same time in *The Famous Victories* because both characters are required on stage together. This complaint has led to the suggestion that another play was produced on the subject of young Prince Hal in the 1580s,[9] but it would have been a relatively simple matter for professional actors to delete lines 451–52 and 456–58 in the text as a matter of expediency, thus providing for a dual role that Tarlton could have managed with a quick costume-change.[10] The dramatic action described in the jest book parallels the scene from *The Famous Victories* so closely that the probability of the Queen's Company being involved in a production of that play during the 1587–1588 winter season is great. This season is the logical *terminus ad quem* because both William Knell and Richard Tarlton were dead before September 1588.[11]

It would seem then that *The Famous Victories* was written between 1583, when the Queen's Company was formed, and 1587, when it was described by the jest-book author. During this period there were serious problems and dis-

putes among the citizens of the Blackfriars precinct over the
occupancy of the large Parliament chamber in the friary
that was being used for practice rooms and for occasional
preview productions of plays which the boys' companies
were preparing for court entertainment. Both the earl of
Oxford and William Brooke, Lord Cobham, were indirectly
involved in these disputes. Out of these disruptions in
Blackfriars arise plausible explanations for the exaggerated
role of the historical earl of Oxford in *The Famous Victories*
and for the belittling role of Jockey or Sir John Oldcastle
in the same play.

The exaggerated role created by the author of *The
Famous Victories* for the historical earl of Oxford at the
Battle of Agincourt is fabricated from almost pure air.[12]
This aggrandizement of particular historical figures is an
early example of the montage technique, but in this instance the author does not conflate several historical
events or characters; rather he simply spins fiction to glorify his subject. The historical earl of Oxford was a child or
youth when the Battle of Agincourt was fought, but Hall
mentions in a list of names of noblemen who were camped
nearby the king, "the earles Marshal, Oxforde, Suffolk, War-
wicke and the other lordes." And Holinshed followed Hall's
account of the battle; he too mentions Oxford, but only in a
listing. Neither chronicler gives the earl of Oxford credit in
the warfare. The author of *The Famous Victories,* however,
makes Oxford the rare right hand of the king. He replaces
the duke of Exeter as the principal adviser in the strategems
of war, and his role in the battle is splendid. It is he who
supervises the palisade of stakes that stopped the French
horsemen and ultimately gave the victory to Henry's forces.
Not one of his heroic actions comes from the chronicle
sources. And certainly there were no heroic actions of this
order in the life of Edward de Vere, the Elizabethan earl of
Oxford, that could have inspired the montage technique in
the drama. In the 1570s the seventeenth earl of Oxford had
associated himself with the young Catholic rebels, Charles
Arundel, Francis Southwell, and Lord Surrey, but in 1581
Oxford made a violent break with his friends and accused
them of a conspiracy against the crown. Oxford himself was
arrested and placed in the Tower; finally, he was charged
with attempting to murder his former associates and also

with plotting to do away with Leicester, Walsingham, Sidney, Raleigh, and Sir Henry Knyvet. In addition, he was accused of conducting treasonable correspondence with the Spanish ambassador as well as with the English fugitives in Rome. The accusations against Oxford include a reference to his "perjury, mercenary habits, butcherly bloodiness, dangerous practices, dishonesty, unnatural propensities, drunkenness, and undutiful dealings toward the queen."[13] With accusations of this kind, Oxford needed more than a pinch of civet to sweeten his reputation. The playwright who wrote *The Famous Victories* obviously intended his play to compliment the contemporary earl. Even Oxford's brother-in-law receives aggrandizement through the enlargement of the description of Lord Willoughby's role at Agincourt. There was, however, recent historical activity to warrant the montage technique at this point.

The earl of Oxford's brother-in-law, Peregrin Bertie, Lord Willoughby d'Eresby, remained in the Low Countries after Oxford returned home in the fall of 1585. Oxford had accomplished little on his mission, and he had been replaced by the earl of Leicester in December of that year. Leicester appointed Lord Willoughby governor of Bergen-op-Zoom in May 1586. No sooner had he taken his new station than he and his forces were engaged in combat with the enemy. Willoughby's victory earned him praise from his fellow soldiers and commendation from Leicester. In a letter to the queen Leicester described the heroic actions of the new governor:

> I have received even now word from my Lord Willoughby, who writes to me that upon Tuesday, hearing of a great convoy going to Antwerp of four hundred and fifty waggons, he went himself with two hundred horse and four hundred footmen and met with them, being a thousand footmen, and set upon them, slew three hundred, took eighty prisoners and destroyed all their waggons, saving twenty-seven he carried away for his soldiers' relief. This is a notable piece of service, and puts Antwerp in a danger of present revolt, and it is thought it will forthwith send to me and submit themselves, which I pray God grant.[14]

These heroic actions in the Low Countries may possibly have inspired the anonymous author of *The Famous Victories* to amplify the roles of Lord Willoughby and the earl of Oxford in the play. In the process he also added the names of other noblemen of the Elizabethan period, names which did not occur in his sources. Thus the earls of Derby, Kent, Effingham, Huntingdon, and Northumberland are mentioned in the drama (lines 1525-28, 1534-37).[15] But the greatest glorification goes to the unhistorical character of the earl of Oxford. The natural assumption from this fact is that the writer of the play was one of the group of players and directors associated with the Elizabethan earl of Oxford after 1580 when he began to patronize both adult and youth companies.[16] Among those professional dramatists were William Hunnis, Henry Evans, and John Lyly; these men were at the center of the whirl of emotional friction that occurred in Blackfriars precinct when the acting companies invaded the quiet and aristocratic Liberty.

The tensions began in the Blackfriars community in 1576 when the large Parliament chamber in the old friary once more was available for lease. From 1571 to 1576 William Brooke, Lord Cobham, held the lease on the old Parliament hall, which had been temporarily divided into six rooms. His father George, sixth Lord Cobham, had been an inhabitant of Blackfriars from the early years of Henry VIII's reign when his family had moved from Cobham Inn in Eastcheap to the buildings on the west side of Water Lane.[17] In April 1536 Lord Cobham leased from the crown the large building that had been the porter's lodge and had served as a guest house to accomodate important foreign visitors during Henry VIII's reign. This building lay to the north of the old Parliament chamber and was joined to it by the pantry and buttery, which had served the friars as a refectory.[18] In 1546 Lord Cobham purchased the building from the king.[19] And in April of 1554 Cobham added to his holdings in the old friary. He paid Sir Thomas Cawarden, the master of the Revels, sixty pounds "of good and Lawfull monye of Englond," plus his title to the buildings on the west side of Water Lane, for the fifty-two by twenty-seven-foot extension lying to the south of his rooms.[20] This sale included the "neythere rome," the lower space, some forty-seven by twenty-one feet in dimension. In the 1555-1556 survey of the precinct, Lord Cobham's house is noted as a "howse and gardens w' many fayer greate Edifices & c[er]-ten londs & teneme[n]tes."[21] The nobleman had good cause to be proud of his property in the exclusive Blackfriars precinct.

When the sixth Lord Cobham died in 1558, his eldest son and heir became the owner of this property. The great hall to the south of the Cobham rooms had served Parliament as a convenient meeting place even in the reign of Henry VIII, but it housed the Office of the Revels in the reign of Edward VI; it had also been used for private lodgings, first by Sir John Cheke and later by Sir Henry Neville. In 1571 William Brooke, seventh Lord Cobham, leased the great hall from its owner, Sir William More. The contract contained a provision for Cobham "to breke the walles w'in the p[re]misses aboue letten."[22] (We do not know to what use the new leasee put this additional space abutting his house on the south.) For almost six years he used the whole length of the upper floor of the western range of buildings in the old friary, a grand space some 231 feet in length and 46 feet in its widest areas. He also used the rooms on the lower floor at the north end of the building.

In the early years of Elizabeth's reign Lord Cobham maintained an acting company of his own. A few records of this dramatic troupe remain; in these fragmentary documents the group is called either "the lorde of Cobhames players" or "my Lord Wardens plaiores." It had become traditional in Henry VIII's reign for the lord warden of the Cinque Ports to maintain a company of entertainers, and when the seventh Lord Cobham was appointed to the post in December of 1558, he apparently sponsored a group which performed in Faversham and Lydd (1558-59) as the "lorde wardens mynstrelles."[23] These could have been Sir Thomas Cheyney's servants, or perhaps they were members of the company that the elder Lord Cobham had patronized much earlier. The records are too fragmentary for complete documentation. We know that in 1563-1564 the company went on tour as far as Gloucester; the mayor's records for that year list a payment of five shillings for "the lorde of Cobhames players."[24] In January of 1570 or thereabout, the company played in Dover for the sum of eleven shillings, and on 3 February the "lorde wardens playeres" received "a rewarde" of ten shillings, eight pence in New Romney.[25] In July of 1570 they performed in Bristol "at the commd'mt of m' mayer & the alderemen" and were paid ten shillings.[26] In the spring of 1571 the Lord Warden's Players performed again in Canterbury for ten shillings.[27] Unfortunately, further records of this company have not been found. What happened to the troupe? We do know that Lord Cobham's social stature and eminence increased after 1572. Perhaps his acting company remained intact and continued to be a part of his growing household, but this is speculation. We also lack evidence to suggest the composition of the group or the plays they performed. Whether the entertainment they provided was limited to music, juggling, and brief interludes, or they were professional in the sense of being capable of producing a full dramatic production is, alas, unknown. One would like to speculate that in the grand Blackfriars home of Lord Cobham (a home which included the great chamber where Sir John Oldcastle was condemned to death) the acting company performed a tragedy starring the famous martyr of Henry V's reign, but this would be imagination at play in a leisure hour. There is no record to tie such fancy to the Elizabethan scene. One thing is certain, however, William Brooke, Lord Cobham, was no Puritanical advocate of the antitheater faction. He obviously respected the pleasure and power of patronizing an acting company. His own family had developed a tradition over many years, it would seem, of keeping and using a troupe of its own.

In the summer of 1576 Sir William More was faced with a delicate problem. He received two letters in August, one from Sir Henry Neville, who had been his former tenant in the great chamber, and one from Richard Farrant, master of the Children of Windsor, who was closely associated with the royal entertainment for the queen. Neville recommended Farrant in his letter, assuring More that "no man shalbe redyer to requit yor fryndship then he, I dare answer for hym."[28] Farrant's letter contained an inquiry about the availability of the great chamber and an offer to lease it. Neither letter makes clear whether Lord Cobham had given up his lease on the Parliament hall or whether More was quietly searching for a more profitable tenant. The lease that Farrant signed in December specified that he should have the "sixe vpper Chambers loftes lodgynges or Romes" which "were latelye amongest other in the tenure & occupacion of the right honorable S' Willyam Brok Knyght lorde

Cobham."[29] Farrant's lease was for an annual rent of fourteen pounds. Sir Henry Neville on the other hand had
leased approximately the same space for six pounds per
annum. Cobham seems to have had the best bargain of the
lot, for he had the great hall for four pounds yearly rent.[30]
More's profit in signing the lease to Farrant was, therefore,
a considerable one.

Richard Farrant and his boys' company apparently
moved into their new quarters in the fall of 1576, before their
lease was signed. It was understood that he would train the
boys under his command for their performances at court,
but Farrant, in need of extra financial resources, began to
use the Blackfriars rooms as a theater. More complained
later that "fferrant p[re]tended vnto me to vse the howse
onlie for the teachinge of the children of the Chappell but
made it a Continuall howse for plays to the offence of the
p[re]cincte." In addition, More continued, Farrant had
"pulled downe p[ar]ticons to make that place apte for that
purpose."[31] Farrant had specified in his contract that he
wished to remove one of the partitions remaining in the
chamber; however, in the litigation which followed, after
everyone concerned in the venture had grown unhappy
with its results, More complained that Farrant had removed
far more than had been contracted in the lease. Farrant's
wife, Anne, complained after her husband's death that he
had "greately indepte[d]" himself "to make it comodius for
his purpose" and that only with the queen's gracious bounty
had that debt been discharged. If Anne Farrant's statement
is correct, Queen Elizabeth was aware of the proceedings in
Blackfriars and apparently was encouraging Farrant in his
activities.[32] Farrant died in 1580, leaving his widow to
struggle with the complex arrangements. He left her the
lease in his will, but the contract with More contained a
clause prohibiting any sublease. Through the efforts of the
earl of Leicester, More was brought to consent to the sublease that Anne Farrant arranged with William Hunnis,
master of the Children of the Chapel Royal, and with his
assistant, John Newman. The new contract was to her advantage in that she was to collect twenty nobles above the
rent she had to pay More for the building.[33] Legally, things
were becoming snarled for all concerned. Hunnis
apparently continued the public performances, using both

boys' companies, but when Sir William More began to make efforts to reclaim his property, Hunnis signed his lease over to Henry Evans, the Welsh scrivener, who was assisting in training the children. Evans continued the public performances "and reaped farr greater profytt then the saide yerely rente amounteth vnto," claimed Mistress Farrant.[34]

By 1583 all parties concerned in the proceedings were eager to seek equity and justice in the law courts. More signed a new lease (perhaps fictitious) to one Thomas Smalpeece of Guildford, thus forcing Evans into court. Anne Farrant filed charges against Hunnis and Newman. In her long petition to the Court of Requests she complained that the masters of the children had failed again and again to pay their rent on time, so that she had been forced into desperate measures on several occasions. She described how in one such emergency she had been driven to make "humble and pittifull suite to the righte honourable Lord Cobham to obteyne such fauo' and helpe of his good Lordshipp" that she might pay her rent[35]—Cobham seems to have been drawn into the friction by assisting the beleaguered Anne Farrant. The boys, who lived in the south part of the space Farrant and Hunnis had rented, were doubtless annoying; the youthful mischief and exuberance of extroverted boys seems to have irritated the long-term residents of the Blackfriars precinct. More said the boys were both noisy and destructive. Cobham complained that the boys climbed out upon the roof and bored holes in the tiles with "bodkins."[36] Quarreling also erupted over the water conduit, the cocks, and the mutual sharing of the water supply. Lord Hunsdon complained later after he had rented the rooms that the water had been diverted from the premises to serve Lord Cobham's house.[37] It would seem that Cobham had tried to dry up the boys in one way or another.

How long the friction continued we can only guess. Evans, with some knowledge of law derived from his earlier activities as a scrivener, was able to delay the court hearings. In June of 1583 or shortly thereafter Evans sold the lease of the great chamber to the earl of Oxford who in turn gave it to John Lyly. Sir William More complained later in his petition that "Imediately after she [Anne Farrant] lett the howse to one Hvnnis & afterwarde to one Ne[w-man] or Sutton as farre as I remember & then to Evans whoe sould his in[terest] to the Erle of Oxforde whoe gave his interest to Lyllie & the t[itle thus] was posted over from one to another from me Contrarie to the said [Con]dic[ion]."[38] It should be noted at this point that the boys' companies were amalgamated and combined during this period of transition when their masters were being changed frequently. Farrant had trained the Children of Windsor, but when Hunnis took over the Blackfriars lease the boys are called the Children of the Chapel Royal. Later with Evans and Lyly supervising the training of the youths they are presented at court sometimes as "the Children of Therle of Oxford."[39] We also know that Lyly was writing for the combined chapel children and the Paul's boys, so that it would seem that "the Children of Therle of Oxford" was the title used in the Revels' records for payment to Evans and Lyly. The Windsor children disappear during this period. The earl of Oxford also was sponsoring an adult company which was on tour frequently in the provinces throughout the 1580s. His involvement with the drama at this time was complex. That he attempted to protect both Lyly and Evans by purchasing the lease of the Blackfriars rooms seems evident. But even his influence and actions ultimately failed. In Easter term of 1584 Sir William More received a favorable judgment in the courts, and he proceeded with the sheriff's assistance to take possession of his long-sought property.[40] At the last moment, however, Lyly sold the lease of part of the space in Blackfriars to Lord Hunsdon, who maintained a large home just south of the old Parliament chamber. Two years later Hunsdon was quarrelling with More over the bad faith involved in the leases that More would not extend.[41]

It is out of this bickering, ill feeling, and "vnfrendly and harde dealings" that the topical references in *The Famous Victories* had their beginnings, I believe. The glorification of the earl of Oxford's ancestor is a flagrant but witty violation of history. In a presentation at court, amusement must surely have been evoked by such misrepresentation. We know that *The Famous Victories* was presented by the Queen's Company in the 1580s. If we assume that the play was written by one of Oxford's men, it remains to be suggested how the play moved from the Evans-Lyly group to the Queen's Players.

In 1586 the earl of Oxford was the recipient of a one-thousand-pound annuity from his royal mistress. Such a large grant to an individual in her court was an unusual gesture on the part of the queen. B. M. Ward, Oxford's modern biographer, has suggested that Oxford received the money for use in improving the activities of the Office of the Revels and the general entertainment at court.[42] If this suggestion is correct, the earl of Oxford was involved in supervising all the plays given at court during this period, and this perhaps will explain how *The Famous Victories* was performed in 1587 or thereabout by Tarlton and the Queen's Players.

Who among the Oxford group of dramatists could have written *The Famous Victories?* Certainly not John Lyly. His plays are of a different cut. Both the language and the structure of Lyly's dramas preclude such a suggestion. It has been theorized that the earl himself wrote the play,[43] and this is an attractive idea. Edward de Vere was an arrogant, aggressive, and uninhibited young man. In later years he was said to have written comedies, and certainly we know that his interest in the newly developing English drama was keen and that he was generous in patronizing the acting companies, both adult and boys. But among the Oxford group of dramatists, I think the most probable candidate for the authorship of *The Famous Victories* is Henry Evans, the Welsh scrivener. My speculation is based upon the very bold use of Hugh Evans and the children a dozen years later in *The Merry Wives of Windsor*. But before we proceed with this theory, Shakespeare's name should be eliminated from the line-up of possible candidates for authorship of the old play.

The latest editor of *The Famous Victories* has suggested that it is "reasonably presumptive" that Shakespeare wrote the old play in his earliest attempts at the craft of playwriting.[44] Pitcher bases his theory upon the similarities between the plot of the older drama and the content of Shakespeare's *Henry IV* and *Henry V* plays. But similarities in the use of source materials, particularly in the Elizabethan period, are not weighty enough for authorial conjecture. Shakespeare's dramas are characterized by a complex management of thematic statement; the magnitude of *ethos* and *dianoia* in each of the major characters is created by a subtle relationship between language, imagery, symbolism, and thematic ideas. This wealth of artistic accomplishment was a product of Shakespeare's genius, and it is his indelible signature in a work of art. *The Famous Victories* is barren of such artistic qualities.[45] We do not know where Shakespeare was in the mid-1580s or what he was doing, but it is safe to say that he was not writing *The Famous Victories of Henry V.*

Henry Evans and John Lyly presented their boys at court a number of times in 1583–1584, and in April of 1585 we know that Evans received over six pounds for a performance of Oxford's boys before the queen.[46] We wish for more information about these activities, but we wish in vain. We do not know the date of the court performance of Lyly's *Endymion*, nor do we know who played the role of Sir Tophas in that play. The role was a plum, from any comic actor's point of view. The fat knight is the first of the great presentations in English drama of the stock character of the *miles gloriosus* or braggart soldier that had been handed down the centuries from Roman comedy. Sir Tophas is vain, comic, outlandishly brazen, and equally foolish; moreover, he is delightfully funny as the butt of all the jokes of the young pages or boys in the play. The climax scene for Sir Tophas is the one in which the boys dance around his sleeping figure, poking at his large bulk and singing:

> Holla, Holla in his eare.
> The Witch sure thrust her fingers there.
> Crampe him, or wring the Foole by th' Nose,
> Or clap some burning flax to his toes.
> What Musique's best to wake him?
> Baw wow, let Ban dogs shake him,
> Let Adders hisse in's eare
> Else Eare-wigs wiggle there.
> No, let him batten; when his tongue
> Once goes, a Cat is not worse strung.
> But if he ope nor mouth, nor eies,
> He may in time sleepe himselfe wise.
>   [III.iii.116–27]

Earlier in the play the fat knight declares war on the boys, threatening to destroy them when they tease and mock him.

In this study we are of course taking a total view of the character of Sir John Falstaff. It is important to recognize that Lyly's Sir Tophas lies in the immediate background of Shakespeare's great Sir Jack. In the scene in *Endymion* in which the boys dance around the prone figure of Lyly's *miles gloriosus* we have an archetypal image which is repeated when Evans and the boys dance about Falstaff's prone figure in *The Merry Wives*. Once the relationship is established between these two scenes, it becomes relatively easy to address Lyly's dramatic situation and place it within the context of the bickerings within the Blackfriars precinct in the mid-1580s.

We have established, I think, that Falstaff is a satiric figure created to lampoon Sir William Brooke, Lord Cobham. I believe that Lyly started this line of satire in the 1580s with the creation of Sir Tophas and the boys who caricature the situation in the large Blackfriars building in which Lord Cobham's hostility had annoyed the masters and their charges; or perhaps the reverse was true, and the hostility of the boys irritated Lord Cobham. I would like to think that the actors were witty enough to allow Henry Evans to play the role of Sir Tophas. At court the performance of the comic scenes in *Endymion* would have been intensified if the master of the boys played the role in which the youths could tickle and torment him. We have no way of knowing whether Evans had a talent for mimicry. I suspect that he did and that he used it in voice and gesture to present Lord Cobham in a comic fashion on the stage. This is speculation, of course. We do know for certain, however, that Lord Cobham was soon satirized through the character of Sir John Oldcastle in *The Famous Victories*. I believe that this play followed *Endymion* and that Henry Evans wrote it. It was first performed, I would suggest, by Evans's boys, or, as they are listed in the Revels' records, "Oxenford his boyes." In the play Sir John Oldcastle carouses with the riotous crew that surrounds the young prince. He is called Jockey by his colleagues in crime, and humorously he rides a bay horse named "Hobbie." We know that he is not an innocent bystander to the mischief, for in the robberies which the comic characters have been conducting, Oldcastle has taken a sizable loot of one-hundred pounds. Soon afterwards he willingly sallies off toward the old tavern in Eastcheap to celebrate the success of the adventures with the prince, Ned, and Tom. Furthermore, he apparently participates in the hurtling at the tavern described by the boy as "a bloody fray." The fact should not be overlooked that Oldcastle definitely is presented in the play as one of the major dissolute characters. When the news comes of King Henry IV's death, Oldcastle rejoices, "Dead, then gogs blood, we shall be all kings" (sig. D₁). He is therefore ill-prepared for the rejection that follows the coronation of Prince Hal. When the new king commands the unruly knights to change their ways or else be made to reform, Oldcastle responds, "Gogs wounds how like you this? Sownds tis not so sweete as Musicke" (sig. D₂). That is his last line.

The Oldcastle role is not a major one in the drama, but it is an important one from the point of view of the satire. It seems to have been intentionally created to present a ludicrous figure of the famous Lollard ancestor of William Brooke, Lord Cobham. Against the explicit aggrandizement of the ancestral earl of Oxford, the contrasting denigration of the ancestral Lord Cobham stands out like a sore thumb. The satire appears to have originated with the dramatists patronized by the Elizabethan earl of Oxford. A dozen years later Evans and the boys apologize for tormenting Oldcastle-Falstaff-Cobham in *The Merry Wives of Windsor*. Evans assures Falstaff that the boys are not fairies and that they cannot harm him. Looking backward from Shakespeare's scene, it would appear that Evans was responsible for the first dramatic lampooning of the Lollard martyr in *The Famous Victories of Henry V*.

In addition to the tensions created by the disagreements within the Blackfriars precinct, there were larger tensions created by the political factiousness of the period. The earl of Oxford was a kinsman of Thomas Howard, fourth duke of Norfolk. He was greatly upset when Norfolk was placed in the Tower, and in 1571 rumors floated abroad that the young Oxford was ready to storm the Tower to release the duke from imprisonment.[47] Lord Cobham's bungling in the management of Ridolfi's packet containing the letters to Norfolk and the queen of Scots was one important factor in Norfolk's downfall. We know of Oxford's violent reaction to the execution of the duke. And it was rumored that the

serious marital problems that arose between Oxford and his
new wife, Anne Cecil, were the result of Oxford's anger
over the fact that Lord Burghley had refused to save the
duke of Norfolk's life. A total rift developed between Oxford and the Cecil circle, which of course included Lord
Cobham. In 1585 Cobham was installed as a knight of the
Garter, and in the fall of that year the earl of Oxford
returned from the Low Countries. His military exploits had
not been great, but, in contrast to his earlier activities, he at
least had been trying to serve his queen and his country.
There were vacancies in the Privy Council, and those positions were among the most powerful posts in the political
hierarchy surrounding the queen. Oxford, with his new-
found ambition, wanted the appointment to one of the
vacancies. But so did Lord Cobham. In the spring of 1586
the three vacancies in the Council were filled. Lord Buckhurst and John Whitgift, archbishop of Canterbury, were
two of the appointees, and the third was Lord Cobham.
Cobham's star was rising, and there were many in England
who resented his rewards and successes, particularly since
he merited nothing from their point of view. The queen, in
what was to become a traditional pattern of behavior with
her, apparently chose to console Oxford with the annuity of
one thousand pounds and control over the entertainments
at court. Oxford used his new power to his best advantage,
it would seem, and Lord Cobham was soon derided through
the attack upon his famous ancestor. The rejection scene in
The Famous Victories in which Oldcastle, Ned, and Tom
are charged to reform or be sent into exile appears to have a
salient message buried just under the surface of the text.
The removal of unworthy councillors is the duty of the ideal
king, the play asserts. And there is no doubt about who
those unworthy councillors were in the court of Queen
Elizabeth.

Such a usage of the topical in drama is propagandistic.
The twentieth-century reader may be both disillusioned and
repelled at the mundane content and meaning, but it is
there. A decade later Shakespeare was to resort to the same
technique in very similar circumstances. His victim was to
be the same family, the lords of Cobham.

The second figure of interest within this context of satire
is that of the clown Dericke. This comic figure was devel-

oped out of an embroilment that was even more heated than the one in the Blackfriars precinct, and it lasted many years longer. The unhappy financial circumstances within the College of Arms, plus the volatile natures of the Tudor heralds made that supposedly dignified office a seedbed of contention, physical violence, and acrimony. In this present study the most important figure within the herald's office at that time was William Dethicke, Garter king of arms, and certainly Dethicke would have agreed with that estimation of his worth. He was both arrogant and paranoid, and there seems to have been sufficient hostility within the College to activate all of Dethicke's antisocial traits in the 1580s and 1590s. His family name had been Dericke, but that name had been changed in the mid-sixteenth century to hide the base Dutch origins of the distinguished Garter kings of arms. The most acrimonious opponent of William Dethicke in the office of the heralds was Ralph Brooke, Rougecross pursuivant, who became York herald in 1593 and who gave both Camden and Dethicke trouble over the issuance of John Shakespeare's coat of arms. Ralph Brooke had also falsified his family line to make himself a distant relative of William Brooke, Lord Cobham. Many vitriolic charges were brought by Dethicke and Brooke against each other in the last two decades of the sixteenth century, and this unruly state of affairs continued into the reign of King James. Since it seems probable that Shakespeare's character of the host in *The Merry Wives* was derived from the comic satire inherent in the role of the clown Dericke in *The Famous Victories*, we should examine carefully the role of that clown and the character of William Dethicke, Garter king of arms.

In *The Famous Victories* Dericke appears first on stage shouting, "Whoa! whoa!" He has lost his horse to the thief Gadshill (whom he recognizes later). Robin Pewterer and John Cobbler confront him in amazement, and Robin evidently grapples with the excited Dericke. In addition to acting in a frantic passion, Dericke is wearing a strange silk garment. The low-lifers do not recognize its significance, for Robin exclaims, "Why, I see thou art a plain clown." And Dericke derides their ignorance heatedly: "Am I a clown? Zounds, masters, do clowns go in silk apparel? I am sure all we gentlemen-clowns in Kent scant go so well.

Zounds! you know clowns very well!" We cannot tell at this point what kind of "silk apparel" Dericke is wearing, but I would suggest that he is cloaked in the herald's colorful tabard. Such a garment was distinctive, and if the satire which I think is inherent in the role is accurately assessed, such costuming would have revealed the meaning of the lampoon even to the pitlings.

As the comedy unfolds, both John Cobbler and Dericke go to France, where neither is competent in speaking the language, so that the playwright can exploit some simple punning in the linguistic breach. Dericke, playing the clown, avoids capture by the French soldier, and indeed, avoids all the warfare. Instead he collects shoes from the fallen soldiers as his fair booty. In the final comic scenes Dericke plans a speedy return to England by marching in front of the duke of York's funeral cortege like a pursuivant or herald.

Even such a skimpy summary of the comic scenes reveals that many of the ideas in this old play were adapted by Shakespeare in the second Henriad group of dramas. The later exploits of Falstaff and his comic crew absorb much from the older play, but Shakespeare reasserts ideas and actions and divides and redistributes comic roles, so that in the *Henry IV* plays Falstaff takes over not only the character of Oldcastle in *The Famous Victories* but also the roles of Dericke and John Cobbler as well. The character of Dericke does not reappear in Shakespeare's plays as an entity until the host walks on stage in *The Merry Wives* as a much more genial character who is given humorous but good-natured lines of raillery. The Garter context for *The Merry Wives* makes explication of some of the host's lines relatively simple, but to understand the pointed satire in the role of Dericke in *The Famous Victories* the reader must know as much as possible of William Dethicke in the early and middle years of his career in the heralds' office.

Sir William Dethicke (who was knighted in 1603 when King James arrived in London) appears to have come from Dutch stock who migrated to England early in the reign of Henry VIII. His grandfather was Robert Dericke, a yeoman armorer who worked as a craftsman for ten pence a day. But Robert's three sons did better for themselves. In 1543 Gilbert Dericke, the youngest son, procured an act of Parliament that made him and his brothers English citizens. In the papers of denization Gilbert said that his wife was the daughter of one Leonard, a Dutch shoemaker who lived at the sign of the Red Cock in St. Martin's Lane.[48] Gilbert rose through the ranks in the heralds' office from Rougecross pursuivant to Richmond herald, then to Garter king of arms. In the records of the day his name is spelled either "Deryke," "Diricke," "Dericke," "Dyriche," or "Diryk."[49] With his rise to prominence Gilbert faced a problem with the rules of the heralds' office. The traditional regulations stipulated that none should be admitted into the offices of the College without "a Purity of Extraction, a Competency of Age, a previous Examination of their Abilities, and a Certificate of their Moralities and Conversations."[50] The problem of "Purity of Extraction" was easily surmounted by a professional genealogist such as Gilbert, and soon the Dericke name was being spelled Dethicke. The Garter king now insisted that he was descended from the ancient English family seated at Dethicke Hall in Derbyshire and that his father had served as steward to Edmond, earl of Suffolk.[51] Dethicke took for his coat of arms argent, a fesse vairy of or and gules, between three water-bougets, sable.[52] Henry VIII rewarded his services with a grant of the mansion and land at Popular in the parish of Stepney, which became the home of the Dethickes for two hundred years. Gilbert remained in his post as Garter king of arms, supervising the advancement of his two sons in the College, until the fall of 1584 when he died at the age of eighty-one. Nicholas Dethicke rose to become Windsor herald, and William Dethicke replaced his father as Garter king. But that replacement was delayed by a vigorous resistance to Dethicke's advancement on the part of the other heralds in the College.

In the spring of 1584 Gilbert Dethicke had carried the news of their election to the Garter to Lord Cobham, Lord Scroop, and the earl of Rutland, but he died in October of that year. The formal initiation of the new K.G.s in April of 1585 was also scheduled to include the installation of the new Garter king. But Somerset, Clarenceaux, and Norroy heralds created "a great Outcry" and working "with distinguishing Eagerness and Animosity," charged that

Dethicke had falsified his charter and privileges, thereby usurping power from the other officers.[53]

William Dethicke was not sworn in as Garter king at the installation held on 21 April 1585, and his patent and charter were examined for corrupt passages. At the Garter ceremonies in 1586 Dethicke presided as Garter king on the command of the queen, but he was never formally installed in the office, an omission his enemies used against him the rest of his life. All of this turmoil was occurring when the author of *The Famous Victories* was writing his satiric scenes with Dericke the silk-draped clown who draws his dagger upon the slightest provocation and who would usurp the function of the herald in the funeral cortege of a nobleman.

We should look even closer at the personality of William Dethicke, Garter king. In addition to being called a man of courage and firmness, William Dethicke has been termed "a Gentleman of an haughty warm Spirit . . . which was too apt to be suddenly enflamed."[54] And it is true. Once he had secured his position as York herald in 1569 and had begun to exercise the rights and privileges of his office, he seems to have used little discretion and no discipline over his violent temper, a negligence which endangered his life a number of times. Even the members of his own family felt the burden of his wrath. He was accused of striking his father with his fist and of wounding his brother with his dagger in Windsor Castle. To his fellow heralds he was a tyrant (they insisted): "Some he sued, some he Charged with Felony, some he Beate, others he reviled, and all he wronged."[55] His enemies insisted that his "Assaults and Batteries were too longe to write," but they listed them anyway. He appears to have struck the minister at Sir Henry Sidney's funeral at Penshurst, and at the countess of Sussex's funeral in Westminster Abbey he stabbed two persons with his dagger, one man named Brown and another, the brother-in-law of Sir William Wade. In Dethicke's letter of explanation to Lord Burghley he describes how one of the "base fellows" had intruded upon him and how he had "thrust him away, Whereupon he strake me with his fist on the face: Which I could not endure." Dethicke continued by reviling his fellow heralds: "And this cause hath Claren-

[cieux], the Drunkard, M' Wade, the vaineglorious, Chester the taverne Hunter, Richmond that escaped to be excused at Barwicke, and Brookesmouth with the burnt hand, so persev[ere] against me, to my discreditt & undoing." And as to the charge of overweening pride, Dethicke tosses it aside, "And for the other point of Pride: my demeanor hath bene acceptable to Noble and Gentlemen in England & beyond seas."[56] He was sent to Newgate prison for his offenses but was released by Fleetwood, the recorder. Soon afterwards he was again sent to prison and fined one hundred pounds for striking a clergyman and calling him "a bald, rascally priest." Later, at Lord Mordaunt's funeral "he stroke York herauld on the face, and now goeth about to hinder the said York of his dew course in law, contrary to an expresse order of Starr Chamber."[57] Dethicke's enemies complained of his insolent behavior in France and insisted he could not speak the French language with intelligence or grace. But Dethicke returned the charges and reviled his colleagues for their ignorance.[58] He was accused of having withheld the fees of the other officers in the College, and it was said that he "abuseth them with wordes, and offoreth them violence when they come to serve with hym."[59] And so on and on. The complaints are endless. But they give us some graphic pictures of Dethicke's actions and character. And they are necessary to help elucidate the satire in *The Famous Victories*.

Just as the earl of Oxford's ancestor was gorgeously arrayed in borrowed deeds of heroism to glorify his Elizabethan descendant, and just as Lord Cobham's famous ancestor was demeaningly stripped of his religious piety and martyr's glory by being presented as a riotous reveller and pickpurse, so too is Sir William Dethicke's ancestral past presented to reflect upon that Elizabethan herald. The clown Dericke is no more historically valid than the character of Oxford or Oldcastle in *The Famous Victories*. The comic scenes include Mistress Cobbler and her husband with whom Dericke the clown resides. This comic situation, exaggerated by the great bundle of shoes which Dericke collects as his booty, anticipates at least a future vocation for the clown, if not a future wife. The hidden shoemaker in William Dethicke's past had become common knowledge because his enemies taunted him with his base origins. And the playwright of *The Famous Victories* creates a fifteenth-century setting for the imaginary ancestor who is quick with a dagger and a witty response. When Dericke enters in "silk apparel," he is wearing a costume of some distinctive kind. I believe that it is a tabard. He is referred to as a pursuivant a number of times in the play. In the Elizabethan period the term was used for a messenger, but it was also used in the heralds' office to designate one rank among the junior officials. When Dericke plans to precede the funeral cortege of the duke of York like an officer of arms, he is a presumptive fifteenth-century ancestor of a very presumptive sixteenth-century Garter king of arms. Then finally, the name *Dericke* is a killing blow. Sir William Dethicke had tried hard to bury that name with his inglorious past, and the satiric playwright tosses it out to public view upon a brazen stage.

The Famous Victories is loaded with ideas and topical satire. We are too far away to catch all of the meanings, but Shakespeare apparently understood much of what was presented in this old play, crude as it was, and he utilized the ideas and images most effectively.

CHAPTER SEVEN

The Merry Wives of Windsor

SHAKESPEARE'S *Merry Wives of Windsor,* THE BROAD
comedy in which Falstaff's amorous adventures are exploited, is considered by most modern scholars to be a
Garter play.[1] Throughout the drama Shakespeare utilizes
well-known topographical features of the Windsor area:
the castle and castle ditch, the chapel, Herne's oak, Datchet
Lane and Datchet mead, the park, the Garter Inn, the road
to Frogmore, and so on. In addition to this specialized setting, we find Mistress Quickly remarking at one point that
the town is filling with courtiers for a special event (II.ii.
64), and Doctor Caius mentions "la grand affaires" which
he plans to attend at the castle. These lines and the implications of the setting suggest the time and occasion of the
annual Order of the Garter celebration on St. George's Day.
This assumption is strengthened by the famous paean to
the honor of the Garter and to its mistress, the queen, which
is given in act V when Mistress Quickly, garbed as the
queen of the fairies, instructs the dancing boys to protect
"euery sacred roome" of Windsor Castle:

> About, about:
> Search Windsor Castle (Elues) within, and out.
> Strew good lucke (Ouphes) on euery sacred roome,
> That it may stand till the perpetuall doome,
> In state as wholsome, as in state 'tis fit,
> Worthy the Owner, and the Owner it.
> The seuerall Chaires of Order, looke you scowre
> With iuyce of Balme; and euery precious flowre,
> Each faire Instalment, Coate, and seu'rall Crest,
> With loyall Blazon, euermore be blest.
> And Nightly-meadow-Fairies, looke you sing

Like to the *Garters*-Compasse, in a ring,
Th' expressure that it beares: Greene let it be,
More fertile-fresh then all the Field to see:
And, *Hony Soit Qui Mal-y-Pence,* write
In Emrold-tuffes, Flowres purple, blew, and white,
Like Saphire-pearle, and rich embroiderie,
Buckled below faire Knight-hoods bending knee;
Fairies vse Flowres for their characterie.
Away, disperse:

[V.v.56–75]

The activities within the play indicate that this special
Garter celebration is a fifteenth-century one. Two references provide this time setting. The first is the Q_1 reference
in Falstaff's lines in the fairy-dancing scene: "Ile lay my life
the mad Prince of *Wales* / Is stealing his fathers Deare"
(lines 1522–23), and the second one is the reference to Fenton's association "with the wild Prince and Poins" in the
first folio edition (III.ii.66–67). From these basic clues we
know that Shakespeare's *Merry Wives* continues the general setting and the comic *dramatis personae* of the *Henry
IV* dramas, but the latter are greatly changed. The character of Falstaff in particular is a new comic creation. His wit
seems eroded as he repeatedly plays the dupe for the
shrewd wives of the town. But neither Falstaff nor the play
as a whole is as simplistic a farce as it is at times depicted to
be in modern criticism.[2] When the drama is placed within
its proper context as part of the Oldcastle-Cobham satire
extending from *The Famous Victories* to *Henry V,* it
becomes an unusually complex comedy with both mythic
and symbolic overtones. The pragmatic problem of the date
of the play's composition provides a realistic entry into an
analysis of the satire of *The Merry Wives of Windsor.*

Since Leslie Hotson published his study of *The Merry
Wives* in 1931, many editors and critics of the play have
accepted his suggestion that Shakespeare wrote the drama
for either the Garter feast or the Garter installation in
April and May of 1597.[3] The suggestion is an unusually
appealing one. We know that in April of 1597 the knights
of the Order elected five new members to join their
honored ranks. These men were George Carey, Lord Hunsdon; Thomas, Lord Howard of Walden; Charles Blount,
Lord Mountjoy; Sir Henry Lee; and one foreign nobleman,
Frederick, duke of Württemberg.[4] The feast of Saint George

was celebrated at Westminster on 23 April when the knights-elect were created; the official investment was performed at Windsor on 24 May. By a decree of the queen in 1567 Windsor had been declared the locale for the investment ceremony; the feast itself, which was far more elaborate, was to be celebrated on Saint George's Day wherever the court was in residence.[5] Hotson was the first to recognize the "illuminating fact" that Hunsdon's own acting troupe was perhaps in attendance upon their lord as he "flaunted it gallantly" at the 1597 celebration accompanied by three hundred gentlemen and retainers dressed in their blue and orange livery, and that *The Merry Wives* was in all probability written and performed for this occasion as Shakespeare and the Lord Chamberlain's Men honored their patron. The acuteness of Hoston's observation brought instantaneous popularity for the theory that Shakespeare wrote the play in April or May of 1597, so that Chambers's earlier suggestion that the play was written in 1600 or 1601 was completely superseded. To supplement Hotson's theory Hardin Craig suggested that the provincial tour of the summer and fall of 1597, which the London acting companies made after the closing of the theaters on 28 July, was the occasion of the alteration and abbreviation of the original text to provide a compressed script for the tour, and that this cut version furnished the copy for the 1602 quarto edition of the play.[6] These suggestions are compatible with each other, but to accept them is to ignore several larger problems that stand out like bold-face type among the italicized ideas. The relationship between Jonson's *Every Man In His Humour* and *2 Henry IV* indicates that Shakespeare wrote Part Two *after* September 1598, when Jonson's unusually innovative play was first produced. *The Merry Wives,* with the continuation of the humors of Nym, seems clearly to have followed *2 Henry IV*.[7] Even more important for dating the play is the embedded Oldcastle-Cobham satire. When this satire is understood and placed within the context of the court activities of the period, the play appears to have been written in 1599 between 23 April, when Henry Brooke, eighth Lord Cobham, was elected as a new knight of the Garter, and 6 June when he was installed at Windsor. The play, I believe, was first performed at Windsor for the Garter installation in 1599.

The Merry Wives of Windsor is a play about the Cobhams, not about, or even for, Lord Hunsdon. The Oldcastle-Cobham satire remains overtly evident in a few places in the text and covertly evident throughout the drama. W. W. Greg noted in his edition of the 1602 quarto version of *The Merry Wives* that the host's bantering line, "Sir *Iohn*, theres his Castle, his standing bed," spoken to Simple, who has just inquired for Falstaff (line 1305), is an allusion to the original name of Falstaff.[8] This I believe to be true. It is similar to Hal's reference to Falstaff as "my old lad of the Castle" in *1 Henry IV.* Similarly, near the end of the play in the famous fairy-pinching scene (act V, scene v), an element of the Oldcastle satire appears to have existed in the quarto text and remains partially in the later text. In the earliest version Mistress Quickly instructs the children to approach Falstaff with their tapers.

> Go strait, and do as I commaund
> And take a Taper in your hand,
> And set it to his fingers endes,
> And if you see it him offends,
> And that he starteth at the flame,
> Then is he mortall, know his name:
> If with an F, it doth begin,
> Why then be sure he is full of sin. . . .   [lines 1492-99]

Evans joins in the merriment and says, "Giue me the Tapers, I will try / And if that he loue venery." At this point he and the fairies touch Falstaff with the candles. The stage instructions add that Falstaff "starts." Evans then exclaims: "It is right indeed, he is full of lecheries and iniquitie." Only by turning to the folio text is Evans's remark clarified. The later text prints Falstaff's startled response to the flames. He cries out, "Oh, oh, oh!" John Crofts suggested some years ago that in the midst of these candle flames that lick at Falstaff's kneeling figure, Mistress Quickly's original line apparently included an *O* rather than an *F*: ". . . know his name: / If with an O. it doth begin, / Why then be sure he is full of sin." Such a construction makes Falstaff's exclamation and Evans's knowing response both logical and meaningful.[9] This scene with its "tormenting flames" carried by Evans and his boys is

one of the most important in the drama as far as the satire
is concerned; the meaning can be understood if *The Merry
Wives* is placed within the context of the Oldcastle lampooning in *The Famous Victories*.

Henry Evans, the Welsh scrivener who had become one
of the masters of the children employed for court entertainment in the 1580s, taught those boys not only acting,
dancing, and singing but also the standard grammar-school
subjects. After Evans, Hunnis, and Lyly left the Blackfriars'
precinct in the mid-1580s, they continued to train the boys,
though their place of residence is unclear.[10] William
Hunnis died in June 1597, and his successor as master of
the Children of the Chapel Royal was Nathaniel Gyles, an
Oxford graduate who had been functioning as master of the
Children of Windsor.[11] Either just before or soon after he
received his patent as master of the chapel boys Giles
formed a partnership with Henry Evans to help him train
the youths for their court performances. It has been suggested that from September 1597 Evans leased the Blackfriars Theatre from the Burbages, who had been frustrated
in their attempts to open the newly remodelled Parliament
chamber as a theater for the Lord Chamberlain's Men.[12] We
do know that Evans had the lease of the Blackfriars Theatre
by September 1600 and that he was involved in litigation
over his practices with the children for years to come.[13] The
important point to be made within this context of satire is
that Henry Evans was occupied as schoolmaster to the
children who entertained the queen in this period. And it
would appear that it was this Welsh Henry Evans and his
boys who played the roles of the "Wealch Fairie" and his
dancing elves in the court performance of *The Merry Wives*.
To presume otherwise seems illogical to me.

The role of Sir Hugh Evans in the play is an affable one.
His position as schoolmaster in the town is also respected,
and by the end of the play he leads in the revenge motif
that is centered on Falstaff. He is eager to help initiate the
revenge; when Master Ford suggests that the children perhaps are not capable of carrying the trick off successfully,
Evans responds eagerly, "I will teach the children their
behaviours; and I will be like a jack-an-apes also, to burn
the knight with my taber." In the quarto text Evans is
described as being costumed "like a Satyre" for the fairy

pinching scene, and he performs a satiric function (to use the Renaissance connotation of the word). But there is an element of apology in this grand comic scene. When Evans and his boys end their dance and the other characters appear upon the stage, Falstaff looks at the children in amazement and inquires, "Why then these were not *Fairies?*" And Mistress Page replied, "No sir *Iohn* but boyes." Falstaff, with relief, responds,

> By the Lord I was twice or thrise in the mind
> They were not, and yet the grosnesse
> Of the fopperie perswaded me they were.
> Well, and the fine wits of the Court heare this,
> Thayle so whip me with their keene Iests,
> That thayle melt me out like tallow,
> Drop by drop out of my grease. Boyes!

At this point Evans admits his role in the jest, "I trust my boyes Sir *Iohn:* and I was / Also a Fairie that did helpe to pinch you." If I am reading this situation correctly, Evans had indeed been responsible for pinching the comic buffoon, both in *The Merry Wives* and in *The Famous Victories* some fourteen or fifteen years earlier. The scene ends in the quarto version with a handshake and "all's forgiuen at last." Falstaff concludes: "It hath cost me well, / I haue bene well pinched and washed." In the folio text, however, this scene is sharpened with an outpouring of colloquial language. When the others confront him, Falstaff exclaims,

> Have I laid my brain in the sun and dried it, that it wants matter to prevent so gross o'er-reaching as this? Am I ridden with a Welsh goat too? Shall I have a cockscomb of frieze? 'Tis time I were choked with a piece of toasted cheese.

Evans responds with a line about cheese and butter (similar to a line in the quarto text), and Falstaff continues,

> 'Seese' and 'putter'? [mimicking Evans's Welsh dialect] Have I lived to stand at the taunt of one that makes fritters of English? This is enough to be the decay of lust and late-walking through the realm.

Then the other characters heap coals upon him: they call

him "a hodge-pudding," "a bag of flax," "a puffed man," "Old, cold withered, and of intolerable entrails," "one that is as slanderous as Satan," one that is "as poor as Job and as wicked as his wife," and one "given to fornications, and to taverns, and sack, and wine, and metheglins, and to drinkings, and swearings, and starings, pribbles and prabbles" [that last from Evans], and so on. Falstaff in defeat responds, "Well, I am your theme . . . I am not able to answer the Welsh flannel . . . use me as you will." Nor is there any remission of the money owed to Master Brook, as the quarto text indicates when Mistress Ford says, "Nay husband let that go to make ame[n]ds, / Forgiue that sum, and so weele all be friends." In the folio text Ford taunts Falstaff about the repayment: "I think to repay that money will be a biting affliction.'' There is a distinct difference in tone between the two endings of this scene. The folio text is not only longer; it is harsher and more corrosive in its comic denouement. Since this text is the more nearly complete one, and since it contains the paean to the queen as mistress of Windsor Castle and of the Order of the Garter, we assume that this is the version presented before Elizabeth, possibly at Windsor. The folio text contains, then, not only more satire but more virile satire. It will pay to look more closely at the three comic episodes of Falstaff's detection or near-detection, for they contain an adumbrative survey of the history of the Cobham satire. Shakespeare's most farcical play is, upon close examination I think, one of his most evasively symbolic dramas.

Falstaff undergoes three comic trials of endurance in the play as he pursues the wealthy wives of Windsor: the buckbasket episode in which he is dumped into the ditch at Thames-side, the second episode in which he is soundly beaten as the old witch of Brainford, and the third in which he is burned as a "man of middle earth." All three episodes contain mythic elements that relate them to the Oldcastle-Cobham satire. Falstaff describes his frightening experience in the buck-basket to Ford (who dissembles as Master Brook). The reader should keep in mind the history of Sir John Oldcastle's experiences in the early years of Henry V's reign as Falstaff relates the comic episode.

But mark the sequel, Master Brook: I suffered the pangs of three several deaths. First, an intolerable fright, to be detected with a jealous rotten bell-wether; next, to be compassed like a good bilbo in the circumference of a peck, hilt to point, heel to head, and then to be stopped in like a strong distillation with stinking clothes that fretted in their own grease—think of that —a man of my kidney—think of that—that am as subject to heat as butter; a man of continual dissolution and thaw: it was a miracle to 'scape suffocation. And in the height of this bath, when I was more than half stewed in grease, like a Dutch dish, to be thrown into the Thames and cooled, glowing hot, in that surge, like a horse-shoe—think of that—hissing hot—think of that, Master Brook!

[III.v.98-113]

These lines are replete with grotesque wit. Beyond the literal meaning lies an allusive realm where associations of the past float free, giving broad satiric dimensions to the comedy. The "three several deaths" set the exaggerated tone of martyrdom, while the detection by the "Jealous rotten bell-wether" seems to indicate not only Ford the enraged husband but at a more furtive level the clergy of Henry V's reign who discovered Oldcastle's heresy and treasonous dealings. The language is reminiscent of that used in Bale's *Brefe Chronycle* to describe the Catholic clergy of that earlier period. In similar vein, the confinement "like a good bilbo" refers to both the constrictions of the buck-basket and the incarceration of Oldcastle after he was finally captured in Wales. It should be noted at this point that *bilbo* means a type of slender sword, as editors usually indicate; however, the term also was used for a singular kind of shackles in the Tower of London which pressed a man's head down to his ankles and kept him in that encircled position. The bilbo was a cruel instrument of torture.[14] And finally, it is difficult to consider Falstaff's reference to his being "half stewed in grease," to being "glowing hot" and "hissing hot"as innocent remarks with only one dimension of meaning. The playwright is apparently once more playing with satiric fire.

Falstaff's description of his trip to the ditch in the buck-basket is even more complex with allusive meanings. The image of the fat knight, bound in "like a horse-shoe," being dumped unceremoniously into the castle ditch at Thames-side is iconographically potent within the Garter context. The ceremony of the degradation of a knight found guilty of treason was performed a number of times in the Tudor period. The arms of the duke of Norfolk had undergone such degradation in Queen Elizabeth's reign, and shortly after *The Merry Wives* was written the Cobham arms were dealt with in the same humiliating manner. We cannot insist naively that Shakespeare was clairvoyant; he does appear however to have known much about the underhanded political machinations of Henry, eighth Lord Cobham. In this passage in *The Merry Wives* which anticipates Lord Cobham's future, Shakespeare probably was thinking of the Garter episode in his own early play of *Henry VI* in which Sir John Falstaff or Fastolf was involved. The possibility of treason in *The Merry Wives* is introduced in the elaborate paean to the Garter in act V. The lines are spoken by the fairy queen herself: the fairies must search the Castle to ward off evil influences, and they must cleanse each stall and coat of arms.

> The several chairs of order look you scour
> With juice of balm and every precious flower;
> Each fair instalment, coat, and sev'ral crest,
> With loyal blazon, evermore be blest; . . .

The element of anticipation is here. The knights of the Garter were and had always been the greatest nobles and gentlemen of the kingdom. But some had fallen from their high eminence. Elias Ashmole describes in his seventeenth-century history of the Order the traditional ceremony of degradation that occurred after a Knight was found guilty of treason.

> First Garter [King of Arms], in his Coat of Arms, (usually before Morning Prayer, if the Grand Feast, or Feast of Installation be then held) standing on the highest step ascending to the Brazen Desk, place in the middle of the Choire in St. George's Chappel at Windsor, the Officers of Arms standing about him, and the Black Rod also present, reads aloud the Instrument for Publication of the Knights Degradation. . . . This being read, one of the Heralds deputed thereunto (a Ladder being raised to the backside of the convict Knights Stall, and he, in his Coat of Arms, placed there before hand) when Garter pronounceth the words, *Expelled and put from among the Arms*, &c., takes his Crest, and violently casts it down into the Choire, and after that his Banner and Sword, and when the Publication is read out, all the Officers of Arms spurn the Atchievements out of the Choire into the Body of

the Church, first the Sword, then the Banner, and last of all the Crest, so out of the West-Door, thence to the Bridge, and over into the Ditch.[15]

I would suggest that Falstaff's trip in the buck-basket, circumscribed in a bilbo (like a Garter crest), and his dunking in the ditch are symbolic ritual. The Cobham crest and arms with Henry Brooke's achievements as knight of the Garter were taken down and kicked out of the west doors of Saint George's Chapel on 12 February 1604. The officers did not kick the crest into the castle ditch because King James prohibited this final act of debasement, probably because Sir Robert Cecil's dead wife had been Henry Brooke's sister, and the Cecil children quartered the Cobham arms.[16]

Eleanor Cobham was one of the few women elected to the Order of the Garter. Her installation in 1436 probably was the result of the great influence of the duke of Gloucester, and it has been suggested that Gloucester introduced his new wife to his peers in the colorful ceremonies at Windsor.[17] The record of her later debasement at the chapel does not appear to be extant, but something of her conduct is mirrored in the second episode of Falstaff's humiliation at the hands of the witty wives of Windsor.

In spite of his being "a man of continual dissolution and thaw" Falstaff survives his "three several deaths" to become involved again with the merry wives. In his second encounter with angry Master Ford, Falstaff dons female disguise and becomes the "fat woman of Brainford" who is thought to be a witch.[18] Certainly Master Ford thinks her to be a practitioner of the black arts. He cries out to the disguised Falstaff,

> A witch, a quean, an old cozening quean! Have I not forbid her my house? She comes of errands, does she? We are simple men; we do not know what's brought to pass under the profession of fortune-telling. She works by charms, by spells, by th' figure, and such daubery as this is, beyond our element; we know nothing. Come down, you witch, you hag, you; come down, I say!
>
> [IV.ii.158–65]

The beating which follows is pure slapstick comedy, and the scene is a commonplace one in domestic farce. But when Falstaff is disguised in woman's garb and is called a witch and practicer of magic and fortune telling, he becomes a symbolic figure as well. In the transmission of the spirit of rebellion in the Oldcastle-Cobham line of descent, the second famous historical character was Eleanor Cobham, who had practiced withcraft, so her enemies insisted, in an effort to gain the crown. Shakespeare appears to be creating in his succession of comic episodes in *The Merry Wives* a symbolic transmigration of the Cobham spirit of evil as it descended through the chronicles to his own day. Thus by the time Falstaff dons the stag's horns and finds himself surrounded by fairies who burn him, we have not only the reference to the burning of the Lollard Martyr but a reference to the toasting of the Elizabethan Cobhams by the poets of the period, as well.

Shakespeare's consummate art is almost never a monotonal or monochromatic achievement. None of the plays exists only in its surface or literal meaning, which, I hasten to add, does not diminish the importance of that literal meaning. Renaissance art in general is complex and polysemantic, and intentionally so. If a reader wanted direct frontal knowledge in those days, he turned to history or mathematics. Art taught pleasingly by indirection, as every schoolboy knew. There is no doubting that the pleasing indirection of Shakespeare's fairy-pinching scene offers the reader a wealth of allusive suggestions. One almost resorts to Falstaff's enthusiastic response with such abundance: "Let the sky rain potatoes; let it thunder to the tune of 'Greensleeves,' hail kissing-comfits, and snow eringoes!"

The moral significance of the disguises Falstaff assumes—the buck's head, the buck-basket, and the witch's garb—has been recently explained: the metamorphosis in each ordeal is a symbolic expression of lust and its chastisement.[19] In addition, we find in the beleaguered Falstaff a composite image of the ancestral Cobham dishonesty, a dishonesty wrought in the symbols of unchaste ethical and sensual desire. The montage effect is achieved in the play with symbolic costume and images. Especially is the stag's headpiece fitting for Falstaff. The ritualistic dance around the "man of middle earth" in which the fairies burn and pinch the "corrupt heart" till "candles and starlight and moonlight be out" appears to have mythic elements which go far beyond the Oldcastle immolation theme. There is an element of pre-Christian ritual and pagan sacrifice in the scene. The imagery stems from the ancient cult of the stag king. Elements of it survive in the myths of the moon goddess Britomart, a character whom Spencer had introduced into the Elizabethan milieu with a special nod toward the queen. The image of the horned king survives in the Greek myth of Artemis and the metamorphosed Actaeon, a myth Shakespeare obviously is utilizing in the scene. The image of the horned king survives in many other figures, in the antlered Gaulish king, in Cernunnos, "the horned one," in the horned Dionysus, and even in the image of Alexander wearing the horned crown as shown on Alexandrian coins. The horned Moses of the artists is also involved here. The cuckold's branching horns are a survival of the ancient myth of the betrayed stag-king.[20] The ceremonial May Day stag-mummers of Abbot's Bromley in Devonshire are descended from this body of prehistoric myth, and the chase there is sometimes explained as a punishment for trespassing. Part of Falstaff's punishment in the fairy scene is perhaps related to his trespass on Justice Shallow's deer park. In the quarto version of the play Herne the hunter is spelled "Horne," and perhaps such a spelling is meaningful. Falstaff becomes Horne when he dons the stag's headdress. He also becomes Auld Hornie, the Scot's term for Satan; he becomes an outlaw who is "put to the horn"; he is the image of the cuckold, and at the same time he is the image of a king. The meanings of the scene extend beyond the ethical and moral into the realms of the political and the mythic. Where the end lies is almost beyond encompassing.

It is the fairy queen who instructs the youthful "fairies" to guard the castle, and a few lines later she urges them to test Falstaff:

With trial-fire touch me his finger-end:
If he be chaste, the flame will back descend,
And turn him to no pain; but if he start,
It is the flesh of a corrupted heart.

[V.v.85–88]

This is a curious situation. Mistress Quickly is of course playing the role (the confusion over Ann Page's activities need not blur the implication here). The expressed purpose of the fairy queen's appearance in this little tableau within the play is relatively obvious, or so it seems to me. Queen Elizabeth was the archetypal fairy queen after Edmund Spenser created his epic poem earlier in the 1590s and in it prefigured Elizabeth as the monarch of his land of imagination. I believe that Shakespeare is making an overt gesture at this point in his play toward the queen. It is *she* who commands the testing of Falstaff. If I am sensitive enough to read this situation in the text correctly, it places a firm foundation under the old legend that Queen Elizabeth commissioned Shakespeare to write a play showing Falstaff in love. We ought to reexamine that old legend and the court milieu behind it.

The reader will recall that John Dennis rewrote *The Merry Wives of Windsor*, turning it into his own version of what a true comedy should be, and that when he published his play as *The Comical Gallant* in 1702, he added an epistle dedicatory in which he remarked on Shakespeare's play: "I knew very well that it had pleas'd one of the greatest Queens that ever was in the world." Then he continued by describing Queen Elizabeth's request for the play. "This comedy was written at her Command, and by her direction, and she was so eager to see it Acted, that she commanded it to be finished in fourteen days: and was afterwards, as Tradition tells us, very well pleas'd at the Representation."[21] In Nicholas Rowe's edition of Shakespeare's plays we find the additional information concerning the subject matter of the play. "She was so well pleas'd with that admirable Character of Falstaff, in the two Parts of *Henry* the Fourth, that she commanded him to continue it for one Play more, and to shew him in Love."[22] It should be noted that Rowe's phrase concerning Falstaff's character, "in the two Parts of *Henry* the Fourth," indicates an important point of chronology: if he is accurate in his remark, *The Merry Wives* was written after both parts of *Henry IV* had been completed and performed. Charles Gildon, in the supplementary volume to Rowe's *Works of Mr. William Shakespeare*, repeated the story, conflating the accounts of Dennis and Rowe.

The story is an attractive one, but it is in the category of hearsay; however, if Dennis and Rowe got their accounts of the play from Dryden, who had been acquainted with D'Avenant, there is a strong possibility that the legend is a true one. We do know from the title page of the 1602 edition of *The Merry Wives* that the play had been acted before her Majesty. In the drama we have the fairy queen commanding the fairies to test Falstaff. I believe that this dramatic action underscores the viability of the old legend. Moreover, when the court milieu of the last two years of the sixteenth century is examined closely, it appears that there were practical reasons for Queen Elizabeth's curiosity about a representation of Falstaff in love. Those reasons have nothing to do with delight in the characterization of the fat knight.

Students of Elizabethan history are aware of the hostility with which Queen Elizabeth greeted the news of the "unlicensed" marriages of the young men and women in her court. The cases of Sir Walter Raleigh, the earl of Essex, and the earl of Southampton are perhaps the most widely known. Their marriages sent Elizabeth's anger to the boiling-point for brief periods of time. Raleigh and Essex were in turn banished from the court, and Southampton later was sent to the Fleet for marrying without the permission of the queen. We cannot ascribe all of this royal anger to neurosis. Queen Elizabeth was a conscious image-builder. She had endeavored for years to create a court famed throughout Europe for its virtue and idealism. In the last half of her reign she was fighting the Counter-Reformation image that Rome had created for her as an illegitimate ruler of an heretical people given to the practice of scandalous and ungodly habits. Her own white costuming, her use of pale cosmetics, her insistence upon the image of the virgin queen, her attempts at rigorous control over the handsome young people who surrounded her in her later years, all were part of the public image-building in which she had become a skilled director. This is not to deny that possibly there was an unwarranted amount of meddling in the private lives of her courtiers. In the sixteenth century, however, it was taken for granted that the monarch should control alliances between the great families in the realm. Marriage was a political as well as a social instrument, and the queen carefully planned the contracts between the noble houses. She also kept a wary eye upon the high-spirited young women who were under her charge and care as maids of honor in the court. Elizabeth was "Our radiant Queene" who "hates sluts and sluttery" (V. v. 47). She insisted upon high standards of social carriage and conduct, and she was not above slapping a pretty face for an oversight or a careless word. In 1598 and 1599 the court gossips were busy with talk of the new Lord Cobham's activities, particularly his romantic associations. He was an attractive bachelor, aged thirty-two, when his father died in 1597. He seems to have exploited his good standing with the queen and perhaps with a number of the young ladies of the court. Soon after he became the new Lord Cobham, his name was linked romantically with one of the daughters of the earl of Oxford, but that talk was superseded before the end of 1597. Margaret Ratcliffe, daughter of Sir Alexander Ratcliffe of Ordsall, and one of the prettiest of the maids of honor who surrounded the queen, fell in love with Lord Cobham. From this beginning the story grows pathetic and somewhat sordid, but the information we can gather from the fragmentary sources is important for understanding the queen's desire to see a representation of Falstaff in love.

Rowland Whyte, in his gossipy letters to his employer, Sir Robert Sidney, included a number of references to the affair that seems to have developed between Mistress Ratcliffe and Cobham. In the spring of 1597 he described the maid of honor in detail. "Yesterday did Mrs. *Ratcliffe* weare a whyte Sattin Gown, all embrodered, richly cutt vpon good Cloth of Siluer, that cost 180 £. But the Fairest doth take Pleasure in nothing since the Departure of her beloued." He continued with more details of her quiet ways. "Her Garments, her Countenance, and Jestures, witnes no less; besides a Kynd of vnwonted Solitarines, which is familiar vnto her."[23] The next bit of information we have is that teasing line which the earl of Essex added in his letter to Sir Robert Cecil, a letter dated in February 1598. "I pray you commend me allso to Alex. Ratcliffe," he wrote, "and tell him for newes his sister is maryed to Sr. Jo. Falstaff."[24] We have no way of knowing whether Essex was writing about a marriage which had

taken place in the Court but which was being kept a secret from the queen or writing in jest. Almost a year and a
half later the young countess of Southampton wrote to her
husband, who was with Essex in Ireland, that "Sir John
Falstaff is by his Mrs. Dame Pintpot made father to a godly
milers thum," and then she added, "but this is a secrit."[25]
We have only this gossip to indicate that a tragedy was
brewing in the court. The countess of Southampton wrote
her letter in July 1599; in August Rowland Whyte described the unhappiness of Mistress Ratcliffe over a rival
who had caught the eye of Lord Cobham.

Frances Howard, daughter of the lord admiral and
now the widowed countess of Kildare, was taking a serious interest in Lord Cobham. Margaret Ratcliff's health
at this time was poor, and the queen was keeping the
news of her brother's death in Ireland from her. Whyte,
after noting that fact, continued, "Mrs. *Ratcliffe* hath kept
her Chamber these 4 Daies, being somewhat troubled at
my Lady *Kildares* vnkynd vsing of her, which is thought
to proceed from her Loue to my Lord Cobham."[26] In a few
weeks the young woman was dead, and Whyte sent that
news to his master also: "Now that Mrs. *Ratcliffe* is dead,
the Lady *Kildare* hopes that my Lord *Cobham* will proceed on his Sute to her."[27] A more detailed account of
Margaret Ratcliffe's death is given in a letter written by
Philip Gawdy to his brother. Gawdy describes the London
talk over the strange events:

> Ther is newes besydes of the tragycall death of Mrs. Rat-
> cliffe the mayde of honor who ever synce the deathe of Sr.
> Alexander her brother hathe pined in suche straunge man-
> ner, as voluntarily she hathe gone about to starve her selfe
> and by the two dayes together hathe receyved no sustinaunce,
> which meeting withe extreame greife hathe made an ende
> of her mayden modest dayes at Richmonde uppon Sater-
> daye last, her Majestie being [present?] who commanded
> her body to be opened and founde it all well and sounde,
> saving certeyne stringes striped all over her harte. All the
> maydes ever synce have gone in blacke. I saw it my selfe at
> court, wher I saw the quenes majestie talke very long withe
> my L. Henry Howarde and your oncle Fra: Bacon.[28]

Out of what appears to have been an unhappy love affair
we have, I think, the probable explanation of the queen's

command for another play on Falstaff. She was completely aware of the way the satire in the *Henry IV* plays
had been directed toward the elder Lord Cobham and then
toward his son, who was using all his friends to solicit
his suits before the queen.

The younger Lord Cobham wanted all the important
posts his father had held, and those posts included the
lord chamberlain's position, the wardenship of the Cinque
Ports, and membership in the Privy Council. In April 1599
Cobham was elected K.G. Soon after 23 April, I believe
that the queen asked the Lord Chamberlain's Men to produce another play "shewing Falstaff in Loue." And she
wanted that play ready for production on or before 6 June,
the time set for the installation of the new knights-elect.
I believe the queen was upset over the gossip concerning
Cobham's behavior. Then too she may also have wanted
to test the actors. The satire of the martyred Lollard had
been carried to the edge of propriety in Shakespeare's
plays and had been dumped into the limbo of scandalous
wit by Jonson and Nashe. I believe that Shakespeare was
suddenly faced with an unpleasant task in writing the
comedy for the queen. He could not and would not depict
the recent activities in the court. His alternative was to
adapt a comic plot from *Tarlton's Newes Out of Purga-
torie* and to arrange his contrived episodes to represent
a mythic history of the Oldcastle-Cobham satire from beginning to end.[29] And I do mean *end*. For under the pressure of the queen's close observation and under the pressure of having to depict something which I think he did
not care to write, Shakespeare appears to have determined to rid himself of his fat knight who had suddenly
become more of a problem than a witty tour de force. Instead of proceeding with his plans to carry Falstaff into
France in *Henry V*, as he had promised in the epilogue of
2 Henry IV, Shakespeare resolved to make an end of the
comic character as soon as possible. The satire had become
uncomfortable, and it was getting out of hand.

In addition to the few incidents found in Henry Brooke's
personal life which help to date the composition of *The
Merry Wives of Windsor* and to explain in part some of the
satire of the play, there are a number of political aspects
of this same period that function in a similar way. Henry

Brooke, the new Lord Cobham, was an ambitious man, and he fought the earl of Essex on almost every political issue in the last years of the sixteenth century. The feud between the two men broke into open hostility early in 1597 when the elder Lord Cobham was seriously ill. It was during this winter (November-February 1596–1597) that Shakespeare apparently wrote the first part of *Henry IV*. There was need then to denigrate the Cobham name, and the playwright turned to the Oldcastle lampoon that the actors had used in the 1580s as they shafted Lord Cobham in *The Famous Victories*. With the elder Lord Cobham dying, the court was filled with speculation over the possible candidates for the important post of the lord chamberlainship. Naturally the acting companies were concerned in this coming appointment; the lord chamberlain had direct control over the Office of the Revels and the entertainment at court. Cobham had held this white staff since Lord Hunsdon's death the summer before, and his son Henry wanted to succeed in the position. But George Cary, now the new Lord Hunsdon, wanted the office also. Old Rowland Whyte has left us a description of the tensions as they mounted in the court. Writing to Sir Robert Sidney in Flushing, he noted on 21 February that "My Lord Cobham is ill in Deed, and much fallen away." Then he added, "I heare his Sonne Mr. Harry comes daily to the Queen, and the Father is willing to make Resignacions of such Places he holds by the Queen, to his Sonnes."[30] And the next day White wrote again to inform that "my Lord Chamberlain growes weaker and weaker, and the Doctors are doubtful of his recovery." Whyte also added that Henry Brooke was using "all the Frends he hath" to sue for the major appointments his father held.[31] By 2 March Whyte was stationing himself outside of Cobham's Blackfriars home each day to pick up the news. He relayed his information to Sidney: "This morning I was at Blackfriars, and their I fownd my Lord Admirall had bene with my Lord Cobham: yt is now feld certain he cannot live."

Whyte was interested more in the lord wardenship of the Cinque Ports than in the lord chamberlainship because Sidney wanted the wardenship for himself if it could possibly be arranged. He had encouraged the earl of Essex to press his suit with the queen. Whyte informed his master that "Yf my Lord of Essex is able to doe any Thing, yt will now appeare: for certainly he opposes hymself against thother, laying before her Majestie his Unworthines, and Unableness to doe her Service."[32] Essex even spoke to the Council concerning his contempt for Henry Brooke, using strong language: "I made it knowen unto them, that I had just Cause to hate the Lord Cobham, for his villanous Dealings and abusing of me; that he hath bene my cheiffe Persecutor most injustly; that in him their is no worth."[33] And then of course we learn that Henry Brooke returned ill-favor with ill-favor: "Hearing how disdainfully my Lord of Essex speaks of him in Publiq, [he] doth likewise protest to hate the Earle as much."[34] The earl of Essex created every diversion and hindrance he could think of to prevent Cobham's rise at court. George Cary, Lord Hunsdon, received the lord chamberlain's white staff in April, and the actors of the Lord Chamberlain's Company were secure once more in their premier position at court. They apparently continued to produce their profitable and popular play on *Henry IV*, but they changed Oldcastle's name at this time to Falstaff, probably at the queen's direct or indirect request, for there is the taunting element of Cobham's failure to keep the white staff his father had held in the new comic name. In September 1598 the company produced Jonson's *Every Man In His Humour*, a play that contains a broad stratum of Oldcastle satire.[35] The popularity of this play's humor characters seems to have encouraged Shakespeare to exploit such characters in *2 Henry IV*. In the continuation of Falstaff's comic crew Shakespeare introduces Pistol, capitalizing upon the conception of the irregular humorists in Jonson's play. And in this continuation he adapts the final rejection scene from *The Famous Victories* with all its implications that the Oldcastle-Cobham line is unworthy of promotion. In the meantime the Essex-Cobham feuding had not diminished.

When Essex left for Ireland in February 1599, he remarked, "I provide for this service a breast plate and not a cuirass: that is, I am armed on the breast but not on the back." And after he had arrived in Ireland, he wrote to Queen Elizabeth: "Is it not lamented of your Majesty's faithfullest subjects, both here and there, that a Cobham or a Ralegh (I forbear others for their places' sake) should have such credit and favour with your Majesty, when they wish the ill-success of your Majesty's most important action, the decay of your greatest strength, and the destruction of your faithfullest servant?"[36] Essex feared his enemies at home.

In the literary milieu of London something else had happened to make the Lord Chamberlain's Men apprehensive once again. Thomas Nashe published his scalding satirical work called *Lenten Stuffe, or Praise of the Red Herring* sometime after 11 January 1599, when he entered it in the *Stationers' Register*.[37] This ribald attack on Lord Cobham, though cloaked in animal allegory, was unrestrained. As we know now, Nashe's career was ruined by this work. It was his last book, for on 1 June the stationers' warden received orders to burn all of Nashe's works. In the early spring of 1599 the Oldcastle satire had become a destructive thing. This was doubly important now because the new Lord Cobham was developing a position of power in the court. He was elected K.G. in April, and he was busily working for momentum in his drive to become a member of the Privy Council, a position his father had held. The whole atmosphere was changing within the court.[38] That is why, I am convinced, Shakespeare created a new set of characters for *The Merry Wives of Windsor*. True, the old comic crew from the *Henry IV* plays are transported to the Windsor setting, but a metamorphosis has occurred. Rather than proceed with a forward development of his witty Falstaff, Shakespeare creates a stylized comic figure who becomes the center of a backward-looking survey of things that had been before. The comic episodes of *The Merry Wives* are scenes of explication of what had happened with the Oldcastle figure. And in spite of the harsh tone of the folio exodus, there is a comic explanation and a general sense of amelioration at the end of the play. Shakespeare had had enough of his brilliant satire. He was trying with some grace to bow out of the contest.

Another area within the play is tied closely to the political milieu of 1599. It should be mentioned at this point while the dating of *The Merry Wives* is under examination. The large arena of political activity concerned with the problem of the succession to the throne can be detected in the outer limits of the play. This vague outline flows around the romantic part of the plot. I hasten to add that only in the most general way can we consider the political function of the marriage of Ann Page in Shakespeare's drama. In both the quarto and the folio editions of the play there is confusion in this romantic action, but there is enough stability in the plot as we have it to warrant a probe of the possible implications of the play. First, it is to be granted that the youthful action within *The Merry Wives* is grafted onto the satiric plot to add the element of romance needed to leaven the broad farce. I am of the opinion that Shakespeare, working against time in constructing his comedy for the queen, adapted an old marriage play from the early years of Queen Elizabeth's reign, a play in which the queen's own serious considerations of marriage (either with the French, Austrian, or native English suitor) were depicted upon the stage, perhaps by the Inns of Court men or by some nobleman's company, possibly Leicester's troupe, since the young native suitor wins the lady's hand. I make this highly speculative suggestion because a similar situation had arisen at the end of Elizabeth's reign with young Arabella Stuart as the marriageable woman who was a serious candidate to play the role of the fairy queen. I believe that Shakespeare, capitalizing upon the queen's sentiment and nostalgia, endeavored to present this loaded topical problem in as appealing and light-hearted manner as he possibly could. We can only surmise whether this was the playwright's maneuver to distract his queen's attention from a complete absorption in the Falstaff episodes.

From the Talbot scenes in *1 Henry VI* we can assume that Shakespeare had at least a few charitable thoughts about the earls of Shrewsbury. I believe that he turned again in 1599 to that family for a subject that would make *The Merry Wives* a drama relevant to his own time. In 1596 Queen Elizabeth sent Gilbert Talbot, seventh earl of Shrewsbury, to France to take the Garter to Henry IV and also, it was rumored, to offer the French king the hand of Arabella, his niece, as a suitable bride. Queen Elizabeth was searching for an answer to the diplomatic problem of the young Arabella's marriage, for the young woman was an attractive candidate for the English crown. This problem had been creating tensions for a number of years. Arabella was the daughter of Charles Stuart, younger brother of Darnley, King James's father, it will be remembered. Arabella's mother was Elizabeth Cavendish, Bess of Hardwick's daughter, and it was Arabella's birth that ended the friendship between Mary Stuart and Bess years earlier. As a child, Arabella was the center of political attention; in her sixth year she was secretly engaged by her grandmother to Leicester's young son. In Scotland James VI was constantly concerned with the young Arabella as a competitor for the English crown, and he asked Queen Elizabeth a number of times for assurance that Arabella would not be matched without his approval.

In 1590 the old earl of Shrewsbury, still full of anger as death approached him, uttered warnings that "he feared the Lady Arabell would bring much trouble to his house, by his wife and her daughter's devices." He insisted that they thought him a great hindrance in their way.[39] As though indeed he were a prophet, in this same year Arabella was imprisoned for listening to overtures of marriage from Henry Percy, ninth earl of Northumberland. De Thou, the French historian, said they were married; his information appears to have come from Sir John Colville.[40] Henry Percy was himself a pretender to the throne through his line of descent from Edmund Crouchback, brother of Henry III. In Robert Parson's *Conference About the Next Succession* (1594) Lord Burghley was said to "especially favor Arbella,"[41] and in that year it was also rumored that the pope was backing a plan of Sir William Stanley, the Catholic exile, to kidnap Arabella and take her to the Continent for a marriage with the son of the duke of Parma.[42] In 1595 the new countess of Shrewsbury (Mary, Gilbert's wife, daughter of Bess of Hardwick) was imprisoned for treating in a marriage proposal for Arabella with Catholics on the Continent. Burghley intercepted letters in the same year which stated that "the traffic of Arabella is accepted, Allen is the merchant."[43] Queen Elizabeth wanted a French connection, and in 1596 she sent Shrewsbury to France with the Garter and with instructions to seek an opening on the subject of Arabella's marriage. Henry IV remarked to his minister, De Sully, that he had no objections to "the Princess Arbella of England, if, since it is publically said the Crown of England really belongs to her, she were only declared presumptive heiress of it."[44] The earl of Essex was also interested in Arabella's title, and Sir John Harington remarked in his tract on the succession that Essex commended Arabella to such an extent as to have "both himself and his honourable friends to be suspected of that, which I suppose was no part of their meaning."[45] Arabella's name was linked with those of a number of foreign suitors, and at home the name of Sir Robert Cecil was rumored to be under serious consideration after the death of his wife in 1597. As late as 1602 Queen Elizabeth was still overtly bent on arranging a French marriage for the young lady, considering, it was said, the young prince of Condé, nephew of Henry IV. In this complex web of schemes and counterschemes we find Arabella developing ideas of her own. She and her grandmother had been approached in 1599 or earlier by Edward Kyrton, a lawyer of the earl of Hertford, who suggested a marriage between Edward Seymour, Hertford's elder grandson, and Arabella. Edward and William Seymour were the grandsons of Catherine Grey, the heiress of the Suffolk claim to the crown. And it was William Seymour whom Arabella finally wed in 1610, much to the disapproval of King James, who feared the dangerous combination of claims that the marriage created.

The romantic plot of *The Merry Wives* should be placed against this complex political background for at least a partial understanding of what is going on in the fairy queen scene. Shakespeare pulls the touchy problem of Arabella's marriageability into the realm of comic fantasy where she wears the mask of Mistress Ann Page who has a French suitor (sponsored by Mrs. Page), a suitor in Slender (sponsored by Master Page), and a wild young lover sponsored only by herself and the host of the Garter. Within the political context the role of Ann Page as the fairy queen becomes important. Mrs. Page thinks that her sweet Nan "shall be the Queene of all the Fairies, finely attired in a robe of white." And Fenton is aware of the plan: "Tonight at Herne's oak, just 'twixt twelve and one, / Must my sweet Nan present the Fairy Queen." But the roles are switched, and love rules the out-come. Ann Page is won by her lover, as any reader of comedies would expect. The stylized comic situation, however, fits into an extremely complicated political situation that had developed in 1599 as a result of Arabella Stuart's willfulness in seeking a suitor of her own choice, and Shakespeare seems once again to exploit particularized incidents in a very generalizing art.

The final aspect of the Oldcastle-Cobham satire in *The Merry Wives* is the Brooke-Broome interchange between the quarto and folio texts. And this problem takes us back into the College of Arms controversy, the Dericke-Dethicke characterization, and the fustiness of old Ralph Brooke, York herald, and his complaint about the issuance of Shakespeare's arms. First, the problem of the texts.

In the 1602 edition of *The Merry Wives* Master Ford assumes the alias *Brooke* in order to gain Falstaff's confidence. The trick works, and Falstaff eagerly responds to the cup of sack which accompanies the introduction: "M. *Brooke,* hees welcome: Bid him come vp, / Such Brookes are alwaies welcome to me" (lines 542-43). And in the folio version of the play an additional phrase is added, "Such Brookes are welcome to me, that o'erflow such liquor" (II. ii. 158). This joke is spoiled in the folio text, however, because Ford's alias is changed to *Broome* throughout the play. This name-change is important because the family name of Lord Cobham was Brooke, and there appears to be some extension of the Oldcastle satire in Ford's original pseudonym. The wit of Ford's alias builds to a climax in the final scene of the play in which he mocks Falstaff while revealing his identity:

Now, sir, who's a cuckold now? Master Brook, Falstaff's a knave, a cuckoldly knave; here are his horns, Master Brook: and Master Brook, he hath enjoyed nothing of Ford's but his buck-basket, his cudgel, and twenty pounds of money, which must be paid to Master Brook; his horses are arrested for it, Master Brook.

The pertinence of this scene, which is the comic anagnorisis for Falstaff, would have been exquisitely witty in the

performance at Windsor on 6 June 1599, with Henry
Brooke, Lord Cobham in the audience. I am of the opinion
that the actor who spoke these lines addressed them directly to Lord Cobham, for the lines make a clear distinction between Falstaff and Brook: "Master Brook, Falstaff's
a knave, a cuckoldly knave; here are his horns, Master
Brook."[46] Moreover, it is Ford who is speaking, so that the
passage becomes illogical (it is Ford who has assumed
the alias of Brook) unless we assume that Ford is ad-
dressing the speech to someone in the audience. I suggest
that Shakespeare is obeying the royal command and offering a comic palinode, or at least an explanation, to
the offended nobleman sitting before him. The irony is
heavy; but the speech is a superbly witty retraction. It is
superficial; but within the comic mode, it is fitting, and I
think it was in all likelihood a successful ploy. Lord Cobham, on the day of his investiture in the Order of the Garter, reached a pinnacle of which he could be proud.

William Dethicke, Garter king of arms, has left us a
description of the ceremonies at Windsor that day in
June. He pictured the knights of the Garter gathering in
the chapterhouse with the three newly elected knights,
the earl of Sussex, Lord Scrope, and Lord Cobham, sitting
down "on a forme neere the Chapterhouse dore." With
the beginning of the formal ceremonies, all the regular
knights marched into the chapel following the officers of
the Order, Garter king, Register, and Black Rod. Then
Garter king went to fetch the new knights, one at a time.
Sussex was installed first as he was led into the chapel by
Garter king "bearing his Mantle hood & Coller upon a
Crymson Velvett Cushion." The new knight was placed
before his stall, and then the dean of Windsor read him
the oath. His mantle was placed upon his shoulders by the
lord admiral and the earl of Northumberland; then they
put his hood and collar about his neck and laid his book
of the Order before him on a velvet cushion. Lord Cobham was installed in the same way, and last came the
Lord Scrope. Dethicke describes the three new knights in
their stalls and the others retiring to their stalls also, then
"The Queene begunne Service." Queen Elizabeth rarely
attended the installations at Windsor in her later years,
but this year the hatchments and arms of two special

knights were being removed because of their deaths in 1598. The two had been friends of hers—important friends. The first was Philip II of Spain, whose arms had remained above his stall in the chapel in spite of the hostility of the Armada and the tensions of the last twenty years of Elizabeth's reign. The other arms were those of Lord Burghley, Elizabeth's anchor and strong right hand since her coronation almost forty years earlier.

Dethicke also describes toward the end of his account how the new knights-elect had ridden into Windsor the evening before their installation. First, about five in the evening, came the earl of Sussex, "riding over the bridge from Colbrooke ward very well accompanied and well horsed." A few minutes later Lord Scrope came from the same direction with a colorful group of attendants. Then last, about a quarter of an hour after Scrope, came the Lord Cobham, "although the last yet most bravest: his Gentlemen in purple velvett breeches, and white satin doubletts and chaines of gold: And his Yeomen in purple Cloth breeches, and white fustian dubletes, all in blew Coates, faced with white taffeta, and fethers of white and blewe."[47] Wednesday, 6 June 1599, was a glorious day for Lord Cobham. When the knights of the Order left the chapel after the ceremonies and proceeded into the castle for dinner and entertainment, Cobham surely must have been ready to forgive the lowly actors who had taunted his family in their whimsical make-believe.[48]

But Ralph Brooke, York herald, was a man with a grudge. He had been quarrelling with the Garter king of arms for many years, and that quarrel had become more virulent at the end of the century. The litigation between Brooke and Dethicke moved from the Court of Common Pleas into the Star Chamber in 1594.[49] A list of interrogations for Dethicke includes accusations that he had circulated "infamous writings" about his colleague Brooke; that he had been proved to be "foresworn"; that his patent as Garter king of arms had been taken from him; that he had stolen books of arms from the heralds's corporation, and so on.[50] Dethicke was found guilty of some of the charges and was fined "xx markes damages for that he hit ye said Yorke by chance with the chape of his rapier in the Court at Easter last past."[51] One of Dethicke's "infamous writings" against Brooke is extant in the Lansdowne manuscripts. It probably is a fair example of the Garter king's outrageous wit. He describes "Raffe Brokesmouth, paynter, called Rougecrosse, al[ia]s Brokes al[ia]s Brookes" and his dishonesty, incompetence, and immorality, as well as his association with one "Robert Bolton a comon cutpurse called Bolton with the great Legge" which resulted in Brooke's being "justly condemned and Burnde in the hand at Newgate for being accessarye unto twoe notable Buglaryes."[52] The Star Chamber proceedings did not end the bickerings; instead, the enmity between the two men was intensified. Dethicke wrote in 1595 to Sir John Pickering, lord keeper of the Great Seal, to complain of his colleagues, especially Brooke, who, Dethicke claimed, was "twyse disgraded, & the Queenes Maties coate of Armes pulled over his eares."[53] In 1596 or shortly thereafter, Brooke wrote to the earl of Essex who had become earl marshall and as such was in charge of the College of Arms. Brooke complained of Dethicke's ignorance and listed thirty-one "guiltes of Armes" for which the Garter king was responsible.[54] In the fall of 1596, while all this squabbling was going on, William Dethicke granted John Shakespeare the coat of arms which Clarencieux king of arms had tricked earlier for the Stratford-upon-Avon family in the first decade of Queen Elizabeth's reign. Ralph Brooke, continuing his habit of faulting the Garter on every issue, compiled a manuscript of twenty-three names he considered ineligible for arms. Among that list was the name of "Shakespear ye Player."[55] In 1597 William Camden was appointed Clarencieux king of arms. Camden had established himself as England's premier historian, and apparently Lord Burghley and the earl of Essex in choosing him for the appointment were determined to place someone of authority in the heralds's office to bring order out of chaos. But Camden had never been a pursuivant or a herald, and his jump into the king of arms position without the traditional apprenticeship intensified the jealousy and friction that was rampant there. Ralph Brooke began to compile his notorious *Discoverie of Certaine Errours,* an attack upon Camden's *Britannia.* The quarrelling was now enlarged to include everyone, and accusations were made against

Ralph Brooke, Esq., York Herald.

both living and dead who had been associated in the College of Arms. Camden and Dethicke prepared a document between 17 November 1599 and 24 March 1600, which verified the Shakespeare arms and the right of the bearers to impale those arms with the Arden Coat.[56] And in 1602 Dethicke and Camden replied to the earl marshall's interrogation concerning Brooke's complaint over the issuance of the Shakespeare arms.[57]

Ralph Brooke's cantankerous behavior continued for more than twenty years after this controversy over Shakespeare's coat of arms. He made a destructive enemy of the printer William Jaggard in 1619 when he published his *Catalogue of Nobility* and faulted Jaggard for all the errors. John Crofts has speculated that the alias in *The Merry Wives* was changed from *Brooke* to *Broome* at Jaggard's suggestion when the first folio was being put to press in 1622–1623, that Jaggard feared the "notorious old make-bate," Ralph Brooke, York herald of arms.[58] Crofts's suggestion is pertinent in one respect only. Old Ralph Brooke may certainly have taken offense at Shakespeare's satire in both the *Henry IV* plays and *The Merry Wives*, but that Jaggard feared Brooke's ill temper is highly unlikely. In 1622 Jaggard printed a vicious attack on Brooke compiled by young Augustine Vincent, Rougecross pursuivant. And in the commendatory poems which preface the volume, Shakespeare's puns from *The Merry Wives* reappear. One of the poems echoes the song of "Shallow Rivers" that Evans sings in act III.

> *Brookes-mouth* is stopt, for shallow brookes are soone,
> That runne not under ground, as Spanish doon,
> And as this did, before it was espyde
> By Lince-ey'd *Vincent*, who it saw, and dryde
> Before it grew a Sewer; as sure it would,
> If this Commissioner had it not controul'd
> And turn'd another way, into the Mayne
> The Marshall-sea, Mediterr-Ocean:
> Where he's confin'd gainst good Philosophie.
> But with good Logicke, Art, and Heraldrie,
> Triumphant *Vincent*, thou hast shewne the South
> His Northerne Errours, and hast stopt his mouth
> To open mine; in praise of such strong sence,
> For he was Herald, ere thy selfe was *ens*:
> That so much cast behinde, can so out go,

Argues what Diligence, not Age can do;
That shot'st him with a Cannon from the Towre,
Who was not Pistoll-proofe, by this good howre.
They say, he's curst euen from his mothers wombe,
That from the Cannons mouth deriues his Tombe.
Ile tell no Fortunes, least I rub a sore,
He's none of us indeede, his hand shewes more;
Or if he be, his writings so untrew,
Will make him Herald to the Wandring Iew:
Whose shame, doth doubly let thy honor in,
To doe us right, and to detect his sin
In so much fraude: and we account thee wise,
That canst speake truth, and say another lies:
Let truth in euery Science have his proppe;
More *Vincents* Lord, or fewer *Mouthes* to stoppe.[59]

That Samuel Lennard, Blue Mantle pursuivant, the
author of this commendatory verse, was aware of some
mockery of Ralph Brooke in *The Merry Wives* is perhaps
too much to expect in 1622. The merriment in Shakespeare's comedy is too broad-based for that. But Ralph
Brooke *was* sensitive about his name. Just as William
Dethicke changed his name and created a fictitious line of
descent for himself, so Brooke undertook to establish himself as a descendant of the Brookes of Leighton in Ches-
hire.[60] In truth, he was the son of Geoffrey Brookesmouth,
a tanner or shoemaker. He was admitted to Merchant
Taylor's School in 1564; in 1576 he had completed his
apprenticeship as a painter-stainer; and in 1580 he was
appointed Rougecross pursuivant in the College of Arms.
Early in 1593 he progressed to the position of York herald.
Traditionally, the next step above York was Garter king
of arms, but Brooke was never promoted to this office.
When Dethicke left his position in the early years of King
James's reign (James learned that Dethicke had been a
sponsor of the Suffolk line as heir-apparent to the crown),
William Seegar replaced him. John Anstis described
Brooke as being a "Person of a fierce, impetuous Temper,
unwearied and implacable in Malice, who to gratify his
Appetite of Revenge stuck at no Design or Practice, how
vile soever."[61] And this was the man who objected to a
player bearing arms.

The Brookes of Leighton were related to the fifteenth-
century Sir Thomas Brooke who had married Joan Bray-

brook, daughter of Lady Cobham. In the Tudor period the
Brookes of Leighton had become a distinguished legal
family. Sir Richard Brooke or Broke (d. 1529), chief baron
of the exchequer, was the fourth son of Thomas Broke of
Leighton. He had studied at the Middle Temple and had
become recorder of the city of London, a judge of the
Common Pleas Court, and so forth.[62] There were other
Brookes who attended Oxford and the Inns of Court and
were "called justice there." Sir Robert Brooke, author of
the *Abridgement* or abstract of the year books till his
own time, who became speaker of the House of Commons
and chief justice of the Common Pleas, was a famous
jurist of that line. David Brooke of the Inner Temple became chief baron of the exchequer also. In other words,
old Ralph Brooke, who seems to have been constantly
in a paranoiac state, could easily have extended the satire
of the Ford-Brooke role to the Justice Shallow, Simple,
Slender complex with its banter on heraldry and legal
terms. Or, more likely, he simply was incensed by the im-
pertinence of the actors in satirizing Lord Cobham, who
bore the Brooke name as well as he. Ralph Brooke had
neither power nor influence at court. He could, however,
question an issuance of arms, and that he did before November 1599. It is difficult at this point to prove that he was
angered over the Oldcastle-Cobham-Broome satire, but in
the realm of speculation it is an attractive and plausible
idea. He could not have been responsible for the change
of Ford's alias in *The Merry Wives*. Someone more powerful by far than the crotchety old York herald seems to have
been responsible for that revision. As I have speculated
before, Sir Robert Cecil had become King James's principal adviser before November 1604, when the King's
Men performed *The Merry Wives* at court. Cecil quartered
the Cobham arms because he had married William
Brooke's daughter, Elizabeth. I am of the opinion that the
acting company decided against using the name of Brooke
for this performance, and the substitution was initiated
at this time. It continued to be transmitted in the prompt-
books; after all, Henry Brooke was a prisoner in the Tower
of London, where he resided for the remainder of his life.
He was no longer a subject for comedy; he had become a
pseudotragic figure to all concerned.

Shakespeare's host of the Garter remains to be examined as a part of the comic crew. I believe that the playwright turned to the witless clown of *The Famous Victories* for his basic figure. I am assuming also from what we know of William Dethicke's quick-tempered character that the original character of Dericke in the old play irritated him. Shakespeare appears to have reworked the comic character, using as a model Chaucer's good-natured host of the Tabard Inn.

A semely man Oure Hooste was withalle
For to hav been a marchal in an halle.
A large man he was with eyen stepe—
A fairer burgeys is ther noon in Chepe—
Boold of his speche, and wys, and wel ytaught,
And of manhode hym lakkede right naught.

How much symbolism the Elizabethans read into this irresistible master of ceremonies I do not know, but from it Shakespeare produced a genial character of some strength. If William Dethicke's sense of humor functioned at all, he was flattered by the new dramatic portrait. As the principal officer of the Order of the Garter, the new comic image of the host of the Garter fit him well. In the play the host is genial. Some of his language is specialized; it comes from the terminology of the heralds' office. The title "Cavaleiro" which he applies to Master Page (II. i. 197) and to Slender (II. iii. 76) comes from the formal offices in the College of Arms. The lowly foot messengers were called "knightes caligate of Arms," but when they were promoted to the next rank and could ride on horseback, without spurs, they were called "knights Chivallier."[63] I assume also that the term "bully rook" has a double meaning, with the "rook" portion alluding to castle, just as the term "castallian" apparently does. These words are part of the Oldcastle satire that remains overt in the host's line concerning Falstaff, "Theres his Castle, his standing bed."

How much the horse-stealing scene from *The Famous Victories* influenced the complicated business of the missing horses in *The Merry Wives* is difficult to assess. In the old play Dericke's horse is taken; in Shakespeare's play Evans and Caius plot revenge by making away with the host's horses (which presumably are the same horses Falstaff has pawned). This part of the drama is incomplete as we have it, but the nucleus appears to come from the comedy of *The Famous Victories* rather than from an incident with the post horses in the 1590s.

It is also difficult to tell whether Shakespeare's good-humored host influenced William Dethicke's decision to defend the Shakespeare arms before the earl Marshall's inquiry in late 1599 and again in 1602. Certainly the comic role did no harm, for Shakespeare used his coat of arms thereafter. The queen also appears to have approved the comedy; at least the old legend reports her as having been "very well pleas'd at the Representation." *The Merry Wives* was a popular play in the seventeenth century, and critics such as Dennis and Rowe considered it an excellent example of what a comedy should be. If my analysis of the three-dimensional structure of the play is accurate, and if the wealth of symbolism which I find in the drama is viable, *The Merry Wives* was an exciting comedy for its Elizabethan audience. Had Francis Meres been writing his *Palladis Tamia* after 6 June 1599, he would have remarked on the excellence of the play, I am sure. The fact that he does not list *The Merry Wives* in his 1598 work indicates to me that Shakespeare's robust comedy had not yet been written. It was to be an occasional piece, and the occasion was to be the Garter installation of the following year.

CHAPTER EIGHT

"Enter: Sir John Russell and Harvey"

THE PROBLEM OF NAME-CHANGING IN SHAKESPEARE'S *Henry IV* plays is dominated by the Oldcastle materials, which are complex and admittedly difficult to organize into coherent evidence. Possibly because of the frustrations encountered in dealing with the Oldcastle problem, modern editors of the two plays have done little to provide explanations for the additional name-changes that occur in the dramas, changes which complicate the original problem even more. It is apparent upon close examination of the earliest texts of the plays that the excisions in the original script or scripts of the plays included not only Oldcastle's name but those of Harvey and Russell as well, for these character names remain in the early printed texts along with that of Oldcastle. In the first quarto of *1 Henry IV* (1598) Poins mentions both Harvey and Russell as colleagues in the planned Gads Hill robbery; he remarks in one speech to the prince: "Now my good sweete hony Lord, ride with vs to morrow. I haue a ieast to execute, that I cannot mannage alone. Falstalffe, Haruey, Rossill, and Gadshil, shal rob those men that we haue already waylaid, . . ." (I. ii. 180–83). This speech with the names of Harvey and Russell appears in all six quartos, and it survives in the first folio text of the play. In the robbery scene that follows, the names of Bardolph, Peto, and Gadshill are used, but Harvey and Russell do not appear, nor are they mentioned by the other members of the comic crew. But in the tavern scene that follows the robbery at Gads Hill, three lines have the speech prefix, *Ross.*, for "Rossill" (II. iv. 193. 195, 199); these appear

221

in all the quartos, but in the first folio the speech prefixes
are changed to *Gads.*, and the lines are given to the character Gadshill. This confusion is carried into the text of
2 Henry IV in which a stage direction at the beginning of
one comic scene states: *"Enter the Prince, Poynes, Sir
John Russel, with other"* (act II, scene ii). This cue disap-
pears in the first folio; a substitute replaces it: *"Enter
Prince Henry, Pointz, Bardolfe, and Page,"* yet Bardolph
and the boy enter the scene later at line 64. None of the
speeches in this scene is given to Russell in either the
quarto or the first folio text.

Shakespeare editors have supplied various commentary on these extraneous names. Theobald noted long ago
that Harvey and Russell were possibly the names of actors
who played the parts of Bardolph and Peto; the idea
proved popular.[1] In the nineteenth century Fleay suggested that perhaps Shakespeare intended to make a
reference to contemporary Elizabethans because in the
1590s Russell was the name of the earls of Bedford, and
Harvey was the name of the third husband of the dowager
countess of Southampton. But Fleay carried the idea no
further.[2] Allison Gaw has suggested in the twentieth century that the names Harvey and Russell are "ghost names"
that occur in the texts because Shakespeare changed his
mind about naming the comic crew; in his search for more
distinctive names, this critic speculates, Shakespeare altered Harvey and Russell to Bardolph and Peto.[3] A. E.
Morgan has assumed that the appearance of Sir John
Russell's name in the Shakespearean text is a reference
to the historical John Russell who achieved some stature
in the reign of Henry IV as a member of the household of
Humphrey, duke of Gloucester.[4] Meanwhile, Sir Edmund
K. Chambers found credible Theobald's theory that the
actors' names had inadvertently crept into the text, but
Chambers later changed his mind and accepted with reser-
vations Fleay's suggestion. Since he found Fleay's hasty
speculations at times irresponsible, he generalized that
older critic's theory of topical reference by remarking
that both Russell and Harvey were familiar names in Elizabethan England. Chambers's conclusion was that the
name of Peto had replaced that of Sir John Russell, and
that Bardolph's name was used as a substitute for Harvey

when the Oldcastle revisions were made in the texts of the *Henry IV* plays.[5]

Modern editors are inclined to agree with Chambers's conclusion, but if one turns to the Dering manuscript, Chambers's theory will not stand; in that version of the *Henry IV* plays the characters of Harvey, Russell, Bardolph, and Peto are all spoken of as members of Falstaff's crew. In the comic scene that precedes the robbery Poins speaks to the prince concerning his jest, but the list of names he recounts differs from that used in the quartos and the first folio text. Poins remarks to Hal after Falstaff's exit: "Now my good sweet hony lord, ride with us to morrow I haue a jest to execute that I cannot manage alone. Falstaffe, Harvay, Peto and Bardoff shall rob these men y' we haue already waylaide . . ." (I. ii. 139-41). A short time later in the scene of the robbery itself, Poins exclaims to Falstaff: "Sirra Jack, thie horse stands behind the hedge: when thow needest hime there thou shallt find hime And there stand ready Harvey, Peto and Rossill: goe thow and Bardoffe thether: Prince Hall and I will make good the foote of the hill and between vs they cannot escape: farewell and stand fast" (I. v. 64-68). In the quartos and the first folio this speech is cut to eliminate the names of the crew; Poins remarks curtly: "Sirrha Iacke, thy horse standes behinde the hedge, when thou needst him, there thou shalt find him: farewel & stand fast" (II. ii. 73-74). It would thus appear from the Dering manuscript that Harvey and Russell were *not* replacements for Bardolph and Peto but rather were additional characters who at one time enlarged the comic crew. If we could date the Dering manuscript with some accuracy, it would be helpful at this point, but we do not yet know the date of transcription of the work.

When J. O. Halliwell-Phillipps edited the manuscript for the Shakespeare Society in 1845, he suggested that between 1626 and 1630 Sir Edward Dering corrected the manuscript that had been transcribed earlier in the reign of James I.[6] This same editor noted later that Dering may have purchased the manuscript in 1619; one item in Dering's household books of that year lists twenty-seven playbooks purchased at the price of nine shillings.[7] S. B. Hemingway concluded after his examination of the manuscript

that the transcriber used a copy of the fifth quarto of *1
Henry IV* (1613) and a copy of the second issue of the
1600 quarto of *2 Henry IV* as his sources; he also concluded that Dering acquired the manuscript sometime
after October 1622.[8] G. Blakemore Evans examined the
manuscript in 1955 and concluded that Sir Edward Dering
drafted the first page of the manuscript himself; Evans
prefers to date the entire manuscript "not earlier than
1622."[9] Hardin Craig, however, examined the manuscript
in 1956 and concluded that the Dering version contains a
number of differences and peculiarities which remain
unchanged by any contacts with the fifth quarto. In addition, Craig notes that the manuscript is written in a normal late Elizabethan hand with no obvious Jacobean in-
termixtures. His final conjecture is that the Dering version
may be older than the earliest quarto of the *Henry IV*
plays, that possibly it is a manuscript of Shakespeare's
drama when it was one not two plays, but that it was written after Oldcastle's name was changed to Falstaff.[10]

It is in this unsettled state that the problem of the name-
changes in Shakespeare's *Henry IV* plays remains today. A partial solution to this entangled crux can be found
in Elizabethan history. Some evidence suggests logical
reasons for the appearance of the Harvey name in the
history plays. This historical matter relates, I think, the
satiric usage of the name of the contemporary Elizabethan to the theatrical and political tensions of that age.

Sir Edmund K. Chambers has suggested, as noted earlier, that neither Harvey nor Russell was a singular name
in Elizabethan England, and certainly Chambers's observation is true, as any leafing through the *Calendars of
State Papers* will reveal. Frederick Fleay attempted to
pinpoint the name of Harvey long ago when he suggested that possibly Shakespeare's usage indicated a
reference to Sir William Harvey, who married the dowager
countess of Southampton in the 1590s. Fleay offered no
documentation for his suggestion or any evidence to explain why the name of a prominent Elizabethan should
appear as a member of the entourage of Falstaff. Fleay's
speculation, however, can be confirmed as a strong probability by a reference to the historical milieu. There were
personal hostilities that apparently produced the satiric

caricature on the Elizabethan stage. Lampooning may be decadent, but it was a thriving art in the 1590s, and Harvey apparently became a target for the satirist's shafts.

Elizabethan England was not only a place for foreign intrigue; it was a setting for domestic broils as well, as every general reader knows. The divisive political competition at home made England a nest for homegrown treasons; many of the nobility became diplomatic entrepreneurs. In this complex situation in the last decade of the sixteenth century, the power of Lord Burghley began to pass into the hands of his wizened son, Sir Robert Cecil. Cecil's play for power both above and below board was opposed by the earl of Essex, and the competition between the two men extended to their followers. With the marriage of Sir Robert Cecil to Elizabeth Brooke, Lord Cobham's daughter, the Cecil-Cobham tie became one of kinship. This marriage strengthened a friendhsip between Lord Burghley and Lord Cobham that had survived turbulent days; Burghley had protected his untrustworthy friend, "loved him as a brother," his letters reveal. Sir William Harvey was a member of the Cecil-Cobham faction; when his name appears in the chronicle accounts of the 1590s it is usually in conjunction with one of the younger Brookes, sons of Lord Cobham.[11] It is among these ties and tensions that we will find, I believe, the motivation for Shakespeare's satire.

Sir William Harvey courted and eventually married the twice-widowed dowager countess of Southampton in the late 1590s, much to the chagrin of her young son, Henry, the third earl of Southampton, Shakespeare's patron. The countess, Mary Browne, daughter of the first Viscount Montague, had married Henry, the second earl of Southampction, in 1566. The involvement of that earl of Southampton in the affairs of Mary, queen of Scots, and the dissident Catholics of Elizabeth's reign led to his imprisonment, first in 1570 and again in October 1571 when he was implicated in the Ridolfi conspiracy.[12] The reader will recall that Lord Cobham had also been implicated in the Ridolfi plot. His bungling in the affair turned it into a fiasco; furthermore, when he was trapped, he apparently turned state's evidence to avoid dire punishment. As a result of this episode in diplomatic intrigues, the duke of

Norfolk was executed and the earl of Southampton, the earl of Pembroke, and others spent months of imprisonment in the Tower of London. The dissident Catholic lords had ample reason to be irate with William Brooke, Lord Cobham.

The second earl of Southampton died in October of 1581, and his wife remained a widow for thirteen years. In 1594 the dowager countess married Queen Elizabeth's vice-chamberlain, Sir Thomas Heneage; unfortunately, however, Heneage died in the following year. This second marriage seems to have brought even more complicated financial problems to the Wriothesley estates, and in 1597 a final financial settlement still had not been made concerning the inheritance of the young earl of Southampton, Shakespeare's patron. The dowager countess of Southampton was being courted at this time by Sir William Harvey; the tensions caused by this courtship and by the financial problems of the family seem to have been heightened by the personal dislike between the earl and his mother's suitor.

Sir William Harvey was a Kentishman, as was Lord Cobham. He was the son and heir of Henry Harvey of Kidbrooke. This Henry and his older brother George (who later became lieutenant of the Tower) were the sons of Sir Nicholas Harvey of Ickworth in Suffolk, whose second wife (mother of Henry and George) was Bridget, daughter of Sir John Wiltshire. This Sir Nicholas Harvey (paternal grandfather of William) had distinguished himself as a participant in the jousts and tournaments of Henry VIII's reign; he had also served as a royal ambassador for that king in Continental affairs.[13]

William seems to have inherited something of this grandparent's courage, for he became a soldier and an adventurer in his youth. We know that he was on the Continent at some time during the early years of the ferment between Spain and the Low Countries. He had a mature head on his shoulders when he wrote directly to Queen Elizabeth in December of 1585; the letter indicates that Harvey was an astute observer of the politics of the international scene. In addition to advice on the fighting around Brielle and Grave, he sent the queen a detailed list of the common people in Calais (brewers, inn-keepers, ex-soldiers, and the like) who could be considered safe to use in espionage. He also advised that it would be a simple matter to capture Count La Motte at Graveling "as he rydes on honting weakely accompanyed." And he was particularly insistent upon the advisability of planting "sufficient Colonies under discreete governors in the aptest places of *Terra Virginea*" in order to annoy Philip II and to "enrich your ma*tie* notably sondrie waies, and the whole Realme in traffick and Commodities." Harvey's interest in the New World remained with him; it was revived in James's reign when the Virginia Company became an active reality. Harvey's services seem to have been solicited by the queen; indeed, he states as much in this letter which he closes gracefully:

> Thus Right Gracious Soueraigne in obeyeng your Commandment I have sett downe my knowledge in the promised [intelligences], commending them most humbly to your ma*ties* high wisdome, censure, and secresie, wherwith in all lowlie dutie I finishe. London the 20 of December, 1585.
>
> <div align="right">Your Ma<i>ties</i> loyall devoted
Pore servant</div>
>
> W. H.

In a postscript Harvey added a plea for advancement: '. . . ffor I have none to behold, nor trust to but your self, nor after your .lyffe, anie assurance in earth to build on. Be good to me therfore in tyme least I perish by necessitie."[14] Harvey was a fortune hunter, but it was an age that encouraged such pursuits.

Whether or not the queen rewarded him for his attentiveness to duty we do not know. We do know that he was involved in the feverish preparations for defense against the Spanish Armada in the summer of 1588. Harvey's name survives in the "official" account of that famous battle; moreover, he appears to have been aboard the lord admiral's own ship, the *Ark Royal*, which was in the midst of the fighting (". . . the fight was very nobly continued from morning until evening, the Lord Admiral being always [in] the hottest of the encounter"). The primary accounts of the famous battle reveal that after Howard had set fire to the Spanish ships, he pursued the crippled *San Lorenzo*, one of the largest of the Spanish galleons, into Calais Roads where he sent his men to board her:

. . . whereupon the Lord Admiral sent his long boat under
the charge of Amyas Preston, gentleman, his lieutenant, and
with him Mr. Thomas Gerrard and Mr. [William] Harvey, together with other gentlemen, his Lordship's followers and
servants, who took her and had the spoil of her.[15]

The printer Richard Field published for the English reading
public an account of the defeat of the Armada soon after
the event, and his pamphlet contained a description of this
episode. The author of the work eulogizes Harvey and Gerrard, and he states that they were among numerous young
Englishmen who volunteered service "without charge"
during the Spanish attack:

. . . I remember that the names of some of them were these:
Master *Henry Brooke* sonne and heire to the *Lord Cobham*, Sir
Thomas Cecil sonne and heire to the Lord Threasurer, Sir
William Hatton heire to the Lord Chancellour, Sir *Horatio
Pallauicino* a Knight of *Genua*, Master *Robert Carie* sonne to
the Lord *Hunsdon*, Sir Charles *Blunt*, brother to Lord *Mountjoy*.
But much speech is of two Gentlemen of ye Court that went to
the Nauy at the same time, whose names are *Thomas Gerard*
and *William Hervie*, to me not knowen, but now here about
London spoken of with great fame. These two adventured out
of ship boate, to scale the great *Galliasse* wherein *Moncade*
was, and entered the same only with their Rapiers: a matter
commonlie spoken, that neuer the like was hazarded afore, considering the height of the Galliasse compared to a ship boate.[16]

This successful boarding action can be explained from
another historical source; the *San Lorenzo* had run afoul of
her own anchor cables, "which caused one of her sides to
lie so hie that her ordinance could not play, and so xxv.
Pinases came and battered her."[17] The English seamen and
soldiers were able to board the ship on her low side, which
lay near the surface of the water. The legend that Harvey
himself fired the shots which killed the commander, Don
Hugo de Moncada, cannot be borne out, but the English
soldier did return to London an acclaimed hero.[18]

Replete now with glory, Harvey appears to have aspired
even higher toward the Renaissance conception of the perfect courtier. It has been suggested that he became a poet
and a literary critic as well. If scholars have been accurate
in attributing the verses "by Mr. W. Har." to him, then he
did achieve fame (from the modern point of view) by pen-

ning the lines which allude to Shakespeare's "golden stile."
These verses were written in memory of Lady Helen Branch
whose husband had been mayor of London. The small volume was published in 1594 and was entitled *Epicedium, A
Funerall Song*. The author suggests, as a means of "insti-
gating" greater poetry, that Shakespeare has wasted his
talents upon foreign themes while greater subject matter
lies neglected at home:

> You that to shew your wits haue taken toyle,
>   In registring the deeds of noble men:
> And sought for matter in a forraine soyle,
>   (As worthie subiects of your siluer pen)
> Whom you haue rais'd from darke obliuions den.
> You that haue writ of chaste *Lucretia*,
> Whose death was witnesse of her spotlesse life:
> Or pend the praise of sad *Cornelia*,
> Whose blamelesse name hath made her fame so rife:
> As noble Pompeys most renouned wife.
>   Hither vnto your home direct your eies:
>   Whereas vnthought on, much more matter lies.
>
> Matter that well deserues your golden stile,
> And substance that will fit your shadowes right,
> Whereon his wits a Schollar well may file:
> Whereof a Poet needs not blush to write,
> When strangers causes should be banisht quiet.[19]

Harvey extended his poem then by praising the Lady Helen
Branch whose virtues and beauty were comparable, he
said, with those of Helen, Cleopatra, Judith, and so on. If
the "Rape of Lucrece" is as symbolic and as meaningful a
poem as I think it is, then Shakespeare must have been
amused with this bumptious criticism from a soldier who
would read a work of art as though it were a military man-
ual. The question arises: was this bit of obtuse criticism the
reason for the appearance of Harvey's name among the
Falstaffian crew? I doubt it. Shakespeare's own character
appears to have been far too magnanimous for this kind of
pettiness, and besides, the verses were intended as commendation. The Harvey problem lies beyond this early
incident.

Harvey's aspirations appear to have been boundless; and
he was rising in the heady whirl surrounding the queen in
London. It has been suggested that perhaps he had become

a helpful friend of the dowager countess of Southampton
before her second marriage to Sir Thomas Heneage in
1594.[20] Of this I find no documentation. There is evidence,
however, that Harvey was looking for preferment at court.
He sought the comptrollership of the navy when the death
of Sir William Borough left that office vacant, but, unfortunately for him, Sir Henry Palmer won the appointment.
Harvey did receive the keepership of St. Andrew's Castle in
1598, an appointment which brought the aspiring parvenu
a fee of nineteen pounds a year.[21] It seems, however, that
lucrative reward through patronage was not yet in store for
him. He *had* participated in the successful sacking of Cadiz
under the command of the earl of Essex and the lord admiral in 1596, but how much wealth he acquired in that military adventure is not known. We know only that in this
encounter with the Spanish, Harvey served as a captain
with one hundred soldiers in the regiment of the earl of
Sussex. Sussex, his captains, and their men were aboard the
Swiftsure, the vice-admiral ship of Sir Walter Raleigh's
squadron. We know that in the Cadiz action Harvey was rewarded with knighthood, but the knighting occurred in an
unexplained, delayed dubbing. Accounts of the battle relate
that on Sunday, 27 June, Howard and Essex created some
fifty-odd knights for their gallantry performed in battle. The
Slyngisbie manuscript describes the dubbing of the unusually large number of men that morning before divine services, but this first-hand account of the events also states
that it was on the following Monday morning that "the
lords general knighted Sir William Harvey."[22] Whether or
not this "extra" accolade was an afterthought performed to
correct an oversight we do not know. It possibly was
another manifestation of the exaggerated feeling of competition between the two leaders. The incontinent thirst for
glory tantalized most Elizabethans, and neither Howard nor
Essex was immune to its goad.

    At home Essex's enemies were soon decrying not only the
excessive number of knighthoods made by the generals but
also the entire Cadiz affair. Record of such attacks is extant
in the Bacon papers; Ed Reynolds, one of Essex's secre-
taries, made bold to write to his employer concerning the
calumny   being   poured   into   the   queen's   ear:

One malicious suggestion of H. Brooke *I forgot in my former letter*, which was, that this service [at Cadiz] was but a matter of chance: that your lordship went to seek blows at adventure without any certain knowledge: *and* saith he, *what if the fleet of Cadiz had been departed? what service then should your majesty have had, and to what purpose had your 50,000£. been consumed?*[23]

Henry Brooke, who became the eighth Lord Cobham in 1597 when his father died, was the object of Essex's contempt. Rarely did the earl descend to the debilitating emotions of hatred; he was normally honorable and compassionate, but with this one man he allowed himself the language and feelings of vilification, as I have noted above. Essex's explosive remarks to the privy Council concerning Cobham are extant:

I made yt knowen unto them [the Council] that I had just cause to hate the Lord Cobham for his villanous dealing and abusing of me, . . . that in hym their is no worth. If theirfore her Majesty wold grace hym with Honor, I may have just cause to thincke myself litle regarded by her.[24]

These statements were made as Essex attempted to stay the appointment of Henry Brooke to the offices at court which the elder Lord Cobham had held. It is among these emotional rancors that the relevancy of the Shakespearean satire lies.

During this time Sir William Harvey's relationship with the Cobham faction was developing. We know that Gawen Harvey, son of Sir George Harvey (William's uncle) had married Lord Cobham's niece, and we know that Gawen Harvey was more than content with the marriage arrangements; at a later date he wrote a letter addressed to the Privy Council in which he exclaimed on his earlier good fortune. The letter was written under adverse circumstances in 1603 after Gawen had been apprehended carrying messages for Lord Cobham, who was then a prisoner in the Tower accused of complicity in the famous Main and Bye plots of that year. Gawen pleaded as his excuse his indebtedness to Henry, Lord Cobham: "I appeal to your lordships whether any man living being in my case could have done less for him [Lord Cobham] which had given me his niece, a handsome young gentlewoman, for a wife, that would be worth to me 10,000£. in portion."[25] But these troubles were later events; let us return to the year 1597. Sir William Harvey rose to command in this year. He joined the abortive Islands voyage as captain of the *Bonaventure,* and the unpleasant features of this historical event *are* important for this study. Harvey's ship was in Sir Walter Raleigh's squadron, and when Raleigh made the unlicensed attack on Fayal, both Harvey and Sir William Brooke (captain of the *Dreadnought* and third son of the elder Lord Cobham) joined the rear admiral in the adventure. Purchas records the story, as told by Sir Arthur Gorges, an eyewitness:

> Our Rear Admirall [Raleigh] in his Barge rowed to Sir William Brookes Ship, and to Sir William Harveyes, and desired them, and some other Sea Captaines, to accompany him in landing, with such men as conveniently they could furnish. . . . Sir William Brooke, Sir William Harvey, and some others, very willingly assented, and presently there were made ready with shot, and Pike one hundred and sixtie men more in Boates.[26]

When Essex arrived in the harbor, Raleigh's forces had established a beachhead and had taken the town, though not the stronghold above it. Essex's anger at the unlicensed attack, which had been made (Raleigh's enemies assured the earl) "to steal honor and reputation" from him, led Essex to consider court-martialing and beheading his rear admiral. The captains who followed Raleigh were cashiered and imprisoned. It was through the conciliatory efforts of Lord Thomas Howard that these explosive tensions were somewhat eased. One Essex partisan, however, claimed that "the Generalls goodness would not suffer him to take any extream course, but with a wise and noble admonition forgave the offence."[27] Essex seems to have been able to moderate his anger, Raleigh made an apology, he and Essex dined together the next day, and the restrained captains were released. But the embers of resentment continued to smoulder in all breasts, and spirits were poised to flare at any given provocation.

The hostilities created during the Islands voyage were fanned by ensuing events, as everyone knows. The hasty marriage of the earl of Southampton with Elizabeth Vernon, Essex's cousin, angered both his mother and Queen

Elizabeth. Southampton was in Paris when the news of his
secret vows with a maid of honor reached the queen's ears.
He had received the long-sought-for permission to spend
two years abroad and was planning to proceed toward Italy
when Queen Elizabeth ordered his immediate return to
London.[28] The queen's sensitivity concerning the "unlicensed" marriages of her courtiers and maids of honor is
well known, and certainly there was some cause in this
marriage for her displeasure. We know less about the anger
of the dowager countess of Southampton. In her letter of 6
October to the earl of Essex she mentions her son who was,
from her point of view, both unnatural and undutiful.[29] This
feeling of unhappiness, however, was a mutual one between mother and son, for Sir William Harvey's courtship
of the dowager countess of Southampton had proceeded to
such a point that gossips were bandying the subject about
London. As early as the spring of 1597 rumors of such a
marriage were a-wing, and Rowland Whyte relayed the
gossip to Flushing where his employer, Sir Robert Sidney,
was governor: ". . . and a Speach goes, that my Lady
Southampton will have Sir William Harvey."[30] A year later
that indefatigable letter-writer, John Chamberlain, adver-
tised to his friend Dudley Carleton that "Sir William Harvy
is sayde to have married the Countess of Southampton."[31]
The news at this point was premature, but the court was
filled with the gossip.

We know that the earl of Southampton objected stren-
uously to Harvey's courtship of his mother, and he enlisted
Essex's assistance in staying the marriage. Essex in turn
sought the aid of the glib Lord Henry Howard, who was sent
to question the countess concerning her marital plans. Following his interview with the dowager, Howard wrote to
Essex, informing him that the marriage had not taken
place: ". . . she did assure me on her honor that the knot of
marriage was yet to tie, although she wold be staied at no
certain time, but ever reserve her owne liberty to dispose of
her selfe where and when it pleased her." Howard assured
Essex that he had begged the countess not to create any
scandal by marrying during her son's disgrace, and he continued his letter by relating how he had explained to the
lady why such a timing was bad—the whole world would
wonder at her contempt of her son, and everyone would

"tax" her very judgment. Howard blandly relayed the countess's spirited response to his admonition: she had said she hoped her son would expect no account from her of her marriage when he had made her such a stranger to his own. She did however remain tractable enough to promise Howard that she would send her suitor to speak with Essex whom (she assured Lord Henry) Harvey honored.[32]

When Southampton returned from Paris, he was imprisoned in the Fleet, and Essex continued his role as mediator, attempting to soothe the ruffled feelings of mother and son. He wrote to the young earl concerning his own interview with the dowager countess, and he described the forthright manner which he had used in the discussion: "I have according to my promise to your Lo: been this morning with my La: your mother. I have told her how sadd I found you, how the grounds of yt ware her unkindness—the discomfort and discontentment you tooke in her marrage and scorn that Sr Wm Harvy shold thinke to ofer any scorn to you." Essex described the warnings he had given the countess of future troubles likely to ensue from her marriage to Harvey, and he was scarcely diffident when he informed her that he would have reacted much as her son had done to such unpromising events. He concluded the interview by praising Southampton as an honorable and commendable son in an attempt to placate the countess's undue umbrage.[33]

The following day Essex talked with Sir William Harvey; that evening when he again wrote to Southampton, he described the tense interview in detail. He had, he declared, "delt freely" with Harvey and had accused him of unkind and unmannerly carriage toward the young earl. The intrepid Harvey had answered by denying that he had spoken disrespectfully of Southampton except when he was threatened, and then he added wittily that "they thatt wer angry without cause must be pleased without amends." At this point Essex apparently lost his temper; he described in his letter his heated response: "After I had told him whatt I thought of his words, I bid him think advisedly now having geven you advantage allredy and being cause of a mischief to you, how he did cross my sollicitation of her giving of satisfaction to you before she married, for I did assure myself they wold both repent it." Essex concluded his letter

by stating his own opinion of Harvey's intentions: he was
sure that Harvey would not "deal truly" with Southampton,
nor would Harvey "thank" the countess if she proved fair
and equitable in the financial settlement with her son.
Essex concluded magnanimously by reassuring his young
friend that he would stand by him as far as any bond of
honor, nature, or reason could move a man.[34]

As historians know, the dowager countess of Southampton did not alter her plans of marriage with Sir William
Harvey. It was with the queen's approval that the wedding
was performed in January of 1598/99. John Chamberlain
sent the news to Carleton that month: "Sir William Harvies
marriage with the old countess of Southampton that hath
lien smothering so longe, comes now to be published."[35]
The "old" countess was forty-four, her new husband was
apparently thirty-three, and her twenty-six-year-old son
was very unhappy with the match.[36]

The unpleasantness between the earl of Southampton and
Sir William Harvey started possibly as early as 1596. We
know from Rowland Whyte that the gossips were discussing the courtship of Harvey and the earl's mother in the
spring of 1597. We date the *Henry IV* plays as composi-
tions of 1596-1597 and early 1598 (*Part One* was registered
with the stationers on 25 February 1598). And in these
plays the name of Harvey is used for one of the comic crew
surrounding Falstaff. I wish to suggest that the tensions
between Southampton and Harvey at this time, tensions
which developed into downright hatred in 1598, are reflected in the satire of the history plays. Shakespeare's
assumed devotion to Southampton ("The loue I dedicate to
your Lordship is without end: . . . What I haue done is
yours, what I haue to doe is yours, being part in all I haue,
deuoted yours") and the young earl's love of the plays
(gossips relate later that he did nothing but "pass away the
tyme in London merely in going to plaies every day") add
strength to this conjecture. The playwright appears to have
been sensitive to the immediate conflicts within the restive
court of Elizabeth. The young earl of Southampton was
under stress at the time of the writing of the *Henry IV*
plays; he was unhappy with his mother because of her
apparent willingness to remarry without first completing
the financial settlement of the Wriothesley estate in his

favor. And he was particularly incensed with Sir William Harvey, who was pressing his courtship of the older countess with a conscious eye to her wealth. Harvey's political alignment with the Cobham-Cecil faction only compounded the grievance. I believe this personal friction explains why the topical lampooning in the *Henry IV* plays extends beyond the Falstaff-Oldcastle satire to include some of Lord Cobham's associates in the wrangling court of the English queen.

The Harvey problem does not end with the history plays, however, because the name of Sir William has entered Shakespearean studies through another crux made famous by scholars. All readers know that the "Mr. W. H." of Thomas Thorpe's dedication of his 1609 edition of Shakespear's sonnets has provoked speculation for many decades. Charlotte Stopes published her tentative theory that "Mr. W. H." referred to Sir William Harvey in her 1904 edition of the sonnets; she suggested that Harvey had very likely acquired the manuscript of the poems after the dowager countess of Southampton died in 1607. In her will the countess left "the best part of her stuff" to her son and "the most part" to her husband.[37] A. L. Rowse has accepted Mrs. Stopes's idea and has concluded in his theory of the sonnets (1964) that Harvey, who recognized the value of the manuscript, sent it to Thomas Thorpe for publication in 1609. Both scholars speculate that Thorpe acknowledged his indebtedness to Harvey by writing the problematic dedication to "the onlie begetter of these insving sonnets, Mr. W. H."[38] I am inclined to agree with the identification of "Mr. W. H." with Sir William Harvey, for I believe the man was moving tangentially in the literary scene. I do *not* think, however, that Harvey was benignly motivated if and when he sent the valuable manuscript to the printer Thorpe as has been suggested. Rather, I believe that Harvey had at last by good luck found the means to revenge the lampooning he had suffered earlier at the hands of the famous playwright. My own reading of the sonnets has convinced me that they are far too personal to have been intended for the "clapper-clawing" public, and I say this with full knowledge of the prototypal elements of the sonnet tradition. That some of the sonnets had circulated in manuscript we can assume from the statement of Francis Meres in 1598, but that the total sonnet sequence was written for the general reader is beyond my belief. This speculation is admittedly assumptive, but I think it is also probable. I believe that Harvey's revenge was achieved by the most effective means he could possibly have found. To censure him for his apparent ill will, however, would be hypocritical. Harvey's supposed action, ungracious as it appears, resulted in the multiplication of our great good; we might never have had the sonnets had Harvey been a more upright man.

The name-changes in the *Henry IV* plays are small editorial problems that will ultimately be explained as the primary historical materials continue to reach print. But these textual cruxes are also related to the larger problems of the meaning and function of Elizabethan historical dramas. We are coming nearer today to the realization that the dramatists of this period saw history as a pliable medium that could be molded and reshaped to fit the heated form of contemporary affairs, "to show the very age and body of the time his form and pressure." Nor will we long be surprised to find, I wager, that the universality of Shakespeare's art gains its force from being seriously rooted in temporal affairs. Shakespeare was compounding his creations from the common clay of everyday occurrences and events. That he could inform such fabrications with spirit and imagination is another indication of his genius.

The second name with which we are concerned in this study, the name that appeared with Harvey's in the early quartos of the *Henry IV* plays and in the Dering manuscript, is that of Sir John Russell. And again, historical materials reveal the unallayed tensions which appear to have provided the motivating force in this satire. Sir John Russell was the eldest surviving son of Francis, second earl of Bedford, one of Elizabeth's staunchest Protestant peers. History is relatively silent about this young man. We know that on 23 December 1574 he married Elizabeth Hoby, widow of Sir Thomas Hoby, and that he attended Parliament the next year as Lord Russell. He died in July 1584 at Highgate and was buried in Westminster Abbey.[39] We are inclined to ask at this point why the name of a man dead for some thirteen years should appear in 1597–1598 in the Elizabethan historical drama. The answer lies in the tensions developing at that time in the Blackfriars precinct:

Sir John Russell's name appeared in the early versions of Shakespeare's *Henry IV* plays to annoy Russell's widow, the singular and exceedingly voluble Lady Elizabeth Russell, the instigator and promoter of the famous petition of November 1596, which was signed by the residents of Blackfriars and sent to the Privy Council to prevent the opening of the new theater that James Burbage was constructing in the old Parliament chamber. Lady Russell's London house was also in the Blackfriars precinct; it lay on Water Lane just north of these "fayer great edifices" that housed the ancient Parliament chamber and the dwellings of Cobham and Hunsdon. It was Lady Russell, it seems, who sponsored the complaint that temporarily stayed the plans of James Burbage and Lord Hunsdon's players, with whom of course Shakespeare was associated.[40]

We know that on 4 February 1596 James Burbage paid six hundred pounds to Sir William More for the old Parliament chamber in Blackfriars. The contract of sale is extant. Burbage and his heirs were to have

> . . . all those seaven great upper Romes as they are now devided being upon one flower, and sometymes beinge one great and entire rome with the roufe over the same covered with Leade. . . . And also all the stone staires leading upp unto the Leades or Roufe. . . . And also that great paire of wynding stairs with the staircase thereto belonging which leadeth upp into the same seaven great upper romes out of the greate yard. . . .[41]

These premises together with "all Liberties, privilidges, Lightes, watercourses, easiamentes, comodities and appurtenance" and rights of "ingres, egres and regres from the strete" were assigned in the contract to James Burbage and his heirs "for ever." This was the same space that Richard Farrant, William Hunnis, Henry Evans, John Lyly, and the earl of Oxford had leased and subleased between 1576 and 1584 for practice rooms and for the performances of the boys' companies.[42]

The friction during this period had created unpleasant tensions in the Blackfriars district, and the inhabitants seem at length to have united in signing the petition of 1596 to keep the adult players out of the precinct. The petition cited lewd crowds and dangers of the plague as good reasons for complaint:

Humbly shewing and beseeching your honors, the inhabitants of the precinct of the Blackfryers London. That whereas one Burbage has lately bought certaine roomes in the same precinct neere adioyning unto the dwellinghouses of the Rt Honorable The Lord Chamberlain and the Lord of Hunsdon, which roomes the said Burbage is now altering and meaneth very shortly to convert and turn the same into a common playhouse which will grow to be a very great annoyance and trouble, not only to all the noblemen and gentlemen thereabout inhabiting but allso a generall inconvenience to all the inhabitants of the same Precinct both by reason of the great resort and gathering together of all manner of vagrant and lewde persons, that under cullor of resorting to the Playes will come thither and worke all manner of mischeefe and allso to the greate pestering and filling up of the same precinct, yf it should please God to send any visitation of sicknesse as heretofore hath been, for that the same Precinct is allready growne very populous. . . .[43]

The petitioners continued their complaint by noting that the "Playhouse is so neere the Church that the noyse of the Drumms and Trumpets will greatly disturbe and hinder both the Ministers and parishioners in tyme of devine service and sermons." Moreover, they suggested that the players were attempting to circumvent the Lord Mayor's edict and "plant themselves in Liberties." The first signature on the petition was that of Lady Russell; below her name was that of Lord Hunsdon. Scholars have been puzzled by George Carey's signature; in November of 1596 he was the patron of the acting company that planned to occupy the new theater in Blackfriars.

We know that the plans for the new theater were made and the purchase completed in February of 1596 when the old Lord Hunsdon, George's father, was lord chamberlain and patron of Shakespeare's company. But Henry, Lord Hunsdon, died on 22 July 1596, and the theaters in London were ordered closed the same day. The former lord chamberlain's players went on tour during the remaining summer and early fall months, returning to London in late autumn for court performances during the Christmas season. George Carey, the new Lord Hunsdon, owned the rooms under the south end of the old Parliament chamber, and although he was now the patron of his father's acting company, Hunsdon seems not to have relished listening each night to the turmoil of the battle of Bosworth Field or of Cade's Rebellion in the apartment above his own.

240   SHAKESPEARE'S TYPOLOGICAL SATIRE

Richard Field (Shakespeare's publisher) seems to have responded in like manner, for his name also appears on the petition. The letter written by Thomas Nashe in the fall of 1596, shortly after Essex's return from Cadiz, reveals the strait circumstances in which the members of the acting company found themselves at this time. Burbage and his sons spent a considerable sum refurbishing the playhouse; years later Cuthbert Burbage remarked on the expense of converting the Parliament hall into a theater: "Now for the Blackfriars, that is our inheritance, our father purchased it at extreame rates, and made it into a playhouse with great charge and trouble."[44] It is evident that the citizens' petition of 1596 was a serious blow to the acting company with which Shakespeare was associated, and the instigator of that petition was Lady Elizabeth Russell, a woman of strong will and indomitable tongue. She deserves closer examination.

Lady Russell has been called an aristocratic termagant—a woman of intelligence who so domineered her acquaintances and kin that everyone in London, from queen to lodge porter, attempted in vain to avoid her. A recent biographer has described her with acid pen:

> She was free to interfere with everybody's business, to point out everybody's faults and her own virtues, to lay about her right and left, to let her personality rip, uninhibited, released, without fear or consideration, like some rich, rank vegetation running to seed with an acrid odour in the air. She was one of those old women: a perfect specimen of the female egotist, domineering, not without her good qualities—plenty of courage and always ready to step into any breach—whom everyone conspires to circumvent since there is no dealing with them, hence often checked, never wholly defeated. Since she was literate and very expressive she stands out naked in her letters, fully revealed.[45]

Lady Russell's dour character was perhaps caused by the misfortune that had overtaken her, or perhaps misfortune had overtaken her because of the dourness—it is difficult to say. She was one of the five formidable daughters of Sir Anthony Cooke. This Elizabethan scholar had schooled his daughters in the classical languages, and they became famous for their learning. All were aggressive and determined women. Elizabeth Cooke's more forward sisters had married Lord Burghley, Sir Nicholas Bacon, and Sir Henry

Killigrew. In 1558 Elizabeth married Sir Thomas Hoby, translator of Castiglione's *Il Cortegiano*. Her husband and William Brooke, Lord Cobham, were friends; in their youth they had studied together in Strasburg as students of Martin Bucer. In 1560 Lord Cobham visited the Hoby country home at Bisham with the marquis of Northampton (his brother-in-law), Lord Henry Seymour, the ladies Jane Seymour and Katherine Grey, and others. Elizabeth Hoby accompanied her husband to Paris when he was appointed by Queen Elizabeth to be the English ambassador to France, but Sir Thomas died of the plague after two years of service. His young widow brought his body home and interred it at Bisham in an alabaster tomb adorned with her own Greek and Latin verses.[46] Sir William Cecil offered the rich young widow as a wife to the duke of Norfolk in 1570 to relieve the duke of the pressures of debts and the attractions of the queen of Scots, but Norfolk declined.[47] Cecil's widowed sister-in-law did remarry in a few years when she accepted the proposal of Lord Russell, heir to the Bedford earldom. But misfortune continued to plague her steps; her two Russell children were daughters, and her husband died in 1584 while his father, the earl of Bedford, was still living. Thus capricious fortune once again stayed the lady's rise; she failed to become a countess (though she used the dowager title), and she had no Russell son to inherit the name. Taking dourly to her widow's weeds, she set about to place the expense of the care and education of her daughters on the queen.[48] Her constant and interminable letters to Burghley are extant in the Salsibury manuscripts at Hatfield House; in addition, a number of her colorful letters remain among the state papers. She was involved constantly in litigation, and, as might be expected, she supervised her legal affairs with an authoritative hand. Her vocabulary was replete with legal terms, Latinisms, and rhetorical cliches; her pen, like her personality, was both florid and blunt.

In 1592 Lady Russell was still fighting for a greater share of the Bedford estate for her two daughters; in one letter to Lord Burghley she demanded that "the judges opinions be delivered *singulatim* to Her Majesty's own self."[49] She acted frequently as intermediary for persons seeking favors from Burghley and his son, Sir Robert Cecil. She insisted that her cousin, Morrice, be made master of the

Rolls[50]; and she provoked the earl of Oxford to anger by
meddling in the financial arrangements between Elizabeth
Vere and the earl of Derby.[51] She descended full force on
Anthony Bacon for his unfaithfulness to his kin in his friendship with Essex.[52] She urged her crippled son, Sir Posthum-
ous Hoby, "to steal away by force" the young widow of
Walter Devereux, and she succeeded in this endeavor when
the young woman was widowed the second time by the
death of Thomas Sidney.[53] Lady Russell hauled her neighbors, the Lovelaces, into the Star Chamber for forcibly
entering her lodge at Windsor and causing "foul riots"
against her. They had turned against her, she said, because she had jailed two of their servants who "behaved
lewdly" to her.[54] She demanded that the earl of Kent be
made president of the North to replace the earl of Huntingdon, but she insisted that Burghley keep her endorse-
ment secret "bicawse He is a widower and I a widdow."[55]
She took Judge Gawdy to task in no uncertan terms for
"committing her man" in the liberty of Blackfriars, and
she informed this chief justice that she stood as much upon
her loyalty and reputation as he did upon his.[56] She wrote
Sir Robert Cecil in 1595 that she had caught the queen
"as Her Majesty was going to God's house, not being able
through malice to see her face else," and in spite of her
wealth she signed her letter 'By y^r Awnt that hath not
above vj^c ^{li} Declaro in ye world to live on left, Elizabeth
Russell y^t liveth in skorn of Disdayne, Mallice, and Rancor,
Fearing, serving, and Depending only upon God and my
Soveraighne."[57]

The most descriptive evidence we have of Elizabeth
Russell's characteristic behavior is that given in the report
of the Star Chamber case in which she sued Charles Howard, earl of Nottingham, the old lord admiral, for "fowl
riots" against her servants at Donnington Castle. This occurred in 1606 when the lord admiral's men took the castle
by force, but the event is so graphic and colorful in its details that it bears quoting. Lady Russell complained first
to King James, then to the courts, and finally to the Star
Chamber. In this highest court she out-talked her own
counsel and interrupted the judges. An eyewitness noted
the affair:

. . . but the Ladye, interruptinge them, desyred to be hearde, & after many denyalls by the Courte, vyolentelye & with greate audacitie beganne a large discourse, & woulde not by any meanes be stayed nor interrupted, but wente one for the space of halfe an howre or more; & in her beginninge of her speache excepted against my Lo. of Nottingham for that he had not aunsweared upon his oathe, but upon his honor. . . . Then shee did with bitternes, objecte that my Lo. Admirall in the begynninge of his aunsweare had denyed her to be Ladye Dowager to the Lo. Russelle, & that he knewe none suche: for shee sayde shee had bene Lady Dowager before Nottingham was, & that if the Lorde Russelle had lyved, bothe for worthe, honor, & judgemente, he had farre excelled the Lo. of Nottingham.

Lady Russell's tirade continued to some length; she declared that the lord admiral had stolen the castle from her; she insisted that she had had it from Queen Elizabeth as a gift, and so forth. In vain the judges tried to stop her:

The Lordes severallye hereupon woulde have stayde her, & muche distasted theise fonde speeches, but shee still wente one, & all the Courte & presence, murmuringe & makinge greate noyse, gyvings no eare to any thinge shee sayde, her owne Counselle goinge from the barre allso; yet shee wente one without any chaunge, or any waye abashed at all, in a verye boulde & stoute manner, withoute any shewe of any distemperature, or any loude speakinge, but shewinge a very greate spirite & an undaunted Courage, or rather will, more then womanlike, whose revenge by her tongue semed to be the summe of her desyre; in a meaner personage it is usuallye termed 'mallice' & 'envye,' but in her, beinge honorable, learned, & indued with many excellente guyftes, wee grace it with 'a great spirite,' which I feare the worlde conceavethe to be more then blemyshed, if not utterlye extinguished, with extreame pryde.

Finally the Lord Chancellor edged in a word to inform Lady Russell that none below the rank of an earl's wife could properly be designated "dowager."

. . . upon that shee plucked him by the claoke, & tolde him the lawe was otherwyse before he was borne: he, much mislyking of that usage, tolde her in manner of a reproffe that it was never offered to the Courte before, such violente interruption of any Judge in delyveringe his sentence when they had bene formerlye hearde, & bidde her forbeare, & heare him,

"for," sayde hee, "the Lo. Russelle, your husbande, was a
noble gentleman, but ill beseeminge you with so many unfit-
tinge detractions to compare him to the Earle of Nottingham;
& he dyed in his father's lyfetime, so you Coulde not be Lady
Dowager, for your husbande was never Earle."

The case was decided, of course, in favor of the elderly
lord admiral, and the judges "all wyshed it had bene
ended, & never broughte to this, all condemninge greatelye
the pryde & wyllfulnes of the plainteff."[58]

This episode, though it comes late, reveals graphically
the character of the lady who headed the list of petitioners in Blackfriars in November 1596. This was also the
woman whose husband's name appeared in the early quartos of the *Henry IV* plays. Were the players tormenting
her for revenge? This would appear to be the case. Sir
John Russell stalked the stage as a member of Falstaff's
(or Oldcastle's) crew. He had been dead for a number of
years, but his indomitable widow was very much alive and,
indeed, vulnerable to such lampooning, for we know from
her letters something of the intense pride with which she
looked forward to wearing the Bedford coronet and something of the bleak frustration she experienced when she
failed to achieve her ambition because of her husband's
premature death. Whether or not she was ever aware of
the players' lampooning we do not know. Her extant letters
do not mention the actors or the theater. She was a friend
of William Brooke, Lord Cobham; their friendship dated
from the days of their youth. In 1595, however, that
amity was ruptured over a money matter—Lord Cobham
owed her some eight hundred pounds, and she threatened
to confront him in the Star Chamber because of his unkind
usage of her. The anger she felt is revealed in her letter
to Cobham:

> You said a year ago that you would not be my daughters' ten-
> ant without my good will, but broke your promise. I did not
> think you would set against Lady Warwick and my daughters,
> they being so near the Queen. You then promised to discharge
> yourself of the house, but I find you have put in two of your
> own men to keep possession; your father would not have thus
> acted against any of mine. Your motive cannot be affection to
> the Lord Treasurer or Lord Burghley; but something yet con-
> cealed, that must appear on the trial as to who is to bear the

loss of 800 pounds arrears of rent for eight years; you offer rent, but it is refused, as no lease has been acknowledged. I think the Queen will not suffer the virgins that serve her to be wronged.[59]

It is tempting to see in this historical episode a Fang and Snare "exion" with Falstaff and Mistress Quickly heading toward litigation. Could Lady Russell's overbearing mannerisms, her pretentious intellection, her colorful and eclectic vocabulary have had an important bearing on the creation of that wondrous and voluble character, Mistress Quickly?[60] There is no positive proof, only a tantalizing suggestiveness. There is, however, enough historical evidence to firm up the case for Sir William Harvey and Sir John Russell. These two men apparently were caricatured in Shakespeare's history plays, and the very appearance of their names indicates the broad sweep of the topical satire of the comic scenes of the *Henry IV* dramas. That allusive satire apparently began with Oldcastle, Lord Cobham's ancestor, and extended through parts of the comic crew. Where it ended we have yet to discover.

CHAPTER NINE

Nashe, Jonson, and the Oldcastle Problem

JUST AS THE SATIRIC LAMPOONING IN SHAKESPEARE'S *Henry IV* plays (with its extension in the witty attacks upon both Sir William Harvey and Sir John Russell) is denser than scholars have hitherto suspected, so too is the Oldcastle satire *broader* than we have usually thought it to be, for it spreads outward, intensifying in its virility, in the works of other acclaimed writers of the Elizabethan period. These ramifications of the Oldcastle satire are to be found in certain works of Thomas Nashe and Ben Jonson, works written in 1598 and 1599 when Shakespeare had finished the *Henry IV* dramas and, as I believe, before or while he was writing *The Merry Wives of Windsor*. Nashe's use of the Oldcastle satire occurs in *Lenten Stuffe or Praise of the Red Herring,* and Jonson's experiment in the same vein occurs in his popular play *Every Man in His Humour.* These satiric attacks which appear to be directed at Lord Cobham were provoked, it would seem, by the harsh treatment meted out to the two playwrights for their "seditious" play, *The Isle of Dogs.* The drama is not extant, but I think we can assume from the backlash of satire which followed its censorship that the Cobhams were touched in the "sclanderous" play.

About all we know concerning *The Isle of Dogs* is that some time shortly before 28 July, in the summer of 1597, one acting company, possibly the Lord Chamberlain's performed a "lewd plaie . . . contanynge very seditious and sclanderous matter" in one of the theaters on the Bankside of the Thames.[1] The Privy Council ordered the arrest of the players, and the authorities were successful in apprehending three of the men. "We caused some of the players to be apprehended and comytted to pryson, wereof one of them was not only an actor but a maker of parte of the said plaie."[2] The "maker" appears to have been Jonson, for his name is listed with those of Gabriel Spencer and Robert Shaa in an order of 2 October for their release from the Marshalsea.[3] From the account of the play which Nashe gives in *Lenten Stuffe* he apparently wrote the induction and the first act, and, being frightened by the "monster" his brain had conceived, he took to his heels: "It was no sooner borne but I was glad to run from it."[4] Nashe (if we can believe his story) fled to Yarmouth in Norfolk, and Jonson seems to have finished the play. Francis Meres included a sympathetic reference to Nashe's trouble over the authorship of *The Isle of Dogs* in his *Palladis Tamia* (1598):

> As Actaeon was wooried of his owne hounds: so is Tom Nash of his *Ile of Dogs*. Dogges were the death of *Euripides,* but bee not disconsolate gallant young *Iuuenall, Linus,* the sonne of *Apollo* died the same death. Yet God forbid that so braue a witte should so basely perish, thine are but paper dogges, neither is thy banishment like *Ouids,* eternally to conuerse with the barbarous *Getes*. Therefore comfort thy selfe sweete Tom, with *Ciceros* glorious return to Rome, & with the counsel *Aeneas* giues to his sea-beaten soldiors.[5]

But not all Londoners felt this sympathy for the brash authors of the troublesome play. We do not know who among the Council members advocated the severe action against the players on 28 July. Henry, the new Lord Cobham, had not replaced his father on the Council, but his brother-in-law, Sir Robert Cecil, was an important member of that group. I suspect that Henry Brooke complained to Cecil or to Lord Burghley and that his complaint added considerable weight to the lord mayor's letter, for the Cobhams bear the brunt of Nashe's satire on the great herring or cob that was cooked before the pope. Nashe had no scruples at all in satirizing the burning of the Lollard martyr; he goes far beyond Shakespeare's "rosted Maningtre Oxe."

In his introduction to *Lenten Stuffe* Nashe states that he means to put his enemy, "the silliest millers thombe," in "bryne" and pickle him, and he does. The allegory of

Lenten Stuffe is built upon the wordplay involved in *cob* and *miller's thumb* as fish, a wordplay which Shakespearean scholars will recognize as that used by the young countess of Southampton in her jesting remark about Sir John Falstaff in her letter to her husband in 1599. This letter, written at Chartley on 8 July and sent to the earl in Ireland, apparently refers to Henry, Lord Cobham. It bears repeating: "All the nues I can send you that I thinke will make you Mery is that I reade in a letter from London that Sir John Falstaf is by his Ms^{rs} dame Pintpot made father of a milers thum a boye that is all heade and veri litel body, but this is a secrit."[6] Scholars have been quick to discover that the small fish with the big head is in Latin a *Cottus Gobio* and in English a *cob* or, as early as 1440, a "myllars thowmbe."[7] Nashe exploits this colloquialism that apparently had become an "in joke."

In the summer of 1597 *The Isle of Dogs* was performed, and on 28 July the lord mayor and the aldermen urged that all public stage performances in and about London be stayed because of their "vnchast matters, lacivious devices, shifts of Coozenage, & other & vngodly practizes."[8] The Privy Council issued an edict that was extremely severe. Not only were the plays to be stopped but the theaters were ordered torn down:

> Her Majestie being informed that there are verie great disorders committed in the common playhouses both by lewd matters that are handled on the stages and by resorte and confluence of bad people, hathe given direction that not onlie no plaies shalbe used within London or about the citty or in any publique place during this tyme of sommer, but that also those play houses that are erected and built only for suche purposes shalbe plucked downe, namelie the Curtayne and the Theatre nere to Shoreditch or any other within that county.[9]

These were disjointed times for the players, and it is small wonder that they resorted to satire. Nashe states explicitly in his introduction to *Lenten Stuffe* that he is writing a mock epic in revenge for his discomfiture over the authorship of *The Isle of Dogs*. He places his clue to the identity of his victim on the first page of the work when he calls his enemy, whose "loud bellowing prodigious flaw of indignation" had stirred up such wrath against him, a miller's thumb. He then makes identity clearer (if such metaphoric usage can be made clearer) by a reference to the wardenship of the Cinque Ports, the important office which the Cobhams had held from the reign of Queen Mary.[10] Nashe remarks that when he first contemplated his project of revenge for his unhappy plight he proposed to take for his subject the Cinque Ports of Kent and their keepers, but after much debating with himself he at length determined to forgo the subject: "Mutch braine tossing and breaking of my scull it cost me, but farewell it, and farewell the Baylies of the Cynqueports, whose primordiat *Genethliaca* was also dropping out of my inckhorne, with the syluer oare of their barronry by *William* the Conquerour."[11] The Cobham baronage *was* created in the reign of William the Conqueror, as readers of Holinshed's *Chronicles* may well have known, for Francis Thynne, who later became Lancaster herald, wrote the detailed treatise on the lords Cobham that was included in the second edition of the *Chronicles* (1585-1587). This was the treatise made famous (or infamous) by its excision from the second edition on order of the Privy Council.[12] Nashe is apparently writing at this point in his satire with tongue-in-cheek, for he does not abandon the "Baylies" of the Cinque Ports as subject matter; he narrows the field to the most famous of the earlier Cobhams, the Lollard martyr, Sir John Oldcastle.

Nashe very carefully hides his satire on the Cobhams under a voluble discourse on the city of Yarmouth, the home of the red herring. He praises the hospitality of the city in sheltering him from the tempests recently stirred up by "the turning of the Ile of Dogs from a commedie to a tragedie" and the "troublesome stir which hapned aboute it."[13] And after a lengthy description of the early history of Yarmouth in which he teases his readers with the coming satire ("the better to whet your appetites to taste of such a dainty dish as the redde Herring"), Nashe begins his mock epic by comparing it with older models. Just as Homer's song of the mice and frogs, or certain of Ovid's satires, or the mockery of Skelton, Gascoigne, or Spenser took the form of the beast fable, so too is his satire to be garbed in animal imagery. He will choose, he declares, the legend of a fish for his story.

The mock epic proper begins with a description of the

red herring as a legate of peace. If he comes near a place where there are "trials of life & death, there where that hangman embowelling is," the herring flees the place forever. The "Scotish Jockies" frightened the herrings out of Scotland, Nashe relates, by their "foule ill feud" among their "sectaries and servitours."[14] Even the least informed reader of Nashe's satire should be able to see at this point that the writer has left the zoological realm of fish and has entered the political realm of man. And a twentieth-century reader who has explored English history of the sixteenth century will not miss the apparent reference in this remark to recent Elizabethan and Scottish affairs. To comprehend fully Nashe's satire, however, the reader must recall something concerning Lord Cobham's role in those historic affairs. William Brooke, seventh Lord Cobham, played an active role in the machinations of the adherents of the queen of Scots in the earlier part of Elizabeth's reign, as noted above. His involvement with the affairs of the queen of Scots and the duke of Norfolk, which ended with Lord Cobham's "turn tail and run" tactics (Dugdale says Cobham "upon hope of pardon discovered all he knew therein"), apparently lies behind Nashe's remarks about the squeamish herrings who fled from the "trials of life & death."

With this contemporary reference made and his victim identified (or at least made identifiable to those "in the know"), the satirist leaves the contemporary herrings and begins his story of the adventure of the famous ancestral cob. Nashe insists that the essence of his tale is to be the terrible stench made by the great red herring, the king of fish, when it was broiled for the pope. The linguistic texture thickens here, for Nashe is playing with language and its wealth of connotations as he so frequently does. In addition to the meaning of *cob* as miller's thumb, the definition of the word as a great man or a rich miser is used: "They were rich cobbes you must rate them; and of them all cobbing countrey chuffes which makes their bellies and their bagges theyr Gods are called riche Cobbes."[15] This meaning of *cob* had been in derisive usage since the days of Hoccleve; the etymology of the word relates it to the Frisian or Dutch *kobbe,* meaning top or head. Thus in his usage Nashe can depend upon connotations for both man and fish. We know also that the term *herring-cob* means not only the head of a herring but in addition "a stupid fellow," and the term is related to *codshead* or the sea fish, *Gadus morrhus,* the herring cod.[16] Nashe's choice of the red herring (the king of herrings, the *Chimaera monstrosa)* is gross but witty in view of the Oldcastle satire, because the red herring acquires its color from being cured with smoke. In its natural state the herring is a white fish.

Nashe continues his little allegory by relating how the king of fish was cooked for the pope's table and how the odor that it created was unendurable:

> The fire had not perst it, but it being a sweaty loggerhead greasie sowter, endungeond in his pocket a tweluemonth, stunk so ouer the popes pallace, that not a scullion but cryed foh, and those which at the first flocked the fastest about it now fled the most from it, and sought more to rid theyr hands of it than before they sought to blesse theyre handes with it. Wyth much stopping of theyr noses, between two dishes they stued it, and serued it vp.[17]

This seems a meaningless fable created by Nashe's peculiar imagination until the reader (as I think he was meant to do) places the allegory in retrospection with the Oldcastle legend. The story of the Lollard martyr had become a point of controversy in the sixteenth century, as the reader will recall. William Tyndale's account of the trial and death of Oldcastle, called the "Bok of Thorpe," was ordered burned in 1531, and Sir Thomas More decried the falsity of the work: "He sheweth hym selfe a false lyar in hys rehersall of the mater." But More's ridicule was no deterrent to John Bale, who expanded Tyndale's account of Oldcastle's trial into a vicious attack upon the fifteenth-century Catholics. Bale's torrent of abuse continued to flow in the first English edition (1563) of John Foxe's *Acts and Monuments of the Church,* in which the martyrologist renewed the attack upon the Catholic clergy with energy.[18] The reader will recall Foxe's famous calendar of Protestant saints published in the 1563 edition of the *Acts and Monuments,* which Nicholas Harpsfield attacked as ludicrous in his *Dialogi Sex.* Foxe in turn called his opponent "a liar, a forger, an impudent, a misreporter of truth, a depraver of stories, a seducer of the world," and so on.[19]

It was this kind of riotous, extravagantly accusatory writing to which the Oldcastle legend was exposed in the sixteenth century; the Lollard martyr, as I have noted, became one of the epicenters of the violent and colorful polemics of that contentious age. In *Lenten Stuffe* Nashe allegorizes the polemics of the Catholic-Protestant controversy over Oldcastle's fame by describing it as confusion in the papal palace. He elaborates further concerning the uproar: "The busie epitasis of the commedy was when the dishes were yncouered and the swarthrutter sowre tooke ayre: for then hee made such a ayre, as *Alcides* himselfe that clensed the stables of *Agaeus* nor any hostler was able to endure."[20] Nashe describes the stench as being so terrible that "the Pope it popt vnder boord," and the whole conclave declares that the fish must be the soul of some heretic who has escaped from purgatory: "Negromantick sorcery, negromanticke sorcerie, some euill spirit of an heretique it is, which thus molesteth his Apostoliqueship. The friars and munkes caterwawled, from the abbots and priors to the nouices, wherfore *tanquam in circo*, wee will trownse him in a circle, and make him tell what Lanterneman or groome of Hecates close stoole hee is, that thus nefariously and proditoriously prophanes & penetrates our holy fathers nostrils."[21] The mock epic description continues in this ludicrous fashion for several paragraphs with Nashe's outrageous satire couched in his own untrammeled language. The author then remarks upon the canonization of the famous cob. Because the conclave suspects that the fish is the soul of some departed king, and because the pope wishes "to bee ridde of his filthy redolence," the cob is placed in a jewel chest, given Christian burial, and made a saint of the church. Nashe instructs the reader to seek evidence for himself: "And for his ensainting, looke the Almanack in the beginning of Aprill, and see if you can finde out such a saint as saint *Gildarde*; which in honour of this guilded fish the Pope so ensainted."[22] I do not know whether Nashe created this inversion in the Oldcastle legend to protect himself (he had by this time gone far toward endangering his future with his scalding satire) or simply to beguile his readers with his manipulations of the burlesque and its inherent inversions, but he parodies here an historical element. Oldcastle's name *was* placed in the red-letter calendar of saints, but it was not the Catholic calendar. Rather it was the Protestant calendar that Foxe devised. Both Sir John Oldcastle and Sir Roger Acton (who was executed as one of the leaders of the insurrection of 1413) were named by Foxe in his calendar of new martyrs who, he declared, were worthy substitutes for the "Romish saints" of the old religion.[23] Harpsfield's taunting remarks about this new red-letter list led Foxe to defend his motives in creating the calendar. It seems to me that Nashe had in mind this controversy when he created his burlesque history of the famous cob who was cooked for the pope. Foxe's book was an extremely popular work, and I suspect that more than a handful of select readers understood the point of Nashe's satire. *Lenten Stuffe* was not meant to be open to all eyes, however—it was too dangerous.

That Nashe was aware of the danger he was in seems apparent in the way he attempts to protect himself from the direct assault of the interpreters. In addition to surrounding his allegory with a lengthy history of Yarmouth and the fishing industry, he digresses at one point with a skilful parody of "Hero and Leander" in which the heroes are metamorphosed into the ling fish and the herring.[24] At another point in his satire Nashe adds the description of a mock battle between the land fowls and the deep-sea fish in which the herring is elected king of fishes.[25] And in another digression Nashe relates the story of a modern cob, "one of the refuse sort of herrings" who forces his attention upon a certain Lady Turbut to her disgrace and ruin.[26] These fables, all contrived as mock encomium, surround the "play," as Nashe terms it, of the red herring and its adventure in the pope's kitchen. Nashe is quick to deny that any of his fables has a dual meaning or is allusive (this in spite of his introductory avowal of revenge). He defies specific identification: "O, for a Legion of mice-eyed decipherers and calculaters vppon characters, now to augurate what I meane by this."[27] And he decries those readers who supply devious meanings for his work and "runne over al the peeres of the land in peevish moralizing and anatomizing it." In particular does Nashe attack with vehemence the lawyers of the Inns of Court; he will toss them a riddle or two, he declares, in order to "set

their wittes a nibbling, and their iobber-nowles a working." And he strikes out at one "infant squib of the Innes
of Court" who reads allegory into every passage and "strait
engageth hymselfe by the honor of his house . . . to thresh
downe the hayry roofe of that brayne that so seditiously
mutined against hym."[28] These declaimers of innocence
and disclaimers of ill intent are repeated throughout *Lenten Stuffe*. Disadvantaged as he was by the uproar which
The Isle of Dogs had created among the authorities (and
certainly the Nashe-Harvey exchange had not brightened
his image), Nashe was in great need of skillful and covert
maneuvering in his mocking satire. This is, I think, the reason for the erratic structure of *Lenten Stuffe*; Nashe's dis-
joined fables, his "Romish historie," and his praise of Yarmouth cast shadows for each other, and intentionally so.
Lenten Stuffe is a difficult work. Although he welds the
fragments together with perhaps the most brilliant prose
of his writing career, Nashe was forced by circumstances
to be oblique.

When *Lenten Stuffe* was entered in the *Stationers' Register* to Cutbert Burby on 11 January 1599, the entry was
qualified by the statement that the book was to be printed
only "vpon Condicon that he gett yt Laufaully Auctor-
ized."[29] Burby evidently got the work authorized and
printed before June of that year. It was on 1 June, of course,
that Richard Bancroft, bishop of London, and Archbishop
Whitgift issued the order "that all Nasshes bookes and Doctor Harvyes bookes be taken wheresoeuer they maye be
found and that none of theire bookes bee euer printed
hereafter."[30] That order was the end of Nashe's career. Had
his satirical revenge been deciphered by his enemies? I
suspect that the answer to that question is yes. Nashe had
remarked, "Next, to draw on hounds to a sent, to a redde
herring skinne there is nothing comparable." The "paper
hounds" appear to have caught up with the brash Elizabethan Juvenal. He had threatened to gull his enemies with
the red herring ("better than euer I haue done"), but he
went too far. The episode ends with irony and perhaps
poetic justice (if one sides with the Precisionists), for the
inordinate satire of the roasted cob turned to ashes when
Nashe's books were burned by the stationers' wardens.

After June of 1599 we have little evidence upon which to

base biographical remarks. Apparently Nashe was dead by 1601, for a Latin epigram praising his memory was printed in Charles Fitzgeffrey's *Affaniae* in that year.[31] Soon afterward the Cambridge students remarked upon his wit in *The Return from Parnassus*: "Let all his faultes sleepe with his mournfull chest, And there for euer with his ashes rest. His style was wittie, though it had some gall, Somethings he might haue mended, so may all. Yet this I say, that for a mother witt, Few men haue euer seene the like of it."[32] There are other references in the early years of James's reign to Nashe's unsurpassed wit. Among them is one of particular interest in this context: Thomas Dekker remarked in his *A Knight's Conjuring* that Nashe would have lived longer had he not "shortened his dayes by keeping company with pickle herrings."[33] It is a witty speculation if Dekker was writing metaphorically, as I think he was. We do not know the causes of Nashe's death, it is true; but it is also true that he destroyed his career just as he had made it—with his undisciplined wit and his skill in riotous, exotic language. His classical conception of satire and the frustrating circumstances of his later years seem to have shaped in his mind this final outrageous creation in *Lenten Stuffe*. The contrast with Shakespeare's imaginative efforts in this same vein is illuminating. In the tremendous bulk of Falstaff's character lie so many and so varied elements that the satiric purpose for which the dramatic character was created remains subordinate, buried even. This comparison can also be made with a third poet, for Ben Jonson too mixed ink and gall in the matter of the Oldcastle satire. Needless to say, Jonson fared far better than his colleague Nashe in the adventure of burlesquing the famous cob. Jonson achieved continuing fame with his play *Every Man in His Humour*; and it was for this play, as most readers will remember, that Jonson created the character of Cob, the water-bearer, who brags with inordinate pride of his famous ancestor, the "first herring, that was broil'd in ADAM, and EVE'S kitchin."[34] This was in the fall of 1598, but let us return for a moment to the summer of 1597.

Jonson's participation in the composition of *The Isle of Dogs* is unquestioned, but whether he actually had Nashe's permission to finish the satirical work is another point. The two men may have worked together on the text of the play, or Jonson may have finished the fragment without Nashe's consent. Be that as it may, Nashe's influence upon the young Jonson's conception of satire and comedy appears to have been a strong one. The two men were at least comrades in spirit, for neither believed in making the lion roar "like a nightingale"—as Jonson's modern editors have observed.[36] It was Jonson, however, who appears to have given Nashe the idea of the red herring metaphor—unless, of course, Nashe finished *Lenten Stuffe* before September of 1598, and of this we cannot be certain. We can date the composition of *Every Man in His Humour* with some accuracy because the folio title page states that the play was acted in 1598, and in addition we have the letter that Toby Matthews penned in London on 20 September in that year, in which he remarks to Dudley Carleton about the "new play called Every Man's humour."[39] The quarto edition of the play that appeared in 1601 contained the Italianate characters and setting that Jonson naturalized in the folio of 1616. And standing out in the quarto dramatis personae, as good English peasants would in an Italianate scene, are Cob, the water-bearer, and his truculent wife Tib. When Jonson revised the play for the folio edition, he sharpened the wit of Cob's speeches with minor rephrasing, but the outlines of the clownish character's dialogue remain the same as do his actions.[37]

If we look closely at the character, we find Cob at his first stage entrance exclaiming on his "poore house" and "linage" to Master Matthew, the town-gull (the Matheo of the quarto). His is an ancient and princely lineage, Cob declares, and he relates it royally:

> Why sir, an ancient linage, and a princely. Mine ance'trie came from a Kings belly, no worse man: and yet no man neither (by your worships leaue, I did lie in that) but *Herring* the King of fish (from his belly, I proceed) one o' the Monarchs o' the world, I assure you. The first red herring, that was broil'd in ADAM, and EVE'S kitchin, doe I fetch my pedigree from, by the Harrots bookes. His *COB*, was my great-great-mighty-great Grand-father.[38]
>
> [I.iv.10–17]

Under the questioning of Matthew, Cob insists that his ancestor was a "mightie great Cob" who lived "a mightie while agoe," and when the town gull leads him on, Cob describes how he is aware of his forefather's greatness: "How know I? why, I smell his ghost, euer and anon." At this Matthew marvels, "Smell a ghost? o vnsauoury iest! and the ghost of a herring COB!" Matthew's reproof leads Cob to inveigle the town-gull with a riddle and a pun: "I sir, with fauour of your worships nose, Mr. Mathew, why not the ghost of a herring-cob, as well as the ghost of rasher-bacon?" Matthew recognizes the pun and questions Cob: "ROGER BACON, thou wouldst say?" And the clown becomes secretive: "I say rasher-bacon. They were both broyl'd o' the coles? and a man may smell broyld-meate, I hope? you are a scholler vpsolue me that, now."

Jonson, of course, is letting Cob play with fire. Jonson's modern editors have remarked on this pun; Cob, they declare, "knew his history probably from a chapbook, which may have had him [Bacon] burnt as a necromancer."[39] Obviously Cob is implying such an event. And from the reference a few lines later to the "Brasen-head" it is evident that Jonson has in mind the folklore legend that Bacon was a magician. This same legend was used by Robert Greene in his play, *Frier Bacon and Frier Bungay*, that was published in 1594 though it was acted earlier by the Queen's Company. Greene's play contained a scene in which the famous brazen head spoke, but only in *The Famous Historie of Fryer Bacon* (an early version of this work seems to have been Greene's source) do we find a magician being burned, and here it is *not* Bacon but rather Friar Bungay and the German competitor, Vandermast, who are "strangely burnt with fire" because of their necromancy.[40] We know that something of the persecution of the thirteenth-century Franciscan was known in the sixteenth century, for both John Leland and John Bale included Roger Bacon's name in their lists of illustrious British writers. The church's condemnation of Bacon's "*novitates suspectas*" was accepted history.[41] The very fact that Bacon's work was considered heretical by the authorities of his time commended him to the early Protestant writers, and we find one early biographer rationalizing thus: "Twas the Popes smoak which made the eyes of that Age so sore, as they could not discern any open hearted and clear headed *soul* from an *heretical Phantasme*. The silly Fryers envying his too prying head, by

their craft had almost got it off his shoulders."[42] Modern
biographers agree that Bacon was probably imprisoned by
the minister-general of his order for being a schismatic,
that is, for his resistance to authority, his bitter and per-
suasive tongue, and "above all, his belief in prophecies and
his tirades on the subject of Antichrist."[43] Bale had mentioned with approbation the fact that Bacon refused to
accept certain church doctrine: *"Nec crucis signatio, nec
aqua benedicta, nec ipsa Eucharistia,"* and Jonson, it would
seem, had this idea of heresy in mind also when he created
the macabre comparison between Roger Bacon and the
famous ancestor of Cob, Sir John Oldcastle. Both men were
religious rebels who opposed the orthodox church doctrine of their days; thus Jonson's analogy, satiric though it
be, is an apt one.

In a following scene the subject of Cob's ancestry is again
brought in. The clown bursts out in a tirade upon fasting
days, "Would I had these ember-weeks, and villanous
fridayes burnt." Cash (who in the quarto is called Piso)
questions Cob about his anger, and the latter, after listing
severals evils connected with fasting days, retorts: "Nay,
and this were all, 'twere something, but they are the only
knowne enemies, to my generation. A fasting-day, no
sooner comes, but my lineage goes to racke, poore cobs they
smoke for it, they are made martyrs o' the gridiron, they
melt in passion: and your maides too know this, and yet
would haue me turne HANNIBAL, and eate my owne fish,
and bloud." At this point Cob pulls a red herring from under
his coat and addresses it: "My princely couz, fear nothing;
I haue not the hart to deuoure you, & I might be made as
rich as King COPHETVA. O, that I had roome for my teares,
I could weepe salt-water enough, now, to preserue the liues
of ten thousand of my kin." In the remainder of this speech
Cob places the blame for the far too numerous fasting days
and for the discomfiture of himself upon the calendar or
"filthie *Almanacks*" which cause such "persecutions":
"But I may curse none but these filthie *Almanacks,* for an't
were not for them, these dayes of persecution would ne're
be knowne. Ile bee hang'd, an' some Fish-mongers sonne
doe not make of 'hem; and puts in more fasting-dayes then
he should doe, because hee would vtter his fathers dryed
stock-fish, and stinking conger" (act III, scene iv).

The famous calendar which John Foxe created for his book of martyrs has been described earlier in this work. Foxe's red-letter calendar was made even more famous by Harpsfield's accusation that Sir John Oldcastle and Eleanor Cobham were traitors rather than martyrs. That Jonson was unaware of this calendar is unlikely; Foxe's book was one of the most popular publications of the late Tudor period, and we can guess with some assurance of accuracy, I think, Jonson's response to it, for we know from his later remarks to Drummond that his Catholic sympathies at this time were strong.[44] Cob's "filthie *Almanacks*" seems to point toward Foxe's notable calendar of saints in which Oldcastle was enshrined; and, again, the humor is grisly.

This scene closes with Cash's warning that if Cob loiters longer he will "bee beaten like a stock fish, else."[45] And true to this prediction Cob is soundly thrashed by Captain Bobadill in the following scene. This episode also contains an element of the Oldcastle satire, for in it Cob reveals his great sensitivity to smoke. Of course, it is not the smoke of a human bonfire which irritates Cob; this lies beyond the province of comedy. The smoke which brings on Cob's outburst and results in his beating is from that roguish weed, tobacco. The scene is a topical one. The main characters have gathered before Kitely's house and have begun to light their pipes when Bobadill declaims in a famous speech upon that "most soueraigne, and precious weede, that euer the earth tendred to the vse of man."[46] Cob enters at this point, takes one whiff, and gasps: "By gods mee, I marle, what pleasure, or felicitie they haue in taking this roguish *tabacco*! it's good for nothing, but to choke a man, and fill him full of smoke, and embers: there were foure dyed out of one house, last weeke, with taking of it, and two more the bell went for yesternight." The clown concludes by threatening, "By the stocks, an'there were no wiser men than I, I'ld haue it present whipping, man or woman, that should but deale with a *tabacco*-pipe." And this insult to his favorite leaf leads Bobadill to pick up a cudgel and beat the waterbearer. This is slapstick comedy, but beneath it lies a stratum of symbolic humor. If the reader despairs of such humor, he should remember that it was an age of despair for many of those who tried desperately to cling to the old faith. He should remember, too, that Nashe and Jonson suffered stern treatment for their dramatic efforts in *The Isle of Dogs*. Nashe's lodgings were searched, and he apparently fled one jump ahead of the authorities. The reader should recall what happened to Thomas Kyd in 1593 when his rooms were searched for similar reasons. Jonson spent more than two months in the Marshalsea because of *The Isle of Dogs* episode, and in those days, at least for the common man, prisons were sinkholes of disease, despair, and death. That Jonson and Nashe, after their experience with the authorities, should continue their stiletto battle of wits speaks not only for their convictions but for their courage as well.

There is one final element in the satire which surrounds the character of Cob, and that element lies in the term "water-bearer." In the play Cob wears a collar and yoke from which buckets hang, and he delivers water to the households which lie at a distance from the conduits or wells. Jonson seems to have chosen this menial job for Cob in order to caricature the contemporary Lord Cobham and to reflect a topical incident of importance that happened in Elizabeth's court in the preceding year. Let us for a moment go back a few months to 1597.

When William Brooke, the elder Lord Cobham, died in March of 1597, the court watched expectantly to see how his white staffs of office would be distributed. The reader will recall that the lord chamberlain's staff was keenly desired by the new Lord Cobham (Henry Brooke) and by George Carey, the new Lord Hunsdon. The latter won the appointment. But the second white staff was that of the office of lord warden of the Cinque Ports, and the new Lord Cobham fully expected to succeed his father in this preferment. His appointment was hotly contested, however, by the earl of Essex, who pressed for that post the suit of Sir Robert Sidney. As it turned out, Sidney's suit was a futile one, for the queen refused to consider it. Therefore, Essex swore to keep the office vacant or ask for it himself to prevent Cobham, "who of all Men, is the unfittest," from receiving it. Essex's hatred for Cobham was intense, and he spoke before the Privy Council on the subject, as I have explained above.[47] It was only after many months and after the queen had consoled Essex with an appointment as master of the Ordnance that she at length gave Cobham the lord warden's staff. In August of 1598 Lord Cobham was ceremoniously installed in the office for which he and Essex had striven. John Chamberlain, in one of his letters to Carleton, described the colorful event as it happened in Kent: "The Lord Cobham was installed Lord Warden of the Cinque Portes on Barthemew Day at Canterbury, at which ceremonious solemnitie were assembled almost 4000 horse, and he kept the feast very magnificently and spent 26 oxen with all other provision suitable."[48]

Jonson's play was performed in September. How does Cob, the water-bearer of *Every Man in His Humour,* relate to the lord warden of the Cinque Ports? The Lord Warden controlled not only the five most important harbors of the country but also the most important strip of water surrounding England. The coastline of Kent faces the Channel and the Continent (which was, of course, why Essex wanted a man he could trust in the position). The office was concerned with the waters, harbors, shipping, and so forth, of a developing nation well on its way toward becoming a great sea power. Jonson seizes upon the idea of controller of waters, and in comic inversion makes Cob a peddler of water, a humor-ridden clown. It is a turn of satiric genius.

How did it all end? We cannot be sure. *Every Man in His Humour* was a popular play, but whether or not Lord Cobham heard of the character of Cob we do not know. The Lord Chamberlain's Men performed the comedy, and we know that Shakespeare acted in the production, because Jonson added to the folio edition of the play a list of the actors, and Shakespeare's name is at the top of the list. Nashe's works were burned in June of 1599, and after that he disappeared. In the summer or fall of 1599 Shakespeare unceremoniously rid himself of the character of Falstaff by letting him die of a fever and a sweat in *Henry V,* his play of the ideal king. We know from Henslowe's account books that the Lord Admiral's Men performed their two-part play, *The True and Honourable Historie of the Life of Sir John Oldcastle,* in the fall of 1599. This production made a hero of Oldcastle by unhistorical poetizing of chronicle materials. The Elizabethan Lord Cobham at this time was courting Frances Howard, the lord admiral's daughter; the courtship was successful, and he married her in 1601. But he brought her disgrace and humiliation two years later when he and Raleigh fell to destruction in the Main and Bye plots to overthrow King James. In 1599 John Weever wrote his idyllic poem entitled *The Mirrors of Martyrs,* in which he reflected on the tarnished fame of Sir John Oldcastle, "that thrice valiant Capitaine and most godly Martyre."[49] And that is almost all we know. It appears that for several reasons Shakespeare got himself involved in ridiculing the contemporary lords of Cobham. This ridicule was effected by satirizing and lampooning the ancestral Lord Cobham who was burned at the stake in 1417 for his heresy and treason. Shakespeare did not invent this satiric mode, nor did it end with him. If my analysis of *Lenten Stuffe* and *Every Man in His Humour* is correct, it appears that Nashe and Jonson joined the game. After the debacle of *The Isle of Dogs* and after their severe punishment for that indiscretion, they determined to seek revenge by grinding salt into the wounded pride of the Cobhams; this they accomplished with their own outrageous inventions of satirical wit.

CHAPTER TEN

The Death of Falstaff and the Chronology of the Satire

THE UNDRAMATIC AND OVERLY HASTY DEMISE OF SIR John Falstaff in Shakespeare's *Henry V* has left readers and viewers of Renaissance drama dissatisfied for many years. It has also provided a touchstone for critical wit and ingenuity, as any serious student of Elizabethan drama knows when he surveys the perennial crop of published commentary on Falstaff's death scene. Today it seems unprovidential that Shakespeare should so suddenly rid himself of the most popular comic character he was ever to create.[1] And when we turn to the history plays, we do find textual evidence to indicate that there was some indecision in the playwright's mind or at least some change of dramatic plans, for in the epilogue of *2 Henry IV* Shakespeare promises the audience further entertainment with Sir John in it: "If you be not too much cloid with Fat Meate, our humble Author will continue the story (with Sir John in it) and make you merry, with faire Katherine of France." But, as everyone knows, Falstaff does *not* appear on stage in *Henry V*; his death is described in classic fashion by Mistress Quickly, who functions ironically as a tragic messenger. And even though it is couched satirically in the mode of Greek tragedy with its stylized form, Falstaff's final scene appears adventitious to the modern reader.

Falstaff and death had, of course, been associated in the earlier dramas. Critics have remarked upon the three symbolic deaths that anticipate the demise of Falstaff in *Henry V*: the feigned death at the Battle of Shrewsbury in *1*

263

Henry IV, the "sweating death" of the buck-basket scene
in *The Merry Wives of Windsor,* and the "burning" by
fairies in the same play.[2] Even the intensification of disease
imagery in *2 Henry IV* lends substance to the atmosphere
of death. Moreover, the epilogue of *2 Henry IV* prepares for
Falstaff's death with a proleptic phrase, "Falstaff shall dye
of a sweat, unlesse already he be killd with your Opinions:
For Old-Castle dyed a Martyr, and this is not the man."
The playwright is writing tongue-in-cheek. Many of the
details of Falstaff's death are relevant to the Oldcastle legend, and they can be understood only in the light of the
established satire. Therefore, in spite of the denial in the
epilogue of *2 Henry IV,* the theme of martyrdom *is* present
in the description of Falstaff's death.

Sir John is dead, says Mistress Quickly, of a "burning
quotidian Tertian" (or the quarto reading, "burning tashan
contigian feuer"), a lamentable sight. In an attempt to
stave off sentimentality some of our more conservative
critics today reject any suggestion of martyrdom in this
description, but from the point of view of Falstaff's friends
Sir John is dying of a broken heart. The statements are
explicit in the text. Nym says, "The King hath run bad
humors on the Knight," and Pistol responds, "Nym, thou
hast spoke the right, his heart is fracted and corroborate."
Many a modern heart has also been "fracted and corro-
borated" by the famous rejection scene of *2 Henry IV* in
which Henry V, regal in his coronation robes, commands
his former friend, "I know thee not, old man. Fall to thy
prayers." This scene separates the critics into Ephesians
and Precise Brethren. We become so involved with Shakespeare's four-dimensional characters that we forget he was
using in this play chronicle materials that many Elizabethans knew by heart. The fifteenth-century chroniclers
invariably described the beginning of Henry V's reign by
repeating the story of his rejection of his wanton friends.
One of the more colorful versions is that written by the
anonymous author of *The Brut:*

And before he was Kyng, what tyme he regnyd Prince of
Walyes, he fylle & yntendyd gretly to ryot, and drew to wylde
company; 7 dyuers Ientylmen and Ientylwommen folwyd his
wylle & his desire at his commaundment; & lykewyse all his
meyne of his housolde was attendyng & plesyd with his

gouernaunce, outsept iij men of his howsolde, whiche were
ful hevy and sory of his gouernaunce. . . . And thanne he
beganne to regne for Kyng, & he remembryd þe gret charge &
wourship þat he shulde take upon hym; And anon he co-
maundyd al his peple þat were attendaunt to his housolde,
to come before hym. And whan they herde þat, they were ful
glad, for they subposyd þat he woolde a promotyd them in-to
gret offices, & þat they shulde a stonde in gret favyr & truste
with hym, & neerest of counsel, as they were afore tyme. &
trustyng hereupon, they were þe homlyer & bolder unto hym,
& nothyng dred hym; ynsomoche, þat whan they were come
before hym, some of them wynkyd on hym, & some smylyd, &
thus they made nyse semblaunte unto hym, meny one of them.
But for al þat, þe Prynce kept his countynaunce ful sadly unto
them, And sayde to them: Syrys, ye are þe peple þat I have
cherysyd & mayntynyd in Ryot & wylde gournaunce; and
here I geve you all in commaundment, & charge yow, þat
from this day forward þat ye forsake al mysgouernaunce, &
lyve aftyr þe lawys of almyhety God, & aftyr þe lawys of oure
londe. And who þat doyth contrarye, I make feythful promys
to God, þat he shal be trewly ponised accordyng to the lawe,
withoute eny favour of grace. . . . And so he rewardyd them
richely with gold & sylver, & other Iuelys, and chargyd them
alle to voyde his housolde, & lyve as good men, & never more
to come in his presence, be-cause he woolde have noon occasion nor remembraunce wherby he shylde falle to ryot agen.
. . . and thus was lefte in his housolde nomo but tho iij men,
and meny one of them þat were eydyng & consentyng to his
wyldnes, fyl aftyrward to gret myschefe and sorw.[3]

Without knowledge of the historical context the modern
reader *is* inclined to exaggerate the pathos in the rejection
of Falstaff. Many of us are taken in by the expansive, effusive wit of the character, and we become one of Falstaff's
crew. Falstaff's death is pathetic—until we turn the death
scene over to examine the implications of its verso side.
There are correlatives to this satiric martyrdom, correlatives which may shock the sheltered or the prim, with the
historical Sir John Oldcastle (whose martyrdom *is* touched
in this scene).

The reader will recall that King Henry turned against the
Lollard knight after the insurrection of 1413, which threatened the throne as well as the established church of that
time.[4] And although the playwright denied in the famous
epilogue any allusion to Oldcastle's martyrdom, when one
recalls the historical background, Falstaff's broken heart
and burning fever become, I think, analogous to martyr-

dom. Furthermore, if we credit Rowe's story, the play-wright, having been reprimanded earlier for such allusive-ness, added a ludicrous inversion, changing heat to cold, and in doing so substituted a far more famous martyrdom for parodic purpose. Falstaff's death at one point is pat-terned on that famous scene described in the final pages of Plato's *Phaedo*. Those of the Elizabethan audience who were schooled in classical literature would have recog-nized, I think, the parallel in Mistress Quickly's ingenuous words, "So a' bad me lay more Clothes on his feet: I put my hand into the Bed, and Felt to his knees, and so vp-peer'd, and upward, and all was as cold as any stone" (even the less-focused quarto lines are pertinent: "Then he bad me put more cloathes at his feete: And I felt to them, and they were as cold as any stone: And to his knees, and they were as cold as any stone: And so vpward, and vp-ward, and all was as cold as any stone"). Compare the lines with Plato's description of the death of Socrates after he had drunk the cup of hemlock:

> . . . and the man who gave him the poison now and then looked at his feet and legs; and after a while he pressed his foot hard, and asked him if he could feel; and he said, "No;" and then his leg, and so upwards and upwards, and showed us that he was cold and stiff.[5]

In this instance the problem of Shakespeare's "small Latin and less Greek" need not intervene, though certainly both the original Greek text and its Latin translation were available in Elizabethan England. The *Omnia Platonis Opera* was published in Greek in September of 1513 at Venice, and the first volume of the *Platonis Opera Quae Extant Omnia,* which contained both Greek and Latin texts, was published by Henri Estienne in Geneva in 1578 and was dedicated to Queen Elizabeth. Marsilio Ficino's Latin translation of Plato's writings circulated throughout Europe after 1482, and the vernacular translations of the *Phaedo* were printed in the sixteenth century, the French in 1553 and 1581, the Italian in 1574.[6] More important perhaps is the fact that when William Caxton published Anthony Woodville, Earl River's translation of *The Dictes or Sayengis of the Philosophhres* in 1477, he gave to the English reading public a lusty vernacular version of Plato's description of the death of Socrates. The particular passage reads as follows:

> . . . he went alitil from them / & saide O god have mercy upon me / & anon his synewes shranke his fete wexed colde / and than he leide him down / one of his disciples tooke a boddekyn & prikked him in his feete / and axed him yf he felt eny thing + And he said naye / than he prikked him in his thyghes / and axed him if he felt it / he sayd naye + Anone the colde strake up unto his sydes than Socrates saide whan the colde cometh to my hert I must nedis dye +[7]

That Shakespeare would parody our much beloved Plato will shock the more conservative critics; therefore, I hasten to point out the witty relevance of such usage. The fates of Socrates and Oldcastle are comparable in an important sense: we know that Socrates was accused of maligning the religion of the state (falsifying the ancient gods); likewise Oldcastle's heresy, his rejection of the doctrines of the established church, catapulted him from Fortune's erratic wheel. Moreover, this substitution of a martyr of greater fame is meaningful at the contemporary level, for like Socrates, William, seventh Lord Cobham, was a victim of the comic poets. One should recall that in Plato's *Apology* Socrates explains that one of his greatest enemies has been public opinion and that the opinion had been molded by the comic poets from envy and malice. Socrates derides his accuser, Meletus, saying, "Such is the nature of the accusation: it is just what you have yourselves seen in the comedy of Aristophanes."[8] In like instance the Elizabethan Cobhams bore for many years the satire of the poets. At his trial in 1603 Henry, eighth Lord Cobham, complained that "except the house of Norfolk noe house of Englande received more disgrace and jealousy for many years together in the time past than my poor house." And this is true. Oldcastle walked the stage in the anonymous play *The Famous Victories of Henry the Fifth* and again in Shakespeare's early versions of the *Henry IV* plays. Eleanor Cobham's legend, which had undergone metamorphosis in the chronicles in a fashion similar to Oldcastle's story, was used not only by Shakespeare but by George Ferrers, Michael Drayton, Christopher Middleton, and Chettle and Day. As one might expect, Shakespeare's version of that legend presents an unflattering and treasonable portrait of that noblewoman. Furthermore, Thomas Nashe and Ben Jonson had also used the legend in their macabre portrayal of the ancestral Cob who was roasted before the pope. Shakespeare's allusions to martyrdom in Falstaff's death scene are wittily (if not morally) fitting and we find the fat knight dying like an ancient philosopher, though hell's fire is on his mind.

This inventive use of analogues was a mode associated with Oldcastle's death in the sixteenth century. Both John Bale and John Foxe had used a comparative technique in their eulogies of the Lollard martyr's death. In Bale's *Brefe Chronycle* the author did not hesitate to equate Oldcastle's death with that of Christ:

> Syr Johan Oldcastell was brent in Cheanes at London in Saynct Gyles Felde, undre the Galowes, amonge the Laye People, and upon the prophane workynge Daye, at the Bysshoppes Procurement. And all this is ungloryouse, yea and verye despyseable unto those wordlye Eyes, what though Jesus Christ his Mastre afore him were handeled after a verye lyke Sort. For he was crucyfyed at Hierusalem, without the Cyte and without the holye Synagoge, acursed out of Churche, amonge the prophane Multytude, in the myddest of Theves, in the Place where as Theves were commonly hanged, and not upon the feastful Daye but afore yt, by the Bysshoppes Procurement also.[9]

And Foxe found the details of Oldcastle's death analogous to the Biblical description of Elijah's ascent into heaven:

> Thys is not to be forgotten which is reported by many that he should say that he should die here in earth after the sort and manner of Helias, the whyche whether it sprang of the common people wythoute cause, or that it was forshewed by him, I think it not without with some gift of prophecy, the end of the matter doth suffyciently proue. For lyke as when Helias should leaue this mortal life, he was caryed in a fiery charyot into immortality: even so the order of thys mannes death, not beinge muche unlike, followed the fygure of his departure. For he fyrste of all being lyfted up upon the galowes, as into a chariot, and compassed in round aboute wyth flamynge fyre, what other thyng I pray you dyd thys most holy martir of Christ represent then onlye a fygure of a certayne Helias flying up into heauen. The whych went up into heauen by a fiery chariot.[10]

The flames that torment Falstaff's slipping mind are, of course, those of mental anguish—the flea on Bardolph's red nose becomes "a blacke Soule burning in Hell." Within this satiric context, this reference to flames is too hot for comfort.

Hostess Quickly's insistence that Falstaff had not gone to hell but was safe in Arthur's bosom is possibly another reference to Oldcastle's death. In the fifteenth-century accounts of the Lollard's execution his final prophecy was usually repeated: Oldcastle promised his followers that he would be resurrected on the third day after his death. Thomas Walsingham's version of this prophecy was turned into English by John Stow and was printed in the 1592 edition of Stow's *Annales*:

> The last words that he spake, was to Sir *Thomas of Erpingham*, abjuring him, that if he saw him rise from death to life again, the third day, he would procure that his sect might be in peace & quiet; he was hanged by the necke in a chaine of iron, & after consumed with fire.[11]

The promise of resurrection inspired the faithful Lollards who returned to Saint Giles Field, the scene of execution, on the third morning. When one recalls that the King Arthur of literature and legend was reported to be in Avalon and would return someday "twice as fair" to rule over his people, the relevance of Mistress Quickly's remark is apparent. Similarly, the page's reference to incarnation and the hostess's uncomprehending reply, "a' could never abide Carnation, 'twas a Colour he never lik'd," become a religious reference applicable to the doctrine of transubstantiation and the incarnate Christ of the sacrament. Indeed, Oldcastle could not abide this "carnation." When one recalls the Lollard's famous trial for heresy and the importance attached to Oldcastle's refusal to answer with doctrinal propriety the "murderous question" concerning the bread and Christ's body, Falstaff's mutterings take on new meaning. In addition, Falstaff's profane cries against the Whore of Babylon are also an apparent Oldcastle allusion. The scarlet woman, as most readers know, was an old symbol of derision for the Church of Rome, and Falstaff's outcry is analogous to Oldcastle's final outburst against the "whorish prelates" who condemned him. One of his colorful accusations was repeated frequently by the chroniclers: ". . . *quod Dominus noster Papa est verus Antichristus*, *hoc est caput ejusdem; Archiepiscopi et Episcopi, necnon alii praelati, sunt membra, et Fratres cauda ejusdem.*[12]

The allusiveness of Falstaff's crying out against women goes beyond the Oldcastle legend, I believe, for Shakespeare appears to pick up the earlier reference to Socrates and to make use of it again in these remarks of the page and the hostess. In the sixteenth century the ancient Greek philosopher was noted for his misogyny. William Caxton, as editor of Lord Rivers's translation of *The Dictes or Sayengis of the Philosophhres* (which contained an eclectic gathering of biographical "facts" and quotations derived from the large body of Arabic translations of the ninth century, the works of Diogenes Laertius, and the *Memorabilia* of Xenophon), was faced with the problem of the unkind remarks on women attributed to the ancient philosopher. Lord Rivers had simply deleted them, and Caxton (after some doubts that he describes in detail) gathered the unchivalrous statements into an epilogue and appended it to *The Dictes* with an apology to the "good, wyse, playsant, humble, discrete, sobre, chast" women of England.[13] Caxton's *Dictes* was an extremely popular work; he reprinted it a number of times after 1477, as did Wynkyn de Worde in the sixteenth century. By the time that William Baldwin printed the antifeminist sayings of Socrates in his *Treatice of Morall Philosophy* at mid-sixteenth century, many of the remarks had become jingles. Two examples of the "pithy mieters" should suffice:

> Woman is more pittiful than manne,
> more enuious than a serpent,
> more malicious than a tyrant,
> and more deceiptful than the deuill.

And another:

> Prayer to God is the onely meane,
> to preserue a man from a wicked queane.[14]

This common image of the ancient philosopher as a woman hater was available to Shakespeare, and I believe that he was treating it in comic fashion to increase the allusiveness of Falstaff's death scene. Such an allusion does not, of course, limit itself. Indeed, Falstaff may have had reason to curse women if poor Doll truly were in the "Poudring tub" in the preceding scene.

There are further allusions to the Oldcastle legend in the death scene; Falstaff's frightened cry to his Creator can be paralleled in the stories of the Lollard's martyrdom. Mistress Quickly describes Sir John as a "Christome Child" who "cryed out, God, God, God three or foure times." This is, of course, a natural exclamation, but it is also allusive. In the chronicle accounts of Oldcastle's death the martyr was reported to have cried out Jehovah's name three times when the flames began to consume him. The Jesuit writer Robert Parsons later picked up this image from John Stow when he vilified both Oldcastle and Foxe's glorified image of Oldcastle in the Jesuit book, *A Treatise of Three Conversions*. At one point in his attack Parsons describes the death of a William Hackett who was executed in 1591 for his mad attempt against the realm and the established church, and Parsons brings in the reference to Oldcastle's cries which he apparently got from Stow:

> For that Hackett said, he should rise againe the third day, as Oldcastle did: and went as devoutly to the gallowes, as the other did, cryinge, Jhehova, Jhehova, (as Stow setteth it downe) and at the gallows railed no lesse bitterly upon Queene Elizabeth, than Oldcastle did upon that woorthie King Henry the fift.[15]

But Parsons's use of the Oldcastle legend to denigrate the Cobhams is another part of the long series of events in the lives of that Elizabethan family.

Shakespeare's use of the Oldcastle legend and its analogues is only part of the admixture of satire found in Falstaff's character. Current happenings in Elizabeth's court are mirrored in Sir John's death. Editors have noted the pun on "rheumatic-Romeatic"; it is possibly an allusion to Oldcastle's hatred for the Church of Rome. But the pun is also an allusion, I think, to the furtive intrigues of William, Lord Cobham, with the disaffected Catholics of Elizabeth's reign. Cobham, the reader will recall, played an important role in the intrigues of Mary, queen of Scots, and the duke of Norfolk. He turned informer, it seems, and escaped punishment.

The Elizabethan Lord Cobham seems again touched in

Mistress Quickly's remark that Falstaff died "Betweene twelve and one, Just at turning of the tide," for we know that William Brooke also died "about Midnight" on 6 March 1597. Our information comes from Rowland Whyte, that loquacious steward of Sir Robert Sidney who kept his absent master informed of the details of London life. The reader will remember that Sidney was eager to have Lord Cobham's staff as lord warden of the Cinque Ports, and Whyte watched closely as Cobham drew his final breath.[16] Doubtless the actors were watching too, for the lord chamberlain's staff would also be transferred at Cobham's death.

The preparations for death that William, Lord Cobham, made in 1597 are relevant to Falstaff's final scene in *Henry V*, for in those plans we find, I think, a possible solution for that perplexing problem of the "Table of greene fields" which has intrigued Shakespeare scholars for over two centuries. Debate thrives today as readers supply ingenious emendations or argue for the folio reading of this text. Theobald's emendation of the famous crux holds the field with most editors in this century, but the historical background of the Cobhams provides material to suggest that the "Table of greene fields" is meaningful as it stands, for we know that as death approached, Lord Cobham was concerned with a special project, an endowment that would provide a memorial table or tablet to be erected in his honor in Poppynefelde in Kent.

At the age of seventy, Lord Cobham, being in poor health and despondent at the death of his daughter, Elizabeth, wife of Sir Robert Cecil, wrote and signed his last will on 24 February 1597. He divided his lands, jewels, horses, and books among his three sons and three daughters, but he reserved some five thousand pounds of ready money and certain building materials for the use of William Lambarde, the antiquary, Sir John Leveson, and Sir Thomas Fane, his executors, who were instructed to reestablish the ancient College of Cobham as an almshouse for the relief of the poor in Kent.[17] Lord Cobham died on 6 March, and a few days later William Lambarde wrote to Lord Burghley explaining Lord Cobham's wishes:

His lordship therefore minding an undoubted accomplishment of his godly and fatherly intentions as well towards the poore as his own children, did in his lifetime put into the hands of Sir John Leveson the sum of 5,600 pounds almost, in ready money, over and above rich furniture of his lady's provision amounting to his own estimacion to the value of 2,000 marks. His command to us was that with 2,000 pounds or more of these monies the late suppressed College of Cobham should be re-edified and endowed with livelihood for the perpetual maintenance of twenty poor.[18]

In spite of the nuances of the old faith which clung to the plan, special permission to reestablish Cobham College was granted by an act of Parliament passed in 1597 soon after Lord Cobham's death stating that royal assent had been given to carry out Lord Cobham's wishes to found the New College of Cobham in Kent.[19]

The history of the Old College of Cobham is interesting and unusual; it had been founded in 1362 by Lord John de Cobham, who provided an endowment for a perpetual chantry which was to sing praises for the honor of God and the welfare of the souls of the founder and his progenitors. The endowment provided for the maintenance of five chaplains and a number of brothers from the priory of Saint Saviour, Bermondsey. The college flourished, and some one hundred and seventy-five years later when the master signed the bill of the king's supremacy in 1537 which "dissolved, dis-established, and dis-endowed" the college, the fellowship included eleven chaplains and had in revenues approximately 142 pounds per annum. After the dissolution, the college remained uninhabited, and in this state of abandonment it fell into ruins.

The seventh Lord Cobham wished to rebuild the ancient monument in a new Protestant form, as an almshouse to assist the poor of Kent and, of course, to memorialize his name. The construction of New College progressed rapidly in 1597, and the establishment, with its new rules and ordinances, its order for daily prayers, and its code of conduct for the poor, was finished in September of 1598. The memorial tablet with the arms and quarterings of the Cobhams within a Garter was engraved and placed above the south entrance of the college. It stated that

This new College of Cobham in the County of Kent was founded for the relief of the poore at the charge of the late Right

Honorable Sir William Brooke, Knight of the Garter, Lord Cobham, late Warden of the Cinque Ports, Lieutenant for the same County to the Excellent Majesty of Elizabeth, Queen of England, one of Her Highnesses Privy Councillors and Chamberlayne of Her most Honorable Household. He died 6th March 1596/[97]. This was finished 29th September 1598.

The quadrangle of New College and the ruined Founder's Gateway with its memorial tablet remain standing today adjacent to Cobham Church in Kent. Within the church is a famous collection of monumental brasses which has been called the finest family collection in England.[20] It includes the magnificent bronze and marble effigies which Lord Cobham provided for his parents' tomb in 1561; he was conscious of memorials. Perhaps he anticipated the negligence and misfortune that would keep his own grave unadorned; before a worthy tomb was created for him, his sons and his estate fell to destruction in the plots of 1603. Today, New College stands as sufficient proof that "wasteful Time debateth with Decay." But beyond being a symbol of mutability, this memorial structure may quite possibly be the "Table of greene fields" that Mistress Quickly mentions in Shakespeare's famous passage. Admittedly, the table image is complex, but it is not incomprehensible as some critics insist, nor does it require rearrangement of elements or ellipses or transposed letters or parenthetical enclosures or emendations.[21] I find the folio reading of this famous line both meaningful and consistent. Let us look at it closely in context.

In preceding lines Mistress Quickly describes Falstaff's delirium, his fumbling with the sheets, and his toying with the flowers (I assume that Falstaff mistakes the floral design of the bed coverings for real posies; however, perhaps there were fresh flowers at hand, or there may be a suggestion of Elysian Fields in the hostess's description of Sir John's irrational imaging. There is also some bawdry here.) Mistress Quickly then describes Falstaff as smiling on the tips of his fingers. This is a prayerful pose that fits the preceding image of Falstaff slipping away as a "Christome Child," but such a pose is also a traditional one for the effigies on monumental brasses, and the hostess is quick to recognize that it is time for ultimate things, though she attempts to cheer Sir John.

This realistic description of Falstaff's gestures is followed by a figurative description of his face in its drawn and discolored state. Mistress Quickly compares Falstaff's sharp nose to two things: a pen and a table. She remarks bluntly: "for his Nose was as sharpe as a Pen, and a Table of greene fields." We have here, I believe, two similes and a problem of terminology. Let us proceed carefully.

Critics have noted the realistic death imagery in this passage, the withering of tissue, the green complexion, and so forth. The details are accurate here, and Mistress Quickly as well as her creator apparently knew the commonplace elements of Elizabethan medical lore and of the popular *ars moriendi* literature.[22] But the two similes are allusive— as similes traditionally are. The comma should not confuse us: Shakespeare frequently uses a comma to separate compound elements (subjects, verbs, objects). For a cursory example, the preceding scene in the folio contains several such instances of the playwright's "dramatic punctuation":[23]

(1) Crowned with faith, and constant loyalty.   [II.ii.5]
(2) Doing the execution, and the acte,   [II.ii.17]
(3) With hearts create of duty, and of zeale.   [II.ii.31]
(4) Treason, and murther, euer kept together,   [II.ii.105]
(5) Wonder to waite on treason, and on murther: [II.ii.110]

Modern editors are prone to remove these extraneous commas; however, the punctuation between *pen* and *table* has not been altered because Theobald's famous emendation has convinced most editors that this line contains two independent clauses: "For his nose was as sharp as a pen, and a' babbled of green fields." This reasoning, I believe, is erroneous. I think Mistress Quickly is saying that Falstaff's nose resembles a pen and a table; the *OED* provides clues to the meaning of these terms, and the historical background should provide an explanation for the allusion.

Although the word *pen* can mean a quill-pen or writing instrument pointed and split into nibs at its lower end, *pen* can also mean a hill or mountain, a jutting promontory.[24] Either of these definitions is relevant and will fit the context—the nose and nostrils are pinched by the imminence of death. I prefer the former meaning, however, because of its connotation of writing or inscription—a meaning which links *pen* with *table*. And I think that Shakespeare intentionally juxtaposed these two images for mutual elucidation. The *OED* offers numerous meanings in use in the sixteenth century for the word *table,* and the *Shakespeare Concordance* reveals that the playwright used the word variously in his plays.[25] In this passage, however, I believe the word *table* means a tablet bearing or intended for an inscription or device (*OED: Table, sb.,* 2, a), in other words, a memorial table or monument. The attribute of sharpness is relevant if we limit the category of memorial tables or stones to the famous classical monuments of antiquity such as Trajan's Column or Cleopatra's Needle, a definition which places the image among the classical motifs used in the death scene.[26] To be explicit, I believe that Mistress Quickly says that Falstaff's nose juts from his discolored face like a pointed monument built in green fields. If we place this remark against the topical background, it seems to me that the simile becomes a satiric allusion to the monument which Lord Cobham was planning on his death bed—a monument to be erected in Poppynefelde in Kent. Cobham College was built in the rural village of Cobham, and its site overlooked the green pasturelands to the south called Great Church Field and Little Church Field. The architect for the Old College and for the tower of Cobham Church was said to have been the great Henry Yevele, king's master mason and architect of the nave of Canterbury Cathedral. New College was designed by Giles de Witte, an architect from the Low Countries whom Lord Cobham had hired to assist with the impressive wings of Cobham Hall constructed in the reign of Elizabeth.[27]

I do not know whether Shakespeare was ever in Cobham village or not, but I suspect that he had seen Yevele's tall tower at one time or another and that the image of the older building in its rural setting remained in his mind. Or perhaps he actually saw New College after its completion in 1598 with its arched gateway and the memorial tablet above it. The Founder's Gateway is itself a pointed image with the tablet and crest sheltered by a projecting corbel-table, a pediment, and a peaked entablature which reaches to some height.[28] It does seem to me that Lord Cobham's plans for New College supplied Shakespeare with a simile and an ironic allusion when he wrote the final lines concerning Falstaff. If our dating of Henry V is correct, these lines were written in 1599. The elder Lord Cobham was dead; he had caused the Lord Chamberlain's Men some tense moments when he received the chamberlain's white staff in 1596. As a partial result he was immortalized not by a memorial structure but by a satiric creation which has never been surpassed. Perhaps the modern reader, looking back through the death scene, will find the satire on the Cobhams more gross than unsurpassed. Lest this response occur, let me remind the reader that the actions of William and Henry Brooke, lords of Cobham, throughout Elizabeth's reign made them targets for those who wished to satirize disloyalty and disorder in the political world. Before Shakespeare used it, the Oldcastle legend had become a point of departure from which the barbed shafts of ridicule could be launched at the Cobhams. Our playwright adapted and perfected the satire. If from our distant vantage point such usage appears unseemly, we should remember that in the heat of political contest, the rivalry of court factions placed a number of lives at stake. The satire of Oldcastle's martyrdom with its reflections on the contemporary Cobhams appears to have been part of the propaganda of that conflict. Public pressure (or perhaps private) seems to have prevented the playwright's further development of the Oldcastle legend into the reign of Henry V, as I have noted before. In his play of the ideal king Shakespeare wisely rid himself of an extremely successful but toxic character, and we find Falstaff dying of both a fever and a chill. In this final scene of the Falstaff cycle of plays the idea of martyrdom is not entirely gone, for the scene is densely complex with historical allusions, and the echo of a classical death rings them in. The satire of the tragic mode is pointed. The poignancy and pathos which modern readers find reflected in the death scene are nineteenth-century sentimental affections which turned Falstaff into an amoral demigod of sensuous pleasures—a creature to be envied, not condemned. The ancient Vice, like the historical archetype who was burned at the stake for heresy and treason, has been hidden from view. Twentieth-century critics, or rather those who use the neohistorical approach in the analysis of literature, are successfully attempting the reconstruction of Falstaff as forceful satire on dishonor and disloyalty in the Elizabethan world scheme.

Shakespeare's participation in the Oldcastle satire terminated with the death scene of his great comic character whom he sent out in a blaze of classical wit. So it is now with a backward look that we can determine to some extent the chronology of the Oldcastle satire as it developed in the late sixteenth century. We have no proof that George, sixth Lord Cobham, encouraged his acting company to produce a play on his famous martyred ancestor. But we do know that Thomas Cromwell paid Lord Cobham's players twenty shillings for entertainment in 1539.[29] John Bale, who was interested in the development of a new Protestant form of drama, did not write a play on Oldcastle; instead, he published his *Brefe Chronycle* of the story of Oldcastle's martyrdom about 1544. We do not know what plays were produced by the acting company called the Marquis of Northampton's Players, but their noble mistress was Elizabeth Cobham, marchioness of Northampton. This company was active in the early years of Queen Elizabeth's reign.

The first tangible evidence of satire directed against the Elizabethan Cobhams is in George Ferrers "royal ballads" on Eleanor Cobham and the duke of Gloucester, which Ferrers finally got into print in 1578, although the titles of the poems had been indexed in the 1559 and 1571 editions of the *Mirror for Magistrates*. The poems appear to have been written in the reign of Queen Mary Tudor. In the mid-1580s, if my thinking is correct, the character of Oldcastle, derisively called Jockey, appeared as a clown in the anonymous play *The Famous Victories of Henry V*. This play appears to have been written by someone involved in the disputes among the inhabitants of the Blackfriars precinct, as Lyly, Evans, and their players fought to maintain their lease on the old Parliament chamber in the friary. William Brooke, seventh Lord Cobham, had held the lease of that chamber until 1576 when it was turned over to Farrant for a practice room for the Children of the Chapel Royal. We know that this Lord Cobham kept an acting company of his own called the Lord Warden's Men, but we unfortunately do not know what plays they performed or when they were disbanded. John Lyly appears to have created a satiric caricature of Lord Cobham in the character of Sir Tophas, who fights with boys. Lyly introduces in this role many of the stock characteristics of the braggart soldier, some of which are seen in the role of Jockey in *The Famous Victories.*

Shakespeare's first use of Cobham satire apparently came in *The Contention,* which most scholars date about 1591. Shakespeare was following the lead of George Ferrers and the tradition of the *Mirror* literature with his portrait of Eleanor Cobham. There is no evidence that any of the Cobham family complained about the version of the Eleanor Cobham legend which appeared in *The Contention,* although the appearance of the satire on Fastolf or Falstaff in *1 Henry VI* (produced in March 1592) would suggest that the young playwright was perhaps spurred on by some direct criticism. In November of 1596 the inhabitants of the Blackfriars precinct signed the petition to keep Burbage from completing the new Blackfriars Theatre. The actors were under severe pressure to find a home for their company, for the lord mayor had issued orders for the destruction of the older theaters. I believe that Shakespeare started *1 Henry IV* in the final months of 1596 and that the play was completed before March 1597, when the seventh Lord Cobham died. In the first productions of the play the Falstaff character was called Oldcastle, but when Andrew Wise entered the play in the *Stationers' Register* on 25 February 1598, the name had been changed, for the entry includes a reference to "the conceipted mirthe of Sir John Ffalstoff." It is possible that the players continued to use the name of Oldcastle in some of their productions of the play, because references were made at later dates to the Lord Chamberlain's Men and their Oldcastle play. It probably was the younger Lord Cobham who complained to the queen about the liberties taken in the new drama with his ancestor's name. Queen Elizabeth seems to have favored him not because of his character but because she had loved his mother Frances, Lady Cobham, who had served as mistress of the wardrobe for many years. Certainly it was the younger Lord Cobham who became the strongest contender against George Carey, Lord Hunsdon, for the lord chamberlain's white staff which both their fathers had held. I believe that *1 Henry IV* was being performed in the spring of 1597 when the tensions over the appointment to the lord chamberlain's post were running high. I believe the play became part of the factional striving that occurred at that time and that it served as artistic propaganda to influence the queen's decision on her choice of a new lord chamberlain. The post was of great importance to the actors. The comic satire of the play was an attack upon the integrity of the Cobhams, on both Oldcastle and the contemporary Brookes. The victory went to Hunsdon with the appointment, but the actors apparently were rebuked for their overt satire. Usually Queen Elizabeth tried to keep a semblance of harmony in her court. I suspect that she enjoyed the comedy of the play as much as anyone in the audience but she needed to placate the offended Lord Cobham, who had lost the contest with Hunsdon. She apparently issued a reprimand to the players; certainly, the new Lord Hunsdon as lord chamberlain would have been slow to issue the command. He and Cobham had been too involved in the competition.

The play seems to have been an immediate success with the London public (there were seven quarto editions of Part One before 1623). The stationer Thomas Creede appears to have capitalized on the popularity of Shakespeare's *Henry IV* when he printed an edition of *The Famous Victories* in 1598. Creede was a pirating printer (his name is associated with three of the seven "bad" Shakespeare quartos), and Shakespeare may have agreed to Andrew Wise's edition of *1 Henry IV* early that year because of the danger of piracy. Or, indeed, the play may have been published to offer proof that the Oldcastle name had been changed.

2 Henry IV appears to have been written in the autumn of 1598 after the production of Jonson's *Every Man in His Humour* (ca. September), the latter a play in which Shakespeare acted. The swaggering Pistol is a wonderful version of Jonson's new conception of the humour character. Pistol's introduction in *2 Henry IV* is elaborate, and intentionally so. Jonson, in turn, mentions Justice Shallow in his next play, *Every Man Out of His Humour,* which we date as a work of 1599. Jonson had also used a variant of the Oldcastle satire in the character of Cob in *Every Man in His Humour.* Early in 1599 Nashe made his final grotesque flourish with the Oldcastle satire in *Lenten Stuffe,* and on *1*

June the bishop of London ordered all of Nashe's books burned. In the spring of 1599 while the earl of Essex, the earl of Southampton, and their followers were in Ireland, a number of names were being suggested as probable electees for the Garter. The new Lord Cobham's name was high on the list, and he won election. I am of the opinion that it was in the weeks preceding the Garter investiture ceremonies that Shakespeare wrote *The Merry Wives of Windsor,* which is almost certainly a Garter play, possibly performed at Windsor. Legend has it that Queen Elizabeth commanded the playwright of the Lord Chamberlain's Company to write a play showing Falstaff in love. Perhaps she did. *The Merry Wives* contains a Falstaff strangely altered; vanity has eroded his wit, and the political satire is missing. It is replaced by a broad Chaucerian farce, and yet the topical references are there. Sir Hugh Evans, the Welsh "fairy," appears on stage with his boys. They "burn" Falstaff with their candles, but in jest. Evans explains to Falstaff that the fairies can't hurt him, that they are only boys, and he asks to be pardoned. Shakespeare has ended his game with a glance back to the beginning of the Oldcastle satire in the mid-1580s when Henry Evans was directing Oxford's boys in the early Blackfriars theatre. The promised exploits of Falstaff in *Henry V* were never created, for Shakespeare allows Mistress Quickly to describe Sir John's death in comic pathos. The burning of Nashe's books in June 1599 possibly put a damper on the Oldcastle satire. The incident may have given Shakespeare cause to stop and think perhaps of a similar disaster with his own playbooks. At any rate, in *Henry V* the Oldcastle satire was put to rest, buried as far as the playwright was concerned. That drama apparently was finished before the earl of Essex made his wild ride home from Ireland in September 1599. In November of the same year Henslowe paid Drayton, Munday, Hathaway, and Wilson for writing their Oldcastle play, a drama that eulogized the Lollard martyr. The prologue of this competing play proclaims that its hero is no buffoon: "It is no pamper'd Glutton we present, / Nor aged Councellour to youthful sinne." The competing company of actors obviously understood the raillery of Shakespeare's satire. Andrew Wise published another quarto edition of *1 Henry IV* in 1599, and he and Aspley published Part Two "with the humours of Sir John Ffall-stoff" in 1600. This quarto contained the epilogue of dis-vowal. And that was that.

CHAPTER ELEVEN

The Montage Technique in Macbeth

WHEN SHAKESPEARE HAD RID HIMSELF ABRUPTLY OF fat Jack Falstaff and had turned to the creation of tragedies rather than history plays per se at the beginning of the new century, his unique experimentation with the universal elements in chronicle history was subordinated to his search for motivating forces within character itself. But in the summer of 1606 Shakespeare once more turned to the older chronicle sources for dramatic materials, and he revived all the old techniques he had learned in working with the Falstaff-Oldcastle satire. In reconstituting the conflation design the playwright produced his most subtle and dynamic work of this kind. He began with the montage technique of superimposing one chronicle scene or detail of character upon another. We have known for generations that in writing *Macbeth* Shakespeare chose ideas and actions from various Scottish reigns described in his source materials and that he welded them together to create not only his plot but the characterization of his dramatic protagonist as well. By using the montage process the playwright was able to blend the Scottish past with the lively contemporary English scene: historical characters are enlivened with the mannerisms of their Jacobean descendants, and ancient deeds become reflective foils for current events. In this way the older idea of history as a static exemplum of virtue for emulation and of vice for fair warning is replaced with a more dynamic conception of the past as an active element playing a part in shaping the present. In *Macbeth* we find a conflation of the universal and the topical. Far from distorting history in the tragedy, Shake-

283

speare appears rather to have been abstracting and universalizing human character with his own exciting conception of the function of history. Out of the ancient Scottish chronicles the playwright appears to have wrought a drama closely involved with contemporary events occurring in England in late 1605 and early 1606. As a result *Macbeth* is far more relevant to its Jacobean setting than we have hitherto assumed. The much-printed account of *Macbeth* which Simon Forman left us in his diary lends a ready and easy way into the labyrinthine problem.

Dr. Simon Forman, astrologer, physician, dabbler in necromancy, and sometime drama critic, saw a production of Shakespeare's *Macbeth* at the Globe Theatre in April 1611. Almost all modern editors of the play print Forman's description of that production because it is the first direct record we have from an eyewitness of one of the contemporary performances of Shakespeare's dramas. Forman begins his summary of the action of the play with the "3 women feiries or Nimphes" as he calls them and their encounter with Macbeth and Banquo. Then Forman adds something that does not agree with the text of the play as we have it. He describes the return of Macbeth and Banquo to the court, where "Dunkin bad them both kindly wellcom, And made Mackbeth forth with Prince of Northumberland."[1] This title, prince of Northumberland, becomes singularly significant when it is considered within the context of events occurring just prior to the period in which we think Shakespeare composed *Macbeth*. The archives and chronicles of the Jacobean period as well as the older Scottish records contain materials suggesting that Forman knew what he was writing and that his description of the play is indicative of "more than pierces the eye."

It is customary to explain the inconsistencies between Forman's summary of *Macbeth* and the drama as we have it by saying that he wrote his version of the production long after he had seen the play. This suggestion, however, does not take into consideration the fact that Forman saw the play on 20 April and that on 12 September he was dead. Something else about Forman needs to be remembered. Not only was he a practitioner of necromancy (he was imprisoned a number of times on such charges), but he was also keenly interested in genealogy and had traced his own family line to a relationship to the saintly Queen Margaret, wife of Malcolm, king of Scots.[2] Moreover, he was a practicing physician to a number of the nobility of Jacobean London, including the young countess of Essex, the earl of Cumberland, and Lord Hertford.[3] Forman apparently was informed on titles and rank. Why then that name for Macbeth, "Prince of Northumberland"? The play as we have it contains a loyal lord of Northumberland (Old Siward) who appears with his son in act V. How then is the Forman crux to be explained? The answer apparently is a topical one, and its explanation is linked with the artistic process of conflation. A number of years ago it was pointed out that in Shakespeare's *Macbeth* the character of Malcolm becomes a national representative of the Scottish kings who preceded him and that the character is contrived by "a foreshortening of history."[4] This foreshortening or condensation of images and conflation of episodes is basic to the montage technique. In this process the playwright can be observed manipulating details in unchronological patterns, at times risking anachronisms (or, indeed, exploiting them) for his artistic purposes.[5]

The character of Duncan in *Macbeth* is also the product of the process of conflation. Scholars have noted since the eighteenth century that the murder of Duncan in the play is a patchwork of chronicle materials and that Shakespeare used as one of his chief sources the account of the Scottish reigns printed by Raphael Holinshed. Holinshed used as his primary source Hector Boece's *History of Scotland* in the Bellenden translation, but so did George Buchanan and John Leslie, bishop of Ross, in their histories of Scotland. As a result, all of these chronicle accounts of the eleventh-century reigns of the Scottish kings are interrelated. The sixteenth-century authors elaborate on the murder of King Duff by Donwald at the Castle of Forres in the tenth century, and Shakespeare uses this murder and its grisly details for the dramatic action in *Macbeth*, as numerous Shakespearean scholars have observed.

The saintly, paternal character of Duncan which Shakespeare creates is dependent, however, upon the chronicle descriptions of Malcolm Canmore, Duncan's son. Indeed, if we turn to the chronicles, we find that the historical Duncan was Macbeth's age and that he was noted for his "sloth" and "sluggishness." Hector Boece remarked: "Yit the feble mynd of Duncane (quhen it wes patent to ye pepil) wes not only cause of gret seditions amang the noblis, Bot occasion to Danis [the Danes]to attempt new weris agains ye Scottis."[6] George Buchanan describes Duncan as "a Prince of great Courtesy" and notes that he "wes gevin to piete," but then he adds that Duncan was "of more Indulgence to his own Kindred than became a King, For he was of a mild and Inclinable Disposition." Buchanan also remarks on Macbeth's attitude toward his relative, the king: Macbeth "had always a Disgust at the un-active Slothfulness of his Cousin."[7] Holinshed's description of Duncan is similar: Duncan's reign began peacefully, the chronicler writes, "but after it was perceived how negligent he was in punishing Offendors, manie mis-ruled persons tooke occasion thereof to trouble the peace and quiet state of the common-wealth, by seditious commotions." Holinshed quotes the statement of Macdowald, the Scottish rebel, who maintained that Duncan was "a faint-hearted milkesop, more meet to governe a sort of idle moonks in some cloister, than to have the rule of such valiant and hardie men of warre as the Scots were."[8] All the Elizabethan chroniclers note that Duncan was too lax a king and that Macbeth was too cruel, that their humours needed to be "temporate with each otheris." The chroniclers also note that Malcolm, whose reign followed, was the ideal king. Their praises are hyperbolic: Malcolm is described as taking great pains to amend the public manners of his kingdom; he lived "devoutly and piously" and set an example which inspired others "to a Modest, Just, and Sober life." He did much to strengthen the laws of the land, and he "endeavoured to retrieve Church-affairs, which then began to flag and decay." The great medieval cathedrals at Durham and at Dumferling were constructed at his expense. All writers remark that Malcolm was "noted for no Vice, but was famous to Posterity, for his great and many Virtues."[9]

This pious king was assisted in his reign by his queen, Margaret, the English princess who later was canonized by the church. Her piety seems to have increased that of her husband, the chroniclers noted. "He learned from her also to prolong vigils of the night frequently with prayer; he learned by her exhortation and example to pray to God with groaning of heart and shedding of tears." Turgot, her biographer, added that he "marvelled at this great miracle of God's mercy, when sometimes [he] saw so great application of the king to prayer; and during prayer so great remorse, in a layman's breast."[10] Some of this famous piety rubs off onto Shakespeare's character of King Duncan. Shakespeare was writing for a new Scots-English king who prided himself on his piety. One modern scholar has remarked that King Malcolm and his English queen "stood at the beginning of one new age in Scottish history, as James, heir to the united crowns of Scotland and England, stood at the beginning of another."[11] And of course almost all modern editors of *Macbeth* note that "a royal performance was clearly in view from the very inception of this play" with its glorification of King James's ancestors and its catering to the king's personal interest in witchcraft.[12]

If King James identified with the Scottish history presented in its dramatic form by the King's Men, he possibly was flattered; but if he remembered his own reading of the Scots chronicles, he knew that Malcolm, the most famous of the medieval kings, was murdered at the instigation of a lord of Northumberland, and he may have been alarmed. The story of the death of Malcolm interested the medieval chroniclers, and it was included as a legend of significance in the sixteenth-century chronicles. Hector Boece's description is basic because it influenced many later writers.

Boece's *Historiae Scotorum* was published in Paris in 1527. James V was so impressed with the work that he ordered John Bellenden, archdeacon of Moray, to translate it into Scots, and the Bellenden translation was printed in Edinburgh about 1540. The account of the death of the wondrously pious King Malcolm is related in the following manner:

King Malcolme to resist sic thingis [the slaughter of the Northumbrians by William Rufus, King of England]in the beginning come with ane army in Northumbirland & segit ye castel of Anwik. And quhen ye castel be lang segeing wes reddy to be randerit, ane knycht of Ingland intendyng to do ane hardy vassalage come on ane swift hors out of the castell . . . Beirand ye keyis of the castell on his speir poynt. To signify ye castel reddy to be randerit. The wache seand hym cum in sic maner tuke na suspition. Bot brocht him with gret noyis & clamour to ye kings palzeon [pavilion]. . . . And quhen ye kyng wes luk- and maist deligently yairto, yis Inglishman ran him throw ye left Ee, and fled haistelie to the nixt wod. . . . It is said that king William of Ingland changit the surname of yis hardy knycht and callit him pers E, of quhome is discendit ane noble hous under the same surname, decorit with gret honouris callit the erllis of Northumbirland.[13]

John Leland, the sixteenth-century antiquary and scho- lar, said with contempt that Boece's lies were as numerous "as the waves of the sea or the stars of the sky," but there were many historical sources for Boece's Percy story. The older chroniclers had related with horror the "sle tressoun," the "guilefull killing of the king of Scots," the "slaughter," the "murther," and so on.[14] Holinshed, following closely Bellenden's translation, repeated the Percy story, but at this point he added a flourish or two of his own: "And whilest all mens eies were earnest in beholding the keies, the Englishman ran the king through the left eie. . . . The point of the speare entred so farre into the kings head, that immediatlie falling downe amongst his men hee yeelded up the ghost." Holinshed repeats also the additional remark about the Percies: "It is said, that king William changed the name of this adventurous knight, & called him Perse- eie, for that he stroke king Malcome so right in the eie, and in recompense of his service gave him certeine landes in Northumberland: of whome those Percees are descended, whiche in our daies have injoied the honorable title of earles of Northumberland." In the margin of the page Holinshed denies the last point which had been too good to omit from his history; he adds bluntly, "The name of the Percees had no such beginning, for they came foorth of Normandie at the conquest, Erles of Northumberland."[15] The exciting story was a commonplace in Scottish history; we find it repeated by John Leslie in his *De Origine, Mori- bus, et Rebus Gestis Scotorum* translated by James Darymple in 1596: "Loo, Malcolme, to the skaith of the hail Realme, is slane; slane, I say, throuch a traytorous trick." And Leslie's translator continues with great irony: "Rufus, for that namet him Lord Persie, that sa stoutlie, for his cuntrie, he had put him selfe in sik dainger; and gave him fair fieldes in Northumbirland for his rewarde:

letting him to undirstand, that nevir in Ingland was ane so couragious, so vertuous, or as notable ane Interprise evir tuik in hand."[16] The story continued to be popular. How much of it was used in the history play entitled *Malcolm Kynge of Scottes*, which Charles Massey wrote for the Lord Admiral's Men in 1602, we do not know. The timing suggests that the play may have been a propaganda work with a pro-James slant, but this is speculation, for the play is no longer extant.[17]

William Camden tried to scotch the Percy story in his *Remains Concerning Britaine* (1605) when he insisted that the Percies had come from Normandy and that their name had been taken from the Percy forest in Maen, "not of piercing the king of Scots through the eie, as *Hector Boetius* fableth."[18] As late as 1623 a chronicle published in Aberdeen said that King Malcolm was slain at the seige of Alnwick by a knight surnamed "Pierce-eye."[19] It would appear that Shakespeare was familiar with the story; in *1 Henry IV* he assigns Falstaff the remark about Hotspur (the Henry Percy of that play): "Well if Percy be aliue, ile pierce him." But the pun could be used, of course, without knowledge of the story.

If one looks closely at the ancient chronicle story, some details of it appear startlingly relevant to the events of November 1605. Malcolm, king of Scots, was killed by Archie Morell, the nephew and steward of Robert Mowbray, earl of Northumberland, modern historians tell us.[20] The medieval chroniclers called Morell a comrade or bedfellow of Malcolm.[21] The two men had been friends. The similarity of this fact to the details of the Gunpowder plot is unusual, to say the least. Thomas Percy, one of the chief conspirators (it was he who leased the house next to the Parliament building where the powder was stored in the early stage of the plot), was a cousin of Henry Percy, ninth earl of Northumberland, and Thomas Percy had been in the earl's confidential employment as steward of the northern estates and constable of Alnwick Castle.[22] In the trial of the earl of Northumberland, held in the Star Chamber on 26 June, 1606, one of the most serious charges was that the earl had arranged for Thomas Percy to become one of the king's gentlemen pensioners without having him take the traditional oath of loyalty. Attorney General Coke stated the charge dramatically the day of the trial: the earl "putt the said Piercy into the Roome and Place of a Pensioner, dayly to attende his Majesties Personne with a Halberde in his Hande, a Thinge most daungerous for such a desperate Personne."[23] And indeed it was. Thomas Percy was a furious and fanatic man (old John Speed said that Percy came riding out of the North "as hot as Hotspur"). Obviously the earl had been seriously negligent of his monarch's safety, but Northumberland insisted that he was innocent of any involvement in his cousin's nefarious plot.

Francis Osborne has left us an interesting opinion of the Northumberland case in his *Traditional Memoirs*. Osborne was a young man walking the aisles of St. Paul's during the exciting days following 5 November 1605. He remarked later on what he considered to be the victimizing of the earl of Northumberland in the Gunpowder plot. King James was jealous of the power of the Percies, he said, and the monarch could not forget the carnage of the border conflicts between the English and the Scots. The king began "not only to measure," Osborne wrote, "but to weigh the bloud spilt on the borders, amongst which he found that of James the 5th mingled with his Allies, which prompted him no lesse to revenge, than the many perjuries, cruelties, and perfidious carriages of his [Percy's] Ancestors, still hanging on a file in the English Memory."[24] At this late date it is of course impossible to determine the motives behind King James's actions; he saw to it that the earl of Northumberland spent sixteen years as a prisoner in the Tower of London, and the fine of £30,000 which was demanded of the earl was the largest ever levied on an Englishman to that date.[25] We do know that King James prided himself on his scholarship and that he knew his Scots history. Twentieth-century historians are inclined to vindicate the earl of Northumberland; those who have worked with the important manuscript holdings at Alnwick Castle and Syon House say that the earl was victimized by his political enemies, by a jealous monarch, and by his own arrogant pride. Whether the earl of Northumberland was involved in his cousin's destructive plot is not, of course, to the present purpose. What is of concern for this chapter is Shakespeare's attitude toward the earl while he was writing *Macbeth*.

Shakespeare's use of the Percy rebellions as plot material

in the *Henry IV* plays has been analyzed earlier in this study. Lily B. Campbell was one of the first critics to note that the playwright used conflation in the scenes of the Percy rebellion.[26] Shakespeare was using a montage technique to create a unified dramatic action. It appears that he also changed the superstitious character of the historical Hotspur to one of blatant skepticism in order to stress the relationship between the historical Hotspur and the Elizabethan Percies, who were noted for their skepticism. Shakespeare also changed the name of the historical Lady Percy to Catherine, the name of the Elizabethan Lady Percy, and so on. This is the same process of conflation that I have just described in the character of Shakespeare's Duncan. It is the process which Shakespeare uses, I think, for the character of Macbeth. In the famous protagonist's character Shakespeare depicts, I believe, a contemporary Percy figure. But to recognize this figure and the process of conflation the modern reader must know something of the singular ninth earl of Northumberland.

This special member of the ancient Percy family was known as "the Wizard Earl." Anthony Wood included the description in his praise of "the noble earl of Northumberland, the favourer of all good learning, and Mecaenas of learned men." Wood remarks that the phrase "the Wizard Earl and his three Magi" was commonly used for Northumberland and three of his scientific friends.[27] The "three Magi" included Thomas Hariot, the famous mathematician who worked in the special laboratory built by the earl on the grounds at Syon House. Hariot was looking through a telescope before Galileo; he was speculating about sun spots before the beginning of the seventeenth century. He also served the earl as a collector of rents, and he received a pension from Northumberland from 1598 until his death in 1622.[28] The second "magus" was Walter Warner, who served the earl as secretary and bookkeeper from 1590 until Northumberland's death in 1632.[29] He edited posthumously Hariot's *Artis Analyticae Praxis* and dedicated it to Northumberland. The third member of the trio was Robert Hues, a scientific geographer who had sailed the world with Thomas Cavendish. His pension did not begin until 1616, but he seems to have joined the group much earlier.[30] A contemporary author wrote of this little academy that

SHAKESPEARE'S TYPOLOGICAL SATIRE

"their thoughts were elevated above the common cares of life, where they explored science in all its pleasing forms, penetrated her most intricate recesses, and surveyed the whole globe."[31] We are inclined today to assume that only the illiterate pitlings were superstitious about science, that only they associated experimental physics with black magic, but this is an inaccurate view. An example of the prevailing attitude toward scientific experimentation is to be found in Lord Chief Justice Popham's remark to Raleigh about Thomas Hariot. Raleigh and Hariot were associates on the Virginia voyage, and the Chief Justice knew of the friendship between the two men:

> You have been taxed by the world, Sir Walter Ralegh, with holding heathenish, blasphemous, atheistical, and profane opinions, which I list not to repeat, because Christian ears cannot endure to hear them. . . . let not Heriott, nor any such Doctor [some editors print "Devil"] persuade you there is no eternity in Heaven, lest you find an eternity of Hell-torments![32]

King James's interest in the kinds and classifications of magic is well-known. In his *Daemonologie* he insisted that only a very limited amount of astrological medicine and weather prediction was lawful; other forms of astrology, particularly the probing of the heavens, led to the illicit science of black magic.[33] It is perhaps true, as biographers of the earl of Northumberland have suggested, that the nobleman's scientific interests did little to raise him in the estimation of King James. But the earl's interests in science were formed long before James came to the throne of England. Since this fact is sometimes disputed, it should be pointed out that Northumberland had attracted his circle of intellectuals in the early 1590s. The poet George Peele, in his complimentary poem "Honour of the Garter," written for the installation of Northumberland as a knight of the Order in June 1593, praised the earl for his intellectual qualities and for his patronage of men of science:

> Thrice noble Earle . . .
> (Renowned Lord, Northumberlands fayre flower)
> The Muses loue, Patrone, and fauoret,
> That artizans and schollers doost embrace,
> And clothest *Mathesis* in rich ornaments,
> That admirable Mathematique skill,

Familiar with the starres and Zodiack.
(To whom the heauen lyes open as her booke)
By whose directions undeceiueable,
(leauing our Schoolemens vulgar troden pathes)
And following the auncient reuerend steps
Of *Trismegistus* and *Pythagoras,*
Through vncouth waies and vnaccessible,
Doost passe into the spacious pleasant fieldes
Of diuine science and Phylosophie,
From whence beholding the deformities,
Of common errors and worlds vanitie,
Doost heere enjoy that sacred sweet content
That baser soules not knowing, nor affect:[34]

This is mediocre poetry, but it reveals something of the image that Northumberland's interests and patronage had created for him early in his career.

There is another famous name which belongs on the list of the earl's followers: Northumberland was a patron to Dr. John Dee, the famous physician of Queen Elizabeth's reign who denied vehemently in a petition to King James that he had had any traffic with evil spirits—only with good ones![35] There were other friends of Northumberland whose names are associated with the history of early science: Nathaniel Torperley, Nicholas Hill, Thomas Allen, and of course Sir Walter Raleigh. The earl seems to have eagerly surrounded himself with aggressive and curious minds. His broad range of interests is indicated in the list of books that he had with him in the Tower in 1610. That list includes the titles *Discours des Sorciers* and *Histoire de Magicien de Provence.*[36] In addition, records at Syon House indicate that the earl paid for a "speculative glass" or crystal ball early in his career and that he used the services of a clairvoyant agent in an attempt to recover a stolen jewel.[37] It should be noted of course that Northumberland's interest in occult subjects was a natural part of his interest in experimental science. His reputation with the common people, however, was a shadowy one, and historians reflect on the "strange rumors that went abroad about the dark practices of the Wizard Earl and his three Magi."[38]

In addition to Northumberland's scientific interests and his cultivation of liberal and untrammeled minds, his predilection for sarcasm and wit seems to have endangered his position at court. The earl's open contempt for the Scottish favorites whom James brought with him to London did not endear him to the monarch. One biographer writes that "the great English Earl could never bring himself to yield that subservience, or to permit those familiarities, which James demanded from his ministers and indulged in towards his favourites. . . . [The earl] assumed towards those who enjoyed the royal favour, a disdainful and contemptuous attitude which could not fail to make him many enemies at Court, and to offend the jealous Sovereign."[39] The relationship between the earl of Northumberland and King James turned a cool 180 degrees within two years after the monarch's entrance into London. By 1605 the earl had isolated himself with his own selective group of intellectuals. This isolation made him an easy target once the shattering news of the "Papist Plot" broke the calm of the fifth of November.

John Chamberlain wrote to Dudley Carleton, who was abroad but who had been employed by Northumberland as a private secretary. (Indeed, it was Carleton who rented the house next to the Parliament building to Thomas Percy.) Chamberlain wrote: "Not that Your Lord can be any way toucht with this divelish conspiracie, but that neerenes of name, bloude, longe and inwarde dependance, and familiaritie [with Thomas Percy] cannot but leave some aspersion that will not easilie or lightly be washt off without time."[40] Chamberlain's fears were justified. On 27 November, three weeks after the plot had been discovered and after an intensive investigation by the attorney general and the Privy Council, King James signed the warrant for the commitment of the earl to the Tower to await trial for treason. His brothers, Allan and Joscelyn, also were arrested, as were Lord Montague, Lord Stourton, and Lord Mordaunt, the leading Catholic noblemen in the realm.

The earl of Northumberland's trial was delayed until June 1606, several months after Father Garnet had been executed. The earl was found guilty of "divers Crimes very greate, and highe Contempts, misprisions and Offences commited . . . against his Majestie."[41] It could have been worse. The earl had insisted vigorously that he knew nothing of his relative's heinous plot, and he escaped the death sentence. But many in England thought him guilty of involvement in the Gunpowder treason. Zorzi Giustinian,

Sir Henry Percy, ninth Earl of Northumberland.

Courtesy of His Grace, the Duke of Northumberland.

the Venetian ambassador in England, was kept informed of events by the Privy Council. He relayed the following information to the Doge on 12 July, 1606:

> The Earl of Northumberland has been sentenced at last. He has been condemned to pay one hundred thousand crowns, to be imprisoned for life, and to be deprived of all his offices. The proofs of his complicity in the plot are overwhelming, and he was saved from the capital sentence only by the grace of the King. The Earl had earnestly sought this trial in the expectation of being fully acquitted, but when he saw the case going against him he became so alarmed that he returned unsatisfactory answers, and such as were not expected from a man of his prudence and intelligence. This is a great blow to the Catholics, whose protection the Earl assumed when the King came to the throne, and this was not one of the smallest of the charges that led to his condemnation.[42]

It was during this summer that Shakespeare appears to have written *Macbeth*. Henry Paul, in his extensive study of the topical background of the play, insists that the drama had its first performance before the king at Hampton Court on 7 August, 1606.[43] Kenneth Muir, the New Arden editor of the play, concludes "that the play was performed in 1606, first at the Globe, and afterwards at Court—perhaps with a few minor alterations, and perhaps before King Christian of Denmark, who was in England in July and August of that year on a visit to his brother-in-law, James I."[44] In a more recent review of the evidence for dating *Macbeth*, J. M. Nosworthy has concluded, "It now seems certain, in the face of previous editorial doubts, that *Macbeth* was written in 1606." And he suggests that the actual composition may have extended "from *c.* June 25th to *c.* August 1, allowing about a week for rehearsal." Nosworthy also concludes that the play was an "occasional" one, written at the request of the king.[45] It is a fascinating thought. We know that Lord Salisbury used Ben Jonson as an agent in an attempt to ferret intelligence in the Gunpowder case.[46] What the king wanted in a command performance, if he ordered the King's Men to produce a play in the summer of 1606, we probably never will know. But there is room for speculation.

Simon Forman's statement about Duncan's creating Macbeth the prince of Northumberland early in the action of the play indicates, I believe, the original production's focus on current affairs. Forman's statement indicates that Shakespeare was employing a dramatic technique he had used successfully in the earlier history plays, where he had depicted the Percies of Henry IV's reign with an Elizabethan relevancy. In *Macbeth* Shakespeare superimposes elements from the chronicle accounts of the Scottish reigns of King Duff, King Duncan, King Kenneth, and King Malcolm to create a dramatic protagonist who is susceptible to the influence of witchcraft and necromancy, who is given the title of prince of Northumberland, who is ambitious for the crown, and who is willing to murder the king of Scots to gain it. Since *Macbeth* was written and produced, as we think, shortly after the trials of the Gunpowder conspirators and the earl of Northumberland, a period in which King James was in a state of intense excitement over his own "miraculous powers" in discovering the plot (everyone knows the story of the monarch's perception on the fifth of November), it is naive if not irresponsible to ignore the implications of the tragedy. Northumberland's name was on the list of contenders for the crown compiled by Thomas Wilson in 1600; the earl's claim to the throne of England was based on his line of descent from "Mary, granddaughter of Edmund Crouchback, eldest brother of Henry III."[47] Northumberland had a large Catholic following, and had the Gunpowder plot succeeded, he would have been the Englishman of highest rank left in the kingdom. The crown would have been his. The grotesque story of his ancestor's murder of the king of Scots and of his name "Pierce-eye" being derived from the deed was still alive and popular. Among many people of both high and low estate the earl was known as a wizard and an experimenter with magic. Moreover, if images are important, Thomas Percy's head was impaled on a pole and placed above the Parliament building where it remained for many years.[48]

It is against this grotesque background that some speculative conclusions take shape. I believe that Shakespeare wrote *Macbeth* as a tragedy meant to depict the assumed guilt of the earl of Northumberland in his involvement in the heinous plot to murder James I. This was done by an artistically contrived presentation of ancient chronicle materials, so selectively chosen as to represent characters and actions analogous to the current situation. Today, modern criticism is in a state of hypersensitivity toward topical research in literature. This attitude is understandable because the mode was abused by many writers of past generations. But the situation in criticism today has reached an impasse. It is almost impossible to understand the meaning of an Elizabethan work of art without a thorough grounding in the social and intellectual milieu of the period. Historians of the sixteenth and early seventeenth centuries, and moralists of that day too, insisted that the humours of men were passed on to succeeding generations. The playwright seems to have agreed with them: "There is a Historie in all mens Liues, / Figuring the nature of the Times deceas'd." This was a psychological theory that had proved true, in some aspects, and Shakespeare had used it successfully as a basis for the Falstaff-Oldcastle-Cobham satire in the earlier history plays.

But today we think that the earl of Northumberland was innocent of involvement in the Gunpowder plot. Why did the playwright attack him in such a virulent way? Shakespeare was a sensitive and honorable man, as we all stand ready to affirm. The simple answer is that no one at the time believed in the earl's innocence. Even his own kinsman acknowledged the earl's guilt. Sir William Browne, whose daughter had married a Percy, wrote from Flushing on 9 November declaring, "Seing the Earle of Northumberland hath so vilainously and devilishly forgot himself, I am sory that ever I honored him, and more sory that I have a chyld that carryes his name."[49] The earl's enemies circulated their calumnies at foreign courts so that at home and abroad the Percy name was associated with treason. The earl's own fearful apprehensiveness is evident in his letters to the Council and the king. In one of these letters he begged them to be careful of his reputation: "The world may take jealosy, as things fall owt at this point, and lay a greater imputation to my charge, then ever they can rite me in hereafter."[50] And indeed, the world did just that. In one particularly passionate letter the earl wrote to proclaim his innocence: "I was never Extortioner; I never gayned by Oppression; I was never Perfidious; I never ought [owed] any Man any thinge that he had not satisfaction for; I never sought any Man's Blood; I was ever true to my Prince and Contry."[51] But he was trapped, and the circumstantial evidence against him was impressive.

Other factors may possibly have influenced Shakespeare's attitude toward the earl of Northumberland in 1606. Earlier, in the 1590s, the earl had been a friend and follower of the earl of Essex, but that friendship had soured. Northumberland's own words are extant concerning the breach. In his manuscript entitled *Advice To His Son*, the earl speaks of the advisability of selecting a wife whose friends will help in the advancement of one's own fortunes. And he remarks that in this point he had failed himself. He married Essex's sister, the passionate and high-tempered Dorothy Devereux, in 1594, but he notes in his manuscript that he "grew out of Hope within one or two Years; for Essex and I were at Warres within that Tyme, and Hindrance grew rather than love."[52] This breach led to an open break with the earl of Southampton; the record of the conflict is extant in a letter which Northumberland sent to Anthony Bacon. Southampton appears to have spoken disparagingly of the noble Percy, and the latter "gave him the lie." Southampton sent then the "challenge absolute," but it was "stuffed with strange conditions" according to Northumberland. A duel was in the offing when the queen intervened and sent both young men to the Council, where the dispute was patched up. "And this is the end of an idle tale," concluded Northumberland.[53] This episode occurred early in 1597; by 1600 Northumberland had become an active member of the opposing political faction led by Sir Robert Cecil. He had cut his ties with the Essex-Southampton group.

The nagging problem of the king's prejudices lies dormant behind most discussions of *Macbeth*. The problem is a difficult one because in spite of the high drama of the witches' scenes the play appears to cater to the king's "blind spots." Perhaps with some evidence that the practice was not a singular one, Shakespeare's choice in this instance will be more readily understood. Francis Osborne has left us an interesting statement concerning the influence of the stage upon King James. Osborne was speaking—with more compassion than most Anglican writers—about the plight of the English Catholics in the early years of James's reign. He says that the "frequent Peti-

tions of these plundered people [the English recusants]"
had softened James's heart, "which in its own nature was
not cruell"; but he was influenced by "a lively representation of that northerne *Puppet play* whose Scenes they lay in
the Church of *Rome*, pretending the least candor used to
these *Canaanites* [the Catholics] would call his Mothers
sinnes to a new remembrance, and so conjure up the spirit
of Rebellion."[54] This is of course a seventeenth-century
view. Osborne published his *Memoirs* in 1658. But it indicates a certain sophisticated if not lethal use of the stage
in the early 1600s. Dramas were written to influence the
minds of monarchs. I think *Macbeth* was written on royal
command from King James. I also believe that the drama
plays upon the king's prejudices. It is a disconcerting
thought. Apparently, after 1611 the author of *Macbeth*
found the play disconcerting too. The tragedy seems to
have undergone extensive revision. Twentieth-century
critics have produced an inordinate amount of speculation
about the revisions of *Macbeth*. The truncated structure of
the play, its brevity, and its choppy junctures reinforce such
speculation. To the abundant theories I would like to add
my own. I believe that Shakespeare eventually came to
realize that he had done an injustice to Henry Percy, ninth
earl of Northumberland. I believe that sometime between
1611 (when Forman saw the play) and 1616 the playwright removed the passages that marked the resemblance
between the protagonist and the earl of Northumberland.
This certainly would have included the title "Prince of
Northumberland" that Forman says Duncan gave to Macbeth. I think that Shakespeare then added the characters
of Siward and his son to the action at the end of the play,
added them without proper stage directions in some instances.[55] This historical material is taken from Holinshed
and presents a favorable picture of an early and loyal earl
of Northumberland. In this fashion the original thrust of
the drama was covered over.

There are two more tenuous suggestions that can be
made from other sources. When D'Avenant printed his version of *Macbeth* in 1674, he included a formal argument in
the text, but the argument does not fit his revised play. It
reads like a program note to an older play; indeed, the
argument agrees more with Simon Forman's summary

than with the folio version of the play.[56] In the argument the Hecate scene is not mentioned; rather, wizards are brought in: "And afterwards on some new Fears, [Macbeth] Consulted with certain of his Wizards about his future Estate: Was told by one of them, that he should never be Overcome, till Birnam Wood . . . came to Dunsinan Castle."[57] If there is any accuracy at all in this 1674 argument, it may reveal something of the original play. D'Avenant's argument has been identified as part of Peter Heylyn's description of Scotland published in *Microcosmos* (1625). It has been suggested that Heylyn had an early performance of Shakespeare's play in mind when he wrote of the reign of Macbeth, describing it as "a history then which for variety of action, or strangenesse of euents, I neuer met with any more pleasing."[58] Heylyn was a playwright himself; titles of three of his dramas, written while he was in residence at Magdalen College, Oxford, are known, although the manuscripts have not survived. His reference to Macbeth's consultation with his wizards rather than with the witches leads me to suggest that Shakespeare's opening scene in act IV originally may have been a laboratory scene with three magi instead of a cavern scene with the midnight hags.[59] As Heylyn describes the event, the wizards use their occult arts to predict the future for Macbeth. The possibility of Shakespeare's having used wizards in the first version of the play is strengthened by the fact that Holinshed mentions wizards and their influence upon Macbeth. For emphasis Holinshed prints a marginal note: "Makbeths Confidence in Wizzards," and in the text proper he writes that Macbeth listened to "certeine wizzards, in whose words he put great confidence." And when Macduff prepares to slay Macbeth at the end of the reign, Holinshed quotes him as saying, "I am even he that thy wizzards have told thee of, who was neuer borne of my mother, but ripped out of her wombe."[60]

We have no proof that Shakespeare followed Holinshed and depicted Macbeth listening to his wizards, but if he were looking for correlating elements to link past with present, as I think he was, he would have been blind to have missed the exciting relationship between Holinshed's description of the wizards and the incident which involved the ninth earl of Northumberland and his magi. This bit of

Jacobean history includes the casting of the future through the act of astrology.

King James forbade the casting of his horoscope after he visited Tycho Brahe in the observatory at Hveen in March 1590. Brahe had cast horoscopes for Prince Christian and various nobles of the Danish court, and it is assumed that the famous astronomer pointed out an adverse element in James's natal chart that frightened the monarch.[61] Later when James discovered the Gunpowder treason, he learned that the earl of Northumberland had cast the forbidden horoscope. The king sent instructions in his own hand that Thomas Hariot should be interrogated concerning "what purpose he hath heard his Lord use anent my nativity or fortune," and "if ever his Lord desired him to cast it or tell him my fortune."[62] Hariot was in prison by this time, and his laboratory at Syon House had been ransacked by Sir Thomas Smith and the officers under his command.[63] Hariot's answers to the interrogation have not survived, but similar questions were put to the earl of Northumberland. He denied that he had ever seen a horoscope of the king, although he admitted that he had heard of one being cast in Paris when the monarch came to the English throne.[64] Unfortunately for the earl, Nathaniel Torperley, the scientific friend of Hariot, was also questioned, and Torperley revealed that Hariot had indeed cast the King's horoscope from the astronomical tables that Torperley had brought to him. This had been done at Essex House, where Northumberland was in residence.[65] We know that the earl's interest in astrology had been intensified by his desire for an heir after the first children of his marriage with Dorothy Devereux died in infancy. Torperley admitted that he had helped to cast the nativity of the earl's "son that died," but he denied that the horoscopes had been cast for "judgment" or prediction of the future. All of this came out at the trial of the earl in June 1606, as we know from John Hawarde's legal notes on the Star Chamber case.[66]

In the twentieth century the distinction between astrology and astronomy is precise, but that was not the case in the early seventeenth century, and modern students of that period should not be surprised to find such men as Hariot and Torperley involved with occult ideas and practices. From the king's point of view, however, such men were of "the Devil's schoole," the "Astrologie judiciar."[67] Considering the king's strong feelings, the case against Northumberland on this one point alone was enough to assure imprisonment for years. The Jacobean "Magi" who surrounded the ninth earl of Northumberland and the "wizzards" in whom Macbeth "put great confidence" are then part of the amazing set of coincidences which makes the ancient Scottish reign of Macbeth a parallel for the events of 1605.

Again, it should be pointed out that there is no proof of Shakespeare's use of wizards instead of Hecate and the witches in the apparitions scene, but Heylyn's description of such wizards and D'Avenant's use of Heylyn's account of them are suggestive clues which lead me to think that Shakespeare did follow Holinshed at this point. The critical ambivalence in modern editions of the play about Middleton's witch songs and, indeed, the entire apparitions scene at the beginning of act IV are part of this problem. My own suggestion is that the scene as we now have it is the result of a revision made to eliminate the implied reference to Northumberland's "Magi" in the original version of *Macbeth*. In following Holinshed's account, Shakespeare, I believe, had welded past and present in an exciting way. In the revision all lines were not changed, I would suggest. Those lines which Macbeth addresses to the powers of darkness may well have been in the original version:

I conjure you, by that which you profess,
Howe'er you come to know it, answer me:
Though you untie the winds, and let them fight
Against the Churches; though the yesty waves
Confound and swallow navigation up;
Though bladed corn be lodg'd, and trees blown down;
Though castles topple on their warders' heads;
Though palaces, and pyramids, do slope
Their heads to their foundations; though the treasure
Of Nature's germens tumble all together,
Even till destruction sicken, answer me
To what I ask you.

[IV. i. 50–61]

The imagery and ideas of those lines echo the descriptions used by the terrified public to depict what would have happened had the Gunpowder plot succeeded as it was planned by Thomas Percy, Guy Fawkes, and their companions.

The dramatic scene of magic at the beginning of act IV leads also to the second possible clue in the search for the original version of *Macbeth*. There is a similar scene in the last play written by William Percy, the brother of the ninth earl of Northumberland. He wrote six dramas that have survived in manuscript.[68] The first five plays were written between 1601 and 1603, but the last play is dated by Percy as a work of 1632, the year the ninth earl died. This last play is a comedy called *Necromantes*; its central character, an arrogant wizard, appears to be a satirical figure of the ninth earl of Northumberland.[69] In the play the wizard or necromancer attempts to depose the dog-faced king. At mid-point in the comedy he enters with "Booke and Wand," prepared to use his magic power to call up the future in order to know the outcome of his adventure to usurp the crown. He begins to "divine the greater worlde" by creating astrological figures with Venus in Cancer, Mars in Libra, Saturn in Sagittarius, the Moon in Aquarius, and so forth. As the visions or apparitions arise, he of course misinterprets each of them: one is of a man held in prison watched by armed guards. It is his own future, but he does not realize this. Another vision is of a jovial king sitting at a banquet table. The necromancer misinterprets again, for he thinks his own future enjoyment of the crown is assured. Another apparition is of the head of a young prince crowned with flowers. The magician mistakenly thinks the child to be his own son. And so on.[70] The influence of the apparition scene from *Macbeth* is obvious. Indeed, the influence of Shakespeare is strong throughout the play, with its opening scene modeled on *The Tempest* and its plot on *The Comedy of Errors*. Percy's play is not superb drama; the author's lack of sensitivity with language blurs the aesthetic dimensions of his work. But Percy had some talent with plot structure, and he was fascinated with theatrics. *Necromantes*, in spite of its lack of intrinsic merit, is spectacularly important, I think, for *Macbeth*. The play reflects not only Shakespeare's apparitions scene, but it also reflects Shakespeare's dramatic protagonist from a stylized comic view.[71]

When Peter Heylyn's description of Macbeth's consultation with his wizards is reinforced with William Percy's satiric version of the frustrated necromancer, speculation becomes a necessary adjunct of criticism. I believe it was originally the three magi or wizards who created the bloody apparitions and the pageant of kings in *Macbeth*. I also believe they performed their magic for the inquisitive Macbeth who was called the prince of Northumberland. On 7 August 1606, at Hampton Court, I believe the King's Men presented the most electrifying drama of the Jacobean period, a drama which had been commissioned by the king. I am convinced that Simon Forman, Peter Heylyn, and William Percy later saw this first version of *Macbeth*. If Shakespeare had been a less sensitive man, perhaps we would have this version of the tragedy today. But the playwright's sense of justice compelled a revision, I think. His montage of Scots history had allowed him to present a universal characteristic in human personages; his conflation of past and present had succeeded brilliantly. But Shakespeare's most distinguished experiment with the montage technique was, ethically, a failure. He revised the play, I believe, to hide the topicality that was so spectacular in its incrimination of the earl of Northumberland. Topicality, in this instance, had led to an embarrassment in the ethical mode of his art. But it had not violated either the aesthetic structure of the drama or the philosophical basis upon which the montage technique was grounded. In the Elizabethan dramatic period the playwrights had their own version of our modern demand for relevance. Topicality could, in the hands of an expert playwright, lift drama to the universal. In his plays written after 1606 Shakespeare continued to employ the montage technique, I believe, but he employed it with even more subtle forms, striving for those rarified elements which would unite the microcosm of Jacobean England with the macrocosm of art.[72]

CHAPTER TWELVE

The Typological Pattern

MANY YEARS AFTER SHAKESPEARE HAD ABANDONED his famous comic character, John Dryden remarked to the earl of Rochester on the art of the lampoon as being "that dangerous part of wit."[1] Dryden was thinking of the forms of personal satire in his own age, but his precept is classical. Every thinking man of Dryden's era and of the Renaissance before him knew that the comedies of Aristophanes were filled with wittily pointed attacks upon famous political and philosophical figures; they also knew that Aristotle and the critics who followed him had condemned the use of personal satire as a device more destructive than productive in high moral art. The direct personal attack was condemned as limited, narrow, and detracting in art which strove for a universal applicability among the nations of men. In the Elizabethan period Puttenham described for writers and critics the refining progress which the authors of New Comedy had made when they abandoned the "bitter poeme called the old *Comedy*" with its exploitation of invective and lampoon, and he remarks upon how they had replaced the old form with a dramatic art which was "more ciuill and pleasant a great deale and not touching any man by name, but in a certaine generalitie glancing at euery abuse."[2] But personal lampoon in the hands of the greatest writers has always succeeded with boundless energy, from the image of the comic Socrates swinging in his basket midway between the heavens and terra firma to the image of Cibber crowned upon the Throne of Dullness. The great writers of personal abuse, of course, have been aware of the need to broaden their

306

satire with literary traditions that amplify a singular image without destroying the realistic details of identity and personification. The Elizabethans soon learned that personal abuse within the scope of the lampoon could be welded to the larger satiric aggregate through its integrating function as a structural element within its artistic setting.

In sixteenth-century England the lampoon had proved a most fruitful instrument in social satire, although none would have denied that it was also a "dangerous part of wit." Cardinal Wolsey was convinced (and probably rightly so) that the playwrights were pillorying his image upon the stage.[3] In Edward VI's reign the budget for plays at court was slashed because the players had "come somewhat too close" in their satires.[4] And we have records of the Elizabethan masters of the children's groups being punished with imprisonment because of their employment of topical lampoons.[5] In spite of the peril involved, the use of the personal lampoon reached its height in the Elizabethan age in the nondramatic pamphlets of the Martin Marprelate controversy which spilled over onto the stage. The outrageously witty adaptation of the ancient mode of lampoon was employed by antiestablishment writers to belittle the Anglican bishops with exaggeration, jocular accusations, and scurrility. It is probable that both Lyly and Nashe had a hand in the counterattack which Archbishop Whitgift, Lord Buckhurst, and Lord Cobham initiated in their attempts to outwit the satirists.[6] The language of the Marprelate writers on both sides of the controversy was an extension and amplification of the vibrant and comically flexible style developed by John Bale and John Foxe in their witty exchanges in the mid-century polemics.[7] When Gabriel Harvey and Thomas Nashe indulged themselves in a similar vein with their attacks upon each other, they were extending the mode of lampoon to its limits of public usage, and their experimentation ended in disaster.

By the time that Shakespeare had warmed up to his task of lampooning Lord Cobham in 1 Henry IV, he was wise enough and artistically conscious enough to reach for the universal element with which to adorn as well as modify his comic creation. Before Oldcastle had become Falstaff, Shakespeare had learned that the great girth of his clown ought to be amplified with more than a personal attack upon Lord Cobham. He knew that viable comic art should reflect the composite images of universal folly as well as the vices of one singular man. And, with the natural instincts of the Renaissance artist, he turned to the literary traditions of the past, both classical and native. In Falstaff's comic character we find elements in abundance that go far beyond the allusions to the martyred Lollard figure of chronicle fame. From the classics of New Comedy Shakespeare took the standard stock character of the *miles gloriosus* with his boasting and temerity. In the Gads Hill robbery scene the artist exploited these elements in Falstaff, and he repeated the comic pattern in the character's articulate lines and defensive but insolent actions at the Battle of Shrewsbury. In addition, Falstaff's glib speech, ready flattery, championship of riotous living, and marvelously apt wit are part of the characterization of the classical parasite who worked his way through many of the comedies of Plautus and Terence. The craftiness of Falstaff's wit, however, plus the spontaneity of his mind, comes from the wily slaves of New Comedy, who met each confrontation with an original ploy and an amoral expediency. The image is even more complex, for the dominant ancestor of the Falstaff of *The Merry Wives* is the amorous old man from New Comedy with his garrulity and gullibility and vanity. But none of these literary traditions of Roman comedy dominates Shakespeare's conception of comic character any more than the native English traditions do.

J. Dover Wilson has pointed out with characteristic insight that the morality figures from the earlier English drama, particularly the characters of the prodigal son legend, influenced Shakespeare's conception of the relationship between Falstaff and Prince Hal.[8] There is much of the morality Vice in Sir John's great bulk. The allegorical Vice, that sub-lieutenant of Satan, had evolved through the religious drama of the late Middle Ages into a comic figure of ridicule and mirth. His ancestor had been the Devil himself, but Vice evolved into a clown through numerous adaptations of characteristics drawn from the homilists, from the antics of the rollicking medieval actors, and from legends and folklore.[9] Shakespeare's Falstaff functions as a huge mirth-filled Vice, but there is also something of the professional fool in the fat knight, as he extends his wit to entertain the young prince. Nor is it amiss to see something of the symbolic Bishop of Fools in Shakespeare's comic creation. The sense of a ritualistic scapegoat buried behind the universal conception of the fool remains as a worrisome paradox in the complex characterization of Falstaff.[10] In other words, it is simplistic to a degree of naïveté to insist upon one set of characteristics in Shakespeare's greatest comic figure. In this long study of the Oldcastle problem attention has been focused necessarily upon the element of personal lampoon in order to expose the basic design upon which the character of Falstaff is constructed. But the total conception of fat Jack Falstaff is indebted to more than Shakespeare's initial impulse to lampoon Lord Cobham through the figure of his Lollard ancestor. We cannot overemphasize the fact that in creating Falstaff Shakespeare lifted the comic lampoon to a consummate composite satiric art. And in the success of its achievement Shakespeare's art competes easily with that of Aristophanes and Pope.

In much the same way that Shakespeare overlaid personal lampoon with traditions of comic characterization, making it an aggregate art form, so too he transformed the lampoon from the static literary device which it had been traditionally into a dynamic aesthetic factor by making his satire function as a structural element in his dramas. In examining this transformation we can discover Shakespeare's developing awareness of the ontological nature of satire and of its possible relationship to history. He had only to look back to the earlier English drama for suggestions of a procedural plan.

The typological method of biblical exegesis had a profound effect upon characterization and structure in medieval English drama. Recent scholarship concerned with the art of that era has provided incisive evidence of the broad-ranging influence of that ancient mode of interpretation.[11] The Christian system of typology had developed in the first centuries A.D., when the patristic writers cultivated the older Hebraic conception of types and antitypes. Indeed, the authors of the New Testament appear to have combed the Old Testament prophecies for catenae of *testimonia* to prove the relationship between the older

eschatological visions and the life of Christ in which those
messianic prophecies were supposedly fulfilled.[12] The writings of Isaiah, Ezekiel, Moses, and the Song of Songs became types or figures which prefigured events in the life
of Christ or his church and its future glory. The Exodus
prefigured the soul's escape from sin, the sacrifice of
Isaac prefigured the crucifixion of Jesus, manna prefigured the eucharist, Adam prefigured Christ, and so on.
This was not an allegoric or symbolic prefiguration because
both figures in the typological context were actual or historical persons or events; the later figure was the antitype of the earlier. It was taken for granted by the adherents of typological exegesis that God in his timeless realm
had shaped earlier events in human history to foreshadow
events to come.

When the English dramatists of the Middle Ages created
their great cycles of plays, they adapted the point of view
of the exegetes. On the medieval stage Old Testament figures refer easily to Christ, as Cain does when he swears
"bi hym that me dere boght" in the Wakefield pageant.
Dozens of anachronisms flow from the pens of these early
dramatists, not because they were naive but because time
did not intrude into the typological reality of their stories.
The anachronism became a sophisticated device used to
relate Old and New Testament figures, and to tie the play
to the contemporary scene. In addition, typology provided
the medieval artist with an artistic structural conception
of parallel plots. In the Second Shepherd's Play, in the
Noah play, and in half a dozen other pageants in the Wakefield cycle the dramatists employ a double plot in which
the comic episode parallels the serious one. This correspondence between the comic and the serious elements in
the dramas is the result of the artist's conception of the
typological relationship between his sacred and profane
materials.[13] Secular characters and events are created to
parallel the biblical actions, but these secular elements
function as seriously in the typological mode as do Cain,
Isaac, or Noah in their respective plays. And finally, the
imaginative medieval dramatists developed an inverse
form of typological character by extending the figurative
mode to their dramatic villains. Just as Adam or Isaac
prefigured Christ in the formal exegesis of scriptures, so

the Devil and Cain and their progeny look forward to Pilate, who evolves at the end of this system of diabolical typology as the living symbol of original evil.[14] It is from this typological line that Falstaff evolved.

When Shakespeare began to consider the task of turning English chronicle materials into aesthetic form, he knew, I think, that the secular accounts of the fifteenth-century reigns were volatile materials containing many names and events which had various interpretations, which were ambiguously presented by prejudiced editors, and which were open to dramatic exploitation through a use of the typological mode that the medieval dramatists had developed. With the same noble names descending from generation to generation in English history, and with particular patterns of behavior repeated by colorful figures in those famous family lines, it is small wonder that Shakespeare seized upon the idea of "types" or figurative designs in secular history. Certainly the Northumberland line, with its long list of distinguished Henry Percies to make it an envied family among the new nobility of the Tudor period, was open to typological exegesis in the secular vein. The repeated insurrections of the conservative northern earls seemed repetitious in design, and when they were observed from a generalizing artistic view they could easily be interpreted as proleptic events which prefigured the later insurrections that disturbed the order of Queen Elizabeth's reign as well as that of her father.

Shakespeare's optimistic view of history at this time also helped him to select, assimilate, and transform the linear chronicle materials into artistic form. Shakespeare's idealistic conception of history, in which the unchanging nature of man was centered within an evolving universe, afforded him a basis upon which to peg his homocentric art. The "unchanging nature of man" did not mean for the poet a static uniformity in individual minds. Shakespeare, as well as the theorists, was aware that the individual man developed and matured. Tragic art could not endure if a poet stultified himself with static characters. But human nature itself endures, the sixteenth-century historiographers insisted. Men of the modern world had ambitions, fears, loves, jealousies, disdains, inclinations to worship, and inclinations to disobey just as God's first creatures had, they assured themselves. By reading history one could learn to understand human nature; and with the knowledge that history afforded, wise men could glimpse the future with some degree of certainty. The poet seems to have been thinking in this vein when he wrote the following lines.

> There is a Historie in all mens Liues,
> Figuring the nature of the Times deceas'd:
> The which obseru'd, a man may prophecie
> With a neere ayme, of the maine chance of things,
> As yet not come to Life, which in their Seedes
> And weake beginnings lye entreasured:
> Such things become the Hatch and Brood of Time.
> [2 Henry IV, III.i.83-89]

Shakespeare seems also to say here that certain kinds of people (for example, Northumberland and his friends) will behave predictably under certain circumstances. And, indeed, this proved too true.

The Oldcastle legend presented numerous problems for the sensitive playwright who had chosen to dramatize the first Lancastrian reigns. The author of *The Famous Victories* had of course set the precedent for satirizing the legendary Lollard figure. How then was the more consummate artist to solve the problem? Shakespeare turned to the "diabolical typology" of the medieval dramatists for his answer. The ancient typological mode could be extended to show the demonic evolution of the ancient evil type into its "modern" antitype, as the cycle dramatists had proved with their depiction of Pilate, the descendent of Lucifer. The medieval playwrights had also created comic episodes which paralleled the sacred materials in the pageant shows. Shakespeare adapts the two conceptions and creates a vehicle for his theories of history as he inverts typology into a satiric mode, using secular chronicle materials as types to prefigure Elizabethans who are his antitypes. The old biblical mode of exegesis is converted into a brilliant vehicle for secular satire within a comic frame. The Oldcastle-Falstaff episodes parallel the serious historical scenes in the *Henry IV* dramas just as the comic elements in the cycle plays paralleled the sacred texts. In Shakespeare's dramas the comic crew bears the burden of the moral theme equally with the serious political characters. There is moral disorder in the private sector just as there is political disorder in the public realm. The riotous conditions in the tavern and on Gads Hill parallel the insurrection and treason that erupt in the kingdom at large. Shakespeare creates parody to complement serious episodes, and vice versa, as in the twin interview scenes between Hal and Falstaff, and Hal and the king. The shenanigans at Gads Hill, where the thieves are thieved upon, parallel the king's determination to take Hotspur's hostages. Hotspur's teasing-taunting scene with Kate is matched with Hal's taunting of the drawer Francis. Falstaff's vow to "repent, and that suddenly" parallels Hal's decision to reform "when men think least I will." Hotspur's desire "to pluck bright honour from the pale-fac'd moon" naturally opposes in parallel form Falstaff's famous catechism. Falstaff's refusal to hear the lord chief justice is a parody of Hal's seeming rejection of the same figure of justice. And similarly, Falstaff's plans to fleece Justice Shallow prepare us to expect along with the chief justice that Hal will rape the law. Falstaff captures Colville of the Dale who "gavest himself away gratis" just as the unwary rebels fall naively into Prince John's hands at Gaultree Forest, and so on.[15]

But parallelism through likeness and contrast is only one aspect of the aesthetic procedure that seeks to present multiple perspectives on complex themes. Shakespeare's technique develops depth as the patterns are rendered in triplicate between the rioters, the rebels, and the court with an aesthetic congruence that extends from character groupings to a triadic pattern of action and ideas. The old didactic method of the medieval dramas is revitalized and developed to new heights as the antithetical elements of the comic and serious scenes are juxtaposed. The contrasts in form only heighten the analogies in theme and action, and in the process an aesthetic unity is created, permeating the whole work of art and transforming history, through permutation, into imaginative truth.

This dialectic pattern of aesthetic form is also filled with countermovements that derive power from interactions and implications. Irony, ambivalence, and paradox play their intriguing roles in these opaque mirror scenes that reflect cross-patterns having complex bearings upon each other. The total aesthetic reality of these plays cannot be comprehended without the inclusion of these structural formulae and all their ambivalences, any more than the totality of Falstaff's character can be estimated without seeing him from multiple points of view. He is Sir John to the sober, Jack to the familiar, Jockey to the jesters; he is a pseudofather, a pseudojustice, a pseudoking; he is the old Vice figure usurping authority in both personal and public wealds. But he is also flippancy and wit personified. We must make distinctions for purposes of critical analysis between the magnificent dramatic figure, the world's finest comic role, and both the moral meaning of the figure and its functional purpose within the cosmos of the play. Aesthetic distance is required for this difficult task; but it allows us to see that by adopting the medieval techniques of typology and by exploiting the older dramatists' conception of the relationship between comic and serious materials, Shakespeare has created a new kind of satiric comedy in which characters become structural entities that develop plot, theme, and aesthetic form. The figure of Falstaff is functional satire in its most creative role.

I believe that Shakespeare's confidence in the viability of history, his conviction that in history one could find clues to what the future would unfold, led him to create an image of a treasonable antitype of the historical Lollard of Henry V's reign. The earlier chroniclers had depicted the Lollard as a Satanic figure, a Vice, an ambitious rebel who sought to destroy the king, the church, and the realm. We know that Sir William Brooke, Lord Cobham, was deeply involved in treasonable activity in the early years of Queen Elizabeth's reign. We can only wonder if Shakespeare had heard rumors of Henry Brooke's covert movements in the plots to determine the succession to the throne. Certainly the antitype that Falstaff represents reflects the type of the earlier Lord Cobham of Henry V's reign. That antitype fits both William Brooke and Henry, his son and heir. It was the latter who fell to ruin in the treasonous plots of 1603.

The famous Main and Bye plots that interrupted the midsummer festivities of King James's precoronation days in London are still considered unsolved matters of state.

Involved in the plotting were a number of discontents who saw in the coronation of James the end of all their prospects for reward and advancement in England. Chief among these were Henry, Lord Cobham, and Sir Walter Raleigh. Arthur Wilson in his seventeenth-century history of James's reign described the situation in 1603.

> The Earl of Southampton, covered long with the ashes of great Essex his Ruins, was sent for from the Tower, and the King lookt upon him with a smiling countenance, though displeasing happily to the new Baron of Effingden, Sir Robert Cecil; yet it was much more to the Lords Cobham and Grey, and Sir Walter Rawleigh, who were forbidden their attendance. This damp upon them, being Spirits full of acrimony, made them break into Murmur, then into Conspiracy, associating themselves with two Romish Priests (men that could not live upon lingring hopes) and other discontented persons, which every Change produces. The ground of the Design was to set up the Lady Arbella (a Branch sprung from the same Stem by another line) and to alter Religion and Government; disposing already to themselves the principal places of Honour and Profit.[16]

There is little need here for a detailed account of the involved plots and of the strange dispensation of justice which King James arranged for the guilty men. The king had formed hostile opinions of Cobham and Raleigh as a result of their leadership in the movement to overthrow the earl of Essex in 1601, a movement which had succeeded. James had also had his ears poisoned by the vitriolic letters that Lord Henry Howard and Cecil had sent him in the last years of Queen Elizabeth's reign. Cobham, Raleigh, and Northumberland were called the ."atheistical trinity." And Howard wrote to the king of Scots in 1602 that "hell did never spew up such a couple [Cobham and Raleigh] when it cast up Cerberus and Phlegethon—they are now set on the pin of making tragedies, by meddling in your affairs."[17] At least part of the statement was true. Cobham and Raleigh and their colleagues established ties with the Count d'Aremberg, ambassador for the archduke and the infanta in the Low Countries. It would seem that they had fallen into a trap, for Howard had written to Cecil some short time earlier suggesting the possibility of such a plan.

So must you embark this gallant Cobham by your wit and interest in some course the Spanish waie, as either may reveale
his weakness or snare his ambition. . . . Be not unwilling . . .
to engage him in the traffic with suspected ministers, and upon
the first occasion of further treaty [with Spain] to make him
the Minister. For my part, I account it impossible for him to
scape the snares which wit may set and weakness is apt to fall
into.[18]

Howard's estimate of Cobham seems accurate; he appears
to have been both foolish and ambitious. Sir Anthony
Weldon in his history of the times states bluntly that Cobham was "but one degree from a foole" and "a most silly
Lorde."[19] King James sent a reprieve when the conspirators were on the scaffold; their death sentences were
changed to life imprisonment. And Cobham spent the remaining sixteen years of his life in the Tower.[20] During the
trials of late 1603 and early 1604 there was a resurgence of
the Oldcastle story. Robert Parsons placed emphasis upon
the treason of the Lollard in Harry V's reign when he was
writing his *Treatise of Three Conversions of England.*

Heere only in this place it shalbe sufficient to remember for
example sake, Syr John Oldcastle, Syr Roger Acton, and above
40 more hanged in Saint Gyles field, for treason and actuall
rebellion, & for consperinge the death of K. Henry the fifth
& of his brethren.[21]

Again and again Parsons refers to the Lollard as a traitor,
as "a most disorderly seditious troublesom man in his manner of life." And he stresses the legality of Oldcastle's execution: "he was condemned by orderly judgment of the
church in those dayes, and afterwards of treason and open
rebellion, as well by particular arraignement, as also by Act
of Parliament."[22] In another passage Parsons lashes out
again: "Lo heere another commendation of this Martyr,
who was not only enemy to the Church and Clergy, as before
I have said: but also to the King and commonwealth, & had
devised a new King to set up against the old."[23] Parsons's
timing is important; he was using the old legend of the
martyr as adverse propaganda while the trials of conspirators in the Main and Bye plots were being conducted. Parsons was not an objective bystander at this time. The two

secular Catholic priests involved in the Main and Bye plots, Watson and Clark, had been staunch opponents of Parsons in the Archpriest controversy.[24] Parsons was having his revenge.[25] His insistence upon the treason of an earlier Lord Cobham at a time when the contemporary Lord Cobham was being convicted of treason reveals his dramatic method, in which history is used as a pattern to color a current event—for him history becomes a pointed instrument of propaganda. We do not know whether Parsons's statements about an earlier Lord Cobham who had "devised a new King to set up against the old" reached King James. Old John Speed was shrewd enough to see some resemblance between Parsons's use of the Oldcastle legend and the method of defamation which the playwrights had employed in their treatment of the story. Speed condemned the detractors of the martyr; the negative version of the Oldcastle affair was "more befitting the pen of his [Parsons's] slanderous report, then the Credit of the judicious, being onely grounded from this Papist and his Poet, of like conscience for lies, the one ever faining, the other ever falsifying the truth."[26] Speed was angry, and he was guessing of course. There is no evidence that there was ever any relationship between Parsons and our poet. Parsons had simply found the artistic endeavours of the playwright extremely useful as a weapon against his enemies. Shakespeare had washed his hands of the Oldcastle problem with the Socratic death of Falstaff in 1599. The prophetic element in the plays and the fantastic way in which future events in England had borne out the prediction of treason seem to have convinced the playwright that his conception of history was a valid one. By the summer of 1606 he was prepared to use the montage technique again to present upon the stage an even more fantastic conflation of chronicle materials to mirror the most explosive circumstances in King James's reign. With paralyzing accuracy the technique worked—but the poet was wrong. His confidence in his perception of the meaning of history, his faith in his own genius led him into the over-reacher's trap.

Macbeth is still a brilliant play, just as Falstaff is a brilliant comic character. Knowing something of the underside of each creation does not diminish the glory of either work of art. Perhaps as historical materials continue to come to light and as scholarship in literature continues to take advantage of the new sources, we will learn more of the circumstances that stimulated Shakespeare and more of the inner structure and workings of his unparalleled art.

NOTES

FOOTNOTES TO PREFACE

1. Irving Ribner, *The English History Play in the Age of Shakespeare* (Princeton, New Jersey: Princeton Univ. Press, 1957), p. 21.

2. M. M. Reese, *The Cease of Majesty* (London: E. Arnold, 1961), p. 19.

3. Robert Ornstein, *A Kingdom for a Stage* (Cambridge, Massachusetts: Harvard Univ. Press, 1972), p. 224.

CHAPTER ONE

1. For studies of the changing attitudes toward history in Renaissance England, see: F. Smith Fussner, *The Historical Revolution, English Historical Writing and Thought, 1580-1640* (London: Routledge and Kegan Paul, 1962); Herschel Baker, *The Race of Time* (Toronto: Univ. of Toronto Press, 1967); F. J. Levy, *Tudor Historical Thought* (San Marino, Calif. Huntington Library, 1967); C. A. Patrides, *The Phoenix and the Ladder: The Rise and Decline of the Christian View of History* (Berkeley, Calif. Univ. of Calif. Press, 1964); J. G. A. Pocock, *The Ancient Constitution and the Feudal Law: A Study of English Historical Thought in the Seventeenth Century* (Cambridge: Cambridge Univ. Press, 1957); Beatrice Reynolds, "Shifting Currents in Historical Criticism," *Journal of the History of Ideas* 14 (1953): 471-92; Wallace R. Ferguson, *The Renaissance in Historical Thought* (Cambridge, Mass: Harvard Univ. Press, 1948); H. Weisinger, "Ideas of History during the Renaissance," *Journal of the History of Ideas* 6 (1945): 415-33; James Westfall Thompson, *A History of Historical Writing*, 2 vols. (New York: Macmillan, 1942).

2. Hiram Haydn, *The Counter Renaissance* (New York: Scribner, 1950), p. xvii. This is a sensitive study of the impact of skepticism on the minds of the writers of the sixteenth century. Another competent study of this subject is Richard H. Popkin, *The History of Scepticism from Erasmus to Descartes* (Assen, Netherlands: Van Gorcum, 1960). An older but still reliable work is Paul Hazard, *La Crise de la Conscience Européenne*, 3 vols. (Paris: Boivin, 1935).

3. For a brilliant study of *King Lear* from this point of view, see William R. Elton, *King Lear and the Gods* (San Marino, Calif: Huntington Library, 1967).

4. In a technical sense there are two kinds of historical skepticism: the first is based upon the idea that no knowledge is possible (called academic skepticism); the second is based upon the idea that the means to determine whether knowledge is actually possible are insufficient and inadequate (called Pyrrhonian skepticism). My own use of the term is casual and does not differentiate between the technical categories. For a discussion of the philosophical distinctions, see Popkin, *History of Scepticism*, p. ix.

5. Many of the conceptions of man's dignity are summed up by Paul O.

Kristeller in *Renaissance Concepts of Man* (New York: Harper and Row, 1972), pp. 1-63.

6. The pervasive pessimism of the Renaissance is one of the themes of Charles Trinkaus's large study, *In Our Image and Likeness*, 2 vols. (Chicago: Univ. of Chicago Press, 1970). This author's earlier work, *Adversity's Noblemen: The Italian Humanists on Happiness* (New York: Octagon Books, reprint ed., 1965), contains some of the same basic ideas. See also his article, "The Religious Thought of the Italian Humanists, and the Reformers: Anticipation or Autonomy?" in *The Pursuit of Holiness in Late Medieval and Renaissance Religion*, ed. Trinkaus, with Heiko A. Oberman (Leiden: E. J. Brill, 1974), pp. 341-66.

7. When most sixteenth-century writers use the term, they mean the art of composing narrative history. They do not mean the science of comparative civilizations, as the term implies today. For a discussion of this point, see Pocock, *Ancient Constitution and Feudal Law*, p. 5.

8. *The Praise of Folly*, trans. Leonard Dean (Chicago: Packard, 1946), p. 84. The Italian humanists were not immune, of course, to skepticism. Many statements reveal the despair of some of the intellectuals of the fifteenth century concerning the state of learning in their day. Many of them felt that modern man could never compete with the great minds of antiquity. For a discussion of this point see Paul O. Kristeller, "Philosophy and Humanism in Renaissance Perspective," in *The Renaissance Image of Man and the World* (Columbus: Ohio State University Press, 1966), pp. 29-51.

9. For the influence of the writings of Sextus Empiricus, sometimes called the father of modern philosophy, see especially Popkin, *History of Scepticism*, pp. 17-43. See also the same author's article, "The High Road to Pyrrhonism," *American Philosophical Quarterly* 2 (1965): 1-15.

10. The *Quod Nihil Scitur* was published a few years later at Lyons (1581). For speculation that Sanchez's famous work was perhaps "a youthful ebullition, a momentary reaction and expression of discouragement before the vastness of the field of learning and the perplexity of science's task," see Lynn Thorndike, *A History of Magic and Experimental Science*, 8 vols., (New York: Macmillan, 1923-58), 6:567.

11. *Les Essais de Michel de Montaigne*, ed. Pierre Villey, 3 vols., (Paris: F. Alcan, 1922), 2:179, 214, 302, 349-64. See also Donald M. Frame, *Montaigne's Discovery of Man* (New York: Columbia Univ. Press, 1955) for an important analysis of the "Apologie de Raimond Sebond."

12. For a discussion of François Hotman's influence upon historical thought, see Julian H. Franklin, *Jean Bodin and the Sixteenth-Century Revolution in the Methodology of Law and History* (New York: Columbia Univ. Press, 1963), pp. 46-54. Also see Pocock, *Ancient Constitution and Feudal Law*, p. 14. Donald R. Kelley calls Hotman "one of the first modern revolutionaries," *François Hotman, A Revolutionary's Ordeal* (Princeton, N.J.: Princeton Univ. Press, 1973), p. vii.

13. Henrie Cornelius Agrippa, *Of the Vanitie and Uncertaintie of Artes and Sciences* (London: Henry Wykes, 1569), fols. 13^v-17. In the preface to his translation Sanford reassures his reader that Agrippa is not mad: "And although this Authoure sharply inveigheth against them [the arts and sciences] (which to the rude multitude for that cause, maye seme naught and noysome) yet his intent is, not to deface the worthinesse of Artes and Sciences, but to reprove and deteste theire evil uses, and declare the excellencie of his wit in disproving them, for a shewe of Learning" (sig. *iii.). Hiram Haydn has some perceptive comments on

Agrippa's work in his chapter "The Counter Renaissance and the Vanitie of Learning," *The Counter Renaissance*, pp. 76-103. See also C. G. Nauert, *Agrippa and the Crisis of Renaissance Thought* (Urbana: University of Illinois Press, 1965).

14. Agrippa, *Vanitie and Uncertaintie*, fols. 11-13ᵛ.

15. Ibid., fol. 32.

16. *Succintz Adversaires de Charles de la Ruelle* (Poitiers, 1567), p. 23.

17. For a discussion of Guicciardini's contribution to the theories of history in the sixteenth century, see Myron P. Gilmore, "Freedom and Determinism in Renaissance Historians," *Studies in the Renaissance* 3 (1956): 49-60. See also Patrides, *The Phoenix and the Ladder*, pp. 37-38.

18. Niccolò Machiavelli, *Discorsi*, ed. G. Feltrinelli, Biblioteca de classici italiani, 2 vols., (Milano, 1960), 1:123-25, 194-96, 222-23, 230. See also Roberto Ridolfi, *The Life of Niccolò Machiavelli*, trans. Cecil Grayson (London: Routledge and Kegan Paul, 1963), pp. 195-206, for an analysis of Machiavelli's interests in principles rather than facts. Machiavelli tells us in the "Proemio" of the *Discorsi* that the work was written to "draw mankind from the error" of reading history in an aimless fashion, as though the very cosmos and mankind himself were different from what they used to be (1:125).

19. Sir Walter Raleigh, *The Sceptick or Speculations* (London: W. Bentley, 1651), pp. 1, 30. An older and wiser Raleigh could write in the *History of the World* from another point of view: "In a word, we may gather out of history a policy no less wise than eternal" (London: W. Stansby, 1614), pp. v-vi.

20. Sir John Davies, *Nosce Teipsum* (London: R. Field, 1599), sigs. B1, B4ᵛ.

21. John Norden, *Vicissitudo Rerum* . . . (London: S. Stafford, 1600), sig. A2.

22. *Letter-Book of Gabriel Harvey, A.D. 1573-1580*, ed. J. L. Scott, (London: Camden Society, 1874), p. 78.

23. "An Apologie for Poetrie," in *Elizabethan Critical Essays*, ed. G. G. Smith, 2 vols. (Oxford: Clarendon Press, 1904), 1:156.

24. *Literary Criticism: Plato to Dryden*, ed. Allan Gilbert (New York: American Book Co., 1940), pp. 271, 305, 482, 494.

25. Louis Le Roy, *Of the Interchangeable Course, or Variety of Things in the Whole World*, trans. Robert Ashley (London: C. Yetsweirt, 1594), fols. 127-29. The italics are mine.

26. See Pocock, *Ancient Constitution and Feudal Law*, especially chap. 1, "The French Prelude to Modern Historiography"; and Franklin, *Jean Bodin*, p. 119. For the disintegration in France of the older chronicle view of history, see Paul Archambault, *Seven French Chroniclers, Witnesses to History* (Syracuse, N. Y.: Syracuse Univ. Press, 1974), pp. 1-24.

27. François Baudouin [Balduinus], *De Institutione Historiae Universae* (Halle, 1726), pp. 27-28. See also Franklin, *Jean Bodin*, pp. 116-37.

28. Franklin, *Jean Bodin*, p. 117. For a full-length study of the emerging attitudes toward history in France in the last decades of the sixteenth century, see George Huppert, *The Idea of Perfect History* (Urbana, Ill.: Univ. Illinois Press, 1970), especially chap. 9, "The Sense of History," pp. 151-69.

29. François Patrizzi, *Dieci Dialoghi della Historia* (Venice: A. Arriva-

bene, 1560). For a discussion of Patrizzi's Neoplatonic ideas, see Beatrice Reynolds, "Shifting Currents in Historical Criticism," p. 484. Franklin, *Jean Bodin*, p. 96, says that Patrizzi's fifth dialogue was a major contribution to historical Pyrrhonism, in spite of the fact that Patrizzi was more Neoplatonic than skeptic.

30. Thomas Blundevill, *The True Order and Methode of Wryting and Reading Hystories* (London: W. Seres, 1574), sig. B1. See also Hugh G. Dick, "Thomas Blundeville's *The True Order and Methode of Wryting and Reading Hystories*," *Huntington Library Quarterly 2* (1940): 149-70.

31. *The Six Bookes of a Commonweale Written by J. Bodin a Famous Lawyer*, trans. Richard Knolles (London: A. Islip, 1606), p. 445. This translation is close to the original at this point. For an analysis of Bodin's contribution to historical thought, see Franklin, *Jean Bodin*, pp. 137-55. See also John L. Brown, *The Methodus and Facilem Historiarum Cognitionem of Jean Bodin: A Critical Study* (Washington, D.C.: Catholic Univ. of America Press, 1939).

32. We are inclined today to forget that not only arithmetic ideas but elements of vitalism and pan-psychism were a part of Renaissance Platonism. For perceptive remarks on this aspect of Renaissance thought see Hans Baron, "Toward a More Positive Evaluation of the Fifteenth-Century Renaissance," *Journal of the History of Ideas* 4 (1943):21-49; and Alexander Koyré, "Galileo and Plato," *Journal of the History of Ideas* 4 (1943): 100-128.

33. *The Annales of Cornelius Tacitus*, trans. Richard Grenewey (London: A. Hatfield, 1598), sig. A1. In this context the work of Henry A. Kelly on the providential view of history should be noted. He states that Shakespeare's use of chronicle materials in the history plays was innovative and original: "Shakespeare's great contribution was to unsynthesize the synthesis [of the providential theories of history] of his contemporaries and to unmoralize their moralizations." See *Divine Providence in the England of Shakespeare's Histories* (Cambridge: Harvard Univ. Press, 1970), p. 304.

34. J. H. [John Hayward], *The First Part of the Life and Raigne of King Henrie the IIII* (London: J. Woolfe, 1599). See S. L. Goldberg, "Sir John Hayward, 'Politic' Historian," *Review of English Studies*, n.s. 23 (1955):233-44. Hayward's *Henry IV* contained some forthright statements on the rights of succession to the throne of England. At one point Hayward was bold enough to write: "But it is well knowen to all men, who are not eyther wilfully blinde or grosely ignorant, that there are some now alive, lineally descended from Lionell Duke of Clarence, whose offspring was by judgement of the high Court of Parliament holden the vii yeere of the raigne of King Richard, declared next successour to the Crowne, in case King Richard should dye without issue" (sig. P2). When James entered England after Elizabeth's death, Hayward had ready his *Answer To The First Part of a Certaine Conference, Concerning Succession* (London: S. Waterson, 1603) in which he claimed "these labours were undertaken with particular respect to your Majesties just title of succession in this realm" (sig. A3ᵛ). Hayward had learned his lesson; King James released him from the Tower.

CHAPTER TWO

1. John Dennis, *The Comical Gallant: or The Amours of Sir John Falstaffe* (London: A. Baldwin, 1702), sig. A2. In the Henry E. Huntington Library copy of this play there is written at the bottom of the title page in

old brown ink: "Mr. Dennis, I believe, is the first Writer who mentions
this anecdote." Edward Niles Hooker seems also to have examined this
copy; see his superlative edition, *Critical Works of John Dennis*, 2 vols.
(Baltimore: Johns Hopkins Press, 1939-1948), 1: 492. Most scholars agree
that Dennis probably had his information from Sir William D'Avenant.

2. Nicholas Rowe, *The Works of Mr. William Shakespeare*, 7 vols.
(London: E. Curll and E. Sanger, 1709-1710), 1: viii. This "annotated"
edition presents the collected notes in an introduction rather than in the
traditional annotated form. In the same paragraph in which he mentions
the name-change Rowe tells the story of the earl of Southampton's gift
of one thousand pounds to Shakespeare. Rowe states, "If I had not been
assur'd that the Story was handed down by Sir William D'Avenant, who
was probably very well acquainted with his affairs, I should not have
ventured to have inserted it." It is possible that Rowe also had his account
of the Falstaff-Oldcastle problem indirectly from Shakespeare's "godson."
But there were other sources for the story of the Oldcastle-Falstaff name-
change; see the reference to it in Richard James's statement below, p.
52.

3. Ibid., 7:345.

4. Thomas Fuller, *The Church History of Britain*, 11 vols. (London:
John Williams, 1655), 4: 167-68.

5. Peter Heylyn, *Examen Historicum* (London: Henry Seile and
Richard Royston, 1659), pp. 67-68. This work was answered by Fuller in
The Appeal of Injured Innocence (London: W. Godbid, 1659), p. 40.

6. Sir Richard Baker, *A Chronicle of the Kings of England* (London: J.
Flesher and E. Cotes, 1653), pp. 253-54. Thomas Rymer's *Foedera,
Conventiones, Literae* was first published in 1704-1717 and was reissued
by Tonson in 1729.

7. Sir William Dugdale, *The Baronage of England*, 2 vols. (London:
Thomas Newcomb and Abel Roper, 1675), 2:67.

8. Laurence Echard, *The History of England*, 3 vols. (London: Jacob
Tonson, 1707-1718), 1:455.

9. Jeremy Collier, *An Ecclesiastical History of Great Britain*, 2 vols.
(London: Samuel Keble and Benjamin Tooke, 1708), 2:647. Collier gives
six folio pages to his account of the historical Oldcastle. By this time
John Foxe's *Acts and Monuments* had passed through nine complete
editions and numerous partial editions.

10. John Anstis, *The Register of the Most Noble Order of the Garter*,
2 vols. (London: Jack Barber, 1724), 2:132-33. Elias Ashmole did not mention Shakespeare's distortion of history in the dramatic presentation of
Sir John Fastolf when he published *The Institution, Laws & Ceremonies
of the Most Noble Order of the Garter*, 2 vols. (London: Nathanael Brooke,
1672). But Peter Heylyn did in his *History of That Most Famous Saynt
. . . George*. Heylyn defends Fastolf's honor in spite of the fact that on
"the stage, they have beene pleased to make merry with him" (London:
Henry Seyle, 1631), p. 308.

11. Alexander Pope, *The Works of Mr. William Shakespeare*, 6 vols.
(London: Jacob Tonson, 1725), 3:391. Pope had done some background
research; his comment on *The Merry Wives* reads thus: "This Play was
written in the Author's best and ripest years, after *Henry the Fourth*, by
the command of Queen Elizabeth. There is a tradition that it was compos'd
at a fortnight's warning. But that must be meant only of the first
imperfect sketch of this Comedy, which is yet extant in an old Quarto
edition, printed in 1619. This which we here have, was alter'd and im-

proved by the Author almost in every speech" (1: 233). Pope's philosophic friend Henry St. John, Lord Bolingbroke, threatened at this time to write the memoirs of Sir John Oldcastle. His controversy with the Walpoles over the divine rights of kings aroused great public interest, and the circulation of *The Craftsman* increased immensely, exceeding even that of *The Spectator* for several months.

12. William Warburton, *The Works of Shakespear*, 8 vols. (London: J. & P. Knapton, 1747), 4:102–3. In an article by Rudolph Fiehler, "How Old-castle Became Falstaff," *Modern Language Quarterly* 16 (1955):16–28, the Oldcastle problem, as Shakespearean editors handled it following Rowe's comment, is described in some detail. Fiehler suggests that Warburton was obliged to Lewis Theobald for the Oldcastle information because the two men had worked together much earlier on the text of Shakespeare's plays. This may be true, but I believe that it was perhaps Warburton who led "Tibbal" to this evidence in their earlier association, although Theobald had done some background reading in the Elizabethan and Jacobean chronicles for his book, *The Memoirs of Sir Walter Raleigh*. Sir Thomas Hanmer's edition of the plays also appeared in 1747 (an inexpensive edition of Pope's text and notes), and it too contained the remark that the line, "old lad of the castle," is "proof that the name of Sir John Oldcastle stood first under this character of Falstaff": *The Works of Shakespear*, 6 vols. (London: J. & P. Knapton, 1747), 5: 9.

13. Lewis Theobald, *The Works of Shakespeare*, 7 vols. (London: A. Bettesworth and C. Hitch, 1733), 3: 348–49.

14. Thomas Hearne, *Titi Livii Forojuliensis Vite Henrici Quinti, Regis Angliae* (Oxford: E. Sheldon, 1716); *Chronica Regnum Angliae Per Thomas Otterbourne* (Oxford: E. Sheldon, 1732).

15. John Bale, *A Brefe Chronycle Concerning The Examinacyon And Death Of The Blessed Martyr Of Christ Syr Johan Oldcastell The Lorde Cobham* (London: Charles Davis, 1729). See below, chapter three, for a detailed account of the fifteenth- and sixteenth-century historians.

16. *Biographia Britannica*, 6 vols. (1747–66), 3: 1901–2.

17. "Observations on Shakespear's Falstaff" *Gentleman's Magazine* 20 (1752):459–61.

18. Samuel Johnson, *The Plays of William Shakespeare*, 8 vols. (London: J. and R. Tonson, 1765), 4:116–17.

19. William Gilpin, *The Lives of John Wicliff, and of the Most Eminent of his Disciples* (London: J. Robson, 1765).

20. Edward Capell, *Mr. William Shakespeare His Comedies, Histories, and Tragedies*, 10 vols. (London: J. and R. Tonson, 1767), 1:54–55. There is an interesting article on Capell's critical abilities; see Alice Walker, "Edward Capell and his Edition of Shakespeare," *Proceedings of the British Academy* 46 (1960):131–45.

21. Edmond Malone, *The Plays and Poems of William Shakespeare*, 10 vols. (London: H. Baldwin, 1790), 5:119.

22. James Orchard Halliwell [-Phillipps], *On the Character of Sir John Falstaff* (London: William Pickering, 1841).

23. See in *The Variorum* edition of this play, *Henry IV, Part Two*, ed. M. A. Shaaber (Philadelphia, Pa.: J. B. Lippincot, 1940) the notes to I. ii. 115; see also the editor's comments at pp. 477 ff. The survival of this speech prefix and the other various prefixes for Falstaff's lines (at times *Fa., Fal., Falst.,* and occasionally *John* or *sir John*) indicates that the quarto was probably set up from Shakespeare's foul papers rather than

from a prompt book. The *Old* prefix does not appear to me to be the accident of a transcriber. The epilogue to this play is part of the problem. If the quarto was set up from the foul papers, the double form of the epilogue would indicate, I think, that Shakespeare wrote both versions when he finished the play, one with the denial of the Oldcastle usage written apparently for the court performance (if the story of Queen Elizabeth's reprimand is true), and the other for the public theater. Both were among the foul papers, and both were therefore put into print in the 1600 quarto.

24. In the *Variorum* text ed. S. B. Hemingway (Philadelphia, Pa.: J. B. Lippincot, 1936), the lines fall at I. ii. 40; II. ii. 99; II. iv. 498. In the *New Arden* edition, ed. A. R. Humphreys (Cambridge, Mass.: Harvard Univ. Press, 1960), they fall at I. ii. 41; II. ii. 103; II. iv. 521. It should be remembered that in the first folio much of the prose is printed as verse.

25. *The First Part of the True and Honourable Historie of the Life of Sir John Oldcastle* (London: Thomas Pavier, 1600). The second quarto of this play was printed in 1619 by Jaggard for Thomas Pavier with Shakespeare's name on the title page. The editors of Shakespeare's third folio included the play in that edition, and it reappeared in the fourth folio and in many subsequent editions. This factor perhaps helped to obscure the critical problem for the eighteenth-century editors. It may be noted here that Anthony Munday, one of the collaborating authors of *Sir John Oldcastle*, had, in his earlier writings as a "faithful affected freend to his Country, who desireth God long to blesse it from Traytours, and their secret conspiracyes," repeated the adverse account of Oldcastle's insurrection which he found in John Stow's chronicles. See Munday's *A Watch-Woord To Englande To Beware of Traytours And Treacherous Practises* (London: Thomas Hacket, 1584), fol. 7ᵛ.

26. There is a complete analysis of these allusions in an article by R. S. Forsythe, "Certain Sources of *Sir John Oldcastle*," *Modern Language Notes* 26 (1911):104-7. See also M. G. M. Adkins, "Sixteenth-Century Religious and Political Implications in *Sir John Oldcastle*," *University of Texas Studies in English* 20 (1942):86-104; L. M. Oliver, "*Sir John Oldcastle*: Legend or Literature?" *The Library* 5th ser. 1 (1947): 179-83. J. William Hebel, editor of *The Works of Michael Drayton*, 5 vols. (Oxford: Basil Blackwell, 1961), has noted a number of such allusions in his notes to the play; his conclusion is that Drayton and his fellow dramatists were consciously exploiting the box-office possibilities of a lively existing controversy about Oldcastle (5:45). Henry Tyrell, in *The Doubtful Plays of Shakespeare* (London, 1853), states that "the death of the unfortunate Cobham was followed by a storm of ridicule upon the stage, for the clergy encouraged the players to burlesque him as a buffoon and a coward" (p. 30). I have found no evidence to indicate that the clergy were involved after Cobham's death in 1597 or that there were players involved after Oldcastle's death in 1417.

27. John Weever, *The Mirror of Martyrs* (London: W. Wood, 1601), sig. A3ᵛ. Weever's background study for his poem was negligent; he makes Reginold Cobham the father of Oldcastle, and he uses the unhistorical statement about Oldcastle's being a page of the duke of Norfolk in his youth—a statement which he apparently took from Shakespeare's play. Weever's knowledge of Shakespeare's plays was better than his knowledge of the historical Oldcastle. See his sonnet "Ad Gulielmem Shakespeare," in his *Epigrammes in the Oldest Cut and Newest Fashion* (London: Thomas Bushell, 1599), sig. E6.

28. Leslie Hotson, *Shakespeare's Sonnets Dated and Other Essays* (London: R. Hart-Davis, 1949), pp. 147-60. Hotson states that Essex's

letter was found among the uncalendared papers in the Public Record Office.

29. Arthur Collins, *Letters and Memorials of State in the Reigns of Queen Mary, Queen Elizabeth, King James*, 2 vols. (London: T. Osborne, 1746), 2:118; cited subsequently as Collins. It should also be added that Henry Brooke's name was linked romantically with a number of the young women in Elizabeth's court (see below, pp. 202-04).

30. Great Britain, Public Record Office, *Calendar of Salisbury Manuscripts*, 15:175-76.

31. John Florio defined *Gobbio* or *Ghiozzo* as the fish called a gudgeon, a gullhead, or a miller's thumb. See *A Worlde of Wordes* (London: Arnold Hatfield, 1598), p. 152. Florio was living in the earl of Southampton's household, I believe, in 1598. The *OED* lists *miller's thumb* as a small freshwater fish. The bawdry involved in this wordplay was overt to most Elizabethans. The word may illuminate the two Gobbo characters in *The Merchant of Venice*.

32. Margaret Ratcliffe's death is described by Philip Gawdy in *Letters of Philip Gawdy*, ed. I. H. Jeayes (London: J. B. Nichols and Sons, 1906), p. 104. See below, p. 202 for further reference to this supposed love affair.

33. Great Britain, Historical Manuscripts Commission Report, De L' Isle Manuscripts, 2:445-46.

34. Sir E. K. Chambers, *William Shakespeare: A Study of Facts and Problems*, 2 vols. (Oxford: Clarendon Press, 1930), 2:353.

35. *The Meeting of Gallants at an Ordinarie* (London: T. C. for Mathew Lawe, 1604), p. 16.

36. Roger Sharpe, *Moore Fooles Yet* (London: Thomas Castleton, 1610), sig. E3.

37. Nathan Field, *Amends for Ladies* (London: Matthew Walbancke, 1618), sig. G1.

38. Thomas Randolph, *A Pleasant Comedie Entituled Hey For Honesty* (London: F. J., 1651), p. 28. There are numerous allusions in this play to Falstaff and his crew, and one to the "Spanish Cobbler" who admonishes his son to "let not the ashes of your dead Ancestours blush at your dishonours," which seems aimed at the Cobhams. G. C. Moore Smith, in his biography, *Thomas Randolph* (London: Oxford University Press, 1927), p. 27, suggests that Randolph wrote the play before he left Cambridge.

39. *The Wandering Jew* (London: J. Raworth for N. Butter, 1640), p. 37. This passage echoes Jonson's Cob in *Every Man in His Humour*; see below, chapter eight.

40. William Oldys quotes from the manuscript of this poem in his article on Fastolf in *Biographia Britannica*. Grosart published the poem in 1878; see *The Poems of George Daniel, Esq. of Beswick, Yorkshire*, ed. Alexander B. Grosart, 4 vols. (Boston, Lincolnshire, 1878), 4:112, 135-136.

41. John Speed, *The Theatre of the Empire of Great Britaine*, 2 vols. (London: J. Sudbury, 1611), 2:637. Speed's Puritan contempt for the stage is revealed in a passage he wrote for his commentary on Paul's "Epistle to the Epheseans." In this later work Speed remarked: "Let it not be once named much less acted as in Stage-playes. . . . How *Alipius* was corrupted by them, S. *Austin* tels us. How the youth of *Athens, Plato* complaineth. One of our country-men professeth in Print (*Spec. belli sacri.*) that he found theaters to be the very hatchers of all wickedness, the brothels of bawdery, the black blasphemy of the Gospel, the devils chair, the plague of piety, the canker of the Commonwealth, *etc*. He in-

stanceth on his knowledge, Citizens wives confessing on their death-beds, that they were so impoysoned at Stage-playes, that they brought much dishonour to God, wrong to their marriage-beds, weakness to their wretched bodies, and woe to their undone souls": *A Commentary Upon the New Testament* (London: R. W., 1656), p. 766.

42. N. D. [Robert Parsons], *A Treatise of Three Conversions of England from Paganisme to Christian Religion*, 3 vols. ([St. Omer], 1603-1604), 2: Bviii. For a further discussion of Parsons's use of the Oldcastle story, see below pp. 316.

43. Fuller, *Church History*, 4:168.

44. Thomas Fuller, *The History of the Worthies of England* (London: F. G., W. L., and W. G., 1662), p. 36.

45. John Trappe, *A Commentary or Exposition Upon the Books of Ezra, Nehemiah, Ester, Job and Psalms* (London: T. Newberry, 1657), p. 69.

46. *The Poems of Richard James*, ed. A. B. Grosart (London, 1880), p. 138.

CHAPTER THREE

1. Richard Bentley, *Reflections Upon Mr. Varillas His History Of Heresy* (London: B. Lintott and H. Clements, 1702), p. 464. Bentley attacked Varillas, royal historiographer of France, for his condemnation of Wyclif and the Lollards. Bentley does not mention Oldcastle.

2. Competent scholars have written of Oldcastle in our own time. I am indebted to their research. See James H. Wylie, *The Reign of Henry The Fifth*, 3 vols. (Cambridge: Cambridge Univ. Press, 1914-1929); W. T. Waugh, "Sir John Oldcastle," *English Historical Review* 20 (1905):434-56, 637-58; E. F. Jacob, *The Fifteenth Century 1399-1485* (Oxford: Clarendon Press, 1960); James Gairdner, *Lollardy and the Reformation in England*, 4 vols. (London: Macmillan, 1908-1913); and the *DNB*, 42:86-93.

3. Jacob, *The Fifteenth Century*, pp. 102-3.

4. Thomas Walsingham, *Ypodigma Neustriae* (London: Longman and Company, 1876), p. 429. This petition has not been found in the government records.

5. Waugh, "Sir John Oldcastle," p. 440. This author questions the traditionally accepted view of this Parliament, saying that its notoriety was probably an exaggeration of the chroniclers.

6. It has been suggested that Sir John was the author of the paper "Twelve Conclusions of the Lollards," which was affixed to the doors of St. Paul's in 1395. See J. G. Waller, "The Lords of Cobham, Their Monuments, and the Church," *Archaeologia Cantiana* 11 (1877):92.

7. Reginald L. Poole, "On the Intercourse Between English and Bohemian Wycliffites in the Early Years of the Fifteenth Century," *English Historical Review* 7 (1892):309.

8. Waugh, "Sir John Oldcastle," p. 443.

9. Quoted in ibid., p. 444.

10. Walsingham, *Ypodigma Neustriae*, p. 433; John Capgrave, *The Chronicle of England* (London: Longman, Brown, Green, Longmans, and Roberts, 1858), p. 300; *The Brut*, ed. F. W. D. Brie (London: Kegan Paul, Trench, Trubner and Company, 1906-1908), p. 371.

11. *DNB*, 42:89.

12. Capgrave, *Chronicle of England*, pp. 303-4.

13. C. L. Kingsford has suggested that the proceedings against Oldcastle were begun in March before Henry IV's death. See his review of *The History of England 1377-1485* in *English Historical Review* 22 (1907):577.

14. Walsingham, *Ypodigma Neustriae*, p. 439; Thomas Netter of Walsen, *Fasciculi Zizaniorum* (London: Longman, Brown, Green, Longmans, and Roberts, 1858), p. 434.

15. Walsingham, *Ypodigma Neustriae*, p. 439.

16. Netter, *Fasciculi Zizaniorum*, p. 435; Walsingham, *Ypodigma Neustriae*, p. 439; "Elhami Liber Metricus de Henrico Quinto," in *Memorials of Henry The Fifth*, ed. C. A. Cole (London: Longman, Brown, Green, Longmans, and Roberts, 1858), p. 97. In this latter work Oldcastle is described as a Behemoth whose hard scales could not be pierced by the oil of the king's mercy.

17. *DNB*, 42:88.

18. Netter, *Fasciculi Zizaniorum*, p. 438.

19. Capgrave, *Chronicle of England*, p. 305.

20. Walsingham, *Ypodigma Neustriae*, p. 443.

21. Netter, *Fasciculi Zizaniorum*, p. 445.

22. Ibid., pp. 414-16.

23. Wylie asserts that the Lollard strength has been underestimated, that of the laity "almost all England was now on their side." (*Henry the Fifth*, 1:261). Waugh, however, declares that the sect was by no means popular and was becoming less so every day ("Sir John Oldcastle," p. 646).

24. Jacob, *The Fifteenth Century*, p. 131.

25. Thomas Walsingham, *Historia Anglicana*, 2 vols. (London: Longman and Company, 1863-1864), 2:298. This edition of Walsingham's history should be supplemented with V. H. Galbraith's edition of Bodley manuscript 462, which is the fullest surviving form of the chronicle: *The St. Albans Chronicle 1406-1420* (Oxford: At the Clarendon Press, 1937). Both Bale and Stow owned this manuscript. The marginalia are interesting: a note (identified by Galbraith as in Bale's handwriting) appears in the margin opposite the account of Oldcastle's promise of resurrection; it reads: "Nota de insania Cobam."

26. Wylie, *Henry the Fifth*, 1:263-64.

27. Jacob, *The Fifteenth Century*, p. 133.

28. *Political Poems and Songs Relating to English History*, ed. Thomas Wright, 2 vols. (London: Longman, Green, Longmans, and Roberts, 1861), 2:243-44.

29. Printed in Grosart, ed., *Poems of Richard James*, pp. 139, 151.

30. Wylie, *Henry the Fifth*, 3:85. Dugdale found evidence of this in his research among the Warwickshire records; see his *Antiquities of Warwickshire* (London: Thomas Warren, 1656), p. 382.

31. *Chronica Regum Angliae Per Thomam Otterbourne*, ed. Thomas Hearne, 2 vols. (Oxford: E. Sheldon, 1732), 1:274; Walsingham, *Historia Anglicana*, 2:325.

32. Wylie, *Henry the Fifth*, 3:87.

33. *The English Works of Sir Thomas More*, ed. W. E. Campbell and A. W. Reed, 2 vols. (London: Eyre and Spottiswoode, 1927), 2:274-76.

34. Hearne, ed., *Titi Livii*. See C. L. Kingsford's introduction to *The First English Life of King Henry the Fifth* (Oxford: Clarendon Press, 1911), p. 13, for a discussion of Titio Livio's sources.

35. *Three Fifteenth-Century Chronicles*, ed. James Gairdner (London: Camden Society, 1880), pp. 54, 56, 148; *The Historical Collections of a Citizen of London in the Fifteenth Century*, ed. James Gairdner (London: Camden Society, 1876), pp. 107-8, 116; *Chronicle of the Grey Friars of London*, ed. John G. Nichols (London: Camden Society, 1852), p. 12.

36. *Polychronicon Ranulphi Higden*, ed. Joseph R. Lumby, 9 vols. (London: Longman, Trubner and Company, 1865-1886), 8:549.

37. Kingsford, ed., *The First English Life*, p. 23.

38. *The Examinacion of Master William Thorpe Preste . . . The Examinacion of the Honorable Knight Syr Jhon Oldcastell Lorde Cobham . . .* ([Antwerp?, 1530?]), sig. H7^v. The date of this work may possibly be ascertained by a remark which Tyndale makes in his preface: "Syr Thomas hitton was brente / now thys yere / at maydstone yn Kent" (sig. Aii). But Tyndale's source is uncertain. In his preface he also remarks that he is using a northern manuscript but has put it forth "in the english that now is used in Englande / for ower sothern men / nothynge therto addynge ne yet therfrom mynysshynge" (sig. Aii^v). Tyndale may have been using a manuscript which is no longer extant. I hesitate to question his integrity, but he appears to be using the account written by Capgrave, and he has added some comments and details of his own. For a discussion of the general problem of Tyndale's sources see an article by Rainer Pineas, "William Tyndale's Use of History as a Weapon of Religious Controversy," *Harvard Theological Review* 55 (1962):121-41. Pineas says that Tyndale altered his sources because he considered them biased and corrupt.

39. *The Confutacyon of Tyndales Answere* (London: William Rastell, 1532), sig. Aiiii^v.

40. Bale, *Brefe Chronycle*, sig. Aiiii. Bale had used the Oldcastle story the year before in a polemical work attacking "the Popes olde faythe": see John Harryson [Bale's pseudonym], *Yet a Course at the Romyshe Foxe* (Zurik: Olyver Jacobson, 1543), fols. 46^v-48. Bale says in this work that Bishop Bonner had ordered such books as "a boke of Frythes / & a boke called Thorpe and olde castell" to be burned because he had not been obeyed by the writers of "these wholsom workes of holye churche" (fol. 90). For a discussion of Bale's use of Tyndale's methods, see "John Bale's Nondramatic Works of Religious Controversy," *Studies In The Renaissance* 9 (1962):218-33. The author of this study, Rainer Pineas, remarks that Bale created heroic and godly characters for his martyrs in order to encourage his co-religionists with such examples of endurance (p. 228). See also Millar Maclure's discussion of the books prohibited in 1531, *The Paul's Cross Sermons, 1534-1642* (Toronto, 1958), p. 23.

41. John Foxe, *Actes and Monuments of These Latter and Perillous Dayes Touching Matters of the Church* (London: John Day, 1563), p. 173. Also, *The Acts and Monuments of the Church*, ed. Josiah Pratt, 8 vols. (London: Religious Tract Society, 1877), 3:321. Foxe composed his martyrology first in Latin while he was in exile in Basel, living in the house of the printer Oporinus. The *Rerum In Ecclesia Gestarum* was published by Oporinus in 1559 and contained a dedication to the duke of Norfolk. When the book was issued, Pope Paul IV prohibited Oporinus from publishing any further books. This Latin edition contained ten pages of praise for Oldcastle, "D. Joan, Cobhami, equitis Aurati & Martyris" (pp. 97-107). For a discussion of Foxe's *Acts and Monuments* as history, see Frances Yates, "Foxe as Propagandist," *Encounter* 27 (1966): 78-86. Miss Yates remarks that Foxe's "vast work presents a view of the meaning of history as a whole, worked out with a passion equal to that of Eusebius or

Marx" (p. 78). See also, William Haller, *Foxe's Book of Martyrs and the Elect Nation* (New York: Harper and Row, 1963), and Helen White, *The Tudor Book of Saints and Martyrs* (Madison, Wis.: Univ. Wis. Press, 1963) for discussions of Foxe as a historian. Foxe did search for basic materials on Oldcastle, for his transcripts from the official records of the reign of Henry V are still extant in his collection of papers, British Museum, *Harleian MSS*, I. 420:13 (fol. 69).

42. *Acts and Monuments* (1877), 3:336.

43. Ibid., 3:343, 358.

44. Ibid., 3:367.

45. [Nicholas Harpsfield,] *Dialogi Sex Contra Summi Pontificatus, Monasticae Vitae, Sanctorum, Sacrarum Imaginum Oppugnatores, et Pseudo-martyres* . . . Alano Copo Anglo editi (Antverpiae: ex officina Christophori Plantini, 1566), pp. 434, 832-36, 953-55. Harpsfield's *Historia Anglicana Ecclesiastica* was not published until the seventeenth century; it too contained an account of Oldcastle's treason and heresy and the falsification of the chronicles by Bale and Foxe. See *Historia Angelicana Ecclesiastica* (Douai: Marci Wyon, 1622), pp. 726-32.

46. John Foxe, *The First Volume of the Ecclesiasticall History* . . . (London: John Day, 1570), pp. 536-66.

47. *Acts and Monuments* (1877), 3:378.

48. Edward Halle, *The Union of the Two Noble and Illustre Famelies of Lancastre and York* (London: R. Graftoni, 1548), fol. xxxv; *Hall's Chronicle* (London: J. Johnson, 1809), p. 48.

49. *Prima pars Cronecarum* (London: R. Pynson, 1516), fol. clxxi.

50. *Fabyan's Cronycle* (London: W. Rastell, 1533), fol. clxxi.

51. Robert Fabyan, *The New Chronicles of England and France*, ed. Henry Ellis (London: F. C. and J. Rivington, 1811), p. 583.

52. *Anglicae Historiae* (Basileae: Mich. Isingrinium, 1546), pp. 441-42. For an account of Vergil's sources, see C. L. Kingsford, *English Historical Literature in the XVth Century* (Oxford: Clarendon Press, 1913), pp. 254-55, and Denys Hay, *The Anglica Historia of Polydore Vergil* (London: Royal Historical Society, 1950), pp. xvii-xx. Foxe found it necessary to attack Polydore Vergil's version of the Lollard martyr. He blames Polydore's political beliefs for the distortion of the story: "It semeth the lesse marvell if Pollidorus being a learned man over muche favouring the Popes parte, whose collectour he was sometyme in the Realme, seduced by other mens errours, did erre him selfe or peradventure added some thing of his own head, as we doo see it often tymes come to passe in such, which bearing great affection unto some partes, doo either extoll all thinges or abase them for the favour and good wyll suche whome they desire to please" (1563 ed., p. 174).

53. *The Chronicle of Jhon Hardyng* (Londini: Richardi Graftoni, 1543), fol. ccviii.

54. Robert Redmayne, "Vita Henrici Quinti," in *Memorials of Henry the Fifth*, ed. C. A. Cole (London: Longman, Brown, Green, Longmans, and Roberts, 1858), p. 15.

55. *Coopers Chronicle unto the late death of Queene Marie* (London: T. Berthelettes, 1560), fol. 255^v.

56. Richard Grafton, *This Chronicle of Breteyn* (London: R. Tottyll, 1568), p. 444.

57. John Stow, *A Summarie of Englyshe Chronicles* (London: T. Marshe, 1565), pp. 138-39.

58. Thomas Walsingham, *Historia Brevis ab Edwardo Primo ad Henricum Quintum* (London: H. Binneman, 1574); *Ypodigma Neustriae vel Normanniae* (London: J. Day, 1574).

59. John Stow, *The Annales of England* (London: R. Newbery, 1592), pp. 550–51. Stow's name was abused by his colleagues who resented his independent thinking. The image of Stow as an illiterate fumbler (he was an antiquary and scholar) survived for many years. An example of such abuse can be found in Thomas James's *An Apologie for John Wickliffe* (Oxford: Joseph Barnes, 1608) in a passage which begins: "Master Stow, not to defraud him of his just praise, was a painefull Citizen, by trade a Taylour, by his industrie a Chronicler, so well minded to the publike good, that for fault of better writers, he tooke upon him at the first to record such things. . . . But here his learning failed him: for being not able to understand his Auctors, how should he judge them? And not judging them, how could he write or cite anie thing out of them, judiciouslie, pertinentlie, and as became an Historian? I spare to speake, what I know, concerning his books; his reverend old age, and incredible zeale to the common good, shalbe to me insteed of so many garments, to cover his historicall imperfections" (p. 59).

60. John Stow, *Annales or A General Chronicle of England* (London: R. Meighen, 1631).

61. Raphael Holinshed, *The Chronicles of England, Scotlande, and Irelande*, 3 vols. (London: J. Harison, G. Bishop, R. Newberie, H. Denham, T. Woodcoke, 1585–1587), 3:1499–1516. Thynne notes in his margin that he is following the manuscripts of Robert Glover and John Leland.

62. *DNB*, 47:132.

63. Holinshed *Chronicles of England* (1585–1587), 3:544, 561.

CHAPTER FOUR

1. Le Roy, *Of the Interchangeable Course*, fol. 129. For a pertinent discussion of the relationship of the theme of marriage and children with that of the continuity of history in Shakespeare's plays, see Ricardo J. Quinones, "Views of Time in Shakespeare," *Journal of the History of Ideas* 26 (1965):327–52.

2. Scholars have provided numerous suggestions concerning the meanings of these references to time. For examples of these speculations see, *The New Variorum Shakespeare* (1936), p. 26–27, and *The Arden Shakespeare* (1960), pp. 9–11; see also the more recent suggestions of Paul A. Jorgensen, *Redeeming Shakespeare's Words* (Berkeley and Los Angeles: Univ. of Calif. Press, 1962), pp. 52–69.

3. For an objective account of the charges brought against Oldcastle, see Jacob, *The Fifteenth Century*, pp. 133 ff.

4. This is a difficult point. The Anglican position in the later sixteenth century on the problem of transubstantiation was a Protestant one. If the symbolism which I think I detect here is accurate, Shakespeare was writing from a conservative point of view.

5. Quoted by Wylie, *Henry the Fifth*, 1:275–76.

6. *Calendar of State Papers, Foreign, 1582*, p. 383.

7. *Calendar of State Papers, Scotland, 1588*, p. 639. This letter was discovered among the state papers some years ago by Robert B. Sharpe, who suggested its relationship to Shakespeare's Falstaff. See his *The Real War of the Theaters* (Boston: D. C. Health, 1935), p. 72.

8. John Stow, *The Chronicles of England, from Brute unto this Present Yeare 1580* (London, 1580), pp. 582–83. Stow repeated the story in *Annales*, p. 547.

9. Kingsford, ed., *First English Life of King Henry The Fifth*, p. 17. This editor has suggested that the anonymous translator of the *Vita* intended his hero, Henry V. to be a model for imitation by other princes, indeed, that the deliberate princely design was stressed to afford a political lesson in greatness for Henry VIII (see pp. x–xiii).

10. The Latin *Vita* had simply described the prince as tall, thin, and youthful, a fleet-footed lad who followed the pastimes of youth as long as his father, the king, lived: "Hic erat princeps ultra mediam staturam, facie decora, oblongo collo, corpore gracili, membris subtilibus, miris tamen viribus, cursu velocissimus, ita ut nullis canibus, nullis missibilus, duobus saepe comitibus damam velocissimum animal ipse prehenderit. Musicis delectabatur, veneria & martialia mediocriter secutus, & alia quae militaribus licentia praebere solet quoad rex illius pater visit": Hearne, ed., *Titi Livii*, pp. 4–5.

11. Kingsford, ed., *First English Life of Henry the Fifth*, pp. xvi–xxxii.

12. Hearne, ed., *Titi Livii*, p. xv.

13. This assumption could be erroneous. The anonymous author of *The Famous Victories of Henry the Fifth* includes in his account of the dauphin's gift of a tun of tennis balls to the new king a reference to a carpet that was part of the ludicrous gift: "Meaning that you are more fitter for a Tennis Court / Then a field, and more fitter for a Carpet then the Camp" (London: T. Creede, 1598), sig. D3ᵛ. The reference to the carpet is not to be found in any extant printed source. The one manuscript source which contains the reference is that compiled by John Strecche, canon of Kenilworth. This work has been edited in the twentieth century by Frank Taylor as "The Chronicle of John Streeche for the Reign of Henry V (1414–1422)," *The Bulletin of the John Rylands Library* 16 (1932):137–87. See in particular p. 150. Did the anonymous dramatist have access to manuscript materials? My assumption is that he did.

14. See chapter six below for a detailed discussion of *The Famous Victories* and a possible identification of its author.

15. The only twentieth-century full-length study of the allusions to Oldcastle in Shakespeare's history plays is that of Wilhelm von Baeske, "Oldcastle-Falstaff in der englischen Literatur bis zu Shakespeare," *Palaestra* 50 (1905):1–119. Baeske describes a steady deterioration in Oldcastle's fame until the time of the Reformation, when the Protestant writers drew "one gold-sized portrait, a sacred picture over which the Renaissance diffused its splendor" (p. 69). He suggests that after the 1560s and 1570s Oldcastle's martyrdom faded from view and that Shakespeare was unaware of the heroic possibilities of the character. Baeske thought that Shakespeare finally relinquished the satirical caricature of the folk-version of Oldcastle on aesthetic grounds. Baeske also suggests that the playwright did not allow a moral judgment to arise in his characterization of Falstaff (p. 105). For a summary of Baeske's work, see *The New Variorum Shakespeare* (Part One), pp. 453–55.

16. Lord Cobham became warden of the Cinque Ports in December 1558. See the *Calendar of Patent Rolls, 1558–1560*, p. 103.

17. Edward Arber, ed., *The Stationers' Register*, 5 vols. (New York: P. Smith, 1950), 1:96. Phaer's poem is not extant. Another ballad was entered in the *SR* in September of 1586; this one was entitled "Callino Shryll over Gaddeshill," *SR*, 2:457.

18. *Calendar of State Papers, Foreign, 1558–1559*, p. 288. For other contemporary references to robberies at Gads Hill, see the *New Variorum Shakespeare* (1936), p. 42.

19. British Museum, Harleian MSS. 897, fol. 17^v.

20. *Calendar of State Papers, Foreign, 1558–1559*, p. 13.

21. *Calendar of State Papers, Spanish, 1558–1567*, p. 36.

22. The brothers of Lord Cobham were Thomas, George, Henry, and, it would seem, Arthur Brooke. They preferred to use the titular name of Cobham rather than the family name of Brooke, as I have noted. Historians usually refer to them as Thomas Cobham, Henry Cobham, etc. Thomas achieved fame as a renegade pirate and agent for the imprisoned duke of Norfolk in 1571–72. George achieved fame as a spy in the Privy Council during the reign of Queen Mary. Henry Cobham was later the resident English ambassador in Paris. Arthur Brooke was the author of *Romeus and Juliet*, a poem which later became the primary source for Shakespeare's tragedy of the star-crossed lovers.

23. *Calendar of State Papers, Spanish, 1558–1567*, p. 236. On 24 May De Quadra wrote to the duchess of Parma again. He had questioned the courtier closely and then had complained to Queen Elizabeth about the incident: "I spoke to the Queen about it as your Highness ordered, and she pretended she had heard nothing of it before, but said if the person who had done it could be discovered, she would have him punished. She added however that if she suspected anything was being written from here against her interests she would, in such case, not hesitate to stop the posts and examine what concerned her" (p. 237).

24. Ibid., p. 241. De Quadra also described to Philip the interview with Elizabeth in which she accused him of the intrigues recently found out. "At last I could not deny," he explained, "that I had sent Dr. Turner to Flanders to try to get her turned off the throne and substitute others (meaning Lady Margaret)." De Quadra remarked further about the list of English Catholics that Cecil now had in his possession: "The evil will greatly increase after the summer because just now they are afraid of a rising and of the aid your Majesty might extend to the Catholics and do not dare arrest those whose names are mentioned in the report. I am informed that the Councillors are much annoyed that the Queen revealed to me the secret of this report, as they think I may warn those whose names are mentioned in it." De Quadra did warn the earl of Derby so that when the earl received a letter (Cecil's) reportedly from the Spanish king containing offers of great favor, he dutifully gave it to the queen. See J. A. Froude, *History of England*, 12 vols. (London: Longman, Green and Co., 1902–1910), 6:552.

25. *Calendar of State Papers, Spanish, 1558–1567*, p. 231.

26. E. Harris Harbison, *Rival Ambassadors* (Princeton, N.J., 1940), pp. 317-18.

27. Ibid., pp. 320-22.

28. Margaret Morison, "A Narrative of the Journey of Cecilia, Princess of Sweden, to the Court of Queen Elizabeth," *Transactions of the Royal Historical Society* 12 (1898):211-24.

29. Ethel Seaton, *Queen Elizabeth & A Swedish Princess* (London: F. Etchells & H. Macdonald, 1926), pp. 20-25.

30. Holinshed, *Chronicles of England*, (1585–1587 ed.), 3:1511. Thynne wrote his "Lives of the Lords of Cobham" to compliment his patron, and the work was included in Holinshed's *Chronicles*, but the Privy Council (of which Cobham was a member) ordered the tract excised. Thynne's manu-

script of this work is in the British Museum collection, Additional MSS. 12,514, fols. 58-78ᵛ.

31. *Correspondance Diplomatique de Bertrand de Salignac de la Mothe Fénélon*, ed. Charles P. Cooper, 7 vols. (Paris et Londres: Bethune et Plon, 1838-1840), 1:258-59.

32. Ibid., 2:254-55.

33. Ibid., 2:255-56.

34. Ibid., 2:382. Inside this letter in cipher is written, "J'entendz que le comte de Surampton et le viscomte Montequ sont passez devers le duc d'Alve" (2:362). The earl of Southampton, father of Shakespeare's patron, was deeply involved in the Catholic intrigues. For a detailed account of the evidence see C. C. Stopes, *The Life of Henry, Third Earl of Southampton, Shakespeare's Patron* (Cambridge: Cambridge Univ. Press, 1922), pp. 502-16. The French courier who carried the packet of 27 September was Jehan de Bouloigne; the courier who carried the packet of 5 December was Oliver Champernon. We know nothing else except that La Mothe complained to Cecil on 30 September that the bearer of his official packet had been wounded and his letters stolen; he demanded redress from the queen: *Calendar of State Papers, Foreign, 1569-1571*, pp. 126-27. In March of 1570 it was Cecil's turn to complain; he wrote to La Mothe that the queen was angry with the detention of her courier at Amiens: *Calendar of State Papers, Foreign, 1569-1571*, p. 198.

35. *Calendar of State Papers, Rome, 1558-1571*, pp. 346-48. Ridolfi's own memorandum on the advantages to be achieved by the success of the plan is extant, ibid., pp. 412-13.

36. Ibid., p. 393.

37. Ibid., pp. 393-400. Cobham's name appears on another such list compiled in Rome (see p. 411).

38. *Calendar of State Papers, Spanish, 1568-1579*, p. 322.

39. J. H. Pollen, *The English Catholics in the Reign of Queen Elizabeth* (London: Longmans & Co., 1920), p. 182.

40. Cooper, ed. *Correspondance . . . la Mothe Fénélon*, 2:254-55.

41. William Murdin, *A Collection of State Papers Relating to Affairs in the Reign of Elizabeth* (London: W. Bowyer, 1759), p. 10. Charles Bailley was released from prison after being racked. He returned to Flanders where he remained in the Spanish service until his death at a great age. On his tombstone in a church in Brussels he is called secretary to the queen of Scots: *Calendar of State Papers, Spanish, 1587-1603*, p. 146. Francis Barty, who was also working for the bishop of Ross and who frequented Cobham's house in Blackfriars "to sound my Lord on causes at Court," wrote to Sir Robert Cecil many years later trying to collect a debt of over a thousand pounds "due to him by the king's mother [Mary Stuart] which he had forborne forty years. Was noticed by the late Lord Burghley, but got into trouble for Lord Cobham's sake": *Calendar of State Papers, Domestic, 1603-1610*, p. 490.

42. Pollen, *English Catholics*, p. 164.

43. Edmund Lodge, *Illustrations of British History, Biography, and Manners*, 3 vols. (London: Mitcham, 1838), 1:529.

44. For a detailed description of the evolution of Diana as a symbol of courtly love and the use of that symbol in poetry dedicated to Queen Elizabeth, see Elkin C. Wilson, *England's Eliza* (Cambridge: Cambridge Univ. Press, 1939), pp. 167-229.

45. *Calendar of State Papers, Spanish, 1558-1567*, p. 236.

46. *Acts of the Privy Council, 1596-1597*, p. 38.

47. *The Works of Thomas Nashe*, ed. R. B. McKerrow and F. P. Wilson, 5 vols. (Oxford: Basil Blackwell, 1958), 5:194.

48. For information concerning the structure of the queen's household and the Office of the Revels, see Sir Edmund K. Chambers, *Notes on the History of the Revels Office Under the Tudors* (London: A. H. Bullen, 1906).

49. *Acts of the Privy Council, 1596-1597*, p. 98.

50. Notes to *The New Cambridge Shakespeare*, ed. J. Dover Wilson (Cambridge: Cambridge Univ. Press, 1952), p. 137; notes to *The Kittredge Shakespeare*, ed. G. L. Kittredge (Boston: Ginn 1940), p. 129.

51. Halliwell-Phillipps made the suggestion in his 1850 edition of the play. If Shakespeare were thinking symbolically, as I believe he was, this inn is quite possibly the locale the playwright had in mind for this allusive scene in which a dishonest chamberlain sets the stage for a robbery. The old Crown with its frontage on High Street is said to date from the fourteenth century. It was pulled down and rebult in 1862. See H.P. Haskell, *The Taverns of Old England* (London, 1927), pp. 10-13.

52. For a detailed discussion of this petition, see below, chapter eight.

53. Chambers, *William Shakespeare*, 2:321.

54. *The Variorum Shakespeare* (1940), p. 238.

55. Burghley's manuscripts are in the Public Record Office (SP.XII. 85, fol. 11; 255, fol. 84) and the British Museum, Cotton MSS., Caligula C. 3, fols. 121-23ᵛ. Conyers Read concludes that Burghley did not tell the complete story because parts of it involved disloyal behavior by some important people whom it was not expedient to expose and techniques which it was not desirable to reveal. See Read's *Lord Burghley and Queen Elizabeth* (New York: Knopf, 1960), pp. 35-41. William Camden appears to have had some evidence when he wrote that the bishop of Ross "dealt so carefully and cunningly with the Lord Cobham, who favoured the Dukes purpose, that the sayd packet was delivered unto him": *Annales* (London, 1635), p. 139. For a detailed description of the continental background and the planning behind the Ridolfi plot, see Pollen's *English Catholics*, pp. 162-84.

56. British Museum, Cotton MSS., Caligula C. 3, fols. 103-104ᵛ. The deposition is summarized in the *Calendar of State Papers, Scotland, 1571-1574*, pp. 9-10.

57. See Murdin, *Collection of State Papers*, pp. 73, 77, 79, 156-57.

58. British Museum, Cotton MSS., Caligula C. 3, fols. 61ᵛ, 62, 65-68, 96, 99, 176, 178.

59. *Calendar of State Papers, Foreign, 1569-1571*, p. 353.

60. Murdin, *Collection of State Papers*, p. 29.

61. Ibid., p. 80.

62. Ibid., p. 23. Cobham was related to the Nevilles through his first marriage to Dorothy Neville, daughter of Lord Abergavenny.

63. *Calendar of State Papers, Spanish, 1568-1579*, p. 393.

64. *Baronage of England*, 2:282.

65. British Museum, Cotton MSS., Caligula C. 3, fol. 103. Burghley's agent, William Herle, who worked in the Marshalsea prison, wrote to his master to describe the great anger of Lord Cobham when he discovered that Bailley had been clapped up, and the lord's even greater "marvaileng" that such "sodein intelligence shold procede to ye Counsell": ibid., fol. 178.

66. Galbraith, ed., *St. Albans Chronicle*, p. 117. This manuscript belonged to John Bale and later to John Stow.

67. *Annales* (1592 ed.), p. 572.

68. M. R. James, "Pictor in Carmine," *Archaeologia* 94 (1951):141-66.

69. For one example of typological explication of medieval drama, see Rosemary Woolf, "The Effect of Typology on the English Medieval Plays of Abraham and Isaac," *Speculum* 32 (1957):805-25.

70. *Shakespeare's "Histories" Mirrors of Elizabeth Policy* (San Marino, Calif.: Huntington Library, 1968), pp. 228-38.

71. It should be noted that in Holinshed's account of Hotspur's rebellion the lady is mistakenly called Eleanor. Shakespeare makes a conscious attempt to keep the lady innocent.

72. *Calendar of State Papers, Domestic, 1598-1601*, p. 578.

73. The same information is given in the deposition of Sir Gelly Merrick, ibid., p. 575.

74. Wilbur Dunkel, *William Lambarde, Elizabethan Jurist, 1536*-1601 (New Brunswick, N. J.: Rutgers Univ. Press, 1965), pp. 177-78.

75. Thomas Walsingham, *Historia Anglicana*, 2:256.

76. See the *DNB* article on Thomas Hariot. For further details on the characterization of the ninth earl of Northumberland, see below, chapter eleven.

77. *Advice to his Son, by Henry Percy, Ninth Earl of Northumberland*, ed. G. B. Harrison (London: Ernest Benn, 1930), p. 94.

78. The historical Hotspur died at the Battle of Shrewsbury when a chance arrow, falling from aloft, pierced his brain. He had entered the battle with his visor up so that he could be recognized by both his own men and the enemy.

79. *A True and Summarie Reporte of the Declaration of Some of the Earle of Northumberlands Treasons* (London: C. Barker 1585), p. 13.

80. Gerald Brenan, *A History of the House of Percy*, 2 vols. (London: Freemantle, 1902), 2:24.

81. *Theatrum Crudelitatum Haereticorum Nostri Temporis* (Antverpiae, Anno 1587), sigs. GI^v, K2.

82. *DNB*, 44:410. The English exiles on the Continent published the *Concertatio Ecclesiae in Anglia* ([?], 1594) in which the story of the earl's death was depicted as murder (pp. 204-6). This work is generally credited to John Gibbins and John Fenn, with the enlargement by John Bridgewater.

83. *Calendar of State Papers, Domestic, 1581-1590*, p. 187.

84. Sir Henry Brooke, a handsome man, was a younger brother of William Brooke, Lord Cobham. He was knighted at the famous festivities at Kenilworth in 1575. Queen Elizabeth appointed him to the ambassadorial post in Paris in the late 1570s. Many of his letters to Walsingham and Burghley are extant in the Public Record Office. He signed his letters *Henry Cobham*, and modern historians refer to him in that way rather than as Henry Brooke. He should not be confused with the son of Lord Cobham who was also named Henry.

85. Printed by E. B. de Fonblanque, *Annals of the House of Percy*, 2 vols. (London: R. Clay, 1887), 2:179.

86. Public Record Office, *SP*. 12. 27, fols. 66-67.

87. Throughout the *True and Summarie Reporte of the Declaration of*

the Earle of Northumberlands Treasons Burghley insisted upon the earl's continued involvement in the Catholic intrigues.

88. See especially De Fonblanque's analysis, *Annals of the House of Percy*, 2:184.

89. *Calendar of Carew MSS.*, 2:444.

90. Percy, *Advice to his Son*, p. 79.

91. De Fonblanque, *Annals of the House of Percy*, 2:200.

92. There are two unhistorical characters introduced at this point in the play. The second is "my servant Travers." I have not completed my search of the numerous manuscript letters to the servants of the ninth earl of Northumberland that remain at Alnwick Castle and Sion House, and I have not been able at this point to identify Travers. My conjecture is that he was a well-known servant of the ninth earl.

93. See the editor's remarks, *The Variorum Shakespeare* (1940), pp. 476–88. The editor of the *New Arden Shakespeare* (1966) edition of the play remarks on the probability of censorship in this scene: "The Archbishop's part is reduced to insignificance, and his cause is given far less chance to justify itself than it has in F. Whoever made the cuts did so with a gross disregard of the dramatic niceties. His only concern, it seems, was that two dangerous themes should 'Have their stings and teeth newly ta'en out' " (p. lxxii).

94. Alfred Hart, *Shakespeare and the Homilies* (Melbourne: Melbourne Univ. Press, 1934), pp. 203–7.

95. Some critics remark upon the relevance of these lines to the tensions of the Essex insurrection, but, as the editor of the *New Variorum* points out, this play was registered with the stationers in February 1598 before Essex fell from grace at court.

96. Holinshed, *Chronicles of England* (1587), 3:528.

97. William Camden, *Annales* (London: T. Harper, 1635), p. 219.

98. *The Execution of Justice in England* (London: C. Barker, 1583), sig. Biii. Lord Burghley published this work as a reply to the polemical writings of Nicholas Sanders, Richard Bristow, and other Catholic authors who were describing the rebels of 1569 as "true Catholic martyrs." Burghley's work was the official defense and justification of Elizabeth's treatment of the English Catholics who were being executed for treason. See below, chapter five, for the way the Arden-Somerville case entered this controversy. Cardinal William Allen's answer to Burghley's tract was published in the following year. Allen concedes that Pope Pius V sent Dr. Morton to England to inform the earl of Northumberland that Queen Elizabeth was to be declared, in an official papal bull, an heretical and unlawful ruler: *A True, Sincere and Modest Defence of English Catholiques that Suffer for their Faith* ([Ingolstadt, 1584]), p. 135.

99. Morton landed secretly on the coast of Lincolnshire and proceeded northward to the earl of Northumberland at Alnwick Castle. He was assured of shelter with his relatives, the Markenfields and Nortons, who were to be leaders in the uprising.

100. *De Visibili Monarchia Ecclesiae* (Lovanii, 1581), p. 730.

101. Sir Cuthbert Sharp, *Memorials of the Rebellion of 1569* (London: J. B. Nichols, 1840), pp. 41–42.

102. James K. Lowers, *Mirrors for Rebels* (Berkeley and Los Angeles, Calif.: Univ. of Calif. Press, 1953), p. 17.

103. Sharp, *Memorials of the Rebellion*, pp. 204–5.

104. *Calendar of State Papers, Foreign, 1572-1574*, pp. 223-24.

105. *Calendar of State Papers, Foreign, 1569-1571*, pp. 183, 186, 206, 213.

106. Compare the letter which Pope Pius V wrote to the earl of North-unberland: "We with due benignity receive and welcome, exhorting you in the Lord, and with our whole heart's yearning beseeching you, with all constancy to persevere in this noble resolution and laudable design. . . . And even if in maintaining the Catholic faith and the authority of this Holy See you must needs meet death and pour forth you blood, yet better far were it, confessing God, by the short trial of a glorious death to wing your flight to life eternal than by a base and ignominious life to pander to the lust of an abandoned woman, to the loss of your souls": *Calendar of State Papers, Rome, 1558-1571*, p. 327.

The importance of Nicholas Morton's actions in the Rising of the North was known to the general public through such popular publications as George Whetstone's *The English Myrror* (London: J. Windet, 1586): "Doctor *Morton* with a commission, or ambassage from the saide Pope *Pius* to the like effect, stirred the rebellion in the North. 1569. He blasted his commission, and had soone moved *Thomas Percy, Earle of Northumberland, Charles Nevel, Earle of Westmerland*, and other Gentlemen of account in the North, unto rebellion" (pp. 141-42).

107. See particularly, Paul A. Jorgensen, "The 'Dastardly Treachery' of Prince John of Lancaster," *PMLA* 76 (1961):488-92.

108. The two-volume study *The Pilgrimage of Grace* by Madeleine H. Dodds and Ruth Dodds (Cambridge, Cambridge Univ. Press, 1915) is thorough but emotional in tone. More recent studies of the episode can be found in J. J. Scarisbrick's *Henry VIII* (Berkeley, Calif.: Univ. Calif. Press, 1968). This author argues that the movement was of "an essentially religious character" (p. 341). A. G. Dickens, in *The English Reformation* (London: B. T. Batsford, 1964), insists that "the roots of the movement were decidedly economic, its demands predominantly secular, its interest in Rome almost negligible" (p. 128). All historians acknowledge that the Pilgrimage of Grace was an extremely serious crisis in Tudor history.

109. Great Britain, Public Record Office, *Letters and Papers of the Reign of Henry VIII*, 6 (1536):347.

110. Ibid., p. 353.

111. For a discussion of the king's more or less open deceit, see Scarisbrick, *Henry VIII*, p. 344; Dickens, *The English Reformation*, p. 127; J. D. Mackie, *The Earlier Tudors, 1485-1558* (Oxford: Clarendon Press, 1952), pp. 390-92.

112. *Letters and Papers of the Reign of Henry VIII*, 12, Part 1: 496. In a "note of remembrance" of the Percies, Thomas Percy's demeanour during the uprising is described: "How gorgeously he rode through York with feathers trimmed, which shows he did nothing constrained but of a willing malicious stomach against the king" (p. 504).

113. Printed by Thomas Wright, *Queen Elizabeth and Her Times*, 2 vols. (London: Henry Colburn, 1838), 1:432-35.

114. *Calendar of State Papers, Venetian, 1558-1580*, p. 656.

115. The letters of Hunsdon, Burghley, Mar, and the queen are summarized in the *Calendar of State Papers, Scotland, 1571-1574*, pp. 230, 257, 284, 291, 293, 301-12, 317, 333, 337, 383.

116. This topical allusion was suggested some years ago in the unpub-

lished thesis of M. A. Taylor, "Falstaff and Contemporary Life" (Iowa State University, 1931). I might add that there was a Sir John Colville who served as Henry IV's envoy to Pope Gregory XII in 1409. A detailed account of the various incidents in the public life of the sixteenth-century Colville can be found in Andrew Lang's *A History of Scotland*, 4 vols. (Edinburgh: W. Blackwood, 1929) 2:333-400.

117. *Calendar of State Papers, Foreign, 1583*, p. 139.

118. *Calendar of State Papers, Foreign, 1584-1585*, p. 322.

119. *Original Letters of Mr. John Colville, 1582-1603*, ed. D. Laing (Edinburgh: Bannatyne Club, 1858), p. 233.

120. Ibid., p. 235.

121. Ibid., p. 236.

122. Ibid., p. 235.

123. Ibid., p. 295.

124. Ibid., p. 292.

125. Ibid., p. 208.

126. Ibid., p. xxxv.

CHAPTER FIVE

1. Gilbert Talbot, seventh earl of Shrewsbury, was elected K.G. on 23 April 1592 and was installed at Windsor on 19 June the same year. I am assuming that the new play, "Harey the vj," listed by Henslowe as a production of "my lord Stranges mene" in the spring of 1592, is Shakespeare's *1 Henry VI*. The dates of performances, fifteen in all between 3 March and 19 June, lead me to suggest that the acting company was being used to help ameliorate the gloomy political atmosphere surrounding the new earl of Shrewsbury. We do not know which of the knights of the Garter nominated Gilbert Talbot in April; the nominating process was secret. See Elias Ashmole, *The History of the Most Noble Order of the Garter* (London: A. Bell, 1715), pp. 268-70. Ashmole remarks upon an unusual occurrence at the election of 1584 (the year William Brooke, Lord Cobham, was elected to the Order) when the earls of Derby and Rutland demanded to see the list of nominees. Their request was denied because of the rules of the Order. In the political factions of the day, both Derby and Rutland belonged to the group opposing Lord Cobham. There is a strong possibility that Gilbert Talbot's name was nominated for the Garter in 1592 by the earl of Derby.

2. In the Syon House accounts for 1593 is the item: "Deliver to Mr. Warnour, at my Lord's appointment, to give to one George Peel, a poett, as my Lord's liberalitie, £3": De Fonblanque, *Annals of the House of Percy*, 2:195.

3. Shakespeare used the spelling *Falstaff* rather than *Fastolf*. The fluid orthography of the period permitted great variance. Both forms of the name appear in the state papers, and in 1631 John Weever was still using the form Falstolfe in reference to the monuments of that family in Norwich, *Ancient Funerall Monuments* (London: T. Harper, 1631), p. 863. Even in 1715 Elias Ashmole was using the spellings *Falstoff* and *Falstaff* indiscriminately with *Fastolf (History of the Most Noble Order*, pp. 242, 281). Shakespeare's preference in spelling appears to be based upon allusive meanings. The white staff of office in Queen Elizabeth's court and the breaking of it were symbolic. The very name Falstaff indicates unfaithfulness to the queen, and Lord Cobham held two white staffs, the

lord chamberlain's and the lord warden's. In this one name we find the function of all the Falstaffian scenes: the portrayal of disorder and infidelity, both moral and political.

For a discussion of the thematic structure and unity of this play, see the introduction by Andrew Cairncross, editor of *The New Arden Shakespeare* edition of the play, pp. xxxviii-lvii. I have accepted the theory of Shakespeare's sole authorship of the drama, a theory that is reinforced by modern criticism concerned with the aesthetic and artistic accomplishments of the play. For an article on Talbot's honor, see James A. Riddell, "Talbot and the Countess of Auvergne," *Shakespeare Quarterly* 28 (1977):51-57.

4. See T. W. Baldwin, *On the Literary Genetics of Shakspere's Plays 1592-1594* (Urbana, Illinois: Univ. of Illinois Press, 1959), pp. 334, 353-54; see also *The Cambridge Shakespeare*, pp. xviii-xix. Baldwin comments dryly that Essex was no more successful in capturing Rouen in the autumn of 1591 than he was in bringing back the Irish rebellion broached on his sword in the summer of 1599. Essex's failures were not, however, due to an absence of enthusiasm and devotion in his followers.

5. C. W. Scott-Giles, *Shakespeare's Heraldry* (London: J. M. Dent, 1950), p. 150.

6. For an analysis of the distinctive qualities of the language of the scene, see Sigurd Burckhardt, "Ceremony and Design in *1 Henry VI*," *Modern Language Quarterly* 28 (1969):139-58.

7. Jacob, *The Fifteenth Century*, p. 247; A. F. Pollard, *The Political History of England from Edward VI to the Death of Elizabeth* (London: Longmans, Green, 1910), p. 309.

8. R. W. Bond, *The Complete Works of John Lyly*, 3 vols. (Oxford: Clarendon Press, 1902), 3:93-94. Some modern critics, frustrated with the difficulty of the problem of political allegory, disenchanted with the carelessness of older historical critics, and ill-prepared to handle the political background of the era, condemn the whole process.

9. The date of composition of *Endymion* is disputed. My own research in this area leads me to conclude that Lyly wrote the play after he was involved in the disputes over the Blackfriars theater in the mid-1580s.

10. *Leycesters Commonwealth*, ed. F. J. Burgoyne (London: Longmans, Green, 1904), p. 202.

11. Lodge, *Illustrations of British History*, 2:153.

12. Ibid., p. 237. Mendoza was sending Philip II a side-line account of what was going on in England. He related that Walsingham and Leicester both wanted Mary Stuart placed in more capable hands, but being unable to prevail upon Queen Elizabeth, they suggested a severe curtailment in the 200 pounds per month allotted to him for his expenses, "the idea being that, as Shrewsbury was very fond of money, he would give up the charge, and the Queen might then without apparent offence to him, dispose of the Scotch Queen as she thought best." But when Shrewsbury failed to surrender his post after a cut was made in his allowance, Elizabeth told Walsingham, "You do nothing but stir up things to gain other ends, but it all ends in smoke; you see now that Shrewsbury will not leave the Queen of Scotland after all": *Calendar of State Papers, Spanish, 1580-1586*, p. 301. Shrewsbury did, however, feel the financial pinch. His letter to Burghley in complaint of the matter reveals his despair: "I have made sute unto her Hyghnes for sume recompense, in which I doo fynd so colde comfort that I am nere dryven to despere to obtayne any thynge": Lodge, *Illustrations of British History*, 2:270-71.

13. *Calendar of State Papers, Scotland, 1581-1583*, pp. 292-95, 328-29. Andrew Lang, who worked closely with this difficult era, refused to speculate on Lennox's betrayal. He wrote, "Once arrived in Paris, he [Lennox] either betrayed Mary's and Guise's plans, and a scheme for carrying James to France, or he used these revelations as a blind for Walsingham, for he stood to win on either chance": *A History of Scotland*, 2:290.

14. Public Record Office, *SP*. 78, 9, fol. 99.

15. Ibid., fol. 108.

16. The news of Lennox's death was related by William Fowler, one of Walsingham's spies. On 4 June Fowler wrote to his master: "It did fal out verray opportunlie that I was the first advertiser off the Duik of Lennox his death to the French pairtie." Fowler then related that the "pairtie" had responded with a long discourse of the death and slaughter of noble personages and concluded with these words, "The Queene of Scotland heth lost a great and good freind, and be his death I se doeth ensew an alteratioun and stey off al our purposses": *Calendar of State Papers, Scotland, 1581-1583*, p. 489. Sir Walter Mildmay wrote to Walsingham in June that he had told Mary of Lennox's death and that she had replied that she had looked for word from Lennox for three months but had recently been advised that he was poisoned. Mildmay concluded, "It seems she favored and trusted him much": ibid., p. 497.

17. Lang, *History of Scotland*, 2:281-90.

18. Great Britain, Public Record Office, *Historical Manuscripts Commission*, Twelfth Report, Part 4, 1:151.

19. A letter of intelligence dated 11 August 1583 contains information on the duke of Guise's plan of invasion; it names Rutland as one of the earl's followers who was working to further the plot: *Calendar of State Papers, Scotland, 1584-1585*, p. 8. The earl of Shrewsbury's first wife was Gertrude Manners, daughter of the first earl of Rutland. Gilbert Talbot's letter to Bess describing his visit to Worksop and the meeting with Rutland and his father is printed in Joseph Hunter's *History of Hallamshire* (London: Virtue & Co., 1875), p. 119.

20. *Calendar of State Papers, Spanish, 1580-1586*, p. 473.

21. E. Carleton Williams, *Bess of Hardwick* (London: Longmans, Green, 1959), pp. 160-61.

22. *Calendar of State Papers, Scotland, 1584-1585*, p. 5. Mary's letter to Monsieur de Mauvissière, dated 12 November 1583, is printed in Prince Alexandre Labanoff's edition of her correspondence, *Lettres, Instructions et Memoires de Marie Stuart, Reine d'Ecosse*, 7 vols. (Londres et Paris, 1844), 5:389-90.

23. *Calendar of State Papers, Domestic, 1581-1590*, p. 450.

24. Ibid., p. 452. Shrewsbury was said to have concluded finally that he was fortuneate to have been "freed of two devils," his wife and the queen of Scots: *Calendar of State Papers, Spanish, 1580-1586*, p. 546. In her petition to the Privy Council the countess of Shrewsbury denied that she had ever maintained her husband was guilty of treason and said that she knew of the imputations of treason only by the evidence of the witnesses at the York assizes: *Calendar of State Papers, Domestic, 1581-1590*, p. 452.

25. De Tassis, Philip's ambassador in Paris, wrote to the Spanish king in April 1584 that Mary's plan of escape should be attempted immediately. He warned that should the queen of Scots be removed from Shrewsbury's keeping, all would be lost. *Calendar of State Papers, Spanish, 1580-1586*, p. 523.

26. *Dictionnaire de Biographie Française*, 13 vols. (Paris: Librairie Letouzey et Ané, 1933-), 4:755-58.

27. Compare the life of Sir John Fastolf written by H. S. Bennett, *Six Medieval Men & Women* (Cambridge: Cambridge Univ. Press, 1955), pp. 30-68. Bennett vindicates Fastolf's retreat at the battle of Patay, and he prints the account of Fastolf's actions written by "moy acteur estant present" which corrects the misguided chroniclers of the fifteenth and sixteenth centuries.

28. *Calendar of State Papers, Spanish, 1558-1567*, p. 214.

29. Ibid., p. 454. The earl of Sussex also visited de Silva and begged for moderation of the piracy charges brought by the Spanish against Thomas Cobham. Sussex said Lord Cobham "was a near kinsman of his own and of many of the highest people in the land who were attached to your Majesty" (p. 455).

30. *Calendar of State Papers, Scotland, 1575-1580*, pp. 93-94. In July of that year Burghley wrote to Lord Cobham declaring that the queen of Scots's jewels had been slipped out of England via Sandwich, that Elizabeth had sent out search orders, and that the customs officials were to be arrested. Burghley added that he regretted the accident and knew that Cobham was innocent of any knowledge of the deed. He signed the letter, "your Lordship's assured at your Command, as any Brother you can have": Murdin, *Collection of State Papers*, p. 281.

31. Quoted by M. S. Rawson, *Bess of Hardwick and Her Circle* (London: Hutchinson, 1910), pp. 42-43. It should be mentioned that the earl of Shrewsbury's sister Anne had married John, Lord Bray. This Lord Bray was sent to the Tower in 1556 for being involved in a plot to overthrow Queen Mary. Lord Cobham's mother was Anne Bray, sister of John, Lord Bray. See Lodge, *Illustrations of British History*, 1:266.

32. Quoted by Rawson, *Bess and Her Circle*, p. 118.

33. Murdin, *Collection of State Papers*, pp. 489-505. This letter is summarized in *Calendar of State Papers, Scotland, 1585-1586*, pp. 268-70, and in *Calendar of Salisbury Manuscripts*, 3:137.

34. Q. Z., *A Discoverie of the Treasons Practised . . . by Francis Throckmorton* (London: C. Barker, 1584), sig. Biii'. These papers were important evidence at Throckmorton's trial, which is described in the British Museum, Stowe MSS., 1083, fols. 17-18. Thomas Morgan and his group in Paris heard news that the planned insurrection had already started in England, that the earl of Shrewsbury had refused to turn over his royal prisoner to Sadleir, and that the earls of Northumberland, Arundel, and Rutland and Lord Montague were expecting *beau jeu* in England soon: *Calendar of State Papers, Foreign, 1583-1584*, p. 299.

35. John B. Wainwright, "Two Lists of Influential Persons Apparently Prepared in the Interests of Mary, Queen of Scots, 1574 and 1582," *Catholic Record Society* 13 (1913):140. On the list Cobham's religious preference is stated as being neither Catholic nor Protestant but "indifferent."

36. For a brief but competent summary of these events, see J. B. Black, *The Reign of Elizabeth, 1558-1603* (Oxford: Clarendon Press, 1959), pp. 360-64.

37. British Museum, Harleian MSS. 6035, fols. 31ᵛ, 39ᵛ, 40ᵛ, 42. These entries were made in October and November 1583 at the height of the activities of the Throckmorton and Somerville cases. Walsingham intersperses notes on both cases throughout.

38. Lord Cobham was elected K.G. on 23 April 1584 and installed the next year on 15 April. He occupied the vacancy created by the death of the fourteenth earl of Arundel in February 1580. See G. F. Beltz, *Memorials of the Most Noble Order of the Garter* (London: William Pickering, 1841), p. clxxxi. Cobham's appointment to the Privy Council was made soon after Leicester departed for the Low Countries in December 1585. When Leicester heard the news of the appointment, he was furious. He accused Burghley of packing the Council with his own "tools" while Leicester's back was turned. See Conyers Read's *Mr. Secretary Walsingham*, 3 vols. (Oxford: Clarendon Press, 1925), 3:138. Lord Cobham's change in loyalties may have been influenced by the sudden death of his eldest son, Maximilian, who had been serving his uncle, Ambassador Cobham, as a special courier in 1583. Sir Henry Cobham's letters to Walsingham in the spring and summer of that year contain casual references to his nephew, but on 27 July the ambassador tells of the death of Maximilian in Italy. "I beseech your honour to pardon me that I do not write at large unto you, being not well in health and in grief for the death of my dear nephew, who was not only a hope to his father, but to all others of his poor house." In the same letter, in cipher, is written, "It was true that the packets of the king were taken from the courier who was going towards the Duke Joyeuse, which I hear Chatillon had." The duke of Joyeuse had been to Rome and had had a secret meeting with the pope. He left Rome on 3 July. Whether or not Maximilian was involved in this escapade we do not know. A letter of condolence written by Thomas Wotton to Lord Cobham, his kinsman, in August does not state the cause of Maximilian's death. It was given out publicly that the young man had died in France: *Thomas Wotton's Letter-Book, 1574-1586*, ed. G. Eland (London: Oxford Univ. Press, 1960), p. 54.

39. Holinshed, *Chronicles of England* (1585-1587), 1:443.

40. Francis Thynne, *An Apology for Certain Passages in Holinshed* (London: Camden Society, 1909), 17:97-99.

41. The chronology is written in Burghley's hand: Public Record Office, *SP*. 12, 163, item 28, fol. 3^v.

42. Ibid., items 4 through 78.

43. Ibid., item 55, fol. 132.

44. Printed from the Chaderton MSS. by Francis Peck, *Desiderata Curiosa*, 2 vols. (London: T. Evans, 1779), 1:138-39.

45. British Museum, Harley MSS. 6035, fol. 35^v.

46. Public Record Office, *SP*. 12, 168, item 30; *SP*. 12, 185, item 53.

47. Bodleian, Rawlinson MSS., D. 985, fols. 52-54.

48. *Calendar of State Papers, Domestic, Addenda, 1580-1625*, p. 100. In one of Lord Thomas Paget's letters to his mother, written on 2 December, he bids her to send his sister Alleyn to Lord Cobham for passports for his men, "for I hope they will not deale so straightly with me but they wyll suffer my men to come to me": Public Record Office, *SP*. 12, 164, item 5, fol. 9.

49. Public Record Office, *SP*. 12, 163, item 55, fol. 132^v.

50. Ibid., 164, item 77, fol. 172. An account of the Somerville case was published a hundred years later by Robert, son of Sir James Ware. He had access to the records, and he included the testimony of Richard Cade of Norwich, who swore that he was in London and witnessed the trial of Somerville and Arden: "At which Trial he heard Edward Arden confess that this Throgmorton was engaged in the same Conspiracy": *The Second Part of Foxes and Firebrands* (Dublin: Joseph Howes, 1682), p. 59.

51. Public Record Office, *SP*, 163, item 55, fol. 133.

52. British Museum, Cotton MSS., Caligula C. 8, fol. 206.

53. For the story of John Talbot's misfortunes, see *The Catholic Encyclopedia*, 14:432.

54. *The Historical Collections of a Citizen of London in the Fifteenth Century*, ed. James Gairdner (London: Camden Society, 1876), pp. 183–84. See also a similar account in *The Great Chronicle of London*, ed. A. H. Thomas (London: G. W. Jones, 1938), p. 175.

55. *Hall's Chronicle* (1809 ed.), p. 202.

56. *The New Chronicles of England and France* (1811 ed.), p. 614.

57. K. H. Vickers, *Humphrey, Duke of Gloucester* (London: A. Constable, 1907), pp. 269–79, 335.

58. Harpsfield, *Dialogi Sex*, p. 849.

59. Foxe, *Acts and Monuments* (1877 ed.), 3:704–9.

60. Ibid., p. 708.

61. *Grafton's Chronicle* (1809 ed.), 1:622.

62. *Holinshed's Chronicle* (1808 ed.), 4:808.

63. *Annales* (1631 ed.), pp. 367, 381–82.

64. See the introduction to Lily B. Campbell's edition of *The Mirror for Magistrates* (New York: Barnes & Noble, 1960), pp. 17–18. The following quotations are from this edition of the *Mirror*.

65. See Thomas Wright's *Political Poems & Songs*, 2 vols. (London, 1859–1861), 2:205–8; R. H. Robbins, *Historical Poems of the XIV and XV Centuries* (New York: Columbia Univ. Press, 1959), pp. 176–80, 184.

66. *The New Arden Shakespeare*, p. 31. It should be noted that John Hume says he has accepted the bishop's gold to "buz these conjurations in her brain" (I. ii. 99).

67. Lily B. Campbell, "Humphrey, Duke of Gloucester and Elianor Cobham His Wife in the *Mirror for Magistrates*," *Huntington Library Bulletin* 5 (1934):119–55.

68. Information concerning Ferrers can be found in Albert Feuillerat's edition of *Documents Relating to the Revels at Court in the Reigns of King Edward VI and Queen Mary* (Louvain: A. Uystpruyst, 1908); in the supplementary material given by Lily B. Campbell in her introduction to the *Mirror*, pp. 25–31; and in the *DNB* article on Ferrers. The *Calendars of State Papers, Domestic* provide additional materials.

69. It should be remembered that the arms of the family of Ferrers are among the twelve coats quartered in the arms of the earls of Essex. There also were Ferrerses in Warwickshire; William Somerville, brother of John, married an Elizabeth Ferrers. See C. C. Stopes, *Shakespeare's Warwickshire Contemporaries* (Stratford-upon-Avon: Shakespeare Head Press, 1907), p. 83.

70. This news was sent to Madrid by the Spanish ambassador. See *Calendar of State Papers, Spanish, 1547–1549*, p. 253. As were the men in the family, Elizabeth Brooke is referred to as Elizabeth Cobham.

71. William Parr had no children by Elizabeth Cobham or by his third wife, Helen, lady-in-waiting to Cecilia, marchioness of Baden. His heir was his nephew Henry Herbert, second earl of Pembroke, son of his sister, Anne Parr.

72. Eveline Feasey, "The Licensing of the *Mirror for Magistrates*," *The Library*, 3 (1922–23):177–93. This scholar concludes that the authors of

the *Mirror* were concerned, far more than they professed to be, with the events of their own day. There was of course resistance to this type of allegorical performance. Early in Edward VI's reign the "seditiousness" of the common players of interludes and plays caused their inhibition in August 1549. The duke of Somerset retrenched the expenses of court plays in 1550, and in June of 1552 the Privy Council instructed the lord treasurer "to send for the poet which is in the Tower for making plays." See further, C. C. Stopes, *William Hunnis and the Revels of the Chapel Royal* (Louvain: A. Uystpruyst, 1910), pp. 324-25.

73. Feasey, "Licensing of the *Mirror*," p. 175.

74. John Tucker Murray, *English Dramatic Companies, 1558-1642*, 2 vols. (London: Constable, 1910), 2:90; Giles Dawson, *Records of Plays and Players in Kent, 1450-1642* (Oxford: Malone Society, 1965), pp. 13, 43, 106.

75. *Letters and Papers of the Reign of Henry VIII*, 14, Part 2:334.

76. Murdin, *Collection of State Papers*, pp. 30, 43, 46, 51. The deposition of the bishop of Ross states thus: "He sayeth, he hath had Conference with Ferrys sondry Tymes, concernynge the Bouks of the Scotts Quenes Title, and at St. Albons, when this Examinate went to Chattsworth, wherat this Examinate had his Advyse concernynge the Artycles to be noted on at Chattsworth, which Tyme also he shewed this Examinate how longe he had favored the Scotts Quene, and had delte with Lyddyngton and Melvyne in former Tymes. He also was with this Examinate dyvers Tymes, in the last Parlyament Tyme, and brought hym Intelligence, from Tyme to Tyme, of suche Matters as weare propounded in the Parlyament."

77. The disastrous effects of this mission are described by Read, *Mr. Secretary Walsingham*, 1:419-22.

78. W. Elderton, *A Proper New Balad in Praise of my Ladie Marques, To the Tune of New Lusty Gallant* (London: T. Colwell, [1569?]).

79. Michael Drayton, *Englands Heroicall Epistles* (London: P. Short, 1598), sig. Hii.

80. Christopher Middleton, *The Legend of Humphrey, Duke of Glocester* (London: E. Allde, 1600), sig. Dii.

81. John Day, *The Blind Beggar of Bednall Green* (London: R. Pollard & Tho. Dring, 1659); for conjectures on this play, see Sir E. K. Chambers, *The Elizabethan Stage*, 4 vols. (Oxford: Clarendon Press, 1923), 3:285.

82. Hatfield House, Salisbury MSS., 102:34.

83. See below, chapter nine.

CHAPTER SIX

1. *Literary Genetics of Shakespere's Plays*, p. 210.

2. *"The Famous Victories of Henry V:* Its Place in Elizabethan Literature," *Review of English Studies* 4 (1928): 270-94.

3. *Some Problems of Shakespeare's Henry the Fourth*, quoted in *The Variorum Shakespeare* (1936), pp. 282-84.

4. *William Shakespeare*, 1: 383-84.

5. "Shakespeare's Use of *The Famous Victories of Henry the Fifth*," *Notes & Queries* 199 (1954):238-41. See also, J. D. Wilson, "The Origins and Development of Shakespeare's *Henry IV*," *The Library* 26 (1946):2-16.

6. *The Case For Shakespeare's Authorship of "The Famous Victories"*

(Albany, N.Y.: State Univ. of New York Press, 1961), pp. 195–96.

7. Stow, *Annales* (1631 ed.), p. 698. There are numerous records of payments made to "the quenes players" in the early years of Elizabeth's reign, but this company does not appear to have been a regularly constituted group such as that drawn together in 1583.

8. *Tarlton's Jests*, ed. J. O. Halliwell [-Phillipps] (London: Shakespeare Society 1844), pp. 24–25.

9. *The Variorum Shakespeare* (1936), p. 386; see also C. A. Greer, "A Lost Play the Source of Shakespeare's *Henry IV* and *Henry V*," *Notes & Queries* 199 (1954):53–55.

10. References are to the 1598 edition of the play edited by Joseph Q. Adams, *Chief Pre-Shakespearean Dramas* (Boston: Houghton, Mifflin, 1924).

11. William Knell's widow married John Heming, Shakespeare's friend and fellow actor, in March 1588. See Chambers's *The Elizabethan Stage*, 2:107.

12. This point was established some years ago by Ward (*"Famous Victories,"* p. 284). See also, Pitcher, *Case for Shakespeare's Authorship*, pp. 183–95. The earl of Oxford, living at the time of the Battle of Agincourt, was only a youth. "The XI Earl of Oxford made his will on 6 August 1415 and died the same year on the morrow after St. Valentines Day. . . . He was succeeded by John his son of 9 years of age": Arthur Collins, *Historical Collections of the Noble Families of Cavendishe, Hollis, Vere, Harley* (London: Edward Withers, 1752), pp. 248–49.

13. *Calendar of State Papers, Domestic, 1581–1590*, pp. 38–40.

14. *Calendar of State Papers, Foreign, 1585–1586*, p. 677.

15. For a detailed discussion of the addition of these names at about the time of the trial of Mary, queen of Scots, see Pitcher, *Case for Shakespeare's Authorship*, pp. 184–95. The name of the earl of Effingham obviously was added when the play was published in 1598, for the lord admiral received that title only in the 1590s.

16. See below, p. 219.

17. John Stow notes in his *Survey of London* (London: J. Wolfe, 1598), p. 102, that in the fifteenth century there was in Tower Ward in Eastcheap "a Messuage or great house, called COBHAMS INNE." In the Great Britain, Public Record Office, *Calendar of Inquisitions*, 4:38, 155, it is noted that Cobham Inne belonged to Sir John Oldcastle in right of his wife who died seized of it in 1434. There were brothels on the Bankside of various names, including one called the Castle.

18. Chambers, *The Elizabethan Stage*, 2:494–504; Irwin Smith, *Shakespeare's Blackfriars Playhouse* (New York: New York Univ. Press, 1964), pp. 84–87.

19. *Blackfriars Records*, ed. Albert Feuillerat, 2 vols. (Oxford: Malone Society, 1913), 2:12–13. There is some doubt about the date of this document. Its date may be 1545.

20. Ibid., pp. 15–19.

21. Ibid., p. 3.

22. Ibid., pp. 27–28.

23. Dawson, *Records of Plays and Players*, pp. 58, 106.

24. Gloucester Records Office, Shire Hall MSS., G. 21444.

25. Murray, *English Dramatic Companies*, 2:82; Dawson, *Records of Plays and Players*, pp. 14, 138.

26. Bristol Archives Office, Council House MSS., B. 26031, p. 32.

27. Murray, *English Dramatic Companies*, 2:82; Dawson, *Records of Plays and Players*, p. 15.

28. Printed from the Loseley manuscripts by C. W. Wallace, *The Evolution of the English Drama* (Berlin: G. Reimer, 1912), p. 131.

29. Ibid., pp. 132-36.

30. *Blackfriars Records*, 2:19-26. Cobham's lease is printed only in part, pp. 27-28. The undated list of his rental expenses is printed on p. 116.

31. Wallace, *Evolution of English Drama*, p. 175.

32. Ibid., p. 159. The rooms Farrant used for his auditorium appear to have been those lying just north of the great chamber and just south of Cobham's rooms. See Smith, *Shakespeare's Blackfriars Playhouse*, p. 136.

33. Wallace, *Evolution of English Drama*, p. 154.

34. Ibid., p. 165.

35. Public Record Office, REQ 2:246/25. She complained that she had called upon Lord Cobham for help only after she had pawned her "plate and jewelles."

36. Chambers, *The Elizabethan Stage*, 2:498.

37. Ibid.

38. Wallace, *Evolution of English Drama*, p. 176. It should also be added that Lord Willoughby became involved in the leasing problems of the ground floor rooms: ibid., p. 188.

39. Ibid., pp. 209, 255; Smith, *Shakespeare's Blackfriars Playhouse*, pp. 151, 159.

40. Wallace, *Evolution of English Drama*, pp. 172-76; Smith, *Shakespeare's Blackfriars Playhouse*, p. 468.

41. Wallace, *Evolution of English Drama*, pp. 186-87; Chambers, *The Elizabethan Stage*, 2:498.

42. B. M. Ward, *Edward de Vere, The Seventeenth Earl of Oxford* (London: J. Murray, 1928), p. 270.

43. Ward, *"Famous Victories,"* p. 287.

44. Pitcher, *Case Shakespeare's Authorship*, pp. 195-96.

45. In his theory that Shakespeare wrote *The Famouse Victories* Pitcher emphasizes the importance of Richard James's remark concerning the "first shew of Harrie the fift." He suggests that James was referring to *The Famouse Victories* as the "first shew" of Shakespeare's Prince Hal. A closer look at the statement of James within its context will perhaps dispel the ambiguity. James was writing to Sir Henry Bourchier concerning the two appearances of Sir John Falstaff, and he speaks of the reigns of Henry V and Henry VI; thus when he remarks on the "first shew of Harrie the fift," he means the plays of Prince Hal and Falstaff that come first chronologically. The text of James's letter in full reads thus: "A young Gentle Ladie of your acquaintance, having read the works of Shakespeare, made me this question: How Sir Jhon Falstaffe, or Fastolf, as it is written in ye statute book of Maudlin Colledge in Oxford, where everye daye y^t societie were bound to make memorie of his soule, could be dead in Harrie ye Fifts time, and againe live in ye time of Harrie ye sixt to be banisht for cowardize? Whereto I made answeare that this was one of those humours and mistakes for which Plato banisht all poets out of **his** commonwealth: that Jhon Falstaffe was in thise times a Noble

valiant souldier as appeeres by a book in the Heralds office dedicated unto
him by a herald whoe had binne with him if I well remember for ye space
of 25 yeeres in ye French wars; that he seemes allso to have binne a man
of learning, because in librarie of Oxford I find a booke of dedicating
churches sent from him for a present unto Bishop Wainflete and inscribed
with his owne hand. That in Shakespeares first shew of Harrie the fift,
ye person with which he undertook to playe a buffone was not Falstaffe,
but Sr John Oldcastle, and that offence beinge worthily taken by personages descended from his title, as peradventure by manie others allso whoe
ought to have him in honourable memorie, the poet was putt to make an
ignorant shifte of abusing Sr Jhon Falstaffe or Fastolphe . . ." (Grosart,
ed., *Poems of Richard James*, pp. 138-39). I believe that James's reference to the first showing of Harry means the first part of *Henry IV*. Compare the reference to Prince Hal in Halliwell ed., *Tarlton's Jests*, p. 24, in
which the young prince in the ear-boxing scene is called by his later kingly
title, "And Knel then playing Henry the fift, hit Tarlton a sound boxe indeed."

46. Wallace, *Evolution of English drama*, p. 225; Smith, *Shakespeare's Blackfriars Playhouse*, p. 151.

47. *Calendar of State Papers, Domestic, 1547-1580*, p. 478.

48. John Anstis, *The Register of the Most Noble Order of the Garter*,
2 vols. (London, 1724), 2:385.

49. *Letters and Papers of the Reign of Henry VIII*, 18, Part 1:45, and
numerous pages thereafter.

50. Anstis, *Register of the Most Noble Order*, 2:282.

51. British Museum, Lansdown MSS, 860, fol. 396.

52. Mark Noble, *A History of the College of Arms* (London: J. De-
brett, 1804), p. 164.

53. Anstis, *Register of the Most Noble Order*, 2:389.

54. Ibid., p. 387.

55. British Museum, Additional MSS., 25, 247, fol. 293.

56. British Museum, Lansdown MSS, 108, fol. 98.

57. British Museum, Cotton MSS., Faustina, E. 1, fol. 127.

58. British Museum, Additional MSS., 25, 247, fol. 293^v.

59. British Museum, Cotton MSS., Faustina, E. 1 fol. 127.

CHAPTER SEVEN

1. See Chambers, *William Shakespeare*, 1:434; H. C. Hart, ed., *The
Merry Wives of Windsor* (London: Methuen, 1904), p. xix; Leslie Hotson,
Shakespeare Versus Shallow (Boston: Little, Brown, 1931), pp. 111-22;
John Crofts, *Shakespeare And The Post Horses* (Bristol: J. W. Arrow-
smith, 1937), pp. 12, 94; William Bracy, *The Merry Wives of Windsor*
(Columbia, Mo.: Univ. of Missouri Press, 1952), p. 124; Hardin Craig, *A
New Look At Shakespeare's Quartos* (Stanford, Calif.: Stanford Univ.
Press, 1961), pp. 65-75; William Green, *Shakespeare's Merry Wives of
Windsor* (Princeton, N.J.: Princeton Univ. Press, 1962); J. M. Nos-
worthy, *Shakespeare's Occasional Plays* (New York: Barnes & Noble,
1965), p. 124; H. J. Oliver, ed., *The Merry Wives of Windsor* (London:
Methuen, 1971), pp. xlv-xlvi.

2. See especially the article by John M. Steadman, "Falstaff as Actaeon: A Dramatic Emblem," *Shakespeare Quarterly* 14 (1963):230-
44; Mr. Steadman examines the numerous Renaissance interpretations of

Actaeon's fate, of the basket story, and of the lover in feminine costume, and he considers the implications of Falstaff's disguises. His conclusion is that dramatic consistency leads the reader to view all three metamorphoses as symbolic and emblematic devices, that although the drama is bourgeois realism, the underlying technique is one of mythological symbolism.

3. *Shakespeare Versus Shallow,* pp. 113-20.

4. Beltz, *Memorials of the Order of the Garter,* p. clxxxiii.

5. Anstis, *Register of the Most Noble Order,* 2:385; Ashmole, *History of the Most Noble Order,* (London: A. Bell, 1715), p. 268.

6. Craig, *A New Look At Shakespeare's Quartos,* p. 67. The theory of the quarto text as a memorial reconstruction by an actor who played the role of the host was first advanced by W. W. Greg in his edition of the 1602 quarto (Oxford: Tudor & Stuart Library, 1910), pp. xl-xli. This theory has been abandoned by Bracy, Craig, Green, and Oliver, who agree that the quarto text was an authorized version of the play cut for a provincial tour.

7. See below, chapter nine.

8. Greg, ed., *The Merry Wives,* p. 84.

9. Crofts, *Shakespeare and the Post Horses,* pp. 95-96.

10. C. W. Wallace, *The Children of the Chapel at Blackfriars, 1597-1603* (Lincoln, Neb.: Univ. of Nebraska Press, 1908), pp. 68-71.

11. The commissions of Hunnis and Gyles are printed by Wallace, in ibid., pp. 58-63.

12. Wallace's theory of this occupancy depends upon Richard Burbage's later testimony in the legal suit of Kirkham vs. Painton (1612) that Evans kept a company of the boys in the playhouse "in such sort as before tyme had bene there vsed" (ibid., p. 57). I interpret this phrase to be a reference to the 1576-1585 tenure of the boys in Blackfriars, but this is speculation.

13. Ibid., pp. 191-97.

14. *Cf. Hamlet* (V. ii. 6), "Me thought I lay Worse then the mutines in the Bilboes."

15. *Institution, Laws & Ceremonies,* p. 621.

16. Ibid., p. 622.

17. Beltz, *Memorials of the Order,* p. ccxxiii.

18. Greg, ed., *The Merry Wives,* p. 81. This incident seems also to allude to the drubbing Lord Cobham took at the hands of the satirists who used the unflattering versions of the Eleanor Cobham story. The Cobhams were belabored because of Eleanor Cobham's treason *by witchcraft.* This does not obviate the contemporary allusion involved in the old woman of Brainford and possibly the allusion to the obscene "Testament" printed by William Copland.

19. Steadman, "Falstaff as Actaeon," pp. 240-44.

20. There is some discussion of this symbolism in Robert Graves, *The White Goddess* (London: Faber and Faber, 1948), pp. 82, 181-82. See also Ruth Mellinkoff, *The Horned Moses in Medieval Art and Thought* (Berkeley, Calif.: Univ. of Calif. Press, 1970).

21. Dennis, *The Comical Gallant,* sig. A2.

22. Rowe, ed., *Works of Mr. William Shakespeare* 1:viii. Gildon's remark is in 7:345.

23. Collins, *Letters and Memorials of State,* 2:48.

24. Hotson, *Shakespeare's Sonnets Dated,* pp. 147-60. Hotson found this letter among the uncalendared papers in the Public Record Office.

25. *Calendar of Salisbury Manuscripts* 15:175-76.

26. Collins, *Letters and Memorials of State,* 2:118.

27. Ibid., p. 141.

28. *Letters of Philip Gawdy,* ed. I. H. Heayes (London: Roxburghe Club, 1906), p. 104. Margaret Ratcliffe was buried in Saint Margaret's, Westminster; Ben Jonson wrote her epitaph.

29. Shakespeare seems to have known Barnabe Riche's story of the "Two Brethren and their Wives," that comes from Ser Giovanni Fiorentino's *Il Pecorone* as does Tarleton's tale.

30. Collins, *Letters and Memorials of State,* 2:18.

31. Ibid., p. 22.

32. Ibid., p. 24.

33. Ibid., p. 26. A number of years later, Sir Henry Wotton wrote of Essex's hatred for Cobham: "Onely against one man, he [Essex] had forsworne all patience, namely, Henry Lord Cobham, and would call him *(per Excellentiam)* the Sycophant (as if it had been an Embleme of his name) even to the Queene her selfe, though of no small insinuation with her": *A Parallel Between Robert late Earle of Essex, and George late Duke of Buckingham* (London: R. Marriot, 1641), sig. B2ʳ.

34. Collins, *Letters and Memorials of State,* 2:27.

35. See below, chapter nine. The relationship between Jonson's *Every Man In His Humour, 2 Henry IV,* and *The Merry Wives of Windsor* seems obvious to me, although much subjective speculation about the subject is in print because of numerous efforts to force *The Merry Wives* into the period of the Garter activities of April 1597, a date which defies logic. Shakespeare takes for granted in *The Merry Wives* that the audience is acquainted with the character of Justice Shallow, who had received his wondrous introduction in *2 Henry IV.* Part Two was written, I believe, *after* Jonson's *Every Man In,* which appeared in September 1598; the introduction of Pistol in *2 Henry IV* is elaborate, and the character is dependent for success as a take-off on the popularity of Jonson's conception of the humour characters in *Every Man In.* The swaggering Pistol is a spoof. Half of the fun of the character is gone or is meaningless without the exploitation of the background Jonson created in his comedy. Furthermore, to keep the game going Jonson mentions Justice Silence in his next play, *Every Man Out Of His Humour* (V. ii. 22), which we date as a product of 1599. Pistol is taken for granted as an established character in *The Merry Wives,* and Nym is introduced as the totally new character. The full crew then appears in *Henry V,* as we would expect in the last play of the series. None of this rather natural development is distorted when *The Merry Wives* is placed in its proper position within the chronology as a product of that Garter period between 23 April-6 June 1599.

36. Martin A. S. Hume, *Treason and Plot* (London: J. Nesbet, 1901), p. 347.

37. See below, chapter nine.

38. Sir Robert Cecil's power in the court was becoming extensive, and his appointees were moving successfully to encircle London with territorial control. Buckhurst was made lord treasurer in May 1599, while Cecil was granted the mastership of the Wards (a post Essex wanted) in the same month. At midsummer the new Lord Burghley was made president of the North. Later in the year Lord Zouche, Cecil's friend, became warden

of the Welsh Marches. This was a duplication of the power block which Leicester's enemies had bewailed in *Leycesters Commonwealth* in 1584, only this time the Cecils were in control. Cobham's important position as warden of the Cinque Ports was a part of this encirclement movement. Essex had reason to be apprehensive when he turned his back upon the court and sailed westward toward the difficult assignment in Ireland.

39. *Calendar of State Papers, Domestic, 1581-1590*, p. 689.

40. In 1612 King James sent Issac Casaubon to Paris to question De Thou (or Thuanus) about the unflattering description of Mary Stuart which that historian had written. Casaubon returned to London with the information De Thou had consulted with Sir John Colville who was, he thought, a neutral source about Scottish history. See *Original Letters of Mr. John Colville*, pp. xxxiii-xxxv; Lodge, *Illustrations of British History*, 3:28; *Calendar of State Papers, Domestic, 1581-1590*, p. 708; P. M. Handover, *Arbella Stuart* (London: Eyre & Spottiswoode, 1957), p. 89.

41. N. Doleman, *A Conference About the Next Succession to the Crowne of Ingland* (Imprinted at N. [Antwerp?], 1594), p. 249.

42. *Calendar of State Papers, Domestic, 1591-1594*, pp. 255, 259.

43. *Calendar of Salisbury Manuscripts* 4:625, 627.

44. Quoted by Handover, *Arbella Stuart*, p. 115.

45. Ibid., p. 117.

46. I will go further in this speculation to suggest that Shakespeare played the role of Ford and spoke these lines. The idea satisfies.

47. Bodleian, Ashmole MSS. 1112, fol. 17^{r-v}.

48. There is an association between Ford and Brooke at the level of the water symbolism.

49. British Museum, Harleian MSS, 1567, fol. 64, is a paper by Brooke in which he claims that he has been held close prisoner "for 2 days in ye Dungon havinge nether meat nor drinke."

50. British Museum, Lansdowne MSS. 77:84, 86, 87. For numerous records of the conflict in the herald's office at this time, see the British Museum, Cotton MSS. Faustina, E, 1 fols. 125, 127, 128, 159, 161-63, 166-68, 221-25, 269-71. More information is to be found in the British Museum, Lansdowne MSS. 108:95-104. All of Dethicke's abuses are summed up in British Museum, Additional MSS, 25, 247, fols, 291^v-296.

51. British Museum, Lansdowne MSS. 80:22.

52. Ibid., 77:88.

53. Ibid., 80:23.

54. British Museum, Harleian MSS, 1453, fols. 31^v-40. See also Harleian MSS. 3526, fols. 139-44.

55. B. Rowland Lewis, *The Shakespeare Documents*, 2 vols. (Stanford, Calif.: Stanford Univ. Press, 1940-41), 2:346.

56. Scott-Giles, *Shakespeare's Heraldry*, pp. 34-40.

57. Bodleian, Ashmole MSS. 846, fols. 50-51.

58. Crofts, *Shakespeare and the Post Horses*, pp. 103-5.

59. Augustine Vincent, *A Discoverie of Errours in the First Edition of the Catalogue of Nobility* (London: W. Jaggard, 1622), fol. 4.

60. Noble, *A History of the College of Arms*, pp. 242-43.

61. Anstis, *Register of the Most Noble Order*, 2:389.

62. Edward Foss, *The Judges of England*, 9 vols. (London; Longman, Brown, Green, Longmans, 1848-1864), 1:138-40.

63. Gerard Leigh, *The Accedence of Armorie* (London: R. Tottell, 1591), fol. 40ᵛ.

CHAPTER EIGHT

1. Theobald's letter to Warburton, 13 January 1729/30 is quoted by S. B. Hemingway, ed., *The Variorum Shakespeare, Henry the Fourth, Part One*, p. 45.

2. F. G. Fleay, *A Chronicle History of the Life and Work of William Shakespeare* (London: J. C. Nimmo, 1886), pp. 198-99.

3. Allison Gaw, "Actor's Names in Basic Shakespearean Texts," *PMLA* 40 (1925):530-50.

3. A. E. Morgan, *Some Problems of Shakespeare's 'Henry the Fourth'* (London: H. Milford, 1924), pp. 6-7, 29.

5. Chambers, *The Elizabethan Stage*, 3:196; *William Shakespeare*, 1:382; 2: 81.

6. J. O. Halliwell-Phillipps, *Shakespeare's Play of King Henry The Fourth, Printed from a Contemporary Manuscript* (London: Shakespeare Society, 1845), pp. xi-xii.

7. J. O. Halliwell-Phillipps, "A Note on the Recently Discovered Manuscript of *Henry the Fourth,*" *The Shakespeare Society Publications* 2 (1845):86; see also *The Works of William Shakespeare*, ed. J. O. Halliwell-Phillipps, 16 vols. (London: C. & J. Adlard, 1859), 9:253.

8. *The Variorum Shakespeare, Henry the Fourth, Part One*, pp. 495-501. M. A. Shaaber, who has edited Part Two for the *Variorum*, makes essentially the same remarks; see pp. 645-50 of that edition.

9. G. Blakemore Evans, "The 'Dering MS' of Shakespeare's *Henry IV* and Sir Edward Dering," *Journal of English and Germanic Philology* 54 (1955): 498-503.

10. Hardin Craig, "The Dering Version of Shakespeare's *Henry IV,*" *Philological Quarterly* 35 (1956):218-19. The Dering manuscript is now in the Folger Shakespeare Library, Washington. D. C. Plans are being made to provide Shakespeare scholars with the much-needed modern edition of this work.

11. Indeed, Harvey's cousin Gawen had married Lord Cobham's niece.

12. For primary materials related to Southampton's imprisonment, see *The Loseley Manuscripts*, ed. A. J. Kempe, (London: J. Murray, 1836), pp. 229-40. See also Stopes, *Life of Henry, Third Earl of Southampton*, pp. 502-17.

13. *Letters and Papers of the Reign of Henry VIII* 5:320, 323, 325.

14. British Museum, Cotton MSS., Galba C.8, fols, 199-203.

15. *State Papers Relating to the Defeat of the Spanish Armada*, ed. Sir John Laughton, 2 vols. (London: Navy Records Society, 1894), 1:15. Another account of the fighting, one which Richard Thomson sent to Walsingham, contains additional details of the taking and spoiling of the *San Lorenzo*. Thomson describes the "lucky" musket shot which killed the Spanish commander, Don Hugo de Moncada, and how many of the Spanish seamen jumped overboard to escape and were drowned. Following the battle the governor of Calais sent a commission of Frenchmen aboard the captured ship to assure the English they could sack the vessel, but he insisted that since it was in French waters, the ship itself must remain in French possession. Howard appears to have agreed to this,

but unfortunately the English sailors robbed the French commissioners who had come aboard: ". . . some of our rude men, who make no account of friend or foe, fell to spoiling the Frenchmen, taking away their rings and jewels as from enemies; whereupon going ashore and complaining, all the bulwarks and ports were bent against us, and shot so vehemently that we received sundry shot very dangerously through us": *Navy Records Society,* 1:349.

16. *The Copie of a Letter Sent Out of England to Don Bernardin Mendoza* (London: R. Field, 1588), p. 28. This intercepted letter is attributed to Richard Leigh, a seminary priest, who intended the description of the defeat of the Armada for the former Spanish ambassador residing in Paris. It is probable that the letter was written at Lord Burghley's direction to countermand the premature publication of a Spanish victory which Mendoza circulated in Paris. The work was printed twice by Field and again by George Miller in 1601.

17. *A Packe of Spanish Lyes* (London: C. Barker, 1588), p. 11. This pamphlet was printed by Christopher Barker, the queen's printer, who stated that his source was a Spanish letter that had circulated on the Continent. The beached ship was later viewed by Queen Elizabeth's stranded peace commissioners, one of whom was Lord Cobham, when they walked the beach at Calais on 3 August awaiting the voyage home. The diarist in the group described the "mighty huge Ship" with "the Oars all red, the Sails [which] had upon them the bloody Sword, the upper part of this Galleas was also red. . . . Signs & manifest Tokens of their bloody minds": British Museum, Additional MSS. 35,841, fol. 198.

18. I. R. W. Cook has suggested that William Harvey was the "Cap. Harvye" who was captured by the Spanish in 1589 and who was ransomed home by Lord Burghley. See Cook's article, "William Hervey and Shakespeare's Sonnets," *Shakespeare Survey* 21 (1968):97-105. I have examined the primary materials of this case but have not found enough evidence to provide positive identification.

19. W. Har, *Epicedium, A Funerall Song* (London: T. Creede, 1594), sig. A2. This work was reprinted by Sir Egerton Brydges in *Restituta,* 4 vols. (London: Longman & Co., 1814-1816), 3:298. Brydges attributed the verses to Sir William Harbert, but Harbert was dead before this date, and Chambers has attributed the poem to Sir William Harvey. See *William Shakespeare,* 2:190-91.

20. See Stopes, *Life of Henry, Third Earl of Southampton,* p. 104.

21. *Calendar of State Papers, Domestic, 1598-1601,* pp. 19, 95. Harvey received the office of remembrancer of the First Fruits in July 1603, on the death of Sir Edward Stafford. He continued to prosper during James's reign; in 1619 he was created a baronet, in 1620 he became Baron Hervy [sic] of Rosse, and when Charles became the monarch, Harvey was created Baron Hervey [sic] of Kidbrooke.

22. *Sir William Slyngisbie's "Relation of the Voyage to Cadiz, 1596,"* ed. J. D. Corbett (London: Navy Records Society, 1902), p. 83. See also Richard Hakluyt's description of the affair in *The Principal Navigations, Voyages, Traffiques & Discoveries of the English Nation,* 12 vols. (Glasgow: J. MacLehose, 1903-1905), 4:259-60.

23. Birch, *Memoirs of the Reign of Queen Elizabeth,* 2:96, 100.

24. Historical Manuscripts Commission Report, De L'Isle MSS., 2:246.

25. Hatfield House, Salisbury MSS, 102:58. A contemporary copy of this letter is in the British Museum, Additional MSS. 6177, fol. 173.

Gawen's father, Sir George Harvey, was lieutenant of the Tower in 1603, and this fact made it easy for Gawen to have access to the prisoners.

26. *Purchas His Pilgrimes,* 20 vols. (Glasgow: J. MacLehose, 1907), 20:79. Gorges describes the landing amid sharp rocks which damaged two of the long boats: ". . . and so clambring over the rockes, and wading through the water, we passed pell mell, with Swords, Shot, and Pikes upon the narrow Entrance" (p. 81). In this account is also a description of the earlier separation of the English fleet off the coast of Spain when the *Bonaventure,* the *Dreadnaught,* and other ships followed the rear admiral's signal light (p. 39). Sir William Brooke was killed a year later in a duel at Mile End Green by the son and heir of Thomas Lucas of Essex. Lucas fled over seas, one jump ahead of the hue and cry. See *Acts of the Privy Council, 1597–1598,* pp. 198, 205. King James signed a full pardon for him on 18 March 1604 (Huntington Library MSS., Ellesmere 1444).

27. *The Commentaries of Sr. Francis Vere* (Cambridge: J. Field, 1657), p. 53. The earl of Southampton accompanied Essex on the Islands Voyage and was commander of the *Garland.* In the summer of 1599 when the Spanish fright once again seized the English leaders, the *Garland* was given to Sir William Harvey to command.

28. Southampton wrote to Essex from Paris on 22 September that he had received a letter from Cecil which indicated something of "her Majesty's heavy displeasure." Southampton seemed startled with the news: ". . . as it came unexpected so I assure your lo: it was nothing welcome." But the young earl remained sanguine: "Her anger is most grevous unto mee but my hope is that time (the nature of my offence beeinge rightly considered) will restore mee to her waunted good opinion": Hatfield House, Salisbury MSS., 64:43. A letter from Henry Brooke, the new Lord Cobham, to Southampton in Paris is also extant. Written evidently at Cecil's suggestion, it tempered the news of the queen's anger. Cobham wrote, "My lo: in my lov unto you I am bound to advise you that by any means you retourn for I durst almost assur your ls: y' the queenes displesur will not loung continue." He wrongly advised the young earl that no great offense had been taken, that any "conceat" of Southampton's dishonor was "clean taken away": ibid., 64:39. This letter is kindly in tone but smug; considering the fact that Henry, Lord Cobham, had just succeeded in wresting the position of lord warden of the Cinque Ports for himself in spite of Essex's determined contesting of the appointment, it is likely that Southampton was somewhat galled by the condescension of the writer.

29. Ibid., 64:87.

30. Collins, *Letters and Memorials of State,* 2:53. Whyte sent the same news again to Sidney in February of 1598.

31. N. E. McClure, ed., *The Letters of John Chamberlain,* 2 vols. (Philadelphia: American Philosophical Society, 1939), 1:39. The letter is dated 20 May 1598.

32. Hatfield House, Salisbury MSS, 83:71.

33. Ibid., 175:153.

34. Ibid., 179:152ʳ⁻ᵛ.

35. McClure, ed., *The Letters of John Chamberlain,* 1:67.

36. Harvey's age is given as twenty-four in the inquest held at his father's death in November 1589. He apparently was born early in 1565

in the parish of St. Martin's in the Fields. See S. H. A. Hervey, *Dictionary of Herveys,* 5 vols. (Ipswich: W. E. Harrison, 1928), 4:114.

37. C. C. Stopes, *Shakespeare's Sonnets* (London: Alexander Moring, 1904), pp. xliv–xlvi.

38. Ibid., p. xliii; A. L. Rowse, *Shakespeare's Sonnets* (London: Macmillan, 1964), pp. x–xii. See also the same author's *Shakespeare's Southampton, Patron of Virginia* (London: Macmillan, 1965), pp. 199–200; and the speculations in the same vein by I. R. W. Cook, "William Hervey and Shakespeare's Sonnets," pp. 102–5.

39. Lady Russell wrote at the end of a diary the date of her second husband's death: "Lo: Russell departed this lyffe on Thursday the xxiijth of July . . . aboute vj of the cloke in the afternoone . . . at Higate in the house of Mr Cholmeley": British Museum, Egerton MSS. 2148, fol. 184^v. Before his death Sir John Russell was involved in a feud with Sir Henry Barkeley, a feud that was "so deadly a quarrell, as that great bloud-shed was like to have ensued." See Sir George Paule, *The Life of the Most Reverend John Whitgift* (London: T. Snodham, 1612), p. 23. Later, the brother of Sir Henry Barkeley married the second Lord Hunsdon's daughter Elizabeth. Whether or not the hard feelings had extended to Hunsdon's family is impossible to determine.

40. Public Record Office, *S. P.* 2, 260, fol. 116. The handwriting of the body of the petition is small, and the letters *h, r,* and final *s* are typical of the older secretary hand. It is not the handwriting of Lady Russell. But the heading and the signatures, *all* the signatures, appear to be in Lady Russell's own graceful hand. This manuscript is apparently her copy.

41. The contract of sale is printed in extenso in C. C. Stopes, *Burbage and Shakespeare's Stage* (London: Alexander Moring, 1913), pp. 170–74.

42. See above, chapter six.

43. Public Record Office, *S. P.* 12, 260, fol. 116.

44. Quoted by Wallace, *The Children of the Chapel,* p. 39.

45. A. L. Rowse, *The English Past* (London: Macmillan, 1951), p. 29.

46. George Ballard, *Memoirs of Several Ladies of Great Britain* (Oxford, 1752), pp. 194–201.

47. A. F. Pollard, *The Political History of England,* 6:298.

48. *Calendar of Salisbury MSS,* 4:460.

49. Ibid., p. 461.

50. Hatfield House, Salisbury MSS., 170:53.

51. Ibid., 31:106.

52. W. B. Devereux, *Lives and Letters of the Devereux, Earls of Essex,* 2 vols. (London: John Murray, 1853), 1:318–21.

53. Collins, *Letters and Memorials of State,* 1:357, 361.

54. *Calendar of State Papers, Domestic, 1591–1594,* p. 379.

55. Hatfield House, Salisbury MSS., 30:26.

56. *Historical Manuscripts Commission Report,* 8, Appendix, Part 2, p. 158.

57. Public Record Office, *S. P.* 12, 260, fol. 52.

58. John Hawarde, *Les Reportes del Cases in Camera Stellata, 1593–1609,* ed. W. P. Baildon (London, 1894), pp. 271–77.

59. *Calendar of State Papers, Domestic, 1595–1597,* p. 147. The original

letter (Public Record Office, *S.P.* 12, 255, fol. 50) is fulsome with anger. Lady Russell's final hope rested in the queen, and she threatened Cobham: "My only comfort is that there is a Throane of justice that hath ever ben most carefull that justice shoold be yelded to the meanest and therfore being predominant over owre so mighty ennemyes will not suffer her Virgins that serve here to be wronged by myght Contrary to Law and right."

60. Many years ago it was suggested that Lady Russell's quarrels with the Lovelaces and the contention at Windsor Castle were background materials for Shakespeare's *Merry Wives of Windsor*. See V. A. Wilson, *Society Women of Shakespeare's Time* (London: John Lane, 1924), pp. 223-25.

CHAPTER NINE

1. *Acts of the Privy Council, 1597*, p. 313.

2. Ibid.

3. For Jonson's role in the composition of *The Isle of Dogs*, see *Ben Jonson*, ed. C. H. Herford and Percy Simpson, 11 vols. (Oxford: Clarendon Press, 1925-1952), 1:15-16.

4. For Nashe's role in the composition of the troublesome play, see McKerrow and Wilson, eds., *Works of Nashe*, 5:29-34; and G. R. Hibbard, *Thomas Nashe, A Critical Introduction* (Cambridge, Mass.: Harvard Univ. Press, 1962), pp. 234-35.

5. Printed in McKerrow and Wilson, eds., *Works of Nashe*, 5:148.

6. Hatfield House, Salisbury MSS. 101:16.

7. Leslie Hotson has worked with this problem in *Shakespeare's Sonnets Dated*, pp. 147-60. For additional information concerning the Cobhams and the circle that gathered about Sir Walter Raleigh, see E. G. Clark, *Ralegh and Marlowe: A Study in Elizabethan Fustian* (New York: Fordham Univ. Press, 1941), pp. 242-63.

8. Printed in full by Chambers, *The Elizabethan Stage*, 4:321-22.

9. *Acts of the Privy Council, 1597*, pp. 313-14.

10. McKerrow and Wilson, eds., *Works of Nashe*, 3:153.

11. Ibid., p. 167.

12. Holinshed, *Chronicles of England*, 3:1499-1516 (in an unexpurgated copy).

13. McKerrow and Wilson, eds., *Works of Nashe*, 3:153-54.

14. Ibid., p. 188.

15. Ibid., p. 211.

16. See the *OED* under "cod" and "cob," which are closely related words. I should perhaps note at this point that not only Nashe but also Jonson takes full advantage of the bawdry inherent in the terms "cob" and "cod."

17. McKerrow and Wilson, eds., *Works of Nashe*, 3:208.

18. See above, chapter three.

19. Foxe, *The First Volume of the Ecclesiasticall History* . . . (1570 ed.) pp. 536-66.

20. McKerrow and Wilson, eds., *Works of Nashe*, 3:209.

21. Ibid., pp. 209-10.

22. Ibid, pp. 210-11.

23. Foxe, *Actes and Monuments*, (1563) sigs. Aiii'-v'.

24. McKerrow and Wilson, eds., *Works of Nashe*, 3:195-201. G. R. Hibbard (*Nashe, A Critical Introduction*, pp. 244-47) has found Nashe's guying of Marlowe's poem the center of *Lenten Stuffe*; in his sensitive analysis of this episode he examines Nashe's ability to handle the mode of studied indecorum. It seems to me, however, that Nashe's little parody of "Hero and Leander" serves as an introduction to the story of the famous red herring rather than as the center of the satire. Nashe emphasizes the red herring allegory as the *piéce de resistance* of the work in his full title: *NASHES Lenten Stuffe, Containing, The Description and first Procreation and Increase of the towne of Great Yarmouth in Norffolke: With a new Play neuer played before, of the praise of the RED HERRING*.

25. McKerrow and Wilson, eds., *Works of Nashe*, 3:201-4.

26. Ibid., pp. 216-18.

27. Ibid., p. 218.

28. Ibid., pp. 213-14.

29. *A Transcript of the Registers* . . . , ed. Edward Arber, 3:134.

30. Ibid., 3:677.

31. McKerrow and Wilson, eds., *Works of Nashe*, 5:149.

32. Ibid., p. 150.

33. Ibid., p. 152.

34. The following quotations of *Every Man in His Humour* are from the standard edition of *Ben Jonson*, vol. 3, Herford and Simpson, eds., which contains both the quarto and the 1616 folio editions of that play.

35. Ibid., 1:15.

36. *Calendar of State Papers, Domestic, 1598-1601*, p. 97.

37. In their remarks on the revision of *Every Man in His Humour*, Herford and Simpson in *Ben Jonson* state that the language became more colloquial and realistic, more the "language such as men doe vse."

38. In the quarto edition (ibid.) the word "broil'd" is printed "eaten."

39. Ibid., 9:354.

40. *The Famous Historie of Fryer Bacon* (London: F. Grove, 1629), sig. Gi'. In the final pages of this work the writer describes how Bacon "burnt his books of magick, and gave himselfe to the study of Diunity onely; and how he turned Anchorite" (sigs. Gii'-iii').

41. John Bale, *Illustrium Maioris Britianniae Scriptorum* (Ipswich: J. Overton, 1548), fols. 114'-115'. Bale mentions not only Bacon's "*novitates suspectas*" but also his imprisonment: "*Futtque multis annis carceri mancipatus.*"
John Leland's work was well known in manuscript form, but it was not printed until the eighteenth century, when it was edited at Oxford by Antony Hall (see *Commentarii de Scriptoribus Britannicus, auctore Joanne Lelando*, 2 vols. [Oxonii: E. Theatro Sheldoniano, 1709], 2:257-59).

42. *Frier Bacon His Discovery of the Miracles of Art, Nature, and Magick*. Faithfully translated out of Dr Dees own Copy by T. M. (London: Simon Miller, 1659), sig. Aii'.

43. Stewart C. Easton, *Roger Bacon and his Search for a Universal Science* (Oxford: Basil Blackwell, 1952), p. 199. See also *Roger Bacon Essays*, ed. A. G. Little (Oxford: Clarendon Press, 1914), pp. 359-72.

44. Herford and Simpson, eds., *Ben Jonson*, 1:19, 139; 11:577 ff.

45. Stock-fish is another name for dried cod.

46. The relationship of Sir Walter Raleigh and Jonson's character of Bobadill, the tobacco lover, has long been a point of speculation with literary critics. For the reader who is interested in this problem, the friendship between Raleigh and Cobham is well documented in the *Calendars of State Papers, Salisbury Manuscripts*, etc., as indeed are their quarrels. The friendship ended with Cobham's bitter accusations in the trials following the Main and Bye plots in 1603.

47. Collins, *Letters and Memorials of State*, 2:26.

48. McClure, ed., *The Letters of John Chamberlain*, 1:43.

49. Weever, *Mirrors of Martyrs*.

CHAPTER TEN

1. Various dates of composition for *Henry V* and *The Merry Wives of Windsor* have been assigned by scholars. If the latter play was written after *Henry V*, then of course Falstaff was resurrected for his role in that Garter play. Leslie Hotson suggested some years ago in *Shakespeare versus Shallow* (Boston: Little, Brown, 1931) that *The Merry Wives* was written to celebrate the election and/or installation of Lord Hunsdon to the Order of the Garter in 1597. My own study of the Falstaff satire leads me to believe that *The Merry Wives* was written to satirize Lord Cobham (Henry Brooke) when his name was submitted for election to the Garter in the spring of 1599. Most editors suggest that *Henry V* was written later in this same year while the earl of Essex was in Ireland with the English forces. If this dating is correct, the death of Falstaff in *Henry V* is the final scene for that famous comic character.

2. See the articles by Robert F. Fleissner, "Falstaff's Green Sickness Unto Death," *Shakespeare Quarterly* 12 (1961):47-55; John M. Steadman, "Falstaff as Actaeon," pp. 231-44; Philip Williams, "The Birth and Death of Falstaff," *Shakespeare Quarterly* 8 (1957):355-65.

3. *The Brut*, ed. F. W. D. Brie, *Early English Text Society*, 136 (London, 1906-1908), pp. 594-95.

4. See above, chapter three.

5. *The Dialogues of Plato*, trans. Benjamin Jowett, 5 vols. (Oxford: Clarendon Press, 1892), 2:266. Dover Wilson noted this parallel in the Cambridge edition of the play, but no critic that I can find has seen the significance of the satire. We revere Plato and Socrates too much. It may be worthwhile to note that in Elizabethan England the contemporary Lord Cobham had been compared with the noble Grecians by Francis Thynne, Lancaster herald, in his eulogy of his patron which was made suspect because of its excision from Holinshed's *Chronicles of England* in 1586-1587. Thynne used a quotation from *The Republic* which defined nobility as a class of men divided into four degrees: those nobles descended from kings and princes, those descended from good and virtuous ancestors, those who performed great feats of war, and those who excelled in "the prerogative of the Mind." Thynne, of course, concluded his compliment by remarking that Lord Cobham possessed all these virtues: " . . . that Lord Cobham now living, being the glorie of that ancient and honorable familie, not onelie meriteth well of his countrie, as after shall appeare; but is also an honorable Mecenas of learning, a lover of learned persons, and not inferior in knowledge to anie of the born nobilitie of England": Holinshed, *Chronicles of England*, 3:1499. It was an age

of effusive dedications, but this praise must surely have rankled some of the "borne nobilitie."

It should be added at this point that Mistress Quickly's pun upon "stone" is part of the broad native wit.

6. In the French translation of 1581 the relevant passage was printed as follows: "Mais quand Socrates sentit qu'en so promenant les iambes luy failloient, il se coucha a la renuerse, comme auoit dit le ministre, qui en le touchant vn peu apres, regardoit ses pieds & ses iambes: puis pressant fort l'vn des pieds, luy demanda s'il le sentoit, qui respondit que non, il en feit autant aux iambes, & peu a peu montant plus haut, il nous monstra ses parties estre desia toutes froides & roides": *Le Phedon De Platon.* Le tout traduit de Grec en Francois . . . par Loys le Roy Dit Regivs (Paris: Abel l'Angelier, 1581), fol. 103ʳ.

7. *The Dictes or Sayengis of the Philosophhres* (Westmestre: W. Caxton, 1477), [fol. 26].

8. Jowett, trans., *The Dialogues of Plato,* 2:110-11. The allusion is even more complex when one recalls that Oldcastle too was lampooned by the fifteenth-century poets. See the anonymous poem "Against the Lollards," printed in Thomas Wright's *Political Poems and Songs Relating to English History,* 2 vols. (London: Longman, Green, Longmans and Roberts, 1861), 2:243-47; and see Hoccleve's poem which censures the defected knight, printed in Grosart, ed., *Poems of Richard James,* pp. 138 ff.

9. Bale, *Brefe Chronycle,* sig. H4.

10. Foxe, *Actes and Monuments* (1563), p. 281.

11. Stow, *Annales* (1592), p. 572. The italics are Stow's.

12. Walsingham, *Historia Anglicana,* 2:295.

13. Rivers, trans., *The Dictes or Sayengis,* [fols. 74-76].

14. William Baldwin, *A Treatise of Morall Philosophy* (London: R. Tottyll, 1575), fols. 207ᵛ, 246. This work was printed first in 1547; its popularity sent it through numerous editions before the end of the century.

15. N. D. [Robert Parsons], *A Treatise of Three Conversions,* 2:250.

16. Collins, *Letters and Memorials of State,* 2:25.

17. W. A. Scott Robertson, "Six Wills Relating to Cobham Hall," *Archaeologia Cantiana,* 11 (1877):209-16.

18. Printed by A. A. Arnold, "Cobham College," *Archaeologia Cantiana,* 27 (1905):80. It was William Lambarde who established one of the first Protestant "hospitals" or "colleges" in Elizabethan England in 1576 at Greenwich.

19. *Historical Manuscripts Commission,* Ninth Report, Part 1, 286.

20. Mill Stephenson, *A List of Monumental Brasses in the British Isles* (London: Headley Bros., 1926), p. 221.

21. The list of commentators on the famous table is almost endless. The most nearly complete article on the history of the emendations and revisions of this folio line is that of E. G. Fogel, " 'A Table of Green Fields' A Defense of the Folio Reading," *Shakespeare Quarterly* 9 (1958):485-92. See also the series of letters to the editor of the *TLS* in April and May of 1956: Leslie Hotson, "Falstaff's Death and Greenfield's," 6 April, p. 212; Sir Ernest Barker, "The Death of Falstaff," 13 April, p. 221; Oliffe Richmond, "The Death of Falstaff," 27 April, p. 253; N. Young, "The Death of Falstaff," 20 April, p. 237; Sir Ernest Barker, 4 May, p. 269. In addition, see an interesting article which suggests allusions

to heraldry in the phrase: Hilda Hulme, "The Table of Green Fields," *Essays in Criticism* 6 (1956): 117-19. This suggestion was answered by John S. Tuckey, " 'Table of Greene Fields' Explained," *Essays in Criticism* 6(1956):486-91. Philip Williams also considers the problem of the table in "The Birth and Death of Falstaff Reconsidered," *Shakespeare Quarterly* 8 (1957):359-65, and so does A. A. Mendilow, "Falstaff's Death of a Sweat," *Shakespeare Quarterly* 9 (1958): 479-83.

22.   See John M. Steadman's article, "Falstaff's 'Facies Hippocratica,' A Note on Shakespeare and Renaissance Medical Theory," *Studie Neophilologia* 29 (1957): 130-35; see also A. S. Macnalty's article, "Shakespeare and Sir Thomas More," *Essays and Studies by Members of the English Association,* 12 (1959):36-57, which contains a section on the death of Falstaff and Shakespeare's possible use of More's *De Quatuor Novissimis.* In addition see Mendilow, "Falstaff's Death," pp. 479-83; Fleissner, "Falstaff's Green Sickness," pp. 47-55. For a survey of the *ars moriendi* literature of the later middle ages and the Renaissance, see the study by Sister Mary Catherine O'Connor, *The Art of Dying Well* (New York: Columbia Univ. Press, 1942). One of these "courtesy books," the *Cordiale Siue De Quatour Nouissimis* which Lord Rivers translated from the French of Jean Mielot, was printed by Caxton in 1479. This death literature enjoyed tremendous vogue. The signs of death (*quibus signis cognosciture moriens)* are to be found in many books of the sixteenth century, and it is obvious, at least to me, that Shakespeare was aware of this large body of commonplace knowledge. He turns it, it would seem, into a most allusive and suggestive imagery.

23.   The first folio does not contain scene and line numbers for *Henry V.* I am using the facsimile of the British Museum copy (G. 11631) for punctuation, but for line identification I am using the *New Arden* text (1960), that is based on the *Cambridge Shakespeare* text of 1891. The problem of the compositor enters into any discussion of punctuation. We know that Falstaff's death scene falls within the first twelve pages of *Henry V,* that were set by the two folio compositors (Hinman labels them A and B) working from a manuscript copy. If Hinman's observations are correct, sig. h4a was set by Compositor B after he had finished sig. h3ᵛ. Compositor A set sig. h4b (the column in which the "Table of greene fields" occurs), working simultaneously with Compositor B who was setting up the left column of this page to assist his partner. See Charlton Hinman, *The Printing and Proof-Reading of the First Folio of Shakespeare,* 2 vols. (Oxford: Clarendon Press, 1963), 2:14-19. Since the particular use of the comma to separate compound subjects and·objects occurs on both sig. h3ᵛ and sig. h4b, I am assuming that the compositors were following the punctuation of the manuscript. This assumption cannot be proved, of course, because both men may have had the same habits of punctuation, habits which differed in comma usage from the manuscript before them. If we look for additional examples of this use of the comma in the other plays in the first folio, instances can be found. In *King Lear:* "Turne all her Mothers paines, and benefits / To laughter, and contempt" (I. iv. 310-11). In *Hamlet:* "And I do doubt the hatch, and the disclose / Will be some danger" (III. i. 175-76). In *Measure for Measure:* "Your brother, and his louer haue embrac'd" (I. iv. 40). These and additional examples not only from Shakespeare's plays but from Donne and Browne as well are listed by Percy Simpson, *Shakespearian Punctuation* (Oxford: Clarendon Press, 1911), pp. 47-48.

24.   This latter meaning of *pen,* which comes from the ancient Celtic language, was first suggested as a relevant definition by John Tuckey, "Table of Green Fields," pp. 486-91.

25. John Bartlett, *A Complete Concordance* (London: Macmillan, 1956), p. 1512.

26. The technical term *obelisk* in use in England by 1549 apparently was never used by Shakespeare in his writings.

27. I am indebted to Miss Susan Griffiths for the opportunity to examine the crests and memorabilia within Cobham Hall. The officials in charge of Cobham Church and Cobham College were equally helpful to me in my search for historical facts about those early structures.

28. I should perhaps remark that the *OED* lists a specialized definition of *table,* which is an architectural term meaning a horizontal projecting course or molding, as a cornice, usually with a defining word, such as corbel-table, etc. (*Table, sb.,* 12, a). Shakespeare may have had such terminology in mind; my preference of meanings, however, is for the definition of table as a memorial tablet or stone. This meaning, it seems to me, fits more appropriately with the definition of *pen* as shaft.

29. *Letters and Papers of the Reign of Henry VIII,* 14, Part 2, 334.

CHAPTER ELEVEN

1. Bodleian MSS., Ashmole 208, fol. 207^{r-v}. The authenticity of Forman's "Booke of Plaies" was questioned some years ago by Samuel A. Tennenbaum, who suggested that the manuscript was one of J. P. Collier's forgeries. This problem was resolved when Dr. R. W. Hunt, keeper of Western Manuscripts at the Bodleian, presented evidence from the library's records that authenticated Forman's work. See J. Dover Wilson and R. W. Hunt, "The Authenticity of Simon Forman's *Booke of Plaies,*" *Review of English Studies,* 23 (1947):193-200.

2. In his genealogical research Forman found that one sister of Queen Margaret was "Elizabeth the yongest who was maried to Robert Lorde Forman the sonn of Richard that came in with William the Conquerour": Bodleian MSS. Ashmole 208, fol. 215^{v}. In his attempt to find Scottish relatives Forman was following a popular fad which flourished in London after James VI became James I of England.

3. Ibid., 411, fol. 179^{v}. See also the *DNB* article written by Sir Sidney Lee, who remarks that Forman had acquired many powerful friends by 1603 and that "until the end of his life Forman's connection among ladies of the court increased."

4. Charlotte C. Stopes, "The Scottish and English Macbeth," in *Shakespeare's Industry* (London: G. Bell, 1916), p. 101. This critic goes on to say: "The superstition of Duffe, the revenge of Donewald, the guilty imaginations of Kenneth, the vice of Cullen, the covetousness of Gryme, are all added by Shakespeare to Holinshed's picture of Macbeth, as well as 'the manifest vices of Englishmen,' a phrase that Shakespeare was too patriotic to quote."

5. See above, chapter four.

6. Hector Boethius, *Hystory and Croniklis of Scotland,* trans. J. Bellenden (Edinburgh, [1540?]), fol. CLXXI^{r}. For a detailed discussion of Bellenden's translation, which is called "one of the two or three most noteworthy examples of the noble Scottish prose of the sixteenth century not yet contaminated by the influence of Southern English," see R. W. Chambers and W. W. Seton, "Bellenden's Translation of the *History* of Hector Boece," *Scottish Historical Review,* 17 (1919):5-15.

7. George Buchanan, *The History of Scotland,* trans. J. Fraser (London: Edward Jones, 1690), p. 210. The translator follows his Latin source

closely at this point. In Buchanan's version Macbeth *dreams* that three women of ethereal beauty address him as "Thane of Angus, Thane of Murray, and King of Scotland." Henry Paul suggests that Shakespeare knew Buchanan's *Rerum Scoticarum Historia.* See *The Royal Play of 'Macbeth'* (New York: Macmillan, 1950), pp. 213-17.

8. Holinshed, *Chronicles of England* (1587) 2:168-69.

9. Buchanan, *History of Scotland* (1690), p. 219; Holinshed, *Chronicles of England,* (1587), 2:177.

10. Alan O. Anderson, *Early Sources of Scottish History,* 2 vols. (Edinburgh: Oliver & Boyd, 1922), 2:67.

11. M. C. Bradbrook, "The Sources of *Macbeth*," *Shakespeare Survey,* 4 (1951): 35.

12. Ibid.

13. Bellenden, trans., *Hystory and Croniklis of Scotland,* fol. clxxxi.

14. Alan O. Anderson, *Scottish Annals from English Chroniclers* (London: David Nutt, 1908), pp. 110-11. William of Malmesbury said that "Malcolm fell rather by treachery than by strength," and Orderic Vital gave an unheroic account of the king's death. "After some time, when king Malcolm wished to return to his own [Scotland] and was returning in peace, honoured by the king [William Rufus] with many gifts, Robert de Mowbray [lord of Northumberland] with Morel, his nephew, and armed knights fell upon him and slew him, unarmed, unawares. And when the king of the English heard this, and the nobles of the realm, they were greatly grieved, and much ashamed for a thing so base and so cruel, committed by Normans": ibid.

15. Holinshed, *Chronicles of England* (1587), 2:179. The story and marginal note are the same in the 1576 edition. Grafton also printed the Percy story, without the apostil, in his account of the reign of William Rufus. See *Grafton's Chronicle,* 1:172-73. The notes made by Norroy king of arms on his visitation to the north in 1530 included the item: "Be yt notid that Malcolyn Kyng of Scotland was slayne at Andewik by Robert Mowbray, Erle of Northumberland and Foundour of Tynmouth": *Heraldic Visitation of the Northern Counties,* ed. W. H. D. Longstaffe (Durham: Surtees Society, 1863), p. 36.

16. Jhone Leslie, Bishop of Rosse, *The Historie of Scotland, trans. by James Dalrymple, 1596,* 2 vols. (Scottish Text Society, 1888), 1:316.

17. *Henslowe's Diary,* ed. R. A. Foakes and R. T. Rickert (Cambridge: Cambridge Univ. Press, 1961), pp. 199-200.

18. *Remaines of a Greater Worke Concerning Britaine* (London: G. Eld, 1605), pp. 124-25. The statement that Malcolm died at the hands of an earl of Northumberland continued to appear in print in London. See Thomas Milles, *The Catalogue of Honor* (London: W. Jaggard, 1610), p. 715; Ralph Brooke, *A Catalogue and Succession . . .* (London: W. Jaggard, 1619), p. 228. The punning on the name Percy began in the Middle Ages, with "Percy persquitur," "Percy penetrativus," and "Percy penetrans" occurring in the chronicles. Such puns continued in Shakespeare's day. John Davies of Hereford used them in his dedication of *Humours Heav'n* (London: A. Islip, 1605) to young Algernon, Lord Percy, son of the ninth earl:

Reade little Lord, this Riddle learne to reede;
So, first appose; then, tell it to thy Peeres:
So shall they hold thee (both in Name and Deed)
A perfect *Pierc-ey* that in darkenesse cleeres.

A Pierc-ey, or a piercing Eie doth show
Both wit and Courage; . . .
So, Percies fame shall pierce the Eie oi Daies.

It might also be noted that after the Gunpowder plot was discovered, the pun became even more popular. The vicar of Halifax wrote an epigram using it: "Pearcye wold pearce the eyes of King and State and lead them blind w^m his traiterous bate": Hatfield HHouse, Salisbury MSS., 140, fol. 104. See also Edward Hawes, *Trayterous Percyes & Catesbyes Prosopopeia* (London: S. Stafford, 1606), sig. A3^v.

19.   A. J., *A Briefe Chronicle of all the Kinges of Scotland* (Aberdene: E. Raban, 1623), p. 28.

20.   *A History of Northumberland,* 15 vols. (London: A. Reid, 1893–1940), 7:34.

21.   *Scottish Annals from English Chroniclers,* p. 111. In the *Anglo-Saxon Chronicle* Morell is called Malcolm's "Compater": "And then Robert, the earl of the Northumbrians, with his men entrapped him [Malcolm] unawares, and slew him. Morel of Bamborough slew him: he was the earl's steward, and king Malcolm's comrade."

22.   Thomas Percy was a descendant of the fourth   earl of Northumberland. He was retained by the ninth earl for a decade or more before the Gunpowder plot, and he had been the trusted messenger between Northumberland and James before Queen Elizabeth's death, when the earl attempted to gain some assurance of tolerance for the English Roman Catholics should James succeed to the English throne. At the earl's trial this was brought out: "The first [charge] was his employing of Percy a year and halfe before the Queens death into Scotland, to procure of his Majesty a mitigation for Catholiques, and some toleration of their religion; and that the kinges favour in this behalfe might be wholly at the disposition of my lord of Northumberland, that his lordship might hold the Catholiques in a kind of dependency and suspense, till his Majesty might have peaceable entry and quiet possession. By which means (said Mr. Attourny) he went about to derogat from the kings authority, by stealing away the hartes of his subjectes, by making himselfe head of the most factious and traiterous faction in the kingdom" (British Museum, Cotton MSS., Vespasian, C. 14, fol. 451').

23.   British Museum, Harleian MSS, 589 (15), fol. 111. Coke's charges are detailed. His ultimate conclusion was that Northumberland's negligence and duplicity allowed Thomas Percy "the Liberty to execute any his intended Villanyes": ibid., fol. 112.

24.   Osborne, *Traditionall Memoyres on the Reigne of King James,* p. 61.

25.   Northumberland paid only eleven thousand pounds of the fine. By careful management of his estates during his imprisonment he actually was able to double his annual income. See G. R. Batho, "The Wizard Earl in the Tower," *History Today,* 6 (1956):344-51.

26.   *Shakespeare's "Histories": Mirrors of Elizabethan Policy,* pp. 230-38.

27.   *Athenae Oxonienses,* 5 vols. (London: F. C. & J. Rivington, 1815), 2: cols. 229–303.

28.   G. R. Batho, *The Household Papers of Henry Percy, Ninth Earl of Northumberland, 1564-1632* (London: Camden Society, 1962), pp. 90, 95, 154.

29. Ibid., pp. 95, 163.

30. Ibid., p. 155.

31. De Fonblanque, *Annals of the House of Percy*, 2:332-35.

31. David Jardine, *Criminal Trials*, 2 vols. (London: M. A. Nattali, 1846), 1:450-51. In the famous "Baines Note" it was stated that Marlowe scoffed that "Moses was but a juggler and that one Heriots being Sir W. Ralegh's man can do more than he." See a discussion of this in E. A. Strathmann's *Sir Walter Ralegh: A Study in Elizabethan Skepticism* (New York: Columbia Univ. Press, 1951), pp. 41-43.

38. *Daemonologie* (Edinburgh: R. Waldegrave, 1597), pp. 9-14. James makes his own clear distinction between "Astronomia," which he classed as a branch of "the Mathematicques," and astrology, which included "knowledge by the nativities, the Cheiromancie, Geomantie, Hydromantie," and such things that were "Utterlie unlawful to be trusted in, or practized amongst christians, as leaning to no ground of natural reason: & it is this part," he concluded, "which I called before the devils schole."

34. George Peele, *The Honour of the Garter* (London: J. Busbie, [1593]). sigs. Ai-ii. Additional evidence of Northumberland's early reputation as a scholar is to be found in the dedication which Sir John Davies penned for the manuscript copy of *Nosce Teipsum* that he sent to the earl:

> The strongest & the Noblest argument
> To prove the Soule immortall rests in this:
> That in no mortall thing it finds content,
> But seekes an object that eternall is.
>
> If any soule hath this immortall Signe,
> (As every Soule doth show it, more or lesse)
> It is your Spirit, Heröick & divine,
> W^{ch} this trew noate most lively doth expresse.
>
> For being a Prince, & having princely blood
> The noblest of all Europe in your vaines;
> Having youth, wealth, pleasure, & every Good
> W^{ch} all the world doth seek wth endlesse paynes,
>
> Yet can you never fixt y^r thoughts on these,
> These cannot wth your heav'nly mind agree;
> These momentary objects cannot please
> Your winged Spirit, wch more aloft doth flee.
>
> It only longs to learne & know the Truth;
> The Truth of everything wch never dies,
> The nectar wch praeserves the soule in youth,
> The manna wch doth minds immortalize.
>
> These Noble Studdies, more ennoble you,
> & bring more honor to y^r race & Name
> Then Hot-Spurs fier, wch did the Scots subdew,
> Then Brabants Lion, or Great Charles his fame.

(Alnwick Castle MSS., 474, fol. 1^{r-v}). Moreover, Barnabe Barnes dedicated his *Parthenophil and Parthenophe* to the earl of Northumberland. Among the poems in this volume were twelve zodiac sonnets, an ode based on astrologic figures, and a sestine which used magic charms. The modern editor of this volume remarks that these poems probably were included or even written because of the particular interests of Northumberland. See Victor A. Doyno's edition of Barnes's poems (Carbondale, Illinois: Southern Illinois Univ. Press, 1971), pp. xxi, 28-29, 154-55.

35. E. A. Strathmann, "John Dee as Ralegh's 'Conjurer,' " *Huntington Library Quarterly*, 10 (1957):365-72. For a balanced view of the influence of the belief in magic upon the sixteenth century, see A. L. Rowse's discussion of the problem in *The Elizabethan Renaissance: The Life of the Society* (London: Macmillan, 1971), pp. 245-52. For John Dee's relationship with Hariot and Northumberland, see the recent biography by Peter J. French, *John Dee: The World of an Elizabethan Magus* (London: Routledge and Kegan Paul, 1972), pp. 171-72. For comments on the experiments conducted in anatomy, astronomy, geography, and horology, see John W. Shirley, "The Scientific Experiments of Sir Walter Ralegh, The Wizard Earl, and the Three Magi in the Tower," *Ambix*, 4 (1947):52-66.

36. Syon House MSS., W. 2, 1. Some of these books are now in the Alnwick Castle library and muniment room.

37. De Fonblanque, *Annals of the House of Percy*, 2:187-88.

38. Ibid., pp. 331-32.

39. Ibid., p. 308.

40. McClure, ed., *The Letters of John Chamberlain*, 1:212-13. Carleton was called home from the Continent for interrogation. His career was almost wrecked by this episode in history.

41. British Museum, Harleian MSS., 589, fols. 111-34. These are Attorney Coke's foul papers. The term "misprision" is defined by Blackstone as "a term derived from the old French *mépris*, a neglect, or contempt, and it is said that a misprision is contained in every treason and felony whatever, and that, if the king so please, the offender may be proceeded against for misprision only": Sir William Blackstone, *Commentaries on the Laws of England*, 4 vols. (Oxford: Clarendon Press, 1778), 4:119.

42. *Calendar of State Papers, Venetian, 1603-1607*, p. 373.

43. Paul, *The Royal Play of 'Macbeth,'* pp. 317-31.

44. Muir, ed., *Macbeth* (London, 1951), pp. xvi-xxvi.

45. Nosworthy, *Shakespeare's Occasional Plays*, pp. 8-13.

46. C. H. Herford and Percy Simpson, eds., *Ben Jonson*, 1:40, 202.

47. Thomas Wilson, *The State of England, 1600* (London: Camden Society, 1936), pp. 3-4. In describing the Percy claims, Wilson adds: "But yt were too long to tell how many treasons have cutt them of."

48. Osborne, *Traditionall Memoyres* (1658), p. 31. Osborne wrote later that "the heads of the Conspirators Catesby and Percy (if not since removed, and others set in their places, as I have been told) remain still on the house of Lords." Percy's head upon a pole is only another of the strange similarities in this fantastic case; Holinshed described Macbeth's head "set vpon a pole."

49. Collins, *Letters and Memorials of State*, 2:316.

50 Public Record Office, *SP*. 14/16, item 41.

51. Alnwick Castle MSS., 9, item 51.

52. Percy, *Advice To His Son*, p. 94.

53. Lambeth Palace, Lambeth MSS., Bacon Papers, 9, fol. 78.

54. Osborne, *Traditionall Memoyres* (1658), p. 28.

55. Sir Edmund Chambers noted some years ago that the action in the final battle-scenes of the play gives no opportunity for the removal of the dead Siward's body. See *William Shakespeare*, 1:472.

56. J. M. Nosworthy, "*Macbeth* at the Globe," *The Library*, 5th ser., 2 (1947-1948): 109. See also Christopher Spencer, *Davenant's 'Macbeth' from the Yale Manuscript* (New Haven, Conn.: Yale Univ. Press, 1961), pp. 55-77, where that author suggests that D'Avenant was using a pre-Restoration manuscript of *Macbeth* as his source and that the manuscript possibly was Shakespeare's.

57. *Macbeth, A Tragedy* (London: P. Chetwin, 1674), sig. A2. It is worth noting that D'Avenant attempts in his revision of Macbeth to make a pointed relevancy between Fleance and Charles II by altering the return of Fleance from Ireland to a return from France.

58. Peter Heylyn, ΜΙΚΡΟΚΟΣΜΟΣ: *A Little Description of the Great World*, augmented and revised (Oxford: J. Lichfield, 1625), pp. 508-10. The story of Macbeth did not appear in the first edition (1621) of this work.

59. The use of the magi is aesthetically fitting in *Macbeth* because of the overtones of the morality play of Herod and the Slaughter of the Innocents which pervade act IV during the murder of Lady Macduff and her son. For an analysis of this element in *Macbeth*, see Glynne Wickham's chapter, "Out-heroding Herod," in *Shakespeare's Dramatic Heritage* (London: Routledge and Kegan Paul, 1969), pp. 224-31.

60. Holinshed, *Chronicles of England* (1587), 2:174, 176.

61. Muriel Rukeyser, *The Traces of Thomas Hariot* (New York: Random House, 1971), pp. 196-98.

62. Hatfield House, Salisbury MSS., 134:86.

63. Ibid., 113:43. The search was made on 25 November and revealed "bookes of all sortes of learning" but no evidence of value to the authorities. There are two extant letters from Hariot, addressed to the Council and to Lord Salisbury, in which the scientist begs to be released from the "misery" of close imprisonment. He declares that he has never been a "meddler" in matters of state, that his life has been directed only by a love of learning, and that his labors therein have been both "painful and great": ibid., 114:40 and 41.

64. Public Record Office, *SP* 14/216, items 112, 113, 113A, 125; *SP* 14/16, items 102 and 103.

65. Ibid., *SP* 14/216, item 122. The tables were from Joannes Stadius's *Ephemerides*, that gave the positions of the planets during the sixteenth century. Hariot had told Torperley that they could determine the ascendant (the hour of birth) because the cannons had been fired at Edinburgh Castle between nine and ten o'clock on the morning of 19 June 1566 to announce the birth of Queen Mary's son.

66. Baildon, ed., *Les Reportes del Cases in Camera Stellata, 1593-1609*, pp. 292-99. Hawarde condemns those who had "calculated the kinges naitiuitie" and concludes that "par le Canon ley suche persons are excommunicate." He also adds, "Herriott is a funerall beaste." Baildon, the editor, is in error when he identifies Hariot as George Heriot, the king's jeweller (p. 297).

67. *Daemonologie* (1597), p. 10.

68. Henry E. Huntington Library MSS., MS4; Alnwick Castle MSS., 509. Both manuscripts contain evidence of Percy's continued revisions. He frequently added new lines by pasting slips of paper over the original passages.

69. A tense relationship between William Percy and the earl of Northumberland seems evident from the records at Alnwick Castle and Syon House. The earl provided pensions for his brothers Charles, Richard, Allan, Jocelyn, and George, but apparently he provided none for William. In one letter, dated 8 April 1602, Richard Percy speaks of his brother William's abusive conduct and ends with, "I can say no more but God forgive him his offences" (Alnwick Castle MSS., 7, fol. 23). For details of some of William Percy's problems (which included charges of manslaughter and imprisonment for debt) see H. N. Hillegrand, "Willaim Percy, An Elizabethan Amateur," *Huntington Library Quarterly*, 1 (1937-1938):391-416.

70. Henry E. Huntington Library MSS., MS4, fols. 173-74; Alnwick Castle MSS., 509, fols. 176-77. William Percy's use of astrology is complex. I have been able to determine that Mars was in Libra, Saturn was in Sagittarius, and the Moon was in Aquarius on 5 November 1605. See W. D. Stahlman and Owen Gingerich, *Solar and Planetary Longitudes for Years -2500 to +2000* (Madison, Wis.: Univ. of Wisconsin Press, 1963), p. 502.

71. The Malone Society is planning to publish the four Percy plays which have not been previously printed. Two of the plays were published by the Roxburghe Club in 1824.

72. When I began this study, I was convinced that Shakespeare abandoned the montage technique as an artistic device after he had written *Macbeth*. But after hearing Professor Glynne Wickham's cogent arguments, presented in his paper, "From Tragedy to Tragicomedy: 'King Lear' as Prologue," for the Fifteenth International Shakespeare Conference at Stratford-upon-Avon (1972), I have changed my mind.

I should add at this point that Professor G. R. Proudfoot, who is working with the Shakespeare apocrypha, has informed me that he has found what appears to be satire of the Cobhams in *A Yorkshire Tragedy*. I am not surprised; I am certain that Shakespeare's mode of satire was used by other playwrights.

CHAPTER TWELVE

1. *The Letters of John Dryden*, ed. Charles E. Ward (Durham, N.C.: Duke Univ. Press, 1942), pp. 9-10. The late James Marshall Osborn suggested to me that Dryden's observation on the lampoon stemmed from his preference for a composite figure in dramatic satire.

2. *The Arte of English Poesie* (London: R. Field, 1589), p. 26.

3. *Hall's Chronicle* (1809), p. 719. Wolsey was angered in 1527 by a play performed at Gray's Inn: "This plaie was so set furth with riche and costly apparel, with a straunge diuises of Maskes & Morrishes that it was highly praised of all menne, sauyng of the Cardinall, whiche imagined that the plaie had been diuised of hym, & in a greate furie sent for the said master Roo, and toke from hym his Coyfe, and sent him to the Flete, & after he sent for the yong gentlemen, that plaied in the plaie, and them highly rebuked and thretened, & sent one of them called Thomas Moyle of Kent to the Flete." The actors learned their lesson well. In November of the same year John Rightwise, master of St. Paul's School,

produced the entertainment for the French ambassadors who brought the insignia of the Order of St. Michael to Henry VIII. In the entertainment Wolsey was prefigured in a Michaelesque role as guardian of the church. Hall remarks on this topical element: "At this play wisemen smiled & thought that it sounded more glorious to the Cardinal then true to the matter in dede" (p. 735). For further considerations in this area, see William O. Harris, "Wolsey and Skelton's *Magnyfycence*: A re-evaluation," *Studies in Philology*, 57 (1960):99-122; David Bevington, *Tudor Drama and Politics* (Cambridge, Mass.: Harvard Univ. Press, 1968), pp. 54-63. Bevington's book is an important work which presents the viable thesis that "politics is germaine to a remarkable percentage of Tudor plays." His numerous insights into the development of dramatic form and the relationship between that development and the changes Elizabethan society itself was undergoing are excellent. His refusal to admit topicality (as opposed to political ideas) into his study is the only sane approach to a survey of the entire sixteenth-century drama. The book is narrow, however, in its blanket condemnation of specific topical analysis per se. Many of the Tudor plays have internal evidence which indicates topicality, and there is external evidence of weight and merit. That modern scholars have failed in many instances to marshall that evidence satisfactorily, or have abused the historical method in working with topical subjects, does not obliterate the fact that numerous sixteenth-century playwrights were involved with particularized materials as well as the philosophy of political problems.

4.   Glynne Wickham, *Early English Stages: 1300 to 1660*, 2 vols. (New York: Columbia Univ. Press, 1963), 2:54-97; V. C. Gildersleeve, *Government Regulations of the Elizabethan Drama* (New York: Columbia Univ. Press. 1908), pp. 8-9; Chambers, *The Elizabethan Stage*, 2:222-23.

5.   Chambers, *The Elizabethan Stage*, 2:15. For the danger in general which the actors faced, see Wickham, *Early English Stages*, 2:102-5.

6.   I have just read the study of the Marprelate controversy which Professor Leland Carlson is completing. His systematic analysis of the writing styles used in the controversy presents impressive evidence that John Penry was not the author of the witty pamphlets but rather that Job Throckmorton was the principal writer.

7.   In Nashe's *Pierce Penilesse His Supplication To the Devil* there is a pun on *Brooke* which leads me to think that it was probably Lord Cobham (whom Burghley had appointed in the fall of 1589 to investigate the controversy) who hired Nashe and Lyly to write against Martin Marprelate with an equally low and witty style, urging them to fight fire with fire. I am assuming that the poets received no pay for their satire when their work had no effect in deterring the Puritan writers in their attacks upon the bishops. Nashe's pun comes in that famous passage about "brave Talbot" who "triumphs againe on the Stage." He remarks that he will defend the stage plays "against any Colliar, or clubfisted Usurer of them all" who "doe envie any man that is not sprung up by base *Brokerie* like themselves." He then describes Henry V "leading the French King prisoner, and forcing both him and the Dolphin to sweare fealty," and asks why the stingy complainers of stage plays, with "their execrable luker and filthie unquenchable avarice," cannot honor fame. His answer is fascinating: "They know when they are dead they shall not be brought upon the Stage for any goodnes, but in a merriment of the Usurer and the Divel." Nashe continues with a description of their coat of arms; they will buy, he insists, "Armes of the Herald, who gives them the lyon, without tongue, tayle, or tallents" (McKkerrow and Wilson,

eds., *Works of Nashe,* 1:212-13). The original Cobham arms had been singularized by three fleurs-de-lis upon a chevron, but in the thirteenth century the three flowers had been changed to three lions rampant. This passage leads me to think that the Cobhams were complaining about the Talbot play (with its satire on Sir John Fastolfe) in 1592 when *Pierce Penilesse His Supplication* was published. This is, however, slender evidence.

8. Wilson, *The Fortunes of Falstaff* (Cambridge: Cambridge Univ. Press, 1944).

9. Robert Withington, "Braggart, Devil, and 'Vice,' A Note on the Development of Comic Figures in the Early English Drama," *Speculum* 11 (1936):124-29; Daniel C. Boughner, *The Braggart in Renaissance Comedy* (Minneapolis, Minn.: Univ. of Minnesota Press, 1954), pp. 145-78. It is a mistake to think of the morality play influence upon the Elizabethan playwrights as a dark Puritan blanket which smothered the fun of drama. The deity medieval people worshipped had a sense of humor.

10. Enid Welsford, *The Fool* (New York, 1961), pp. 199-219.

11. Homer A. Watt, "The Dramatic Unity of the *Secunda Pastorum*" in *Essays and Studies in Honor of Carleton Brown* (New York: New York Univ. Press, 1940); Woolf, "The Effect of Typology on the English Mediaeval Plays of Abraham and Isaac," pp. 805-25; M. M. Morgan, " 'High Fraud': Paradox and Double-Plot in the English Shepherds' Plays," *Speculum,* 39 (1964):676-89; J. D. Hurrell, "The Figural Approach to Mediaeval Drama," *College English,* 26 (1965):598-604; Walter E. Meyers, *The Figure Given: Typology in the Wakefield Plays* (Pittsburgh, Penn.: Duquesne Univ. Press, 1969).

12. G. W. H. Lampe and K. L. Woollcombe, *Essays On Typology* (London: SCM Press, 1957); Jean Danielou, *From Shadows To Reality* (Westminster, Md.: Newman Press, 1960).

13. Meyers, *The Figure Given,* pp. 7-14.

14. Ibid., pp. 37-55.

15. For extended discussions of Shakespeare's use of parallelism in scene construction, see: A. P. Rossiter, *Angel With Horns* (London: Longmans, 1961), pp. 40-64; Nevill Coghill, *Shakespeare's Professional Skills* (Cambridge: Cambridge Univ. Press, 1964), pp. 61-77; John Shaw, "The Staging of Parody and Parallels in '1 Henry IV,' " *Shakespeare Survey,* 20 (1967): 61-73.

16. *The History of Great Britain* (London: R. Lownds, 1653), p. 4.

17. David Dalrymple, Lord Hailes, ed., *The Secret Correspondence of Sir Robert Cecil with James VI King of Scotland* (Edinburgh: A. Millar, 1766), pp. 68, 131.

18. British Museum, Cotton MSS., *Titus,* 106, fol. 386.

19. Weldon, *The Court and Character of King James* (London: R. J., 1650), p. 17. The remark occurs in Weldon's discussion of Cecil's actions at the turn of the century: "You are now to observe, that Salisbury had shaken off all that were great with him, and of his Faction in Queen Elizabeths dayes, as Sir Walter Rawleigh, Sir George Carew, the Lord Grey, the Lord Cobham: the three first, very able men as the World had, the last, but one degree from a foole, yet served their turnes better then a wiser man, by his greatnesse with the Queen, for they would put him on any thing, and make him tell any Lye, with as great confidence as a truth."

20. Cobham died in 1619. Sir Anthony Weldon printed a description of his last days: "His death [was] base, for hee dyed lousie for want of Apparrell, and Linnen; and had starved, had not a Trencher-scraper, sometime his Servant in Court, relieved him with scraps, in whose house he dyed, being so poore a house as he was forced to creep up a Ladder into a little hole to his Chamber" *(The Court and Character of King James,* p. 37.). This appears to be an exaggeration. A Huntington Library manuscript (HM 4547) is a letter from Cobham, written in the Tower, to the earl of Suffolk, lord treasurer, in which Cobham said he was sending his servant for "my monthly allowens of 32 pounds." We also know that he had his books about him in the Tower; King James confiscated over a thousand volumes which were left when Cobham died.

21. [Parsons], *A Treatise of Three Conversions,* 2: sig. Bviii.

22. Ibid., sig. Qvi.

23. Ibid., sig. Qvii.

24. See William Watson, *A Soaring Discovery of our English Jesuits and of Fa. Parsons Proceedings* (London: F. Kingston, 1601).

25. Parsons's *Treatise of Three Conversions* was answered by Matthew Sutcliffe, *The Subversion of Robert Parsons, His Confused and Worthless Works* (London: J. Norton 1606). Sutcliffe had attacked Parsons in 1600 for having been involved in every practise against Queen Elizabeth's life, and like Watson he accused Parsons and Cardinal Allen of contriving all the treasonable acts of Elizabeth's reign: "William Parry, Somerfield, Arden, Babington, Ballard, Patrick O'Collen, and all those murderers, and empoisoners, that of late time have practised against her Majestie were papists, and set on by papists": *A Brief Reply To A Certaine Odious and Slanderous Libel, Lately Published By A Seditious Jesuite* (London: A. Hatfield, 1600), pp. 147, 154.

26. Speed, *The Theatre of the Empire of Great Britaine,* 2:637.

INDEX

371